116464

371.74
M46

Means, Louis
    Intramurals: Their
organization and adminis-
tration

DATE DUE

INTRAMURALS

SECOND EDITION

INTRAMURALS

Their Organization
And Administration

LOUIS E. MEANS

Former
Associate Executive Secretary
American Association for Health
Physical Education and Recreation

PRENTICE-HALL, INC., Englewood Cliffs, New Jersey

Library of Congress Cataloging in Publication Data

Means, Louis Edgar, 1902–
    Intramurals: their organization and administration.

    First published in 1949 under title: Organization
and administraion of intramural sports.
    Bibliography: p.
    1. Intramural sports. I. Title.
GV710.M4 1972   371.8'9   72-2151
ISBN 0-13-477216-4

Prentice-Hall International, Inc., *London*
Prentice-Hall of Australia, Pty. Ltd., *Sydney*
Prentice-Hall of Canada, Ltd., *Toronto*
Prentice-Hall of India Private Limited, *New Delhi*
Prentice-Hall of Japan, Inc., *Tokyo*

This book is dedicated to the principle that no student should be deprived of his or her opportunity for participation in a great variety of recreational experiences while in school, which may contribute more than we know to a long and happy and normal life.

*It is far more important that a man should
play something himself, even if he plays it
badly, than that he should go to see someone
else play it well.*

THEODORE ROOSEVELT

PREFACE

Intramural sports and activities form a vital link in the pattern of blended educational experiences so necessary for all boys and girls in the modern American school. No young person should be deprived of his or her opportunity for participation in a great variety of recreational experiences in the school program, which may contribute more than we can ever know to a long, happy, and normal life. Recent social and economic trends simply re-emphasize this basic truth.

It has been heartening in recent years to observe that school administrators all over the nation are strengthening their demands to provide more wisely planned school recreation. School leaders have become alert to trends and forces contributing the greatest impact on plastic youth. As interscholastic, intercollegiate, and professional sports have grown apace in public esteem, the reaction has gathered support that the true American concept must also provide the remaining major portion of each student body with balanced sports and recreational opportunities. Leaders are realizing that physical education often lacks meaning without the proper laboratory for recreational practice of skills learned. They are realizing that fitness cannot be attained unless youth can participate in a planned schedule. The searchlight is being directed more and more for trained leadership which can make Democracy in Sports a reality.

There may be some debate as to who should direct this type of program; how it can be integrated with the varsity sports program; how every student can be properly reached and served; how proper facilities and sufficient funds can be developed to meet the challenge; where trained and dedicated leadership can be obtained; but there should be no real debate on the necessity for its inclusion.

The author has given careful attention to the many book reviews, suggestions, and expressed ideas on his earlier publications on this subject. It has been encouraging to observe that most major colleges and universities have used earlier editions of this work as a text; and that the list of institutions offering professional courses in this specialized field is increasing. This revised edition utilizes recent source materials, deletes obsolete practices and ideas, gives more attention to the program for girls and women, and clearly outlines desirable practices for all ages and grade levels.

Those who feel that such a text must indicate THE one ideal program that should be emulated by all schools must recognize that experience has dictated that the best program for any school or college must be founded upon a study of local problems, needs, interests, facilities, climatic and geographical conditions, and leadership possibilities. To that end the author has attempted to point the way to wise and intelligent program planing for any area and any grade level by suggesting over and over again the best practices that have become time-proven over the nation and that are based upon sound principles and objectives that make a maximum contribution to the total educational scheme for every boy and girl, man and woman.

The bibliography of resource materials on this subject, considered by many to be the most complete in the field, has been brought up to date.

The author wishes to extend acknowledgments and appreciation to the individuals and publishers who have given permission to use quotations and program ideas, as well as copyrighted excerpts. The very willingness of these leaders is another indication of the sincere professional interest in this dynamic and maturing phase of physical education and recreation.

The greatest indebtedness goes to the thousands of students whose interest, enthusiasm, and participation in the school recreation program over the years has been the stimulus for the preparation of this book.

Perhaps this latest of a series of revisions would never have been attempted without the persistent urging of countless leaders and associates in the profession who felt that the book has value in the professional preparation of future leaders, and as a guide and constant source of information as programs are developed and set in motion.

LOUIS E. MEANS
Sarasota, Florida

CONTENTS

INTRAMURALS

1

HISTORICAL BACKGROUND
OF INTRAMURAL SPORTS
AND ACTIVITIES

Intramural activities, as employed in the modern American school, represent a very important element of education. In early colonial and pioneer days, youth was necessarily absorbed in the tasks of assisting their elders to clear forests, build houses, and do the heavy daily chores; they had to assume at a very early age a major role in the process of economic survival. As the colonial economy became more prosperous and more stable, children and youth found more leisure time to engage in games and sports. A natural development of organized adult leadership gradually followed. The earliest physical education in American schools was a transplanted European pattern of strictly formal gymnastics. This heritage still persists strongly in some cities where population is predominantly of foreign extraction. It was not until the 1860s that American colleges and universities began to borrow outright the English idea of sports. It was still another generation at least until the American pattern of competitive sports began to show characteristic differences from the English conception of games.

Voltmer and Esslinger[1] had this to say about the origin of sports in America:

> There is ample evidence that boys participated in various sports in our early American schools despite the obstacles in the form of hostile

1

teachers and the Puritan philosophy of the sinfulness and foolishness of play. As educational institutions multiplied and the school population increased, informal play activities among students expanded. The haphazard nature of these activities gradually gave way to better organization. The students conducted their activities by themselves. The faculty was indifferent.

In these early days of sports the students banded together and started their own sports clubs. Considering the later rapid expansion of interschool athletics, often to the exclusion of intramurals, it is signifiant to remember that early American athletics were all intramural in nature. Before long the various sports clubs and groups began to seek competition with other city and school teams. In 1873 the football-minded students of the University of Pennsylvania contacted President White of Cornell University and invited the Cornell players to compete with them at Philadelphia in an interschool contest. President White's answer was preserved for posterity: "I will not permit thirty of my students to travel four hundred miles to agitate a bag of wind."

During the early growth of athletics the total school athletic program was usually accomplished with little or no supervision and institutional administration. Student managers directed the business details of competition, a system still common in England today. Soon these clubs began looking around for star players who could be induced to coach their teams as well as play with them to lend added strength. In those days the coach who could act as pitcher on the baseball team or carry the ball in football was in great demand. Eligibility regulations in that period were almost unknown. Thus, in the period from about 1875 to 1908, school athletics became almost totally interschool in nature, and were often managed by students or players with little regard for sound, centralized institutional control. It has only been since 1930 that high schools have begun to develop real intramural sports programs to suit their own local needs and age groups, rather than to blindly follow the practices of the colleges.

As early as 1859 the undergraduates of Yale University were divided into a dozen intramural boating clubs for competitive purposes. This plan at Yale later gave way to a system of interclass crews. Intramural baseball games are recorded as early as 1865 at Princeton, followed closely by Amherst, Williams, and Yale. The "Caledonian Games" brought to America by Scottish immigrants soon became intramural track and field meets at Princeton and Yale. One of the most striking examples of the rapid progress in undergraduate sports in the American university was at Princeton. As early as 1761 the trustees of Princeton University established a severe penalty for any students caught playing ball in certain areas of the campus. The same body again joined with the faculty in 1787 in objecting to "a game played with sticks and balls in the back common of the college." The faculty further stated:[2]

> ...that this play is in itself low and unbecoming to gentleman students and inasmuch as it is an exercising attended with great danger to health by sudden and alternate heats and colds, and as it tends to accidents, almost unavoidable in that play, to disfiguring and maiming those who engaged in it...the faculty thinks it incumbent on them to prohibit both the students and Grammar Scholars from using the play aforesaid.

Today the students of Princeton are expected to play as much as possible in either intramural or intercollegiate sports, and this university now has one of the broadest intramural programs in the nation.

The records show little competition between classes or other campus groups in those early years of interschool competition. But American youth could not long be satisfied with this narrow conception of recreation and soon sought expression in all kinds of challenge games for those not fortunate enough to "make" the varsity team. Students began to form natural units of competition, even though central school organization was lacking and, in many cases, actually opposed. Class organizations grew on most of the college campuses, with committees and officers beginning a competitive organization. The class unit was naturally most prominent in the early period when enrollments were low and classmates knew each other intimately. Soon the fraternities began to take over more of the campus leadership in intramurals due to the more permanent nature of their organizations; they were later somewhat loath to relinquish this prerogative to central authority. It gradually became apparent to these groups that there were great values in institutional control of the whole program, and the last few years have seen most universities developing a strong program through a director of intramural sports assisted by committees or boards and councils comprised of representatives of all campus groups. This system of organization has gradually been adopted by elementary and secondary schools.

The period of student control was strongest between 1900 and 1914. Intramural athletics under this system soon became too unwieldy and a constant problem to athletic directors and coaches of varsity sports. Most colleges of the early period had athletic associations in control of their varsity program, and they in turn permitted student-controlled groups the use of facilities and equipment, and occasional leadership. Great need for coordination was soon apparent, and it remained for the University of Michigan and Ohio State University to inaugurate the first departments of intramural athletics in 1913, each under the direction of one man who was expected to administer the student demands in the various leading sports of the day. One might note that two trends influenced and characterized the early university program even after separate new departments were created: first, intramurals followed closely the pattern and operation of the existing varsity sports as to sports included, methods of coaching and scheduling, and the like; second, as further expansion seemed necessary, there was a close emulation of existing public recreation programs.

The first important contribution to athletic literature, the proceedings of nationally important athletic meetings, which still has its effect on the intramural sports movement, was by J. W. Wilce,[3] then director of athletics at Ohio State. This report from the Committee on Intramural Sports of the Athletic Research Society had much to do with the start of classification of playing units. Athletic associations immediately saw the value of new intramural control since it safeguarded the use of equipment, eliminated confusion over playing fields and floors, and went far toward meeting the growing demand of restless students for more and more recreational opportunity. It permitted the athletic associations to develop varsity athletics still further and, at the same time, allowed "sports for all" a great opportunity for expansion.

Undoubtedly the early paternalism of athletic associations and varsity coaches toward the intramural program was nurtured by the thought that such competition would develop varsity material as its primary objective. This still remains a strong argument for intramurals in the modern school, but educators are now well aware of the many other benefits of such a program and have lent their support to the realization of other objectives.

The example of one Middle Western college illustrates how rapidly the movement for intramurals grew into the educational pattern of this nation. There a group of students were dissatisfied with the traditional four-sport varsity program and wanted tournaments and leagues in the coming summer term in such sports as tennis, softball, golf, and horseshoes. The athletic director, a product of the older school, refused to spend any time in such promotion and organization. The group of students then proceeded to organize summer tournaments in these sports, conducting various activities and declaring champions in each. The city newspaper carried pictures and stories of the new events and champions. This procedure must have been an eye opener for the college officials, because the college bulletin of the following term gave colorful descriptions and illustrations of the new "sports for all" program that had been inaugurated on the campus. This bulletin carried detailed information on the importance of recreational pursuits for all students, emphasizing with much detail the new program that had been made available.

As schools developed their central administration for intramurals, their first objective was to initiate a sports program only when it was demanded by enough student pressure, or when strong student interest was apparent. World War I with its new emphasis on mass competitive sports, the training so many future athletic leaders received during the war, and the growing impetus of the playground movement in America, provided real stimulation to school sports programs. Even before World War I several schools inaugurated extensive intramural programs following the lead of

Michigan and Ohio State. Among these were Illinois, Oregon State, and Texas, in 1916. Great strides forward were realized soon after the war, and the 1918-1920 period was the start of the great boom in mass athletics, with the high schools showing real progress after 1930. Kansas State College started its intramural program in 1921, Oklahoma University in 1925, and the University of West Virginia in 1928. Institutions were now establishing their programs on a larger and more centralized basis.

It has been only natural that school men in recent years have turned their attention more and more to the recreational and health needs of the student body. It is regrettable that large numbers of our elementary and secondary schools in America are still without proper leadership and program planning for adequate intramurals and recreation for all their students. During World War II intramurals suffered a tremendous temporary setback with so many of our younger leaders in the armed forces. But again the influence of the war was destined to set the stage for a second great revival in intramural sports. It is interesting that many coaches of specialized sports who served in the military units came back to their jobs with renewed convictions on the necessity and value of the total athletic program in the modern school. Their influence in this direction has been invaluable in recent growth.

As schools began the expansion of their intramural programs, it was common practice to talk almost entirely of participating numbers, with little regard for the amount of time spent and the amount of benefit derived by each student in the program. More recently there has been closer scrutiny of quality and quantity, with safeguards set up for the health of the individual through more adequate medical examinations, pretournament conditioning requirements, and skills taught to students to assist in greater enjoyment of the activity. It is now considered essential that the more vigorous sports be closely supervised. Many schools require a medical examination at frequent intervals, thus providing a check on the fitness of students for certain activities. The trend toward adapted sports for the handicapped is significant, and much progress has been made by some schools in broadening appropriate intramural activities to meet their needs and interests.

Schools today are moving toward the objective of skills instruction in large varieties of activities that will either be used in intramurals or will be valuable for recreation in adult life. Junior and senior high schools likewise are beginning to open up greater possibilities for instruction than the loosely organized free play period so characteristic of many secondary schools. The increase in graduate study by physical educators is making a great contribution in the field, both by increased appreciation of the values of intramurals, and by the work of these students as graduate assistants. Public recreation programs have received great stimulation from the National Recreation Association and the American Association for Health,

Fig. 1. Touch or flag football continues to be a favorite American fall intramural feature in secondary schools and colleges. Soccer and speedball could just as easily help diversify the fall program when combined with class instruction on skills and rules.

Physical Education and Recreation—both serving to make the public more appreciative of the value of school recreation and intramurals.

The trend to coordinate the school program with community recreation is bringing to American towns and cities the real import of the community school. The work of committees organized in the various states to set up state courses of study in physical education adds new and needed impetus to the movement. The ever-increasing number of states now employing one or more state physical education supervisors and consultants has helped to bring an adequate intramural program to needy and neglected areas. Better administration of the intramural program is a natural result of the increase numbers of young men and women now taking four- to seven-year professional courses in physical education, recreation, and athletics. The growing tendency for these students to prepare themselves for the recreational field rather than merely for the coaching of one or more varsity sports will have an impact on broader school sports programs.

The depression in the middle 1930's profoundly influenced this development. Out of this period came a new appreciation of recreation as a valuable use of leisure time. Out of this period came new governmental leadership through various agencies, and through them much in recreation was given schools and cities. Out of this period also came federal aid for the building of new facilities such as gymnasiums, swimming pools, play fields, and combined city-school facilities of all kinds. Following World War II there was an increased impetus toward living war memorials in the form of recreational and athletic buildings. A number of gymnasiums and outdoor playing fields, not only on high school and college campuses but also within urban areas, were dedicated to the memory of military figures.

Beginning in the late 1930's, the rapid pace of industrialization and automation, the advances of science and technology, the shorter-work-week policy of labor unions, and the chronic periods of unemployment have all worked together to give the American public more and more leisure time. This situation in turn places a responsibility on modern education, demanding that future citizens be taught hobbies, sports, recreation, and interests that will satisfactorily prepare them for the new leisure. Intramurals and the school recreational program can step forward to meet this challenge with a feeling of confidence and service.

Intramural sports after 1930 more nearly expressed the recreational aspects of sports, and in some institutions the title of Intramural Director was changed to Director of Campus Recreation. Intramural participation became less forced, with students developing sports interests more naturally. Activities were enjoyed more for their own sake. Many students were introduced to activities in physical education classes and, liking them, participated in them extensively.[4]

The American Association for Health, Physical Education, and Recreation has given valuable and timely leadership to the intramural movement with many articles in its *Journal,* sponsorship of national conferences on intramurals (1957), professional preparation of recreation personnel (1956, 1957, 1958), school recreation (1959 and 1962), general professional preparation (1962), and in many district and national convention sessions.

Another significant step forward was taken by AAHPER in 1959 and again in 1960 when they sponsored nationwide clinics on the community-school concept at Flint, Michigan. Hundreds of school and community leaders from many states spent three days of intensive visitations in the midst of one of the nation's finest programs for all ages of children, youth, and adults.[5]

In 1948 and 1949 the author, with the help of Al Lumley of Amherst College, gave intramurals a vital and recognized place in the traditional professional activities of the College Physical Education Association. In 1949, at the CPEA meetings in Chicago, this effort brought about an unprecedented attendance of intramural directors and others interested in the intramural movement. This meeting also produced the first major exchange of intramural handbooks from all over the nation, with more than a hundred institutions sending quantities of their handbooks for exchange. Indeed, many colleges went to press for the first time to meet this challenge.

At this CPEA meeting the need for a permanent intramural organization was clearly recognized and an interim organization was formed, headed by William Scheerer of Wofford College. This effort failed to gain momentum, and a few months later the National Intramural Association was started under different auspices.

The emergence of the National Intramural Association in 1950 from its former minor role in the College Physical Education Association has banded together the nation's most dedicated intramural leaders to strengthen their common purposes and to exchange ideas. This group has largely attracted college leaders, but their catalytic effórts have added strength to intramurals in both elementary and secondary schools.

Each year since 1953 has been marked by a steady and promising strengthening of intramural and campus recreation leadership through the able efforts of leaders in the National Intramural Association.

Many colleges and universities, and a few secondary schools, have increased the scope and potentialities of their programs, with outing activities such as hiking, camping, riding, fishing, shooting, canoeing, picnics, sailing, nature trips, and the great field of winter sports. Thus we are moving toward a rapidly expanding movement of co-recreational intramurals and activities, more social and healthful than competitive. Some of the college leaders in this field have been Dartmouth, Middlebury, Albright, Colorado, West Virginia, Pennsylvania State College, Washington State College, Illinois, and the University of Washington. This movement has been best implemented in areas near mountains or water.

The consistent leadership exerted by women physical educators has been a steadying influence on the growth and quality of girls' intramurals and school recreation through the years. Through girls' clubs or organized groups such as Girls' Athletic Association or Girls' Recreation Association, physical education departments have succeeded in providing a medium for sports participation in after-school hours, which are often blended with social features and outing activities.

Presidents Eisenhower, Kennedy, Johnson, and Nixon added much impetus to the mass sports participation effort through their persistent attempts to persuade American leaders to increase and strengthen physical fitness programs for youth. Each established a President's Council on Youth Fitness, stimulating, exhorting, and demanding that schools and agencies as well as parents and citizens work together to provide multiple opportunities for vigorous activity on a sustained and continuing basis. President Kennedy once told a gathering of varsity sports leaders and the nation at large that the vigor and vitality of this nation in the future may depend upon the degree to which opportunities for all boys and girls in sports are provided. He spoke disparagingly of the tendency of Americans to enjoy their sports largely as spectators rather than active participants and urged a national crusade for vigorous sports participation of all types.

During Lyndon Johnson's presidency the name of the fitness council was changed to "the President's Council on Physical Fitness and Sports" to indicate the value of a broad sports participation program.

Another significant medium for the growth and stimulation of sports for all came through AAHPER's Operation Fitness—USA, which started in 1958 and became the banner under which nationwide professional effort for fitness was mobilized. Through its catalytic efforts and through a number of specific projects a veritable flood of sports festivals, demonstrations, local and national sports programs, sportsoramas, and sports clinics were launched and encouraged. New fitness and sports skills test batteries were scientifically developed and made available to millions. Many printed materials were widely distributed. Through the combination of these many efforts, which were translated into local and regional programs of action, the intramural or mass participation concept has received invigorating rejuvenation which means much to future program development.

With the rapid growth of the intramural movement there has been increasing effort to set standards for its improvement. That it has now become a tremendously important part of the educational scheme can no longer be doubted. Some educators are even going as far as to suggest that interschool athletics be greatly curbed or eliminated, and that intramurals be substituted to enable all students to receive equal attention. It would seem that the modern program would best be served by careful administration of both phases of activity, with the intramural program activating the entire student body, and with interschool athletics representing the peak of skill and specialization, crystalizing school spirit wisely through its representative teams, but with neither dominating the other to the point of unfair exclusion of facilities or leadership. The central emphasis of the future may well be a program for the maximum welfare of the entire student body. This implies a closer correlation between what happens in the required program of teaching and the laboratory of intramurals where teaching may be applied. It is further felt that the required program should not include intramural competition, but should be a preparation for it.

Intramural sports must have a carefully integrated relationship to the total physical education program. The definitely graded, planned, and carefully supervised physical education program cannot be superseded by intramurals, but should be implemented and embellished by it. The department of physical education today forms the basic structure out of which grow intense and constant desires for physical and social activity, best expressed through the medium of informal recreation, intramural sports, outing and co-recreational clubs and events, and the varsity sports program.

We cannot ignore or minimize the importance of this rapidly growing field of intramural sports and school recreation in the modern community. The program merits a place as one of the educational essentials. It is the testing ground of reality. It is life itself. In a modern world all too full of maladjustments, inhibitions, complexes, worries, and fears, youth will profit tremendously from a training and an experience that uses pleasurable activity to teach one the way to relax, the ability to get along with other people, a respect for the opposite sex, and wholesome skills that are never quite lost, to be called upon again and again to relieve the adult tensions and worries of society.

REFERENCES

1 Edward F. Voltmer and Arthur A. Esslinger, *The Organization and Administration of Physical Education* (New York: F. S. Crofts & Co., 1938), p. 252.

2 E. A. Rice, *A Brief History of Physical Education* (New York: A. S. Barnes & Co., 1926), p. 217.

3 "Report of Committee on Intramural Sports," Athletic Research Society, *American Physical Education Review,* XXIII, April and May, 1918.

4 D. B. Van Dalen and Bruce Bennett, *A World History of Physical Education,* 2nd ed. (Englewood Cliffs, N.J.: Prentice-Hall, Inc., 1971).

5 "First National Community School Clinic," *Journal of Educational Sociology,* XXIII, No. 4, December, 1959.

*Far better it is to dare mighty things, to win
glorious triumphs, even though checkered by
failure, than to take rank with those poor spirits
who neither enjoy much nor suffer much,
because they live in the gray twilight that
knows no victory nor defeat.*
THEODORE ROOSEVELT

2

PHILOSOPHY AND OBJECTIVES
OF INTRAMURAL SPORTS

Intramurals are a pleasing combination of the elements of physical education and the modern concept of recreation. They form the physical recreation phase of applied physical education. From knowledges and skills learned in the physical education class to the voluntary utilization of these basic elements in the recreation setting, one realizes the scope and potential of the good program. The rapid surge toward automation, the growing problem of seasonal or prolonged unemployment, and the changed pattern of American living have all conspired to place new importance on recreational sports as an integral and indispensable part of modern living. Thus intramurals as a part of education and preparation for living have taken on deeper meaning.

The word "intramural" is a combination of the Latin words *intra,* meaning within, and *muralis,* meaning wall. When used with "athletics," it carries a connotation of the traditional varsity type of athletics such as football, basketball, baseball, or track and field. When paired with the word "sports," its meaning is much more broad and comprehensive—hence the current acceptability of the term "intramural sports." More recent program directions have brought the term of "intramural sports and activities" because of the great diversity of activities employed. This is the broad program designed for students and faculty of a single school only.

On many college campuses the Student Union also conducts some of the recreational activities for students and faculty, although the activities planned are usually of a social, nonathletic nature such as bridge, cribbage, pool, billiards, dancing, crafts, reading, and quiet games.

Extramurals, or intermural activities, are an extension of the intramural sports concept involving participants from two or more schools. They may be considered to be the intermediate step between intramurals and interschool sports and athletics. They usually retain many of the characteristics of intramurals with less highly organized team structure, greater numbers of participants, and less pressure and coaching, and the sports are conducted on a more recreational plane than those of a highly competitive and organized nature.

No school in America need be without some form of intramurals, regardless of size or grade level. Elementary schools should of course plan their programs carefully around the known growth and characteristics patterns appropriate to the physical capabilities of the age groups served. Organized intramural activities usually begin in the fourth or fifth grade and continue thereafter through the school life of the child.

During the developmental period of intramural sports the emphases have shifted from time to time. There is every reason to believe that both objectives and program emphasis will bear modification in the future. For this reason it is apparent that present-day objectives cannot be definitively evaluated in importance or adjudged as static and final.

Physical educators early saw the great possibilities intramurals and have reason to be proud of past accomplishments. Colleges and universities, through their professional departments, are developing a wholesome regard for the total broad program in the nation's schools, as they prepare a new type of leader for the field. Much more needs to be done in this direction. The future program, as in every phase of educational planning, must be constantly scrutinized and evaluated to make sure that every possible benefit will accrue from soundly directed participation in sports and activities for all.

Many studies have been made of intramural sports, and no unanimity is evidenced in the assessment of objectives. The more than ninety objectives that have been identified and mentioned might well be classified into a few general groups or headings. Students view the matter of objectives with present-day perspective, judging them through the eyes of an active participant. Intramural workers are more likely to be conscious of the ideals of a more remote nature, with emphasis on educational values and an attentive eye to trends of the future.

Six general groupings of objectives can be used in condensing and combining the many now claimed for intramurals. These six objectives are (1) physical and mental health and fitness, (2) recreation, present and future, (3) coordination, perpetuation of skills, and bodily processes, (4) development of varsity material, (5) scholarship, and (6) social values, intramural handbooks, from professional literature, and from the published intramural philosophies of various colleges. The paucity of printed materials in the public schools on the subject forces one to turn to the better organized booklets of higher education, adapting them whenever possible for elementary and secondary school use. Such a study may assist the leader in gaining a more intimate insight into the hopes and ideals of the program as expressed by those with much practical experience.

Physical and Mental Health and Fitness

In this complicated scheme of things called civilization we can seldom be ourselves. We are tied in mental knots because we cannot, as our ancestors did, fight for what we want, or cry out against what we do not like. We usually keep still about what we think and feel, and the attics of our brains become stored with fears, jealousies, disappointments, and unsatisfied yearnings. We may either recognize that they are there and get rid of them, or lock the attic door and let them leak out in what psychologists call inhibitions, complexes, and maladjustments.

Those who value mental and physical poise cast about for a way to take care of these mental hangovers. Most of us find that sport is the best way. Competitive exercise is a splendid safety valve. When a man plays a game—any kind of game—the way it should be played, he lets himself go. He suffers disappointments and experiences triumphs. Inwardly he applauds his good shots and swears at the bad ones. He "lays" on every ball as hard as he wants to. At the same time he works off his pent-up venom against life. His complexes melt away with his perspiration. For a little while he is primitive, with the outlets of a primitive man. He even is able to communicate his state of mind to the bleachers.

When a man's game is over, whether it be tennis, handball, football, or whatever, he lies down in panting relaxation. He has discharged his mental bogies. He is as bereft of complexes as an African native is of clothing. If he goes hunting, or just roughs it, his world of troubles dissolves in thin air.

That is what active sport can do for a person. It can be an outlet and a normalizer. A person who keeps active in his play need seldom fear a nervous breakdown. Breakdown requires a state of nervous muscle tension that derives perhaps from the days of our caveman ancestors, when any cause for worry immediately translated itself into action. Now we meet most of our emergencies with headwork, at any rate without use of muscles. We go on day after day storing up nervous tension, which is communicated to the muscles to get them ready for the physical emergency which never comes. This condition provides no follow-up of relaxation after muscle group cooperation, and spirit. This chapter will elaborate on these six general areas, and will also present significant statements gleaned from effort, such as always came to the caveman, to whom everything spelled either fight or flight, both of which required movement. Finally the accumulation gets to be too much and we have blowups or breakdowns of some kind.

Every one of us can avoid them. Physical play, even short periods of it, will discharge the tension that our complicated living stores up. Even though the attics of our brains will again become filled with pent-up feelings, we can always turn to the safety valve of exercise which will carry us through rough and stormy seas.

It is evident that the draining of surplus energy, particularly at the junior and senior high school age, must figure as one of the real contributions of all sports. When the child goes home from school spent in physical energy, we have eliminated much of his desire to participate, for that evening, in the many possibly harmful and wasteful activities so common to modern society. These values increase with the frequency and repetition of the experience, if carefully directed.

One intramural director has made the following statement:

> We are human beings made of body and soul, and how we act spiritually depends largely on how we feel physically. Physical fitness has direct moral implications. Generally speaking, when a boy or girl is at his best physically he is in better shape to fight temptation, particularly temptations in the realm of chastity.

One *Handbook of Intramural Sports* at the University of Virgina stated: "The development of body, mind, and of character is the keynote of athletics." Healthful play activity and invigorating physical exercise have been cited by the University of Oklahoma handbook as aims of their program for many years. The Iowa State handbook had this to say: "Intramural recreation exercises the fundamental organs of the body and aids in keeping up the physical welfare of the student."

A university president once stated to his student body:

> Now, when we are all seriously looking to the future, I suggest two ways you can each help. One is by supporting the athletic teams which represent your institution. Your nation needs the habit of loyalty. Another is by taking part yourself in intramural sports. Your country needs strong, healthy, young men and women. You cannot become such just by sitting on the sidelines. Boost the varsity teams, yes—but also do something on your own.

Ross Townes, in his foreword for the Intramural Handbook at North Carolina Central University at Durham, made this statement:

> The intramural activities program is an essential part of a college's over-all function of educating and developing all-around students. Intramural activities are fertile fields for maintaining physical fitness and disciplining emotions.

Many handbooks stress the safeguarding of health by choice of activities, preparation for them, medical examinations, safety rules, good equipment, and proper supervision. The University of Oklahoma handbook quoted the words of William James as follows:

> Even if the day never dawns in which muscular vigor will not be needed for fighting the old heavy battle with nature, it will always be needed to furnish background for sanity, serenity, and cheerfulness in life, to give moral elasticity to our dispositions, to round off the wiry edge of our fretfulness, and to make us good-humored and easy to approach.

One of the University of Wisconsin handbooks carried this statement:

> The utilization of opportunities in intramurals will mean more health-giving fun for the student, and will provide him with greater physical, mental, and social training. This program has enjoyed a phenomenal growth because of its appeal to the inexpert and the many, rather than to the expert few.

Fig. 2. Tug-O-War at Everett Junior High, San Francisco.
(Photo by courtesy of George Canrinus.)

It is a truism in America that regular physical exercise is rarely indulged in without organization and without competition. Americans today gravitate to the passive types of work and recreation unless inviting recreational programs can divert this trend at the school age. All physiologists tell us that increased activity of heart and lungs serves to eliminate waste products of the body and hasten rapid assimilation of the nutritive food elements. But it should be emphasized here that physical education and health are not synonymous. Completing brilliant forward passes does not eliminate dental caries. Intramurals as conducted in many schools today are often sporadic and too unregulated to secure the best health outcomes. Best results are noticeable in instances where preliminary conditioning is required for the more strenuous activities, or where students take an active pride in keeping in shape for competition in order to guarantee their best performance at all times. Yet it cannot be denied that intramurals are important in the "keeping fit" program of student life. It is also evident that those intramural departments that provide annual or frequent health examinations contribute to health habits and practices in later life. One of the goals should be the more active use of the intramural sports program in launching young people upon a life career of healthy exercise.

Morgan depicted the life history of Teddy Roosevelt as a great example of the value of exercise and constant physical activities which is well worth emphasis here:[1]

Seated at his desk in school was a frail, fearful boy of eight with a face which bespoke hidden panic. When he breathed he wheezed. When called upon to recite he rose with quaking knees and quivering lips, mumbling incoherently, and collapsed in his seat. If he had handsome features it would have helped a little, but no, his teeth rushed out at you. With all his handicaps, however, this boy had a fighting spirit. He would not be downed by the defects which opened him to the ridicule of his comrades. He turned his wheezes into hisses of determination. He used his handicaps as the very rungs of the ladder on which he climbed to fame.

Instead of falling into the trap of self-pity, and instead of babying himself, "Teddy" set out to overcome these barriers. He noticed that strong boys played active games, swam, rode horses, and did hard physical work. So he became active, rode, played, and worked with a vengeance, so that before he reached college age he had built up his health and strength by constant and systematic exercise and hygienic living. In later years he was known as the man of powerful physique who spent his holidays rounding up cattle in Arizona, hunting bears in the Rockies, and chasing lions in Africa. Furthermore, he observed that others who became engrossed in doing exciting acts seldom had time to bother with an analysis of how they felt or whether they were afraid or not.

Recreation, Present and Future

Much could be said about the recreational objective of intramural sports. There are the *immediate* values to the student, in the development of leisure-time pursuits which enrich school years, and the more *permanent* recreational and sports interests that will contribute to later happy adult living. In this brief discussion the two will be closely associated.

Modern American parents seem to be allowing children much more freedom in the use of their leisure time. If the school does not provide a program to absorb their time and interests, this leisure time may be unwisely spent. Intramural sports clearly have a specific function in solving this important problem with intelligence and discretion. As the student emerges from school into adult life he faces a fast-changing and much different world than that of a few years ago. Before the Machine Age, life solved its own problems of physical development. With the rise of great industrial plants came labor organizations to look after the interests of workmen. Shorter working hours and greater leisure time was the by-product of the depression years of the 1930's. In recent years problems of production again are bringing the nation face to face with leisure-time problems, increased crime, and many social problems that follow in their wake. The school must realize the child should be taught the most advantageous use of leisure time so that as an adult he may have desirable avocations, hobbies, recreation, and interests. Many industrial organizations are providing well-directed programs of recreation. Had it not been for the sharpened crises between labor and management from 1940 to 1948 this movement would have made even greater gains. The future promises tremendous progress in industrial recreation.

John Dewey had this to say about leisure:

> A new concept of the use of leisure has to be created; boys and girls need to be instructed so that they can discriminate between the enjoyments that enrich and enlarge their lives and those which degrade and dissipate.

Schools have made significant progress in recreation and sports as a solution to this problem, but when one carefully searches the actual statistics of program participation of the entire student body, in all too many schools it becomes apparent that many have given the idea mere lip service, others have merely scratched the surface in developing the program, and only a small percentage have actually developed a program that is meeting the real recreational objectives of intramurals and physical education. If the schools are to create a close union between recreation and leisure time, they must shoulder the responsibility of developing habits and interests in the students which will enable them to use their leisure time to the best interests of themselves and society. The total program must be organized in such a way that any student may explore countless activities and sports through frequent participation. Thus one or more of these activities may become a specialty. The student should learn the rules and rudiments of several games as a basis for these wise selections and permanent interests. The student should leave high school and prepare to select his avocational interests as a result of avocational guidance within the school. The modern intramural program is a splendid vehicle for this kind of in-school avocational experience.

Dr. Paul Douglas[2] suggested:

> While the concern for physical strength and skill in sports is now an accepted part of the curriculums, the idea of recreation is neither current in general faculty thinking nor it is fully developed as a habit in the behavior of graduates. The creative use of leisure time remains an undeveloped field in wide areas of higher education. . . . I can conceive that the development of recreation to maturity on the campus easily could be the most important educational event of this decade. At least it has inherent in its genius a philosophy related to American traditions, a method which unlocks opportunity for character growth and a universality of appeal which makes it capable of interesting a general citizen. Just because recreation, in essence, is an individual act of a free man, its therapy of refreshment in relaxation contributes to the health and sanity of living in today's world.

Recreation as an objective of intramurals is well expressed in the following quotations from handbooks of several universities:

> Every student needs some recreation, and that of the physical type is much preferred for the student who spends the larger part of his time in classrooms, laboratories, or at his study desk.

> The intramural sports program should provide an opportunity for recreation and relaxation from strenuous school work and the rapid pace of modern living.

> Intramural athletics are founded upon the fact that every student enjoys the thrill of participating in sports. A relatively small number possess outstanding skill which places them on varsity teams, but the majority must depend upon other means of gratifying their desire for sport. Therefore the intramural program has been planned to give everyone an opportunity to compete in a sport suitable to taste and ability.

> Intramural sports are recognized here as an integral part of undergraduate life. They not only promote recreation for the student's leisure time, but also are an important factor in inducing a state of sound vitality which is regarded as an essential factor in a well-rounded development. Permanent interest in sport is cultivated by intramural activities.

It is significant that very few varsity sports today teach athletic skills that can be used after the school years. Intramural programs can offset this deficiency by providing a great number of sports that will be of permanent interest in adult life. This is more easily possible in intramurals since great specialization is not the objective. We are well aware that adults rarely become interested in sports and recreational activities unless some fundamental skills and pleasures have been obtained in undergraduate days. It is true that some adult education programs are helping older citizens to develop new skills and interests in pursuits adapted to their age. Thus recreational skills and interests must become a central objective in the intramural program. This is one of the objectives best defended to the critical taxpayer and educational administrator. Once we have developed in the student a spirit of play and the ability to relax we have given him an outlet which will continue to demand expression all through life.

A. A. "Sonny" Rooker, Director of Intramurals at the University of Texas, describes the place of intramurals in higher education thus:[3]

> Assuming that a major goal of higher education is the development of men and women with the capacity to live full, productive lives and to make creative, meaningful use of their leisure time, then some conscious effort, planning, and direct programming for leisure-time education experiences are essential, if adequate education for leisure is to be achieved.
>
> Education for leisure at the collegiate level is based upon three assumptions: (1) it is primarily from the colleges and universities that the leaders and architects of tomorrow's world will come; (2) the amount of leisure time people have is increasing; and (3) the uses to which they put such time is of serious consequence to any society. It is, therefore, of deep concern that a society's future leaders be skilled in, and knowledgeable about, leisure-time use; that they be capable of exerting leadership by example and in the direction of other people's uses of leisure time.
>
> An intramural sports program should include the responsibility for *all* voluntary physical and leisure-time activity for the University community to provide for all students, all faculty, staff, and their families, and as many others in the community as possible in a "town and gown" cooperative program.

Social Values, Group Cooperation and Spirit

Perhaps one of the most important objectives of intramural sports is the social value of competition. The newly entered freshman or sophomore in high school or college is often "lost" for months or years, and yearns for contacts and recognition from his fellows. The chance to meet others of similar age is vital to happiness and well-being. Contacts for the college student become one of the greatest values of education at that level, and particularly with students from various sections of the country. The field and floor of athletic competition is the testing ground of reality. It is truly a life situation where the student learns to evaluate the character of others, to gather his own self-assurance and determination, and to know the deeper meaning of group loyalties and responsibilities. He learns to sublimate the self in the best interests of the group, yet to retain the best of individual assertiveness and leadership. Surely intramural sports will provide this opportunity faster and more adequately than any other way, because of the wide and continued contact with so many students in so many activities.

Dana X. Bible, long associated with intercollegiate athletics, made this significant statement at the University of Texas some years ago:

> I do not know of any organization on the campus of the University of Texas that does more for the physical and social welfare of students than the Intramural Department.

Dr. Harold C. Hand, near the conclusion of his excellent book, *Campus Activities,* made this statement:

> Throughout the pages we have written runs the conviction that campus activities can be so conceived, so organized, and so administered that they afford numerous real-life laboratory situations in which the students can learn through purposeful and responsible doing to live democratically here and now, and thus equip themselves for so living in after-college years.

A letter written by one college director stated:

> One of the greatest objectives of intramurals is the spread of acquaintanceship. In a large school it is impossible for a student to know more than a small group. But we have found after several years' experience that intramurals has a decidedly beneficial effect in this respect. Acquaintance ripens fast under the stimulus of bumps and bruises received on the athletic fields and courts.
>
> A second objective somewhat similar in nature is the leveling barrier between the varsity and non-varsity athlete. At our college practically all the varsity athletes take part in intramural games during the off seasons. It is a fine training in values for a great football player to be hopelessly outclassed on the basketball floor by some insignificant freshman. It is a very valuable training in soul-satisfying humility. I have seen it happen time and again with most valuable results. Any tendency toward a feeling of superiority is promptly and efficiently suppressed. I should add that practically all such players have accepted the state of affairs in a spirit of good humor, and have a good laugh when they see the little unknown freshman run rings around them on the court, or strike them out on a baseball field.

Fig. 3. Intramural ski events feature winter activities in the High Sierras near Chico State College, California.

A brochure from the University of California at Berkeley said:

> ...pleasure, wider social contacts, and the character built from friendly competition in skill and strength are considered more important in the intramural set-up, with the main emphasis always directed toward "having a good time."

Participation promotes association. The opportunity for students from all parts of the country to associate with one another on the playing fields and under competitive conditions is a lesson in character itself, and will establish many beneficial social contacts for every individual. Team play fosters the rugged virtues of courage, determination, and self-control. The individual student, when placed in playing units with group interest, also develops his sense of group loyalty and self-sacrifice.

Dean McCown of the University of Texas made this declaration in one of the school's Intramural Handbooks:

> In my opinion, our program of intramural sports contributes more towards the development of a well-rounded person than any other nonclassroom activity. Furthermore, it is my belief that, in the years to come, the firmest loyalties to the University can be traced back to participation in intramural sports.

Coordination, Perpetuation of Skills, and Bodily Prowess

It is evident that intramurals cannot provide all that is desired for the student in coordination, perpetuation of skills, and bodily prowess. It should be the function of the physical education program to teach skills

21

and fundamentals enabling the student to approach the intramural or laboratory part of the school program with sharpened desires and interests. It is also the function of physical education to develop greater coordination, strength, fitness, and prowess through its activities. Assuming that class procedures in our schools partially accomplish this objective, we can safely say that intramurals provide an opportunity for further perfection and use of these skills, thereby increasing muscular coordination and bodily prowess. In schools where little physical education is being taught it becomes the function of intramurals to assume the gigantic task of accomplishing marked progress in prowess and coordination for the student. All educators agree that intramurals provide perhaps the most enjoyable and popular medium for this development. To the student unable to enjoy regular exercise and training in physical education classes, intramurals offer great assistance in developing qualities of strength, endurance, and agility—ingredients that are still useful in meeting the emergencies of life.

A statement included in a bulletin issued by the Des Moines, Iowa, public schools, is worthy of quotation in considering the relationship of intramural sports to physical education and physical outcomes in general:

> Every child who is to attain optimum physical, intellectual, and emotional development must have several hours of enjoyable, vigorous, physical activity every day. It should be out of doors whenever possible and in the company of others much of the time.
>
> The regular physical education period does not satisfy this need. It functions mainly in developing skills, knowledges, appreciations, and desires connected with physical activities. It does not give opportunity for sufficient practice in the things taught, nor self-directed natural use of them as an integral part of daily living. The school physical education period is essentially teacher directed. It is not just a free-play period, but a period of both work and play specifically controlled and directed along predetermined lines.
>
> The intramural sports program partially fulfills the total activity needs of the pupils and motivates further satisfactory types of activity. It provides practice in desirable sports conduct which will affect behavior in such sports away from school. It should be the first and basic extracurricular activity.

Development of Varsity Material

Originally the chief objective of intramurals was to assist in the discovery of varsity material. Today this objective is incidental, with other aims looming far more important in the educational significance of intramurals. It is always gratifying to see the intramural competitor find a place on the varsity team, an opportunity that should be open to every boy. Coaches of every sport should give all possible assistance to the intramural teams. The coach who gives occasional individual suggestion, encouragement, and praise to the intramural player will be consistently rewarded by unstinted student support and a greater desire on the part of all students to graduate to the varsity teams.

Schools contemplating new varsity sports would do well to build the teams from the stars of the existing intramural program. Frequently it has been the intense intramural interest that eventually produced the full-fledged varsity sport. Every well-administered athletic department will guarantee and safeguard a close and constant cooperative working relationship between varsity and intramural programs.

Scholarship

Although participation in intramurals and recreational activities does not always produce proportionally higher academic results, one could hardly deny that intelligent use of leisure time and participation in regular recreation is beneficial to the improvement of scholarship. No studies to date have sought to prove that such activity has a deleterious effect on scholarship. On the other hand, several recent studies give credence and weight to the unity of mind and body, to the close relationship between wise physical activity and scholastic attainment. Studies conducted at the University of Nebraska for several years showed a close correlation between intramural participation and higher scholastic averages. Each year the top-ranking fraternities athletically are also top-ranking organizations academically. This finding is also borne out by studies conducted in other universities.

Washke[4] found that students who participated regularly in intramurals at the University of Oregon over a five-year period had a higher grade point average than did nonparticipating students who paralleled the participants in all control factors, and they had a still higher average than the general male student body.

Hackensmith and Miller came to the following conclusions about students at the University of Kentucky:

1. That freshman participation in intramurals does not have a marked effect upon the student's academic grade.
2. That participants in intramurals as a whole have higher mean intelligence sigma ranking than those who do not participate.
3. That sophomore, junior, and senior participants demonstrate a definitely higher mean academic grade than do nonparticipants of the same classes.

A University of Oklahoma handbook made this statement:

> The man that takes a light, brisk workout, then follows it with a
> light shower is better equipped to attack his academic work than if
> he stays bent over a book all day or wastes his spare time loafing on
> the street corner.

Robert Stumpner made the following significant comments concerning
the broadening program at Indiana University in 1960:[5]

> Our basic philosophy on intramurals arises from a faith in the
> worthiness of competitive sport, although we look in many directions
> with various approaches. Many factors and values are involved, but
> the framework of our program consists of vigorous sports competition.
> We expand from that into all of the fringe areas, but we try not to do
> so at the expense of quality. Indeed, without quality, quantity will
> eventually diminish as well. The expansion that we contemplate should
> therefore be considered in terms of depth as well as breadth. We do
> not favor a broad base without a high peak. In this way, through
> the joint efforts of all who share in our total aims we hope to fulfill
> all aspects of the physical needs of our students.

REFERENCES

1 John F. B. Morgan, *How to Keep a Sound Mind* (New York: The Macmillan
   Company, 1946).

2 "A University President Looks at Recreation," *Recreation* (Editorial), XLV,
   December, 1951.

3 *Intramural Sports for Men,* Handbook, University of Texas, Austin, 1971.

4 Paul Washke, "A Study of Intramural Sports Participation and Scholastic Attainment," *Research Quarterly,* XI, No. 2, May, 1940.

5 "Philosophy of Intramurals at Indiana University," *Eleventh Annual Proceedings
   of the National Intramural Association,* 1960, p. 8.

3

ADMINISTRATIVE PROBLEMS
AND RESPONSIBILITIES

We have noted that the first intramural sports often grew out of a student struggle for recognition and participation. It was only natural that the intercollegiate or interscholastic athletic program often gave rather begrudging financial support, staff leadership, and administrative impetus in those early days. In some instances students administered their own program completely, while in others the school assigned a staff member the leadership duty. Thus we have seen a great variety of administrative procedures in the nation, and intramurals have been promoted successfully by a number of methods. It is significant that the greatest progress in this field has taken place since many institutions placed the administrative authority in the hands of one person, the director, who is especially interested in recreation and competition for all students.

A short time ago only the large universities had an intramural director. Now junior and senior high schools, colleges, and universities have either a full-time intramural director or a staff member working in athletics or physical education who is hired with specific intramural responsibility. Teacher-training institutions have come to realize that their graduates are not equipped for the field of athletics without special courses and actual experiences in the intramural program. It is the purpose of this chapter to point out strengths and weaknesses of the great variety of administrative plans now in operation, and to focus attention on good administrative procedure. The trend is unquestionably in the direction of one-man authority. The interrelationship of the director with other allied departments presents many problems, which will be discussed.

Administrative Plans for Directing
Intramural Programs

STUDENT CONTROL

Many schools still continue the democratic-sounding policy of permitting students full control of intramurals. This is particularly true of girls' and women's programs throughout the nation. For the boys' and men's program it has appeared best to centralize authority in the hands of a director assisted by an intramural board and working closely with a student intramural council. It has been proved that student self-government is better appreciated and much more successful when carefully guided by a director who is wise enough to utilize student assistance and cooperation to the limit.

Objections to a student-controlled program might be summarized as follows:

1. If too few students are asked to shoulder the administrative load, the task becomes too great and laxity in leadership is almost a certainty.
2. If too many students accept the responsibilities involved, there will be a natural tendency to shift responsibility and dodge work.
3. Large student management may tend to bring politics and biased control on the one hand, or impersonal relationships on the other.
4. Students are not trained in the special and peculiar problems of wise administration.
5. Students are transient, and there is too much danger of the program being modified and remodeled according to the whims and special interests of a temporary group.
6. Students are likely to slight some sports which have not been well taught in physical education classes, or not yet had time to gain permanent acceptance, yet which unquestionably belong in the intramural family.
7. There is too much danger of constantly changing policies with resulting confusion.
8. Students are not likely to recognize best procedures in the safeguarding of health.
9. Even though students may possess mature enough judgment and are capable of eliminating bias, it is very difficult for them to settle

disputes, handle protests, and make decisions that will be accepted without prejudice and hard feeling.

On the other side of the controversy, J. Malcolm Simon makes a staunch plea for almost complete student management of intramurals:[1]

> The extra-curricular program at Newark College of Engineering is completely student organized and administered. The program of approximately 90 groups including athletics is financed completely by a required student activities fee of $5.00 per year. Officers are elected for the organizations by students. The program is guided by the Director of Student Activities, members of the physical education department, and interested faculty members. Each group is responsible for its own program, even in the area of budgeting, with the Student Council exercising final approval on all matters. The role of the advisor is solely to guide the students to run their program as effectively as possible, but the students do 99 percent of the work, and do it well. Intramural programs should teach students how to organize and administer as well as provide opportunities for participation. Programs of such scope will promote stability, coordination, sportsmanship, and a quality of leadership leading directly toward the attainment of education's goals. Youth wants challenge and is ready for it. We must give it to them. I believe that the student activities program at NCE has achieved a high standard of performance due mainly to our reliance upon student leadership. Mistakes are certainly made, but by meeting these problems intelligently and cooperatively a learning process is involved.

Perhaps the real solution for effective operation lies somewhere between these two points of view. No one can deny the values that accrue to students as we entrust them with more and more responsibility. Likewise, it is hard to believe that some continuity of trained leadership is not demanded. Students, particularly at lower grade levels, can be enthusiastic participants in the leadership adventures provided through intramurals. This does not imply that all management must be turned over to the changing whims and transient impulses of those who lack experience and who are apt to see only the immediate objectives. A strong director, either man or woman, will eliminate most weaknesses of either plan, and will work with all human and natural resources to produce a functional program that will meet the needs, interests, and hopes of all youth.

VARSITY COACHES

The program for boys in many schools still remains in charge of the varsity coaches in spite of the many arguments against such a plan. The theory behind this plan is to pass around the responsibility so as not to absorb all of any one man's time. Theoretically the leadership of several experts is fine, and would lead one to believe that participants in each sport would receive more instruction and coaching, as well as highly respected leadership, from the coach of that sport. Another argument in its favor is that the coach will be in a strategic position to find potent varsity material. The arguments against such a plan might be summarized as follows:

1. The coach almost invariably will slight intramurals when in the midst of his varsity sport season, in some cases disregarding them almost entirely.
2. A good intramural program will include many sports not usually found on the interschool calendar, and thus a leadership vacuum would develop and have to be bridged by some staff member.
3. The plan would lack unity as each coach would seek to act independently of other staff members.
4. Individual ideas will bring in too many types of intramural organization which might add considerable confusion to a workable program.
5. There would be great confusion on the interpretation of methods, awards, schedules, point systems, and general mechanics.
6. The great amount of detail work so essential to a good program would not be accomplished, and the program would suffer thereby.

In spite of these arguments against having coaches assume diverging authority in administration, it is evident that the best program will utilize all staff members working in athletics in every way possible. The coach out of season can work wonders in the program, provided administrative authority is vested in one person throughout the year.

THE PHYSICAL EDUCATION TEACHER

There is no good reason why the physical education instructor cannot act as director of intramural sports or as one of the staff, provided he is granted enough time from his class assignments to permit adequate administration. If intramurals are tacked on to an already overcrowded teaching load, either the class teaching or the intramural planning will be slighted. There are many excellent intramural programs over the nation directed by very busy physical education teachers just as there are similarly successful situations directed by a very busy coach or athletic director. Unless the teacher is trained and installed as director, with sufficient time for planning and supervision, the following objections might be raised to his leadership:

1. The teacher might be inclined to yield to student pressure in permitting more and more intramural-type activities in the class period to the sacrifice of teaching procedures in skills and other more varied procedures.

2. This plan often fails to give the intramural program an identity of its own, so that it becomes sublimated in the total program of physical education.
3. The instructor is likely to select competitive units almost exclusively from the class units, especially in the junior and senior high shool, thus overlooking more natural units that should be considered in many sports.
4. Unless great care is taken, there will not be adequate precautions for equalizing competition.

In general, it will be found more advisable for the junior and senior high schools to select a physical educator as intramural director rather than one of the major sport coaches, since rightly or wrongly the pressure of winning will predominate in the latter's efforts and time.

The Model Plan of Centralized Administration

College presidents and school superintendents are coming to realize an adavantage in the creation of a distinct department of intramural sports and campus recreation. It would be preferable to select a person especially trained and equipped for the position. He need not spend full time on this assignment. Many of the best programs in large and small schools today do not have full-time intramural directors. They do have an individual in charge, however, who understands the peculiar problems of "sports for all" and is unswerving in zeal and enthusiasm to make this slogan a reality. The leader thus selected should have a broad understanding and appreciation of all sports, but he does not necessarily have to be an expert in all of them. The director might be selected from the academic staff if these qualifications are present. He should be a detailist; he should be energetic, resourceful, and a good organizer; he should be well liked by both students and staff. His administrative duties and prerogatives should be clearly defined. He should not be left to wrangle and fight for a proper distribution of equipment, facilities, and staff personnel with the athletic director or the coaching staff. Mutual planning and cooperation should be carefully arranged and understood as the program is established, in order to eliminate later confusion.

The director will be the court of final appeal in all matters of dispute, and must command respect, confidence, and good will from the students. While the director will call upon the student intramural council to determine mutual policies, selection of activities, and problems relating to the activities selected, he will, nevertheless, be responsible personally for the development of a complete and adequate program. In the larger institutions he must be an executive, and in many cases will become almost totally a desk director, with others on the staff doing much of the actual work on field and floor.

Richard B. Morland, of Stetson University at De Land, Florida, made some interesting comments about the person who is selected to direct intramurals at any school or college (at 1969 N.I.A. Convention):

> In my estimation, the intramural director wears the mantle of the most important man or woman in any department of physical education, recreation, or athletics. Through a program of depth and breadth he is rendering a service to the institution that affects more students in a meaningful fashion than perhaps any other single individual.
>
> The intramural director who gets the job done must be a person of many talents. It takes a person with the executive ability of a General Motors Vice-President, the facility for detail of a bank teller, the persistence of a door-to-door salesman, the optimism of a Norman Vincent Peale, the memory of a Univac, the compassion of a minister, and one who speaks with the finality of a magistrate to administer successfully one of these large scale operations. With balls and foils to be checked out and in, officials not showing, eligibility cases to be resolved, players to be consoled who thought they were "robbed," fields too wet, too hard, too soft, postponed contests to be played, protests to be heard, and a host of other problems that occur daily, I am amazed as to how intramural directors manage to retain their composure.

David Lawson, sports director for the Stromberg-Carlson Company at Rochester, New York, advocated the theory that frequent personal contact by the recreation director with the employees develops a more friendly feeling toward the program and arouses interest much more readily than do mere publicity and motivation campaigns. This theory is just as applicable to the school intramural and recreational program as to industry. The director in the large university is often compelled to devote much of his time to office administrative detail, but should not forget the truth of the above statement.

In most larger universities an assistant director will be necessary. His duties involve actual work with student committees or council, the supervision and training of officials, and much actual detail of the department. The director can then give more attention to interdepartmental relationships, school committees, and correlation of the total program, as well as the establishment of policies. The assistant director will work directly with the field supervisors, who become necessary cogs in the program when different sports are being conducted simultaneously in various places. Many schools have all members of the physical education staff assigned as field supervisors at various times, or graduate assistants selected especially for this type of assignment. Older students can often be selected as field supervisors, and often delight in this kind of leadership opportunity. Most good programs in the larger schools operate at least four sports simultaneously, with games spread over as many locations, making the problem of good supervision imperative.

The supervisors see that all competing teams are properly assigned to their respective playing areas, that all officials, timers, scorers, and others are ready for action, that score sheets and records are turned in to headquarters following all contests, and that proper care is taken of equipment furnished by the department. In case of injury they are on hand to see that medical or hospital care is provided. They are available to settle little problems that often arise in the midst of actual competition. School superintendents in many places have come to realize that faculty members profit much by this kind of relationship with students, and as a result do a much better teaching job. Thus more teachers are being asked to assist the intramural director as supervisors. Often students come to have a much different attitude toward teachers when they enjoy this closer recreational relationship with them.

Joseph M. Forbes, at Humboldt State College, Arcata, California, has developed a plan for leadership preparation which requires that all physical education majors and minors attend a lecture course in the administration of intramurals one day per week. The students are then assigned to intramural programs three hours per week as directors, organizers, supervisors, and officials for practical application of materials presented. The plan has been exceptionally successful.

Dan Kinsey at Earlham College described the director thus:[2]

> A good intramural director neither *stands over* students nor *leaves students alone*. A good intramural director *stands by* students.

First Aid and Care of Injuries in Intramurals

Most schools assume no financial responsibility for injuries received in games and contests. However, almost every school provides some way to care for emergencies that arise whether in varsity sports, intramurals, or regular classes. The smaller school may merely equip a small first-aid room or training quarters where the director may personally handle all first aid, sending the student on to proper medical assistance or home to his parents. Larger institutions have set up more adequate training quarters, where a paid trainer handles all varsity injuries as well as intramural problems. This would seem to be the best procedure in most cases, since there is no good reason why separate facilities should be maintained for varsity and intramural injuries. The trainer should have adequate student assistants who can handle all such responsibilities, and the training room equipment can then be enlarged and more complete, thus also eliminating duplication. In all colleges and universities, the student health service gives the same service to those injured in intramurals as to the student body in general, thus usually taking care of all but a few more serious accidents. Adequate provision should be made for injuries that happen between 4 and 6 P.M., or at night.

In such events as wrestling and football, it is necessary that a member of the medical staff examine all participants, barring any who appear unfit for the strenuous sport. Many schools now require that a student health card be procured by each student every year before he begins intramural competition. A staff physician or medical student should be on hand for all boxing and wrestling matches, and should be readily available for all active team sports. Some schools provide a special intramural student trainer who is available daily at the competitive hours. This is an excellent practice in cases where varsity facilities are not available for the intramural program. The student selected for this assignment should be trained and will receive valuable experience in addition to whatever compensation can be provided. He can usually handle most injury problems and should have close contact with school or town physicians when their services are needed.

The trend is toward the use of some plan of accident insurance which would cover all students in case of serious injury. Many high school state athletic associations have now perfected their interscholastic accident insurance plans to include intramural participation, which is a fine step forward. Several insurance plans are now available at low cost from commercial companies. While the usual health service of the university often provides all that is necessary for its injuries, occasionally on every campus a more serious accident occurs. Some universities have worked out a plan with various campus organizations for one annual fund-raising project, and all work together to create a sizable fund which can be used whenever a needy student becomes the victim of intramural injuries. A special committee handles the fund and decides what appropriation should be made to assist in paying medical and hospital bills.

Intramural Managers

Some schools use a large corps of managers, who actually supervise the various sports year after year. Other schools rely on athletic managers representing the various competing units only, preferring to have the permanent staff handle other administrative duties. The latter plan seems best in most cases, and the director, his board, and his staff can work directly with these unit managers in keeping the program in full swing.

Since the managerial system varies greatly in most schools, the following summary of administrative procedures in several institutions may prove helpful. The director, regardless of what managerial plan he selects, will profit much by having at least a small group of managers who can have regular detail assignments, thus taking a great load off the director's office.

The Intramural Handbook at Washington State University includes "Tips to Managers," which are quoted here in part:[3]

Tips to Managers

Each living group or other organization shall select an intramural manager who will *serve* as the *official representative* for *his group in all matters involving intramural participation.* Past experience has shown a close relationship between the intramural *manager's efficiency and enthusiasm and the success* of his group in intramural competition. Following is a list of procedures that former successful managers have practiced.

1. Check your box in New Gym regularly. Entry deadlines are generally on Mondays with the regular bulletin available by 1 P.M. on Friday of each week. However, there may be additional materials available at other times so check your box frequently.
2. Check this handbook regularly for *deadlines*. These dates are also listed in the University Activities Calendar. Plan on checking these materials periodically. Be responsible for meeting these deadlines.
3. *Be an administrator.* Organize your group so that it is not necessary for you to carry all of the responsibility for meeting schedules. *Recruit dependable assistants (team captains)* to make sure that games are played or postponed and reported on time.
4. *Player eligibility is your responsibility.* Be familiar with the rules in this handbook. Check with the Intramural Office concerning any questionable entrant *prior* to entering his nam ein competition.
5. Establish your *own bulletin board* where the weekly schedule and intramural announcements can be placed. Also a noon lunch reminder is helpful if practical.
6. *Encourage participation* by talking intramurals with the men of your group. With the number of sports offered in the program there should be an activity for almost everyone. A *talent form* for information on past high school athletic participation is helpful in aiding the manager to know more about each individual in his organization.
7. Request and make arrangements for *postponements* when necessary.
8. *Be sensible about the number of teams you enter.* Your success as a manager depends to a large degree on your ability to gather responsible teams. *Forfeits hurt your organization* through loss of points.
9. Cooperate with game officials and demonstrate good sportsmanship.

Administrative Organization in Some Colleges and Universities

A survey of present administrative relationships over the nation indicates four general types of control, although there are minor points of difference in each of the schools described:

1. Athletics, physical education, recreation, and intramurals all combined into a unified administrative unit.
2. The physical education department an entirely separate unit from intercollegiate or interscholastic athletics, and having as one of its branches the intramural program.
3. The intramural department separate from interschool athletics, and largely student-controlled and operated.
4. A separate school of health, physical education, and athletics, including intramurals, with a dean and all necessary department chairmen.

Groups 1 and 4 offer the ideal type of organization, since so much can be accomplished with unified control. They offer great possibilities for more balanced finances, more adequate budgets, greater cooperation of all staff members, and combined and planned use of total facilities. It would be most unfortunate to have this type of organization if the director placed undue emphasis on any phase of the entire program at the expense of the other important departments.

The University of Minnesota is an example of Group 1. The assistant director acts as supervisor of physical education; under him are the director and department of intramural sports. Intercollegiate gate receipts have financed much of the great program expansion at Minnesota due to close harmony and unified administration. Some of the varsity coaches are quite active in intramurals. The secret of cooperation may depend upon the attitude of the athletic director. Unit managers work between the various campus groups and the intramural office. Ohio State, North Carolina, Utah State, Chicago, Cincinnati, Cornell, Syracuse, Harvard, Southern California, Michigan State, Williams, and the University of Toronto are all examples of this unified administrative type. In all of these schools it is evident that varsity and assistant coaches are much more active in the intramural activities and that much saving is accomplished in cooperative use of facilities and personnel.

Schools in Group 2 are numerous, and are developing great programs due to their close-knit organization. While cooperation between interschool athletics and intramurals may not be as close in this type of setup, it is evident that schools are realizing more and more that such correlated effort is indispensable in the modern university, and much progress is being made.

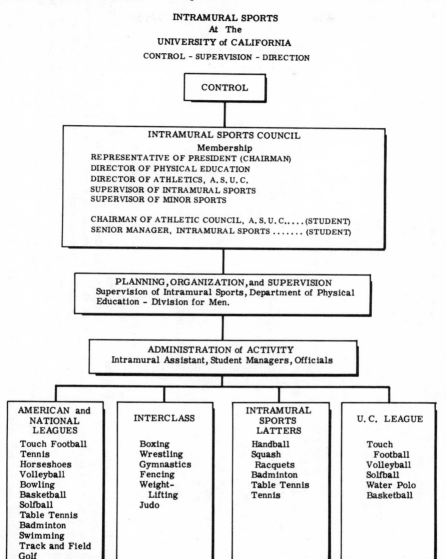

Fig. 4. Administrative chart, University of California, Berkeley.

Universities whose intramural departments are a part of the department or physical education, separate from intercollegiate athletics, are Wisconsin, Illinois, UCLA, Princeton, Nebraska, California at Berkeley, Drake, Western Reserve, Dartmouth, Tennessee, Oklahoma A & M, Washington at Seattle, and Michigan. Each of these schools has a fine, broad program.

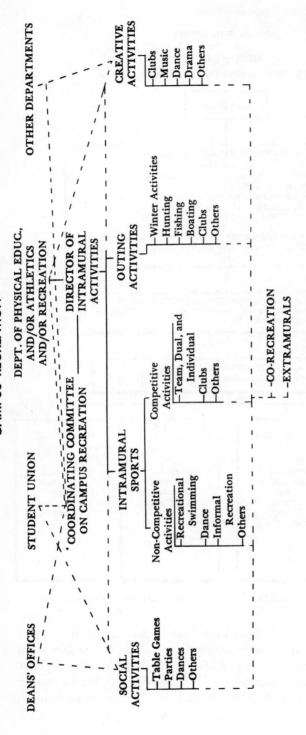

SUGGESTED ORGANIZATION OF CAMPUS RECREATION

Legend:

a. The Director of Intramural Activities is presented as the chairman or adviser of the Coordinating Committee.

b. Dotted lines from departments to the Coordinating Committee show representation on the committee.

c. Dotted lines from departments to activities show some degree of responsibility in that area.

d. Dotted lines from activities to Co-recreation and Extramurals

show that opportunities in these areas are possible for any of the activities.

e. Unbroken line from Department of Physical Education, and/or Athletics, and/or Recreation to the Director of Intramural Activities shows that the Director is directly responsible to this Department.

f. Unbroken line connecting the Coordinating Committee and the director shows the director in an advisory capacity to the committee.

g. Unbroken line from the director to Intramural Sports and Outing Activities shows direct authority and responsibility in those areas.

Fig. 5. Desirable organizational chart for colleges and universities. A plan developed by leaders at a national conference, 1955.

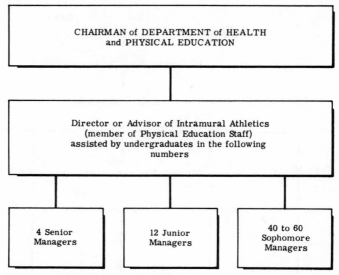

(Princeton University, Princeton, N.J.)

Fig. 6. Intramural Administrative Organization. The Department of Health and Physical Education is responsible to the university for the conduct of wholesome physical activities for all undergraduates. The department sponsors the Intramural Athletic Association, under whose auspices all intramural athletics are conducted. A member of the physical education staff acts as director of the program. He is also a member of the Board of Directors of the Association.

While the trend has been definitely moving farther away from almost totally student-controlled intramurals, several schools still operate with that objective. Noteworthy examples of this type are College of the City of New York, Newark College of Engineering, and Amherst College. Louisiana State University follows the policy of permitting great opportunity for student control and operation of their intramurals. At this institution the students make plans almost independently and proceed to carry them out. The plan is working with considerable success. In 1948 Hartley Price introduced the first Student Leadership Recreational Congress on his campus at the University of Illinois, inviting students from all over the nation to participate in the two-day discussions on the future role of student leadership in campus recreation. The trend being followed in most institutions is to incorporate as much student cooperation and assistance as possible, but closely supervised and controlled by the director and his staff.

Group 4, consisting of schools with a separate school of health, physical education, recreation, and athletics, of which intramurals are a part, is not as widespread. With further growth and expansion of graduate programs

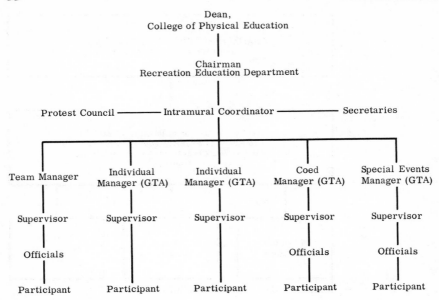

Fig. 7. The plan at Brigham Young University has some differences which should stimulate study before a new administrative plan is adapted.

and professional training, the number will increase in the future. Examples are University of Oregon, West Virginia, Oregon State, Ithaca, Indiana, University of Florida, and Brigham Young University.

College departments almost unanimously make use of some form of student council in administration. It is common practice to settle protests before a board composed entirely or in part of faculty members, or by the director alone. The latter procedure might well put too much direct responsibility on one man, who must, indeed, be a King Solomon to maintain a reputation for unbiased judgment. A board can hear cases as they appear and render decisions impartially, thus escaping any feeling that might revert to any one man. Regulations for protests should be set up in such a way that the desire to register a formal protest would seldom be aroused in students. It would be a wise procedure to have a board administer all protests at a regular meeting time, being presided over by the assistant director or the director. It might be well to provide a "cooling-off" period following the game, which would in some cases eliminate the filing of a protest. With games played in the late afternoon or evening, the rules might provide that protests could not be filed until the following day, though they should be filed, in writing, before a specified amount of time has expired.

The Intramural Council should meet regularly to discuss all kinds of mutual problems and to clarify plans for coming events. Rules and regulations can be discussed at this time. The director takes this opportunity to clear up many details with his campus representatives, who in turn do the same with their organizations. The Intramural Council at the University of Mississippi meets once each week at a specified hour. The attendance here is made more effective by a rule which levies a fine of three supremacy points against any organization whose representative is more than ten minutes late. If a total absence occurs, that organization loses five points. No excuses whatever are accepted.

Larger schools either have full-time intramural secretaries, or part-time services as needed. High schools often assign secretarial and office detail to students or managers. Some students delight in this type of work, and if they are properly organized, can handle hundreds of tiresome details with efficiency.

At Wisconsin, Purdue, and Nebraska a faculty sports supervisor in the department promotes interest in faculty competition and recreation. At Oberlin a director of recreation coordinates all types of recreation, including faculty activities. At Rutgers members of the physical education staff supervise games. Sports supervisors are usually carefully selected older students, or graduate assistants, varsity coaches, physical education staff members, or full-time supervisors of intramurals.

PRE-TOURNAMENT PRACTICE
AND CONDITIONING

Every school should require minimum conditioning preceding some special sports such as wrestling, cross-country, track, swimming, and football. While it is obvious that finely conditioned fitness will not be attained thereby for all contestants, the required preprogram will weed out those physically unfit for such competition, especially when accompanied by the medical inspection. Most varsity coaches are willing to supervise this conditioning period. Some schools provide optional instruction periods preceding most individual sports. A staff member or skilled student works with all who care to report, teaching skills, rules, fundamentals, and playing hints in such activities as handball, badminton, squash, archery, shuffleboard, fencing, golf, wrestling, rifle shooting, and tennis. Some provide reserved practice sessions preceding league schedules in touch football, basketball, water basketball, volleyball, bowling, rifle shooting, track, and swimming. Minnesota has required a five weeks' conditioning period for boxing, wrestling, and cross-country runs. Kentucky requires that cross-country participants run the course at least nine times prior to competition. Ohio State makes no specific requirement, but provides opportunities for practice in most sports. At Pennsylvania State College the varsity coach is responsi-

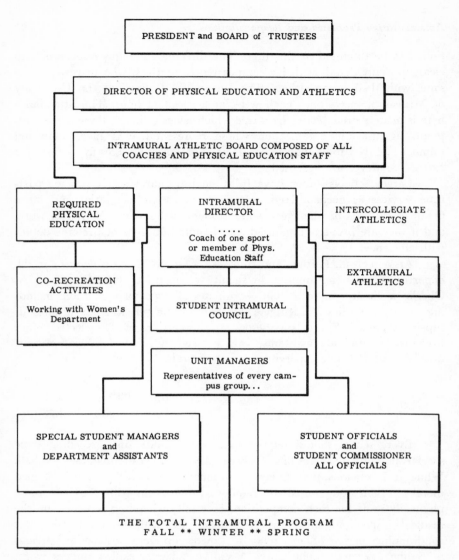

Fig. 8. Suggested administrative plan for a small college.

ble for determining the fitness of all entrants for competition. West Virginia has managers check at least six preliminary cross-country runs. Purdue arranges for practice games in several sports before the championship series begins.

UNIT ATHLETIC MANAGERS

The liaison officer between the department and each competing group and organization is the unit manager. While he is not actually a part of the intramural staff, he represents the most important connecting link in

40

a truly successful program. Each organization will rise or fall in proportion to the efficiency and interest of its own manager. Experience has shown that groups making the best annual showing in sports give special attention to the selection of a capable and enthusiastic manager. He is the athletic director of his group, and may handle most of the duties personally or appoint submanagers to give special attention to various sports. A brief outline of his duties is listed to indicate the scope of his responsibility:

1. Keep all bulletins, notices, and announcements posted on the organization's bulletin board. Use these same bulletins in making oral announcements for all coming events.
2. Attend all meetings of unit managers.
3. File entries for all events before the deadline dates.
4. Promote and stimulate all sports among members of the group.
5. Arrange for practice sessions for the group, and for individual instruction when same is provided by the department.
6. Conduct tryouts for the various teams and events when needed.
7. Coach, or appoint coaches from the group, to direct the strategy of the teams.
8. Have all teams ready for play at the appointed time and place.
9. Be thoroughly familiar with all rules and regulations and be careful that only eligible men participate.
10. File a complete roster of personnel, making changes from time to time as additions and deletions are made.
11. Be responsible for the payment of any dues or fees for the group.
12. Check to see that all competitors have health cards on file.
13. File any formal protests and represent the group when such protests are acted upon by the board.
14. Furnish officials as required by rules of the respective sports.
15. Perform miscellaneous duties, such as keeping individual participation records as desired by the department.

The Intramural Department at the University of Texas publishes and distributes a Handbook for Voluntary Student Managerial System. In the introduction to the 1971 edition the stage is set:

> The men's intramural program is set up for the students and they, in turn, govern, promote, and supervise the managerial system with the guidance of the intramural administrators. With the aim of making the students feel that the program is their own, the student managerial system has been in use at the University of Texas at Austin for the greater part of the program's existence.

The Handbook clarifies duties, bonus points given to organizations, managerial assignments, the merit and promotion system, assistant manager's duties, junior manager's duties, senior manager's duties, and general information.

OFFICIALS FOR THE TEAM SPORTS

The junior high schools have little difficulty getting any number of boys to officiate at their games. The assignment is considered a privilege at that age. Senior high schools often use varsity players since it is considered good experience and increases knowledge of the rules. Faculty members can often be secured to officiate at high school games; unemployed alumni are sometimes available; older students are often willing and well qualified; and staff members themselves often officiate. High schools using a participation point system can also give credit for this assignment.

In colleges and universities the problem may be quite different. Usually plenty of applicants are available, but the players are more critical and rivalry is often more intense. Several schools conduct regular officials' clinics where rules are discussed, written examinations are given, and several devices are used for better results. Clinics at Illinois, Michigan, Nebraska, Minnesota, West Virginia, and Wisconsin are noteworthy in this respect. Nebraska has one of its staff members acting as Commissioner of Officials for all team contests throughout the year, for both paid and voluntary officiating. This plan works very satisfactorily and each year the quality of officiating is improving. Several schools pay their officials in touch football, basketball, water basketball, and volleyball only, with a straight fee per game. Some pay officials an hourly rate. While this amount seems insignificant, a sizable amount of cash can be earned during a season if the official works two or three games in an evening. Officials' shirts should be provided for all contests, and the official held responsible for all game equipment checked out from the cage daily. The field supervisor works closely with all officials in each sport.

In the colleges it has proved better to train and prepare a good staff of student officials rather than to have staff members do the actual officiating. This latter assignment would be impossible with the large number of games running simultaneously every day. Colleges have also made good use of graduate assistants, professional physical education students, and practice teachers. Where special courses in athletic officiating are given, or courses involving intramural administration, officiating is often required as a laboratory portion of the course. Intramural athletic boards should always defend decisions of judgment made by their officiating staff, unless actual rule technicalities have been violated.

Bunker advocated a nonpayment plan at the University of Missouri, suggesting that officiating be made an integral part of student participation. He accorded recognition for participation to the student as an official, just as he now receives recognition as a player or manager. Missouri would have the participating units assuming responsibility for supplying all officials as the schedule demands. This plan probably would be predicated on the assumption that the program provides an individual point system with its individual awards.

The University of Illinois started the following plan a few years ago:

> The Intramural and Recreational Division introduced into its system a clinic for each individual sport. At these clinics all rules and regulations pertaining to that sport are explained and demonstrated. All teams participating in the sport are required to attend and are held responsible for rules explained. This solves many of the disagreements that arise during the games. The referee's decision is then final. Clinics have been held in water polo, volleyball, and basketball. Many players were familiar with the rules, but did not understand clearly local and intramural interpretations. The limited time and facilities are explained and bring the participants closer to the intramural program.

FACULTY ADVISORY COMMITTEE

The Faculty Advisory Committee is not commonly found in most schools. In such a committee, faculty men sympathetic with recreation and intramural philosophy could be selected and undoubtedly could add prestige to the program. They could meet on call, if not too frequently, and would be very helpful in discussing and advising on policies of significant importance. Some universities select outside faculty members to sit on the Intramural Athletic Board.

The Scope of Administrative Details and Duties

While the size of the school will determine the extent and scope of duties that must be performed by members of the intramural staff, it is well here to present a complete outline of all possible functions and details that must be carefully handled in the modern program. Smaller schools may find some value in a study of the outline as a possible check list on their own program, modifying it to their own needs.

It is well known that the broad intramural development will carry with it little of the glamour and headline features that characterize interschool athletics, but as one gets deeper into the workings of a great "sports for all" organization it becomes more apparent that the satisfactions and results are so outstanding that real joys and pleasures accrue to all who work with it. Its potentialities are in direct proportion to the administrative time and attention given to little details. To the casual observer the program seems to move along by its own momentum, while actually this is far from the case. Attention to all the minute and sometimes tiresome details, carefully planned and followed, spells success or mediocrity in the modern program. This rather unspectacular program then almost invariably becomes the largest single department in a college or university, as well as in the junior or senior high school, affecting the lives and educational experiences of more students than any other, and adding spice and zest in the sometimes long and tedious grind of four or more years of school.

The following outline may be helpful to those establishing new departments or reorganizing procedures now in existence:

I. Guiding principles and general policies of the department.
    1. To serve the total recreational needs of the student body by means of a carefully devised program of activities which will reach the largest number of individuals the greatest number of times, and which will have such breadth and variety that all interests will be served.
    2. To emphasize events and activities that will have both in-school value and later adult carry-over attraction. These events must be sponsored and operated in such a way that the maximum in enjoyment, social value, and sportsmanship will prevail. Health is to be carefully safeguarded at all times.
    3. To eliminate any forces that might tend to reduce the maximum of sociability and good will among all students and faculty members participating.
    4. To study constantly the most efficient methods for arrangement of competition, encouraging competition for the fun of playing and not for possible awards.
    5. To provide instruction individually whenever possible, and without fees attached thereto.

II. Staff and departmental administration.
    1. Periodic conferences and meetings of all workers in the program. This involves clarification of objectives and purposes, as well as better understanding of mechanical procedures to be followed.
    2. Regular meetings with the Intramural Board, and with unit managers and other student groups.
    3. Management of the Intramural Headquarters offices, and all the details connected with this busy assignment.

III. Professional responsibilities and public relations.
    1. Constant work with the school administration through individuals and committees, councils, faculty groups, etc.
    2. Addresses before all kinds of civic groups, Parent-Teacher Associations, athletic banquets, school assemblies, state and nationwide meetings, educational and student groups of all kinds.
    3. Radio talks and special programs over the air.
    4. Research and professional studies of best practices, and occasional contributions to professional literature.

5. Close cooperative work with many allied departments of the school such as intercollegiate athletics, health service, graduate school, the physical education instructional and activity program, teacher training, speech, dramatics, and all other departments.
6. Maintenance of memberships and offices in local, district, and national organizations of professional nature.

IV. Relationships with the student body.

1. Constant office and personal conferences with students on many matters concerning sports information, program mechanics, and health problems.
2. Orientation lectures each semester to all incoming freshmen, and the distribution of printed material and activity questionnaires.
3. Arrangement of details connected with special assemblies, meetings, and athletic banquets and special functions.
4. Supervision of actual competition as often as possible.
5. An annual visitation of student groups, fraternity houses, dormitories, and living groups.
6. Arrangements made for special instructional activity courses that will be vital to the program. Teaching professional courses that naturally fall into the administrative sphere.
7. Meetings and conferences with regularly organized managerial groups.
8. Personal assistance in the program of weighing-in and medical examination of competitors for such events as boxing and wrestling where great care should be taken for the health and welfare of the student concerned.
9. Development of an adequate system for selection, training, and assignment of officials.

V. Duties at Intramural Headquarters.

1. Careful attention to all correspondence; proper handling of all institutional regulations, printed forms, requisitions, purchase orders, invoices, requests, and telephone calls.
2. Constant interchange of intramural literature and information; answering questionnaires, preparation of copy for printed forms, mimeographed bulletins, and announcements.
3. Supervision of the office staff and student assistants, to whom usually fall the mass of details, telephone service, card index systems, point charts, office details of all kinds, lost and found, departmental library, permanent records, information, periodicals, etc.
4. Purchase and care of all intramural equipment and maintenance of fields and floors.
5. Inventories of all supplies and equipment taken periodically; preparation and constant checkup of budgets, bookkeeping, reports.

6. Collection and proper processing of all special fees.
7. Preparation of the monthly payroll; keeping records and making payment for all student game officials.
8. Selection of all awards with the assistance of the group representatives, and subsequent purchase of same.
9. Handling of the mass of details connected with promotion, conduct, and business management of all events where admission is charged.
10. Statistical records and summaries of the program in all its phases; maintenance of a clipping service from all newspapers; maintenance of swimming pool charts and testing reports; final summaries of each event giving all pertinent information for the future reference needs of the program; binding of each year's complete statistical records, bulletins, and events summaries for filing.
11. Supervision of special publicity releases, unusual facts, and program highlights.
12. Maintenance of card index systems and point summaries of both individual and group participation.

VI. Supervision outside the headquarters offices.
1. Maintenance and coordination of duties of those working with equipment rooms, towel service and laundry, game equipment, field and floor equipment, preparation of field and floor for contests, janitors, cage attendants, training room, classrooms, first aid supplies and workers, swimming pool sanitation, machinery, etc.
2. Arrangements perfected for special programs, weekend service, field supervision at all times, and staff assignments.
3. Maintenance of proper hygienic conditions throughout the plant.

VII. Organization, supervision, and motivation of the competition.
1. Planning and organization of the year's calendar of events, as well as details connected with each event as scheduled; arrangement of co-recreational events in cooperation with others in authority; planning faculty recreation, outing club activities, and special features; arrangements for extramural athletics; and work with all other campus groups who contribute other recreational features to the year's program.
2. Construction of all schedules in all events after careful study of other campus events, examination periods, building and field conflicts, etc.
3. Preparation of the constant bulletin service and its distribution; maintenance of the bulletin boards and attractive motivating lobby displays.
4. Preparation and planning of championship plaques, lobby record boards, motivating slogans, printed spot announcements, etc.

5. Placing equipment for all events as scheduled; constant notification of teams scheduled; telephone checkup on all organizations not entered as deadlines close for each event.
6. Planning and presentation of special demonstrations, assemblies, sports skills programs, carnivals, public occasions, and exhibitions by outstanding performers in many sports.
7. Making arrangements for instructional periods in various sports.
8. Checkup on problems of eligibility and compliance with health service and medical examination regulations.
9. Distribution of posters, bulletins, and announcements; keeping lobby spot announcement board fresh with coming events; display and presentation of all awards; maintenance of point system lobby charts.
10. Photographs taken throughout the year; preparation of photo displays of permanent nature; preparation of material for school paper and annual.
11. Preparation of copy and maintenance of stock on all printed forms, bulletin heading sheets, cards, score sheets, league standings, and all stock materials.
12. Editing and publishing of the annual or biannual intramural handbook, and any other brochures concerning the program.
13. Sending of reports on the program to the administration and other interested people.

It will be readily observed that the preceding check list partially covers the administrative duties of the large university program. The small school program may not involve as many details of management, but will in lesser degree touch on part or all of these items as the program functions and develops. The junior and senior high school director will undoubtedly employ the willing services of a large staff of students to carry out many of these assignments, and in so doing will gradually develop a program of which the school and the community will rightfully be proud.

Diagrammatic Study of Administrative Organizations

Every director should set up a diagram of departmental administrative responsibility for his own school situation. All staff members should be familiar with the diagram in order to have a clear-cut idea of interrelationship and authority. The typical illustrations offered here present various ideas which might be of assistance in developing or reorganizing a school program at various levels.

For the truly successful program, much work remains to be done after a skeleton administrative organization is perfected. Various staff members have peculiarly different characteristics. If the director permits various individuals to conduct phases of the program in their own hit-and-miss fashion, a veritable hodgepodge will often result. The total administration must be systematized and staff meetings should develop an appreciation for adopted details of procedure. Intramural administration demands constant cooperation between the various departments of the school. In the university it involves related fields of physical education, graduate school, inter-

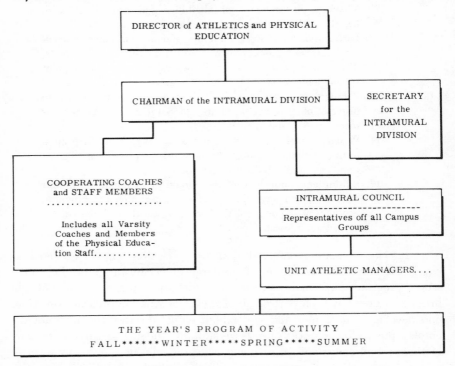

(Courtesy of Milton R. Howard, Syracuse University, Syracuse, N.Y.)

Fig. 9. Organization and administration at Syracuse University, Syracuse, New York.

collegiate athletics, health service, various colleges, chancellor, comptroller, superintendent of building and grounds and his staff, and all the deans and directors. In the junior and senior high school it involves departments such as girls' physical education, janitors, interscholastic athletics, industrial arts, dramatics, speech and debate, library, health service, and the total faculty.

To get the job done effectively, careful attention to details is imperative. All workers in charge of various events may find the following outline helpful in following a carefully organized procedure, which is applicable for every event conducted.

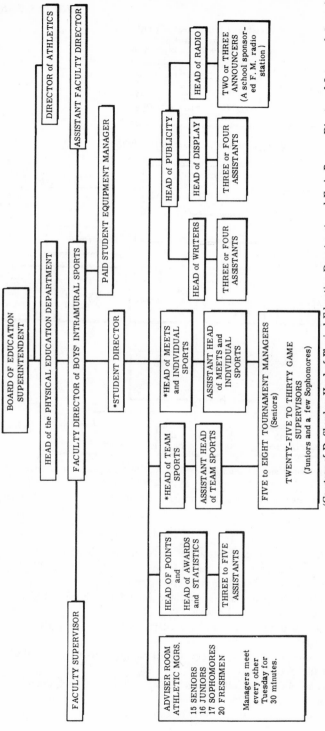

(Courtesy of D. Showley, Head of Physical Education Department, and F. A. Barney, Director of Intramural Sports.)

(Courtesy of D. Showley, Head of Physical Education Department, and F. A. Barney, Director of Intramural Sports.)
Fig. 10. Organization and administration of student leadership in intramurals at the New Trier Township High School, Winnetka, Illinois. The Boys' Intramural Sports Board consists of all boys who are the head or assistant head of a staff and all tournament managers. This totals to about 17 to 19 boys.

Division of Intramural Activities
Organizational Chart
of the University of Louisville

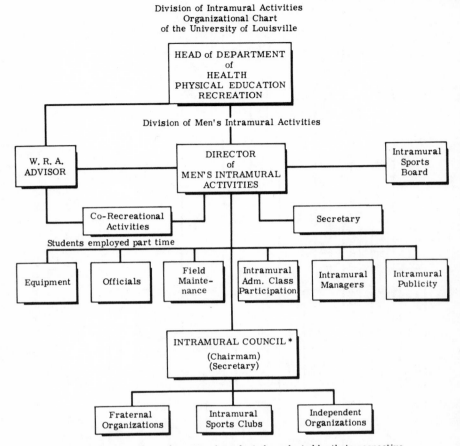

Fig. 11. Division of intramural activities organizational chart of the University of Louisville.

Sports Organization Procedure

I. Preceding competition in any one sport on the calendar:

1. Dates decided well in advance and properly publicized.
2. Deadline date for all entries announced.
3. Bulletin prepared and distributed including all rules, regulations, information, dates, etc.
4. Entry blanks (or method of entry) sent out with early bulletins.
5. At time of deadline for entries, all campus groups who failed to file entries telephoned.
6. Composite list of all entries made, noting preferred times of play.
7. Checkup made on all forfeiture or entry fees paid.

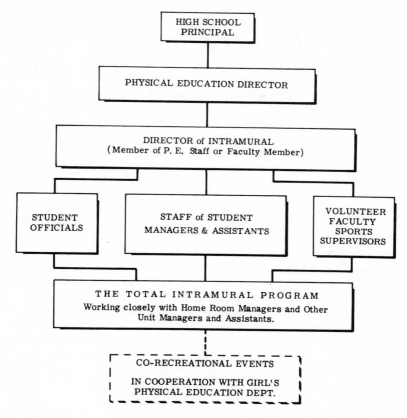

Fig. 12. Suggested plan for large high schools.

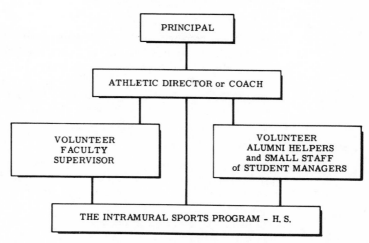

Fig. 13. Suggested plan for a typical small high school.

8. Teams seeded, keeping in mind previous year's champions, and the immediate rivalries involved, and anticipated strength of teams.

9. Leagues established with proper strength distributed.

10. Check list made of all possible facilities and program conflicts noted after conference with those in charge.

11. All available dates and hours set up in dummy fashion, listing all possible games without placement of teams.

12. Separate league schedules (without dates) made up for each league using printed or mimeographed forms for size of league selected.

13. The overall composite schedule drafted with all information at hand.

14. Overall schedule checked and rechecked to avoid duplications and possible errors. It is often wise to have different individuals perform this recheck.

15. Practice period reservations and supervision organized.

16. Schedules mailed or given to all unit managers, field supervisors, and others involved. This can be the composite total schedule or separate schedules for each team prepared.

17. All games scheduled for this activity then placed on the Daily Schedule Sheet.

18. Commissioner of officials for that sport conducts meetings and rules clinics; gets staff assigned and ready for action.

19. Advance publicity written for all sources giving brief and interesting details, previous winners, participation statistics, etc.

20. Score sheets or score books prepared for at least the first one or two weeks' play.

21. Make sure all awards for that sport are ready and on display.

II. On each day of actual competition:

1. Fields or floors prepared and all fixed equipment ready.

2. Game equipment prepared in equipment cage, checked out by game officials who are responsible for its return.

3. Health cards checked as names are entered on score sheets.

4. Scorers, timers, bench officials, scoreboards, etc., readied.

5. Supervisor always available while games are in progress to check procedures and settle problems that arise.

6. Photographs of action taken from time to time.

III. Following day's competition:

1. All score sheets carefully checked for accuracy and neatness.

2. Officials' cards made out and filed.

3. All scores recorded:

   a. On daily schedule sheet in office.

   b. On bulletin board schedules, etc.

   c. Bulletin board league standings revised.

4. Individual participation recorded.

     5. Number of spectators estimated and recorded.

     6. Check made to be sure all team and game equipment was returned.

     7. All movable field and floor equipment replaced to eliminate confusion for following day's physical education classes.

IV. At sport's end—permanent recording:

     1. Bulletins made up (two or three carbon copies) in the standard, adopted form, with all scores, schedules, statistics, point awards, champions, pre-event bulletins, newspaper clippings, etc.

     2. Photographs taken of team champions and others desired.

     3. Supremacy or group scoring charts brought up to date.

     4. Awards presented at the appropriate time following action, with awards entries made in special awards book to avoid later possible confusion and error.

     5. Complete news service; preparation and distribution of stories for all sources, including results, unusual features, etc.

V. At year's end:

     1. Prepare book bindings of all sports and activities bulletins which have been completed and filed (Sec. IV, 1) so that a complete and permanent volume containing the total year's program is available for future reference.

     2. Prepare statistical summaries of the year's activity program, sending copies to all administrative officers, deans and directors, newspapers, alumni periodicals, and to others who should receive same.

     3. Prepare composite photographic displays of year's activities highlights, and frame and hang for future interest and motivation.

     4. Complete news clipping service for the year in either scrapbook for office guests, or composite headline bulletin board displays.

     5. Prepare list of observations and suggestions that have arisen from year's program that will be helpful in planning the following year's program.

     6. Prepare corrected copy for the next year's handbook while pertinent changes and ideas are still fresh, and so printer can have copy in time for early completion.

     7. Check to see that awards, certificates, and individual sports details have all been properly cleared and handled.

     8. Circulate check list of pertinent questions and activities used among all campus organizations to get impressions and suggestions for improvement for years to come.

     9. Organize some one event which will appropriately bring the year's program to a happy and satisfactory conclusion, and which might serve to be the ideal time for final presentation of awards, recognition of outstanding managerial services, and other fitting testimonials.

The casual observer would little realize the great mass of details that must fit into component parts to guarantee the really successful "sports for all" program. But due to the tremendous number of students and departments affected by this program, it is no wonder that intramural athletics may well be considered the largest single program on any campus, and that it is rapidly coming to be recognized as one of the most essential and vital parts of the educational scheme in a modern educational institution.

REFERENCES

1 "Student Leadership—The Urban College," *Eleventh Annual Proceedings of the National Intramural Association,* 1960, p. 19.
2 "Student Leadership," *Eleventh Annual Proceedings of the National Intramural Association,* 1960, p. 23.
3 *Intramural Handbook,* Washington State University, Pullman, 1970.

GENERAL REFERENCE

Intramural Sports for College Men and Women, National Conference Report, Washington, D.C.: AAHPER, 1955.

4

ORGANIZATION OF UNITS
FOR COMPETITION

Differences are bound to exist in the local situation as the director sets himself to the task of organizing competitive units in the school or on the campus. Units that are workable in the colleges may be entirely useless in elementary, junior, and senior high schools. Students who live at home and in their own city present a much different problem than does the college family whose members are gathered from every part of a state or larger area. As the college situation is studied more closely, we again find significant differences: many colleges do not have fraternities, while some demand that every student live in a college-maintained dormitory or club. This problem is the most serious in the organization of group sports, but will also directly affect all individual sports, since we know that group motivation in such activities is very pronounced.

It becomes necessary, therefore, to make a careful survey and acquire understanding of the local situation before competitive units can be set up. Even when these units are established, the director must make a constant effort to organize new types of competitive units from time to time that will entice more and more students into a pleasurable program of rivalry and recreational pleasure. Several programs began with the traditional interclass rivalries, grew into the interfraternity competition, and then slowly sought to develop units for independent students.

The earliest attempts at nonvarsity organization largely conformed to the interclass type, with freshmen, sophomores, juniors, and seniors setting up competition in a limited number of sports. This type of organization should not be overlooked in today's modern program. Another early form was the English tradition of intercollege competition. Some of our oldest Eastern universities and those of Canada still employ this type of organization as the basis of their intramural programs. As one studies the modern college program, it would seem that this natural basis for organization has been too frequently ignored by American schools and could rightfully be utilized along with the many other units favorable for good rivalry.

The Junior and Senior High School Program

While there may appear to be fundamental differences between establishing competitive units in junior high schools and the senior high school, the differences are so slight that the two types of schools will be considered together. We should recognize that the age and interest level of the two groups will naturally modify the program of activities as well as techniques of organization. We shall consider this period as ranging from the seventh to the twelfth grade. At the earlier period there is a great desire to participate in self-testing activities, a greater desire to win simple awards emblematic of individual excellence. We also know it is a period of desire to sample and enjoy the first taste of team and individual activity in a great number of sports, nor does this desire become completely dissipated as college years are approached. The younger students find it easy to become loyal to improvised competitive units, or to shift from one team to another and quickly gain enthusiasm for different groups as each sport approaches.

UNITS THAT ORIGINATE FROM PHYSICAL
EDUCATION CLASSES

The total intramural program should not be carried on in the regular class period—a time all too brief for good skills instruction. However, the class is a perfect medium for stimulation and announcements concerning the total program.

Many team sports can be organized with teams selected in the regular classes. Only a brief beginning can be made here with some early round games played. Most of the schedules would then be played in after-school hours. Larger segments of the student body thereby become team members. New competitive interests are established which carry over into other types of organized activity outside the classes. Using the class as one basic approach to intramural participation is defensible when wisdom is used.

Teams can be set up quickly, team captains and officials selected, and leadership developed. It would usually be undesirable to utilize class periods for scheduled matches in individual and dual sports.

SPECIAL LEAGUE ORGANIZATION

Whether teams and leagues are developed from the gymnasium classes or in some other way, there are many unique ways to stimulate interest at this level. The establishment of color leagues is one example: teams all select a color as the team name, such as Blues, Golds, Whites. The jungle idea is another, with teams named after the animal kingdom, such as Lions, Tigers, Bears, Camels, Rats, Giraffes. The more unusual and bizarre names seem to arouse more interest and enthusiasm, such as Skunks, Anteaters, and similar appellations. Bird leagues carry the idea over into the feathered world. The reptile leagues carry such unusual team names as Rattlesnakes, Cobras, Pythons. Other leagues that have been used are named after cities, leading colleges and universities, professional baseball nicknames, state names, and college athletic nicknames such as Pioneers, Jayhawks, Cornhuskers, Gophers, Uclans, and Boilermakers. As an outgrowth of this constant type of shifting organization, the department should allow some possibility for challenge games which might arise during the year.

INTERCLASS COMPETITION

Interclass competition is one of the best intramural organizational systems for smaller schools, and is easily adopted in larger schools for certain sports. Every junior and senior high school should have some sports organized on the interclass basis, even though some overlapping of personnel and activities may result. It should be remembered also that the interclass idea offers one more place where separate sports records should be maintained as a further motivation for participation and striving for excellence.

HOME ROOMS OR SESSION ROOMS

This type of classification is perhaps the most widely used today. Almost every intermediate and secondary school has this unit for academic or administrative purposes. Since the groups remain set for a whole year, or at least a semester, they become ideal as competitive units, because loyalties and rivalry can be so well stimulated. Some schools now have inter-home room communication systems connected with the principal's office, affording a wonderful medium for announcements of all kinds. The home room also provides a suitable place for trophies, plaques, and team awards not possible in many other methods of organizing competition.

JAMBOREE TYPE OF ORGANIZATION

Announcement is made that a certain tournament will be conducted on a special day, frequently on Saturday. All interested students appear, captains are chosen on the spot, teams are selected by the captains to equalize ability, a schedule is quickly drawn, and play proceeds. This can be developed into a very popular type of highlight for the annual program and can be done in many different sports. This method should not be used to form the backbone of the organizational program, but rather to provide a change of pace and a supplement to other more standard techniques.

RESIDENTIAL DISTRICTS

With a student body scattered about a rather fixed section of the city or town, a division of competitive units by geographical location is often practical. The ward maps of the city can be used, or any arbitrary division of the city can be selected to equalize competition. Care must be exercised not to fan into white heat antagonisms that might be prevalent between certain sections of the city.

CHURCH OR RELIGIOUS GROUPS

Some schools conduct a few activities employing church affiliations as their basis of classification. This plan certainly would not be sound for the bulk of activity, but could be used occasionally to add variety to the program, possibly succeeding in thus reaching new student groups that otherwise might not compete. Care must again be observed in the elimination of friction and bad feeling that might be lurking under the surface between various religious factions of the community.

BOY AND GIRL SCOUT TROOPS

Some consolidated schools, especially in the Middle West, have strongly organized scout units operating and meeting in the school building. Others do not have such an arrangement but the scout organization is strong in the school and community. Some events can then be planned on this basis, which should greatly implement the Boy Scout and Girl Scout program if carefully planned with scouting leaders.

ORGANIZATION BY GRADES

Some of the larger cities have the entire school divided into grade sections such as 7A1, 7A2, 7A3, and 9B1, 9B2, and so on into each semester of gradation. In the junior high schools of South Bend, Indiana, this proved an ideal intramural arrangement, with almost all sports organized by these groupings. True, the younger groups were often at a disadvantage with older classes as the play-off series was reached, but this was usually offset by more youthful enthusiasm and more constant competitive zeal.

MILITARY UNITS

This type of organization cannot be generally used since there are so few junior or senior high schools having military groups. However, schools that do have such a program can satisfactorily work with the military department, furnishing facilities, officials, and league organization as an auxiliary supplement to the other forms of intramural activity.

SOCIETIES AND CLUBS

It is doubtful whether intramurals should ever be organized at the secondary level for social groups. While it is generally known that a few high schools in the nation still have societies of fraternal nature operating *sub rosa,* most states prohibit their existence by law. Attempts to organize other types of societies into athletic units do not often succeed since the groups are specifically organized to devote their interests and time to other things, all of which are equally important to the social and intellectual well-being of the students. Special athletic and sports clubs have been organized with great success in some schools, and intramurals grow out of these club relationships. An example of this arrangement is noted in the Los Angeles public schools. Here competitive units are often based on clubs formed in such sports as tumbling, tennis, golf, fencing, badminton, archery. Several leagues are set up in each sport, classified by the exponent system of height, weight, and age. The midget class might include all with exponent of 71 or below; the minor class those with exponent ranges from 72 to 78; and the major class with exponent 79 and above. Each club is sponsored by a school faculty man who acts as a Big Brother; this brings a large section of the faculty into the recreational life of the school.

FROM INTRAMURALS TO EXTRAMURALS

Cities like Baltimore, South Bend, and Providence have successfully promoted a great variety of interscholastic sports which are not commonly found in the usual interschool program, and which often spring from intramural play in each school. It would seem that all cities of sufficient size could synchronize their intramural and interscholastic sports to include a tremendous number of activities, with intramurals playing a dominant part in the whole structure. Extramurals between various schools within the city or school district could then grow naturally out of the structure, with interschool sports becoming more significant as the extramurals become more firmly established. Extramural athletics will be discussed at greater length in Chapter 15.

Junior Colleges

Intramurals should play a dominant part in the life of all junior college students. This is especially true where intercollegiate competition is difficult with other widely scattered junior colleges. Many of the nation's junior colleges are closely associated with the senior high school, and the intramural program is simply an outgrowth of the secondary program. Since students attending these institutions do not usually live in dormitories or fraternity houses, the problem of establishing competitive units is analogous to the senior high school pattern. Prevocational units offer possibilities, and units organized on the basis of geographical distribution are also possible.

College of the Sequoias, at Visalia, California, has developed a policy worthy of examination. Officials there have decided that almost all physical education classes will be conducted on a coeducational basis, consisting entirely of individual and dual sports or individualized activities. No team sports are included in instructional classes. It is their contention that boys and girls have had ample opportunity in lower grades to learn at least the basic team sport skills. Students are encouraged to enjoy team sports only through intramural and intercollegiate schedules. This places a premium on good intramural organization and operation. An activity period is also provided each day for intramurals and club activities. Late afternoon buses are provided for those who remain to participate in team sports.

Colleges and Universities

Intramural sports challenge the best administrative thought in colleges and universities today. The nation has hundreds of smaller colleges, some lacking adequate facilities and staff, but all having very definite contributions to make to their student bodies through recreational sports. Surmounting these many obstacles, some of America's smaller colleges, with fewer advantages in some ways than the major universities, have made some of the most valuable contributions to intramural development. The smaller institution can often reach a larger percentage of it enrollment more easily, and the possibilities for sociological growth and adjustment can be enhanced through such an intimate and ongoing program. Since competitive units must be selected in light of the local situation, the whole group of colleges and universities will be considered together. Some ideas that will work for the small liberal arts college are not applicable to the teachers' college or the large state university. Competitive units used in colleges might be listed as follows:

Interclass	Curch and religious groups
Interfraternity-Intersorority	Co-recreational groups
Interdormitory	Outing and outdoor clubs
Boarding clubs	Intercollege units
Faculty	Interdepartmental units
Faculty-student units	International groups
Graduate students	Military units
Summer session groups	The ward system of zoning
Purely recreational activities	Groups within various colleges
Gymnasium class units	Interfraternity "B" and "C" units
Geographical units	Units by states or national areas
Professional societies	Units by counties of the state

The modern university program will seek to employ as many of the listed competitive unit possibilities as the situation will permit. Only in this way will the majority of students be reached.

INTERCLASS

The smaller colleges find this method frequently the best, and much of their program is so organized. The larger schools will find many difficulties with such an arrangement, and even if it is accomplished, it will only affect a very small percentage of the students. Class spirit, so pronounced in the earlier years of American colleges, is declining. Competition on this basis is to be commended in that it seeks to break down social distinctions and small group cliques, and places a premium on outstanding ability on the campus. The interclass method can be used as a supplement to other types of organization, coming to a climax where only the best performers merge together to fight it out for the highest school honors next to intercollegiate sport.

INTERFRATERNITY-INTERSORORITY

By far the most extensive organization is by fraternity or sorority units. Since this natural rivalry is so easily developed, too many institutions have allowed it to remain almost their total intramural and recreational basis, thus eliminating all the unorganized students from much of the program. These are usually the students who most need the sociological values of competitive sport and certainly deserve more consideration. Fraternity groups are well organized and strive for excellence at all times. Supremacy

Fig. 14. Elementary school track and field competition, San Mateo, California.

point systems can be administered easily, and unit managers can be very active. It is usually preferable to arrange separate leagues for professional fraternities, since they are wholly or partially composed of graduate students and often include in their membership students who have other fraternal ties.

With the recent explosion of college enrollment it has been found practical to organize "B" and "C" teams in additional leagues in some of the more popular team sports such as basketball, volleyball, bowling, softball, table tennis, tennis, and handball. This would appear to be very desirable in all the more popular individual sports that usually do not require more than from three to six fraternity members to constitute a team in the "A" leagues.

John Longfellow, at Indiana State Teachers College, Terre Haute, has provided leagues in team sports for each skill level. Thus each campus organization may have two or three teams, each in separate leagues, and each an integral part of the total structure.

INTERCOLLEGE OR
INTERDEPARTMENTAL UNITS

English and Canadian universities have for generations maintained the intercollege type of competition as the backbone of their program. Thus many of our earlier American universities such as Harvard and Yale have continued to stress this method of classification with splendid results. Even though many of our colleges now place most of their emphasis on the interfraternity and independent units, the use of interdepartmental leagues in many sports adds much to the program. By careful attention to management of these teams, entirely new groups of unorganized students are brought into the program. There are many problems connected with working out this type of competition since some colleges and departments within the university are very much smaller than others. Sometimes two or more colleges are combined for intramural purposes. Another difficulty with placing too much emphasis on this type of competition is that a large part of the student body may be passing through the first or second year of general academic work, not yet sure what college or department of specialization they will ultimately select. At Temple University one basketball league is composed of teams from the professional schools of Law, Pharmacy, Medicine, and Dentistry.

DORMITORIES

Colleges having no fraternities and requiring all students to live in dormitory units find the interdormitory system ideal. It is, in effect, the interfraternity system under a different guise. Loyalties are fairly permanent, and group organization is easily possible. Team trophies can be awarded. Universities having fraternities, scattered independent individuals, and dormitories, should arrange competition for all these groups, culminated at the end of each sport by all-university championship play-offs.

INDEPENDENTS

Herein lies the greatest challenge to colleges today. The larger the institution, the greater the difficulty in getting independent students interested enough in the program to obtain the recreation they need. Ofter the feeling prevails that intramural athletics do not really exist for them, since so many other social opportunities are denied them. Independents are reached in a variety of ways; and segments of the group are reached when competition is provided in other ways, such as by dormitories, intercollege and interdepartment, church and religious groups, international programs, and through the ward system. This latter plan has been used with success at Iowa State University, Purdue University, and Illinois. The Iowa State Ward Plan is discussed in detail later in this chapter. Independents are often reached through the required physical education program. Constant use of all publicity techniques will draw more and more of them into the program. The main difficulty is the lack of permanent group ties, and teams are often organized only for the duration of a sport season. At the college age real rivalries cannot be built with that kind of arrangement. It is unfortunate that many colleges still make little real effort to reach all independent students, which is, at best, an endless task. One of the best methods in the large university is by use of the sports interest questionnaire which is distributed at the first of the year, either through freshman orientation periods or to registration lines for all classes. The student fills out the questionnaire as he would all other registration materials. The form contains spaces for name, address, telephone number, affiliations if any, and provides a check list for the student to indicate sports and activities he has enjoyed previously in high school or college, activities that he would like to select for class participation or sports instruction, and activities that he would be interested in intramurally. It becomes the task of the office during the year to send him all bulletins and announcements for sports in which he has shown an interest or preference. This method will secure many new entries for all individual tournaments, and will provide the medium through which many independent teams may later be organized.

MILITARY UNITS

Due to the close association of student life with the several military units during World War II on college campuses, the present existing military units provide another natural basis for competition as a supplement to other competitive relationships. In the military school this basis would become dominant, whereas in the general type of institution it would be incidental. Almost all military units stand ready to conduct such events as rifle shooting for the general student body as well as for military personel.

RELIGIOUS GROUPS

Every large campus has several church-affiliated groups that have rather close student relationships. It should be the function of the department to provide organized competition in whatever popular sports the groups might select. Even if this takes place in only one or two sports, the effort is very much worthwhile. It is usually welcomed by the religious leadership, since it is helpful in solidifying their own membership in a common cause and it adds recreation to the many other reasons why students enjoy the fellowship of others of similar religion.

INTERNATIONAL STUDENTS

Larger universities always have fairly large groups of students from foreign countries on the campus. Unless these individuals are made to feel that the program has something to offer them the group feels recreationally lost. Naturally it takes some time to interest these groups in typically American sports. On the other hand, their interest is easily aroused for soccer, swimming, table tennis, handball, volleyball, and other sports that are popular in their own countries. Sometimes competition can be arranged only by means of challenge or matched games in soccer, etc. Sometimes regular leagues can be organized especially for these students in such activities as table tennis where large numbers are not necessary. Again, it might be best to try to include their teams in independent leagues in many of the sports. Every effort should be made to interest them in the program in some way.

GRADUATE STUDENTS

The larger universities have the responsibility of providing recreation for graduate students. Some permit these individuals to compete along with undergraduates, while most schools declare them ineligible for such competition. If the latter is done it becomes imperative that special arrangements be made for them. Team sports are usually not as popular, individual activities being favored. Sometimes competition can be provided combining faculty and graduate student groups.

THE SUMMER SESSION

Since we are constantly striving to inculcate the recreation idea into the life of the undergraduate during the regular college year, we must then care for the summer leisure of both graduate and undergraduate students. The location will determine the extent of the program. Usually most interest develops in a very few team sports, principally softball, and centers around individual tournaments in such activities as tennis, golf, co-recreational events, handball, squash, badminton, shuffleboard, and various methods of arranging recreation through swimming. Often the usual competitive units of the academic year must be completely revamped for the summer session, with an attempt made to gather team and individual entries from any source possible. Noncompetitive outing activities are usually popular during spring and summer months.

COMPETITION WITHIN
THE VARIOUS COLLEGES

This is a source of intramural competition that has not been sufficiently tapped by most schools. Often it is the opening wedge for great interest and participation in many other phases of the campus program. At the

University of Nebraska, in addition to all other units and organized events, separate competition has been carried on as desired by students and faculty combined in the Dental College, the Agricultural College, the College of Engineering with its seven separate departments, and the School of Medicine situated in another city. Participation on teams within the college does not bar the same students from entering many other leagues and tournaments, but does provide a natural unit which can expand as rapidly as the department stimulates and provides leadership.

GENERAL RECREATION

ON A VOLUNTARY BASIS

Every college department should provide a portion of its time and facilities for the numerous students who thoroughly enjoy a bit of recreation and exercise whenever they have a moment of leisure. This program will grow in proportion to the administrative stimulation given and allowance made for use of facilities. Naturally these individuals will not continue activity when it is apparent that they are in the way. Special picnic and party kits of equipment should always be made available for weekend and evening parties and groups, with no charge made unless material is lost or damaged.

Purdue University has developed an extensive nonorganized program and officials there feel this is basic to the total intramural program. Campus recreation, housed in new and superior facilities, has attracted much attention. Some intramural directors feel this type of program is excellent, but is not really a part of intramurals. Nevertheless, this trend is gaining momentum, and arrangements should be made for it on every campus whether administered by the intramural department, a campus recreation director and staff, or by the Student Union. This point of view is equally valid for elementary and secondary schools.

FACULTY UNITS

The enterprising director and his staff are always awake to the possibility of serving the faculty group recreationally. In the smaller college, team groups are almost impossible. However, some schools have solved this problem in a number of ways. Amherst College allows faculty teams to compete with the undergraduate units in all sports. The record shows that occasionally they win games, and once in a great while a championship. Certainly close and profitable friendships are fostered in this way. Other schools provide match games with city adult teams. Bowling and golf are perhaps the easiest sports to introduce on a purely faculty basis. Faculty recreation prospers where separate shower and dressing room facilities are provided, thus affording some privacy and relaxation from the noise and drive of large student participation, and tournaments can be easily devised in tennis, golf, badminton, shuffleboard, squash, handball, table tennis, and the more individual recreational type of activities.

If a school could plan a part of the building unit for the faculty, with dressing and shower room, lockers, reading and smoking room, and a small buffet luncheon counter for coffee or tea and light lunch, the noon period of two hours daily would see appreciative interest on the part of the faculty. Here a class could be developed on the floor for conditioning with accompanying music, a quick game of volleyball or some other sport, followed by a restful shower and light lunch. In such an environment the faculty might quickly develop new appreciations for the role of exercise and recreation in the academic life of the student body.

Purdue conducts faculty competition in squash, handball, tennis, golf, horseshoes, and softball. At the University of Toronto faculty intercollege competition is strongly entrenched. The University of Florida permits faculty members to participate with fraternity groups in the total program, but will not allow fraternities to pledge added strength from faculty ranks. Florida conducts special faculty tournaments in shuffleboard, handball, volleyball, tennis, golf, and softball. Amherst College provides for the faculty to compete with adults of the town and community in the gymnasium every Thursday night. Michigan provides organized activity in a few informal sports, always being willing to add more when desired. Coach Charles Mann of Michigan devoted every noon hour to the faculty men for years. Every Monday, Wednesday, and Friday noon he taught swimming to faculty beginners, with swimming and water polo for the faculty on Tuesday and Thursday noons.

The University of Illinois provides a special recreational program for faculty men and their families. The gymnasium and swimming pool are available to them in late afternoons and early evening hours, on a scheduled basis. Co-recreational faculty events are carried on at the gymnasium during certain evenings. For these events two recreation assistants are on hand for program planning, instruction, and supervision. The faculty there enjoys such activities as archery, archery-golf, bicycling, badminton, rifle, golf, tennis, swimming, handball, horseback riding, weight lifting, square dancing, softball, and several splash parties each year. Purdue operates a fitness program for faculty children.

At Oberlin College two nights each week during the winter are reserved for faculty and local business men to participate in volleyball, basketball, and other sports. A schedule of volleyball games is arranged with business men's groups of neighboring towns, and with Oberlin College student teams. In addition, free golf lessons are given the faculty. A faculty-student golf tournament takes place each fall, and each spring features a faculty-senior softball game. Badminton is a popular activity at Oberlin.

League and recreational bowling is also part of the program. During commencement week the faculty is eligible for competition in the annual alumni golf tournament. Faculty bowling leagues on an interdepartmental basis are carried on at the University of Nebraska from October to May.

West Virginia University has provided leagues for many faculty bowling teams which bowl throughout the entire year; faculty members participate in basketball leagues; archery is a feature for faculty as well as students; Faculty Activity Nights, with faculty guests included, offer a diversity of activities; special fitness and weight training opportunities are provided for the faculty; and a Saturday activity program for school-age children of faculty members includes tumbling, wrestling, gymnastics, basketball, fitness activities, and selected activities for girls.

Other Methods of Establishing Units for Competition

The University of Michigan and several other schools utilize Orientation Week for conducted tours of the athletic plant for new students. During the week special tournaments are held to get the new students competition-minded. Purdue University sets up an intramural program during its Short Course for agricultural students while they are on the campus. Nebraska does the some for the statewide programs such as Four-H, State Music Festival, and Cornhusker Boys' and Girls' State.

Many other more scientific methods have been suggested for the classification of students for competition. Some of these plans offer educationally sound practices for the equalization of ability, often resulting in better competition. A Coefficient Plan could be recommended for elementary and secondary school use. Details of these plans are not given here since those desiring to make use of them should investigate the literature for a more complete understanding.

Richardson proposed a classification based on experimental work at Kessler Junior High School, Longview, Washington, which combines the Cozens-Neilson formula and the McCloy Classification Index, and weighs factors of speed, strength, and power to arrive at a new classification formula.[1] Others have come forward with similar scientific studies which can be helpful in physical education activities at younger age levels. These various plans hold much promise for future experimentation and development. It is doubtful at this time whether the recreational program needs to concern itself so much with scientific classification which might become so involved as to deter the needed wholesome planned competition on a mass scale. If every health safeguard is closely watched, and every possible method for the organization of more and better units of competition exploited, the school program will grow and become increasingly meaningful in the educational experience of Young America. The problem in most junior and senior high schools today is to find time and facilities to carry on as wide a program as possible, and the many details concerned with the superior program take much staff time. After programs have become deeply rooted and staff personnel becomes more ample, the profession will do well to devote more and more time to scientific classification formulas in an effort to improve the quality of competition.

Some Units of Competition
Used by Typical American Universities

As a further assistance to informed directors, who are always anxious to study the needs of their own program, the competitive units employed and utilized in several colleges and universities in the nation are briefly outlined here.

The University of California at Berkeley conducts tournaments open to all in wrestling, fencing, gymnastics, and weight lifting. Seasonal leagues are maintained in most team sports in three classifications: the National League, composed of fraternity organizations; the Dormitory Leagues for dormitory residents only; and the American League for all other independents and individuals.

The University of Tennessee uses three units: individual open events, independent leagues, and fraternity leagues. Wayne University of Detroit maintains an all-campus individual unit, interfraternity, interclass, and separate events for the Law College. Syracuse University uses the all-university open, fraternity, living center, and interclass units. Cornell University features an interdenominational unit in addition to all the others.

Ohio State University uses the following units:

Fraternity	Independent	Military
Church affiliation	Intercollege	Counties of the state
Faculty	Dormitory	Interclass

Princeton University has used the following mode of classification:

1. Individual open (badminton, cane spree, sculling, fencing, golf, tennis, track, squash, cross-country).
2. Interclass (baseball, cane spree, lacrosse, crew).
3. Clubs (juniors and seniors only) (baseball, bowling, fencing, swimming, softball, tennis, golf, crew, squash, table tennis, touch football, track, hockey).
4. Dormitories (sophomores only) (basketball, bowling, hockey, softball, squash, touch football, track).
5. Independents (sophomores, juniors, seniors) (any sport not handled in any of the above).

The University of Illinois conducts all-campus open tournaments and leagues, has interfraternity competition, maintains a recreational service for all kinds of competition, and has a campus-zoned independent division much like the ward system used elsewhere. Illinois has employed about fifty different zones, based on geographical locations for the students in Champaign and Urbana, all teams using Indian names.

Oklahoma A & M College, in addition to the traditional units, features R.O.T.C. military units for much of its competition. Dartmouth College uses dormitory and fraternity units, conducts many open tourneys for all students, and has the active cooperation of outing clubs which greatly complements the program. Harvard University, in addition to the famous intercollege competition, conducts graduate school leagues, interhouse competition, and a separate program for the six dormitories that serve the business scool.

The University of Michigan sets up competitive units as follows:

Graduate—all campus	Independent
Undergraduate—all campus	Interclass
Extension	Co-recreational
Faculty	International
Fraternity	Dormitory

The University of Nebraska has employed competitive units for the following:

1. Interfraternity, with sports approved by the fraternities annually, usually about twenty-four.
2. Open all-university tournaments in fifteen sports.
3. Dormitory leagues. Separate supremacy race and point system, with sports decided upon annually by representative group.
4. Agricultural College. Separate program maintained for these students in some twelve annual sports. In addition, individuals and groups of the Agricultural College (situated 1½ miles from city campus) participate in all other university sports as desired.
5. Independent leagues and tournaments. Every sport sponsored by the department has independent teams and leagues, winners meeting all other divisions in that sport for final championship in all sports.
6. Dental College. Both faculty and students combine as desired to participate in optional sports they elect each year. They are also eligible for independent competition in all other events.
7. College of Engineering. Seven departments of that college compete separately as desired in championship series in sports they select. Also eligible for all other events on campus.
8. Interdepartmental or intercollege. Separate competitive units established and sports selected by representatives of these units each year. Also eligible for all campus events.

9. Faculty. Leagues and tournaments created as interest indicates, and usually conducted informally or by interdepartment.
10. International. Series of match and challenge games and any other sports desired by representatives.
11. Medical College. It has its own intramural program due to its location sixty miles from city campus.
12. Law College. Four groups have own tournaments in sports elected each year. Also eligible for any campus events.
13. Co-recreational. Consists of mixed sports, parties, social-recreational events, mixed tournaments open to all in golf, tennis, shuffleboard, badminton, bowling, swimming, and splash parties.
14. Church and denominational. Composed of campus religious groups, with their own program of tournaments and leagues in several sports of their own selection. Men competing with these groups are also eligible to play with other teams except that one man may never play with more than one team in any one sport.
15. Military. Separate tournaments and leagues between units of the R.O.T.C. and N.R.O.T.C. These units meet and decide on the sports to be used each year.
16. Purely recreational. All facilities maintained and available for students who may select their own time and sport at their own pleasure.

Purdue University has used the following units for participation and competition for men.[2]

Cary Hall Program	18 sports
Cooperative Program	15 sports
Courts Program	17 sports
Interfraternity	18 sports
Men's Residence Halls	17 sports
All-Campus Events	25 sports
Co-Recreational	17 sports
Faculty Program	7 sports
Ward Program	6 sports
Sports Clubs	15 sports
Voluntary Recreational	unlimited-unorganized

Culver-Stockton College in Missouri divided all competition into color units, using the school colors, a plan often used by elementary and secondary schools. All students are placed in color units, and ability equalized for better competition.

St. Olaf College, Northfield, Minnesota, has for years used a unique plan. The college has no fraternities, and the dormitory system did not work. Athletic clubs were organized, with athletic managers for each. Freshmen register for an athletic club and remain with that affiliation for the four year period. Constant attempts are made to equalize ability of groups as additions are made to personnel. The plan has proved very successful.

Eastern Kentucky State Teachers College developed a plan for an organization without fraternities. All units are based on counties of the state. It is sometimes necessary to combine counties into one unit. Out-of-state students are grouped by states. Emory University has made extensive use of the athletic club as a medium for competition, with excellent results.

The Yale Plan for freshman unit competition is worthy of mention. In addition to the intercollege competition at Yale, freshman rivalry is next in importance. All freshmen are organized into the program. The Old Yale Campus houses almost all freshmen and they are divided into four competitive units. Twelve sports are offered in the program.[3] Experienced coaches are assigned to coach intramural football teams for each group. An all-year championship point system motivates freshman competition. A freshman athletic council administers affairs of the unit. The system then becomes a "feeder" for the later intercollege competition which is such an integral part of the Yale system.

It is interesting to view some of the ideas on interhouse competition of Dr. James B. Conant, former President of Harvard University. These remarks appeared in newspapers all over the nation in February, 1952:

> The continued significance of the intramural program should be stressed. Visitors unfamiliar with the extent of the program [at Harvard] or the interest it arouses are often struck by the keen competition between the Houses for the various athletic trophies and the fact that every November seven House teams play their affiliated College from New Haven the afternoon before the varsity contest.
>
> We have never reached anything like the goal of "competitive athletics for all." But we do have far more students participating in athletics than in the pre-House days. That such participation is, for a majority of students in our culture, an important part of learning HOW to live together is a premise that has been widely accepted by teachers for many years.
>
> From this premise developed, in the last century, the idea that games between rival colleges should be encouraged. Slowly at first and then with frightening acceleration, intercollegiate athletics developed in the United States in the Twentieth Century. The status in 1952 needs no comment in view of all that has been written on the subject of football and basketball in the last eight months.

The great problem of really reaching the independent students of any large campus has been most satisfactorily solved by the ward system illustrated in the program at Iowa State University. Some details of the program are presented here since it contains many new ideas that might be of assistance to all institutions trying to solve this problem. T. Nelson Metcalf, Director of Athletics at Chicago University until 1956, who was

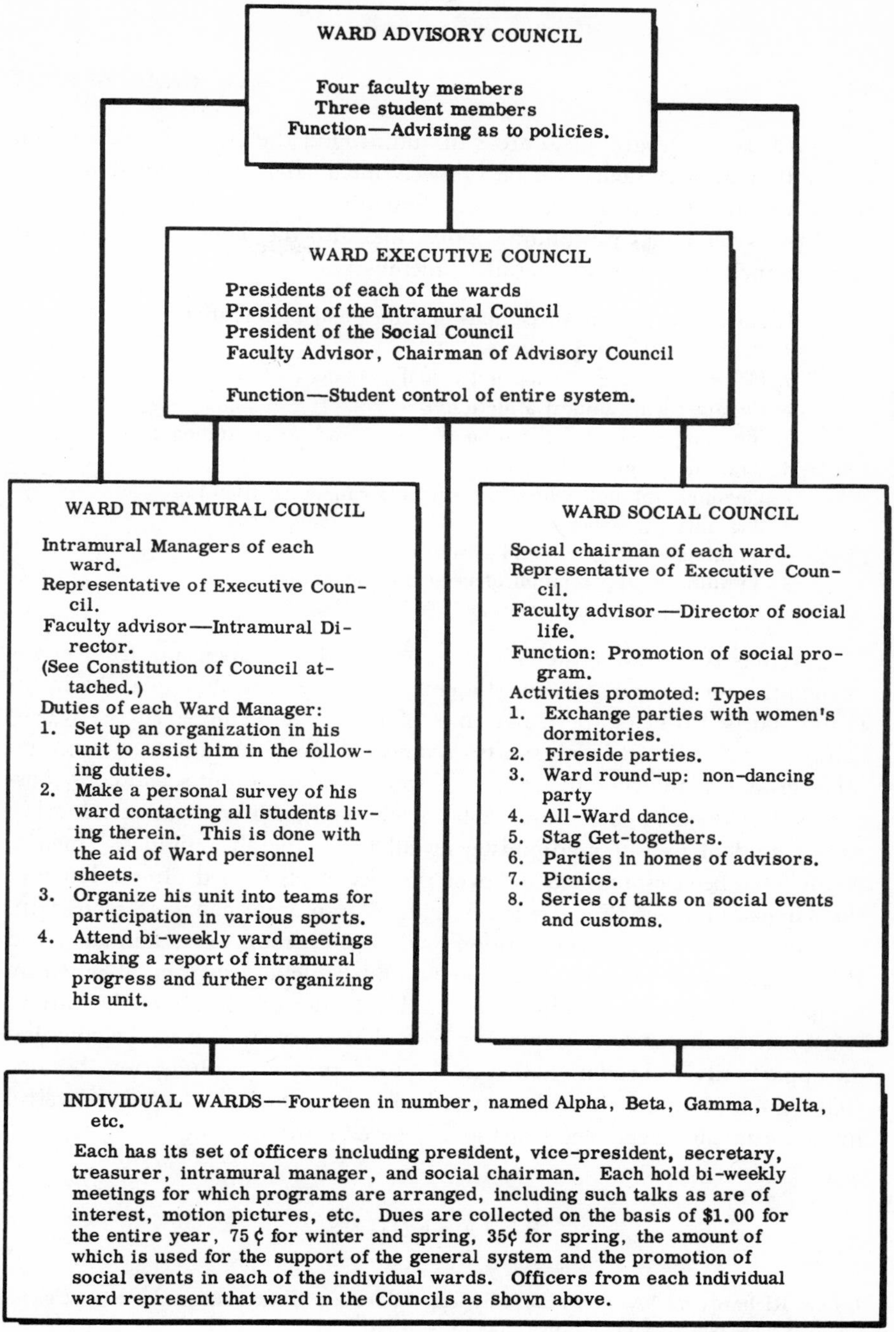

WARD ADVISORY COUNCIL

Four faculty members
Three student members
Function—Advising as to policies.

WARD EXECUTIVE COUNCIL

Presidents of each of the wards
President of the Intramural Council
President of the Social Council
Faculty Advisor, Chairman of Advisory Council

Function—Student control of entire system.

WARD INTRAMURAL COUNCIL

Intramural Managers of each ward.
Representative of Executive Council.
Faculty advisor—Intramural Director.
(See Constitution of Council attached.)
Duties of each Ward Manager:
1. Set up an organization in his unit to assist him in the following duties.
2. Make a personal survey of his ward contacting all students living therein. This is done with the aid of Ward personnel sheets.
3. Organize his unit into teams for participation in various sports.
4. Attend bi-weekly ward meetings making a report of intramural progress and further organizing his unit.

WARD SOCIAL COUNCIL

Social chairman of each ward.
Representative of Executive Council.
Faculty advisor—Director of social life.
Function: Promotion of social program.
Activities promoted: Types
1. Exchange parties with women's dormitories.
2. Fireside parties.
3. Ward round-up: non-dancing party
4. All-Ward dance.
5. Stag Get-togethers.
6. Parties in homes of advisors.
7. Picnics.
8. Series of talks on social events and customs.

INDIVIDUAL WARDS—Fourteen in number, named Alpha, Beta, Gamma, Delta, etc.

Each has its set of officers including president, vice-president, secretary, treasurer, intramural manager, and social chairman. Each hold bi-weekly meetings for which programs are arranged, including such talks as are of interest, motion pictures, etc. Dues are collected on the basis of $1.00 for the entire year, 75 ¢ for winter and spring, 35¢ for spring, the amount of which is used for the support of the general system and the promotion of social events in each of the individual wards. Officers from each individual ward represent that ward in the Councils as shown above.

Fig. 15. Iowa State Ward System organization chart.

formerly associated with the ward system at Iowa State, attempted to set up a similar system at Chicago, but it failed. Metcalf felt that such a plan is most difficult when the university is situated in a large city such as Chicago, and gets its best results in smaller cities.[4]

Wards are geographical areas in and around the city, selected in such a way that most students will be properly included in fairly equal number in each ward. The Iowa State Ward System was an outgrowth of earlier ward plans for men's intramurals alone, and also the Town Girls' Club. It came to include as a service to all its members:

1. An active part in all campus activities and organizations.
2. Better housing conditions.
3. Constructive use of each individual's talents and ambitions.
4. Organized intramural athletics.
5. Training in the appreciation of moral and social standards.
6. Training in group leadership.
7. Channels through which the students can make friends.
8. Training in cooperation.
9. Training in manners and customs.
10. Training in appreciation of personal appearance.
11. An organized social program.

While the Iowa State Ward System seeks to open up tremendous possibilities for the independent student in every conceivable area, the intramural sports aspect of the program is of most interest here. In the wards, competition is offered in all sports. Winners compete against fraternity and other groups at the conclusion of each sport. Fraternal and social consciousness is developed in each ward. A fee is charged each year for membership with a student treasurer administering all funds for all activities. Thirteen wards have been established to cover the city, each named after a letter of the Greek alphabet. Each ward has an intramural manager, who, with assistants, organizes all competition within the group. The annual Ward Round-Up starts off the year's social and athletic program. The entire campus and city are carefully zoned, and duly elected officers of the various wards, with with their assistants, see to it that every student in the zone has an opportunity to become active in the total program. The system became well-organized and thoroughly entrenched at Iowa State and was a powerful influence in the effectiveness of the college educational program.

REFERENCES

1 Len Richardson, "A Scientific Physical Education Program," *Scholastic Coach,* XVII, Nos. 8 and 9, April and May, 1948.
2 *Handbook of Intramural Athletics for Men,* Purdue University, Lafayette, Ind., 1962, pp. 11-19.
3 W. H. Neale, "Intercollegiate and Freshman Intramural Athletics," Mimeo report, Yale University, 1947.
4 T. Nelson Metcalf, Remarks made at Intramural Sports Section Meeting, College Physical Education Association, New York, 1948.

5

PLANNING TIME
FOR INTRAMURALS

Time allotment looms large in the administrative planning of an adequate intramural-recreational program in every school, regardless of size. All of the various departments and interests crowd in for their rightful consideration and emphasis, and all must be balanced and allowed their share of time and facilities. This is not a problem peculiar to athletics and physical education. Every phase of education faces similar difficulties. If intramurals are to be meaningful they must permit frequent participation, and adequate time allotment must be arranged in some way. A student who selects his or her favorite sport, to find that it can be enjoyed only once every two or three weeks, loses much interest, and the real objectives of the program are not attained.

One of the greatest problems confronting the planning of time for intramurals comes directly from the coach or physical education director, who so frequently lacks the desire to plan and budget the entire school year so that intramurals can function along with interscholastic sports. The coach often complains that the public demands he employ his time and energy exclusively to produce winning teams using 5 to 10 percent of the student body. He thereby fails to realize that quite often the public has been deprived of knowledge about the real values which accrue from a program involving all types of competition for 100 percent of the students. Quite often the public has had little opportunity to evaluate his work properly in its broadest and most educational sense. It has been proven time and again that winning interscholastic teams can be produced and even improved with a parallel program of intramural sports operating in close harmony with the girls' program, the physical education classes, and informal recreation of all types.

While the problem is never an easy one to solve, time can always be found for intramurals by a careful study and survey of available facilities, the demands made upon them, and the possibilities for staff help. The season of the year must be considered. Schools farther north must often make extensive use of the indoor plant while the fall and spring varsity squads are outdoors. Schools farther south can arrange many of their activities outdoors, where healthy and pleasurable activities are often more abundant.

Many recent innovations in school organization have helped to provide more time for intramurals and organized or informal school recreation. An example of this is modular scheduling in some secondary schools, which allocates certain hours each week for intramural sports during the school day.

It should be observed that no one time period can be set aside for intramurals, thus achieving a complete or successful program. In the discussion to follow it will be observed that segments of the student body will not be covered in each of the time periods selected, and only a combination of many plans will offer opportunities for all to participate. The director must carefully coordinate all phases of the total program, matching it carefully against the local situation, the year's calendar of events, and each day's potential available time. All of the time periods discussed here have been successfully used in many school environments and may contain some ideas of practical value.

Late Afternoons

Unquestionably the ideal time for intramurals is the period from 3:00 to 6:00 p.m. Most of the students can be reached then. It is the perfect time for recreation, following the crowded academic day and its accumulation of mental fatigue. At this period games can serve best as a safety valve, liberating pent-up emotions, dissolving worries and complexes. After the exercise period the student enjoys an invigorating shower and is ready to go home to dinner, preserving the evening for study and other activities.

Parents of public school students favor the late afternoon period. There could be a conflict between home chores and school recreation at this time, but if the student budgets his afternoons he will usually find that the few afternoons his own teams compete still leave many afternoons for home chores and tasks that are on the academic schedule. In warmer weather the late afternoon, after the midday heat has cooled, is the most enjoyable. This period is also the most economical since no additional heat or light need be used, and it does not require additional janitorial service. Most schools are so organized that janitors proceed with the daily cleanup in other parts of the building, leaving the physical education facilities for the last. A still better arrangement is to have a night crew do all the cleaning of the athletic wing when the day's activities are completed.

In the colleges and universities the late afternoon period is given highest priority. Small high schools that despair of crowded facilities at this time of day have no monopoly on the problem, as the largest universities must face the same difficulties, only in greater measure. The ideal college program would have all physical activities from 3:00 to 6:00 P.M., since dormitories, fraternities, and eating clubs all demand regular dinner hours, and many students must work at that time for their board. After dinner the usual crowded schedule of club and fraternity meetings, plus the heavy requirements at the college level and the usual social events, make night intramurals less desirable.

Many smaller colleges have developed unique and extensive facilities and programs to utilize this period. Swarthmore College not only conducts almost all of its intercollegiate and intramural activities at this period, but its physical education classes as well. They have been able to do this only after a wise and consistent planning of indoor and outdoor plant space, involving numerous play fields, tennis courts, and the spacious field house, gymnasium, and swimming pools. Swarthmore is also favored by its proximity to metropolitan Philadelphia. Thus great numbers of intercollegiate varsity, reserve varsity, and freshman games can be scheduled with teams within a small radius. The planning of extramural activities with neighboring institutions is easy in that environment. However, in the Swarthmore Plan there was an acute shortage of sports supervisors since the peak and almost total load of student participation came in a three-hour period. This problem was solved by supplementary part-time expert staff help from the city, permitting classes and organized events to be properly supervised and instructed. The field house type of arrangement seems to serve all athletic needs best for late afternoon planning, since a combination of dirt and wood floor areas provide more recreational variety, provided all needed facilities are included. Schools having such facilities are indeed fortunate, and the extensive around-the-clock use of such a plant suggests unusual possibilities. Fine field houses are now in use at Minnesota, Wisconsin, Humboldt State, North Central College, Swarthmore, Purdue, Michigan State, Chicago, Lawrence, Beloit, and others. One of the saddest commentaries on athletic administration is to see a fine field house with dirt track and play areas rendered almost unusable during much of the winter season by bleachers permanently erected around the basketball court.

Some universities have segments of their athletic facilities arranged elsewhere. At Wisconsin the track and field annex provides an uninterrupted indoor dirt floor practice area for many sports. At the University of Nebraska and at Carleton College the area under the stadium stands is admirably utilized for dirt floor sports of both varsity and intramural nature. Coe College employs a dirt floor basement area under the large gymnasium. Many schools lacking indoor gymnasium wings and dirt floor areas have designed special rooms where recreational and intramural events can be carried on without conflict from varsity sports, and where social recreation can be had at all hours.

In the public schools the problem of faculty help is made easier when the late afternoons can be utilized. Teachers who might rebel at night assignments are often willing to remain occasionally for supervisory help following the day's classes. In the consolidated rural schools, so universal in the Middle Western states such as Indiana and Illinois, the school buses usually must take all students home before the intramural hours can be completed, but this problem will always be present and it is no excuse for not using that time period. Other time arrangements must be made for the students going home by bus. Some schools provide at least one late bus, allowing larger groups of boys and girls a chance to remain and enjoy the competitive period.

Another regrettable condition exists in too many schools during the fall and spring season: while the varsity teams are still outside, the gymnasium and the indoor facilities are often devoid of organized activity. The fall, just preceeding the indoor season, is an ideal time for late afternoon use of the indoor plant for such sports as volleyball, basketball free throws, basketball golf, bat ball, wrestling, intramural basketball, and many others. In the spring, just after the varsity basketball season has ended, there is another late afternoon period where intramural activity could be packed into the school gymnasium, replacing the almost total lull so often found in many high schools.

Another time of day frequently neglected is the Monday or Friday afternoon when the varsity teams have either been given a day of rest following a hard game, or will need but a short practice period for the day. This should allow adequate time, if planned in advance, for some intramural games throughout the long winter season. Some high schools have also discovered by experience through the years that the varsity squads do not profit by too long a daily practice period. In these situations the gymnasium's weekly time is carefully budgeted so that intramural games can be scheduled for part of the period, with the varsity squad still receiving adequate practice time. Lincoln High School of Manitowoc, Wisconsin, and Shoreline Schools at Seattle, Washington, have had successful basketball teams for years, but have always found it possible to schedule parts of the week's total late afternoon time for intramural games; the schedule is religiously followed with neither program allowed to dominate the other. Another late afternoon time that occasionally can be utilized, but is often neglected, is during the day the varsity teams leave for a trip to other schools. If planned in advance, many intramural games can be arranged and the plant utilized completely.

Twilight Hours

Schools lacking sufficient play area are coming more and more to utilize the period just preceding darkness for such organized sports as softball, touch football, soccer and speedball. Often the varsity squads monopolize the available areas until dinnertime. Rather than do without organized games, most students will enjoy leagues starting play around 6:30, following an early dinner. Since the days are getting longer at that time, the spring season lends itself best to this type of planning. Since larger institutions rarely have enough playing fields for their numerous teams, lighted areas are now being used for nighttime play—a practice which has effectively expanded intramural facilities.

The University of Texas is justly proud of its lighted intramural fields, appropriately named in honor of their long-time director of intramurals, B. M. Whitaker. Texas, like most other institutions, lacked sufficient fields to carry on outdoor competition before nightfall. In an attempt to solve this difficulty, the Inter-Fraternity Council took the matter as its project and raised a very large share of the cost with its annual Varsity Circus. The balance was paid by the Athletic Council. Now it is possible to conduct

Fig. 16. Interesting program features can take place under the lights, at Ponce de Leon Junior High School, Miami, Florida.

fall sport games before dinner, followed by another series of games after dinner, eliminating the threat of diminishing daylight in the fall season, and permitting more teams and more players to enjoy the competitive program. The University of Illinois and the University of Minnesota have also developed lighted areas for ice skating and other sports.

In recent years almost every college campus in the nation has witnessed a growing tendency to take over tennis courts for building sites. The result is that many schools are deprived of as much as 50 to 80 percent of their former tennis facilities. One large university reported that its battery of 42 tennis courts existent in 1925 had diminished to four courts in 1960 with little chance for new tennis court construction except by the purchase of very costly city property, an unlikely possibility. To solve this problem it would be advisable to install lights on tennis court areas, thus immediately doubling the facilities in the same time period. If inadequate funds are available for school maintenance of electricity, a coin-deposit meter can be installed, with the participant inserting a coin for each half hour's use of the court.

The After-Dinner Evening Period

There are, naturally, some objections to extensive intramurals in the evening for youth below college age:

1. Some parents object to the school's providing programs that take students away from home and their studies after dinner.
2. Many other school and community functions take place at this time, creating conflicts in schedule.
3. Interscholastic games are sometimes conducted at night, causing further conflict.
4. Some feel that night is the time school facilities should be used for adult recreation, with the normal school day giving sufficient time for all school recreation.

While night is not necessarily the best time for intramurals, there are many reasons why limited night intramurals are justified in the total school program:

1. If the regular school day is all filled with other activities, and if intramural sports are recognized as not only justified but imperative, it should follow that the night period must be used.
2. Even though there are other community and school activities looming as a possible conflict at night, the fact remains that these conflicts are never continuous, leaving many, and perhaps sufficient, nights for intramurals.
3. It is a recognized fact that many public recreation programs use the

school athletic facilities at night for recreation of school-age youth rather than solely for adult recreation. Since this obligation primarily belongs to the school, part of the nighttime allotment of school intramurals should have priority.

4. While it is admittedly better for all students to remain at home after dinner, the fact remains that all too many students are allowed to roam the streets, get into all kinds of mischief, and otherwise waste their evenings in unwholesome activities which might be better employed in school-supervised competitive sports.

5. It is the best time of the day to avoid conflict with the varsity sports program.

6. With a night program in operation it must be remembered that no one student would be competing too frequently and each could make wise budget of his time on nights when schedules do not include him.

Colleges and universities have found that night intramurals, at least occasionally, are an absolute necessity. This has become particularly true since World War II and the advent of larger enrollments on the campuses, bringing the inconveniences of late afternoon classes and laboratories and complex academic schedules. In too many colleges the problem of having only one or two basketball courts available makes the conduct of a series of games a long and slow process. Night games in this kind of situation cannot be avoided. The larger universities have been trying to provide competition for many more teams, with the result that careful organization at night is demanded. The University of Minnesota and Iowa State University have used a novel system of conducting basketball games to guarantee more games in a limited time. Several games are started and stopped simultaneously with a single timing unit, which conserves valuable time often lost in irregular schedules. Many colleges work out their schedules so that independent teams play all their games on Monday nights, the favorite fraternity meeting night, with fraternities free to compete on other nights. The night period lends itself best also for co-recreational sports nights, where the married student couples find it possible to attend, as well as the faculty families.

At Brigham Young University arrangements for use of facilities has set a policy of scheduling all intramural activities daily from 6:00 P.M. to 10:30 P.M. and from 8:00 A.M. to 5:00 P.M. on Saturday.

Saturdays

The Saturday period is perhaps the top time for elementary and junior and senior high schools to schedule games without interruption from other school activities. Colleges find Saturday their least popular time for games, since too many students leave the campus for the weekened; but they do find that it is an admirable time for individual and group informal recreational activities, and many keep all facilities open and available on Saturday and perhaps Sunday afternoons.

Saturday games often attract the public school boy or girl who has a daily afternoon job or home chores. It is a time when varsity athletes can officiate and take an active part in the leadership of the boys' program. Many coaches want their players to take part in Saturday intramurals as a change of pace from the daily grind, and as a way of becoming more familiar with the rules and conduct of the sports.

The wise director will plan a full Saturday program of intramurals, and will also try to arrange the supervision so that no one staff member must carry the whole load. By a rotation plan, teachers will have only an occasional Saturday assignment, and will conduct the program with more enthusiasm. It is deplorable that too many schools over the nation still lock gymnasium doors to the scores of eager students who crave this natural weekened period for play and competition.

One junior high school planned an annual intramural Saturday afternoon program for its boys with the following time schedule of special events:

1:30	Running high jump and baseball throw for distance
1:30	Wheelbarrow relays
1:45	Stilt races
2:00	Dizzy Izzy relays
2:10	Over and Under relay
2:20	Bicycle relays
2:35	Half-mile walk
2:50	Base running contest for time
3:05	Shuttle relays
3:20	Obstacle relays
3:35	Medley relays
3:50	Shoe scramble
4:10	Tug-of-war as the concluding event

The elementary schools of Rochester, Minnesota, have an excellent Saturday program that runs twelve months of the year. Activities are arranged all over the city for boys and girls of all grade levels with a wide choice of sports and games. The large staff of Saturday supervisors and leaders are all teachers in the Rochester schools. This unique plan requires that every teacher in the system share recreational and leisure-time responsibility in turn during the regular school year, with Saturday emphasis. The plan also demands that every teacher carry recreational assignment for part of each summer, unless excused to pursue advanced professional training.

Noon Hours

The noon-hour period is one of the choicest times in the school day for various types of intramurals. No school should be without some form of recreation at this time. Not so important in the college and university program, the noon hour is an excellent time for the more recreational type of intramural activity for the junior and senior high school. The subject of noon-hour recreation is covered in detail in Chapter 10.

Before School Begins

One of the least used periods in school intramurals is the short period just before school opens each morning. While it is not the purpose of this discussion to urge wholesale use of this time, it is a fact that a short, daily opening period would permit many schools to enlarge and develop their schedules in the face of extremely crowded activities at other times. Scheduled games have been successfully conducted in many places such as South Bend, Indiana, in the junior high schools, Appleton, Wisconsin, in the senior high school, and at Hackensack, New Jersey.

It is not uncommon to see groups of boys loafing on the street in many larger cities early in the morning. Certain precautions must be followed if this period is to be utilized for games. A rigid time schedule must be followed, with games starting and ending promptly, allowing limited but sufficient time for the shower and passage to the first class of the day. Since no one student would be scheduled every morning, occasional games should be included to permit some students to participate who might not otherwise have an available time for competition. To implement the planning for games before school, the stage should be set the night before, so that the time available will not be dissipated with floor and field arrangements before the first whistle.

During School Hours

Some directors have rationalized their school's athletic inactivity by saying that the only available time for intramurals is during the regular school day. While this is rarely, if ever, completely true, it does not follow that some program features cannot be conducted either in the physical education class or during other daytime periods. Physical educators are generally agreed that the class period in physical education should be devoted to instruction in the broad content of the activities field and the teaching of skills, fundamentals, and a great variety of games. They are also agreed that intramurals should be the actual laboratory where previously taught skills and appreciations are utilized and refined. Many schools precede intramural sports with class instruction in that specific activity. The class period is not the best time for intramurals because the time is too short, classes are too large, and the problem of proper employment of after-school leisure time is not adequately solved.

Some schools combine a very limited amount of intramural competition in the physical education classes with the bulk of competition arranged at other times. One practical plan is to start some team sports in the classes, with a champion declared in each section, and final championship series conducted on Saturdays or evenings. Sports that require large numbers on the teams such as speedball, soccer, bat ball, indoor baseball, and softball, fit well into this scheme. In this plan a very small part of the year's class time is used for the actual competition, with other hours used to absorb the awakened competitive interest that comes from the class units. This plan has the weakness of combining into the activity other groups of students who are not enrolled in the classes. This is perhaps offset by the fact that some students who might otherwise never develop an interest are introduced to the intramural activities through the classes.

Many schools have a period each day set aside for activities. Clubs might be sponsored in such activities as archery, bait and fly casting, handcraft, tennis, tumbling, golf, and other sports, and the club period used for actual competition. There are at least two very valid reasons why this plan is not desirable. First, the period is usually short, and the group to be served in the activity necessarily small. Second, it would appear more educationally sound to have students already possessing strong athletic and sports interests taking an active part in club activities in other fields such as art, music, debate, and dramatics. Some of the same objections could be raised against a prominent use of free periods or home-room periods in the school day. In none of these times is it possible to conduct a large league activity, and the very nature of the period limits the activities used.

Vacation Periods

In almost every city and school area groups of students wander aimlessly about during the vacation periods, eager and longing for a place to play. In some instances this problem has led to groups actually breaking into the school gymnasium by force, with resulting destruction of property. Still, it is generally agreed that school staff members are entitled to a vacation from their strenuous duties. Some schools have tried to solve this problem partially by conducting recreational periods and intramural leagues during the Christmas recess and spring vacation, with the assignment of supervision rotated among staff members so no one will be completely saddled with such a responsibility. It is an excellent time for special tournaments, jamboree events, open house recreation, and unusual program features.

A special Orientation Week sports program is used by some universities, notably the University of Michigan. The purpose of such a feature, planned at this short beginning period in the college year, is to acquaint all new students with the facilities available, and to give them a touch of recreation in the first few days of stress and examination when it is usually much appreciated. First, the freshmen are taken on a tour of all recreational and athletic facilities. Then a corps of staff leaders meets the students, divides them into groups, and starts participation in several sports. Brief instruction is provided for those who desire it, games are organized, and each freshman may rotate from one to the other as time permits. In addition, special tournaments in tennis and golf are set up for separate afternoons of the week. The swimming pool is made available to all who want a quick dip during the period. The department furnishes all equipment and all students are asked to come dressed in old clothes and gym shoes.

Special Sports Days

A trend is growing throughout the nation for school administrators to permit the use of half a day once or twice a year in which almost the total student body can participate wholesale in intramural and organized recreation. This idea opens up great possibilities in organization of special point systems, participation in a variety of sports, and real enjoyment that is reflected in renewed school spirit and academic progress. The author has conducted several sports jamborees at Beloit College. Some 300 men assembled shortly after noon, organized so that every man was on a team in one of several sports. Competition began outdoors simultaneously in softball, speedball, track and field, basketball, volleyball, and horseshoes. At the end of thirty minutes of actual competition the whole group was reassembled, leaders reported scores of all games, standings were posted on a large scoreboard, and the second period of competition began. In this period every student was required to select a prearranged different sport. At the end of thirty minutes the entire group was reassembled, scores and results were tabulated, and the same process was repeated for a third period. At the end every student had participated in three different sports; supremacy points were scored, winners declared, and a great competitive period had ended. The event was extremely popular.

Elementary schools in a town, city, or county often select one or more days a year for some wholesale type of competition. Junior high schools

(Courtesy of Harlan G. Metcalf.)

Fig. 17. The perfect weekend sport, roving archery. A scene from the program of Cortland State College.

often look to such a program as a welcome taste of competition denied them in interscholastic games. In every case administrators recognize that the holiday from academic classes, even though brief, adds much enthusiasm to school progress and *esprit de corps.*

Conclusions

There are few, if any, schools in the nation which do not have difficulty in coordinating all phases of the physical education and athletic program for boys and girls, with proper time allotment; however, the aggressive and enthusiastic director will find time to promote an adequate program. He or she will discover that the local situation will modify all planning. It will soon be discovered that no one time period selected will be sufficient to attract all students, nor will it be adequate to provide sufficient time for enough games in enough sports. Every available space during every available day in every available month will be required to achieve comprehensive results. Most school administrators will provide more faculty help, more adequate budgets, and better facilities when they see such a program in actual operation over a period of time. The same administrators, without a chance to evaluate results in operation, would probably never give such support to the same program proposed by the director on paper.

6

THE PROGRAM
OF ACTIVITIES

The program of activities selected for any school must be modified by local conditions. In the North weather conditions are usually favorable to a winter outdoor sports program, featuring many ice and snow activities. In the more southern areas the outdoor sports program will be much more extensive, but with different types of events. Traditional and Old World backgrounds will also affect the program. In Canada the games of English and French background will be featured. In the East such sports as lacrosse, polo, fencing, squash, and Rugby football have deep roots, while parts of the West know little of these sports, since the skills are not well established. Soccer football and gymnastics were formerly more dominant in areas with heavy pre-European populations, but recently they have gained importance in most schools and colleges.

Facilities will modify the selection of activities directly. It is significant, however, that many enterprising directors with meager facilities are operating very successful and comprehensive programs. In the final analysis the enthusiasm and organizational skill of the director and his staff will build an adequate program with existing facilities, eventually proving to school board and community the need for a more adequate plant. It has usually proved more successful to produce a maximum program with available outdoor and indoor facilities, gradually selling the obvious need for expansion, than it is to propose to school authorities that a good program be developed when and if the plant is increased.

Recent trends indicate greater promotional impetus toward the more purely recreational activities, with a balance between team and individual sports and a mixture of the very active and less active sports to stimulate interest and competition for all types of students.

At Vandalia, Ohio, Art Van Atta and his staff have developed an elementary school intramural program that involves hundreds of boys and girls year-round. Archery starts in the third grade. Pupils ascend from short target shooting through field and bow hunting and bow fishing. Badminton starts in the third grade with yarn balls. Baseball, using a batting "T," is organized into leagues for ages 8 through 18. Basketball leagues start in the fifth grade.

Vandalia holds bike hikes every other Friday afternoon all year. They have developed their own 15-mile bike trail. On longer bike hikes a truck goes along to pick up as needed broken-down bikes or riders. Camping starts in the third grade. Fifth- and sixth-grade girls play field hockey. Fishing and casting start in kindergarten and continue with special events through all eight grades. With this activity goes instruction in water safety, canoeing, swimming, rowing, and water skiing. Flag football leagues start in the fifth grade for boys.

Vandalia teaches hunter safety and has intramural competition with air rifles in the third and fourth grades, with pellets in the fifth, and with .22 calibre rifles and trap shooting in the sixth grade, all under close supervision. Soccer, skiing, table tennis, tetherball, Four Square, gymnastics and tumbling, tennis, volleyball, and rhythms are all included at proper grade levels in this comprehensive program.

In the college program the four seasons provide natural groupings for sports. The summer school program is becoming more prominent on most campuses, with a greater recreational aspect. Colleges using the quarter system divide their sports into four divisions. Some, like Minnesota and Iowa State, reorganize leagues in basketball, bowling, and softball for several quarters.

Fall Sports

FOOTBALL

Intramural football, with full equipment and regular rules, was played in only seven colleges in the nation in 1947.[1] Very few more have taken up the sport since that date. Chicago University has stressed football in its recent program more energetically; intercollegiate football was abolished in 1939. Emory University does not have intercollegiate football, but provides intramural football for its men. Amherst is one of the smaller colleges using regular football as an annual sport. There is a growing trend in the nation toward six- or seven-man regular football as an intramural sport. The game is more wide open and less dangerous. The University of California at Berkeley and Eastern New Mexico University feature the six-man game on their calendar. Some high schools conduct six-man football each year.

Beloit College at one time organized eight-man football on an intramural basis. One of the coaching staff conditioned some 150 men four days a week for three weeks on football fundamentals and the development of team offense. Following this period of preparation, regular round-robin games were scheduled with each team playing two games weekly. The coach assisted each team to build its team offense and defense. Pushcarts brought out equipment daily to the playing fields. One-piece pants and shoulder pads were used; football shoes were barred. Each team selected different colored cotton jerseys and colored helmets from the carts. No serious injury was noted at Beloit; the casualty record at season's end was only two sprained ankles. Dozens of boys who had never enjoyed actual football competition received a real thrill out of this experience. It should be observed, however, that regular football should not be played without proper equipment and at least a minimum of actual football pre-game conditioning. Regular football is not recommended below the senior high school level.

TOUCH FOOTBALL

At present the most popular fall outdoor sport in the nation, in one form or another, is touch football. A few colleges have eliminated it in favor of less dangerous fall sports. Michigan substituted speedball, but later returned to touch football. There is little doubt that touch football contributes the bulk of the annual intramural injuries and must be properly taught and officiated to eliminate danger. Rules should be carefully observed, with rules clinics conducted for student officials and with penalties meted out for rough play, vicious blocking, and overenthusiastic tagging. Harry Applequist, former city director at Sacramento, California, utilized an idea for touch football which greatly reduced injuries and facilitated better officiating. This plan demanded that the defensive player stop at once and hold up one hand in the air at point of touch—or two hands if two-hand touch was used. The idea is practical and worthy of trial.

Some schools prefer pass ball or flag football with the thought that fewer injuries will result and the best features of football can be retained. The most notable feature of this variation is that each player carries a colored cloth flag, which has a knot in it 4 inches from one end and 16 inches from the other. The short end is pulled up under the player's belt so that the knot is snug against the lower edge. To "down" a man it is necessary to pull the flag from beneath his belt. Flag football is a fall sport at UCLA. To help reduce the number of injuries, rules were changed concerning officiating, blocking, and reception of kicks.

At Washington State University flag football games consist of two halves, each half being made up of exactly 25 plays. Every play, regardless of penalty or other circumstances, will count, except that a try for point after touchdown does not count in this quota. Also, the last play of each half must be free of penalty on the part of the defensive team.

Indoor pass ball is another form of touch football that could be used indoors with good results. Any size floor may be used. Two restraining lines 6 feet apart are marked or painted across the center of the floor, as shown in Figure 18. The two other lines denote the scoring areas. The

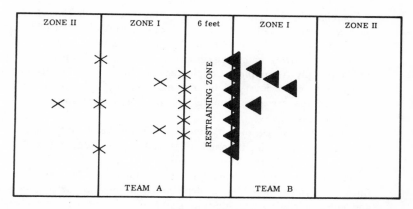

Fig. 18. Field diagram for indoor pass ball.

two teams line up as in touch football. Team A takes the ball and lines up in offensive formation, with team B on defense. The ball is snapped to any backfield man. Any number of laterals may be thrown. The main idea is to pass, not run with the ball. Points are scored by completing a pass into either of the two zones designated in the diagram; one point is awarded for a completion in Zone I, and two points for a completion in Zone II. The defensive team scores one point whenever a pass is intercepted. They also secure possession on this play, or whenever a pass is incomplete. The defense also secures the ball if touch is made before a pass is released. There are no series of downs as in football; the team having possession retains the ball as long as passes are completed. Touch football blocking rules are used. The first team to score 21 points wins. The 6-foot restraining line reduces congestion and gives the passer time to throw. Any number of linemen may be used but only four backs, and positions should be rotated.

The great variety of rules established for touch football in different schools led the College Physical Education Association to survey variations through committee action. A standardized set of rules for high school and college use has been published by The Athletic Institute titled *National Touch Football Rules Handbook.*

Fields should be smaller to increase scoring, as well as to permit more fields in a given space and to decrease fatigue. Some fields are 75 yards long with lines every 15 yards. The need for chains and down markers can be eliminated with the rule that a team must cross the next 15-yard stripe in four tries or surrender the ball.

Stan Fisher, intramural director, Regina Campus of the University of Saskatchewan, advocates the use of floor hockey as. an intramural sport. He describes it thus:

> Combine the cunning of a Master chess player, the speed of a quarter miler, the agility of a gymnast, and the brawn of an offensive tackle and you will aptly describe floor hockey action.
>
> This fast moving game requires skill in passing, pivoting, shifting and, especially, team play. Couple these qualities with no necessary background of previous skill or training, a limited amount of equipment, and you get an intramural activity that is sure to meet with instant success.
>
> The unique aspects of this game lend themselves to many variant groupings. Age, weight, fraternal, rival, and friendship groups may all compete actively in this sport.
>
> Six players comprise a playing team (teammates on the floor at one time), on which there is a center, two forwards, two defense men, and one goalie. Frequent substitutions allow for large team membership; there is a blending of individual talents to form the simple, yet intricate, aspects of a team game.
>
> Using hockey jargon to explain this last phrase, you substitute "lines" of players to give you best operating results. A "line" is usually the three forwards, or the two defense men. Through substitutions you add the speed with the weight; and the eager with the meek (or time-killers in the case of penalty situations).

Regardless of which fall sport is selected for the outdoors, it would be well to give attention to well-marked fields, placement of goal line flags or markers, and proper paraphernalia for all officials. This should include striped shirts, whistles and horns, penalty flags, and stopwatches. In touch football the official rules are usually observed with the exceptions that seem to vary in almost every school in the nation.

To eliminate ties in touch or flag football the number of downs for each team can be counted. The team with the most downs becomes the winner. If the score and number of downs remains tied, one plan is to run eight alternating plays, starting on the 50 yard line. At the end of this alternating series the team that has the ball on its opponent's side of midfield breaks the tie and wins the game.

FOOTBALL SPECIALTIES CONTESTS
OR FIELD MEETS

Several schools use football specialties as a feature of their program. Kansas University has its annual Football Field Meet, Minnesota a Football Field Day, Dartmouth a Football Skills Tourney. These contests are always appealing to students during the fall season and might include a number of events such as the following:

Shuttle relays involving carrying and exchanging the ball
Forward pass for distance
Forward pass for accuracy
Punt for distance
Punt for accuracy
Drop and/or place kicks for goal (established number of tries)
Maze-running for time with football through or around obstacles

Temple University holds an annual forward passing contest during the fall season, open to all university students. Participants are required to throw a football through a suspended target from a distance of 10 yards. All participants sign up at headquarters in advance of action. Individual plaques are presented to the champion and second-place winner.

Temple also conducts an annual extra-point-kicking contest in the fall. All students are eligible. Each is required to kick a football between the uprights and over the crossbar of the goalpost from a distance of 15 yards. Pre-action sign-ups are required. Again, individual plaques are presented to the two leaders.

These events can be arranged on a point system much like the decathlon or similar combination events, or in much the same fashions as a swimming or track meet. This type of competition is excellent for boys in upper elementary and junior high schools.

LACROSSE

Michigan has for years featured this sport, as have many of the private academies and high schools. Some schools, principally in the East, use lacrosse as a spring team sport.

SOCCER FOOTBALL

Soccer is extremely popular in cities having a strong European heritage such as Milwaukee, Philadelphia, Chicago, Pittsburgh, Detroit, Gary, New York. If soccer is to be introduced as an intramural sport in other localities it should be preceded by instruction in the physical education classes. Some colleges provide touch football as the main fall sport, but arrange special soccer games for groups of foreign students and others who desire it. Unless skills are developed, soccer will not be popular. Another fault is the frequency of tie games and low scoring. Some schools use a modified scoring system to eliminate this defect. Corner kicks could be scored for one point; fouls which ordinarily allow free kicks could score one point.

Soccer does not demand more than the usual gym suit, marked fields, goals, and the ball, and is economical to administer. It is becoming more popular in many schools, both as an intramural and interschool sport, and its group of supporters is increasing. Some of its leading exponents are Oberlin, Swarthmore, John Hopkins, Haverford, and Emory University.

SPEEDBALL

Introduced at the University of Michigan in 1921 by Elmer Mitchell, speedball admirably combines the skills and pleasures of soccer, basketball, and football. It provides for handling of the ball, overcoming an American objection to soccer, yet retains many of the soccer skills and employs the passing and kicking of football. Players enjoy its variety and the combination of overhead and ground play, as well as its greater scoring possibilities. During World War II service physical training programs quickly adopted the game because of the constant action and the great possibilities for physical conditioning. Speedball has grown so much in popularity that now many thousands of young men have learned its skills. It is also being used more and more by girls and young women. Specific and detailed rules for speedball and speedaway may be found in many publications.

TENNIS

Many schools divide their tennis programs into fall and spring events, using singles tourneys and leagues in the fall, and doubles in the spring, with mixed and co-recreational tennis in either season. This provides a stimulating program for a great sport, and increases its appeal over the year's program. Potential varsity material can also be discovered early in the year. Tourneys in the fall must not lag, and deadlines must be enforced.

Some schools use singles and doubles tourneys to decide group as well as individual champions. Others schedule team matches between organizations, employing both singles and doubles matches in either round-robin or single and double elimination style. If round-robin leagues are organized, the individual champion can be declared at the same time by compiling the season records of each player, awarding places on the basis of matches won or total games won and lost.

CROSS-COUNTRY

At least one annual fall cross-country run should be included in every school program, starting in the junior high school. The distance need not be long; $\frac{3}{4}$ miles to $1\frac{1}{2}$ miles is recommended. The course should be selected to include variety, some natural obstacles, and fairly comfortable running surface. All competitors should be required to have a minimum number of practices, and a medical inspection of heart and lungs is indicated. The varsity coach should profit from this event, as many potential runners are uncovered annually. Size is no factor, and the sport quite often appeals to a group of students who are less active in other sports. Some schools feature this event near Thanksgiving and offer a variety of prizes in keeping with the season, such as turkeys, ducks, geese, and chickens. Schools giving cross-country runs a prominent place on their calendar are: Texas, Nebraska, Northwestern, Amherst, Oklahoma, Utah State, Michigan Normal, Michigan State, Wofford, Louisville, Washington, Oregon, West Virginia, Williams, Cornell, Princeton, Illinois, Georgia, and Nebraska Wesleyan.

Most schools require a certain number of competitors to cross the finish line in scoring organization team points. All runners should wear numbers on their chests. Two or more officials should check numbers at the finish line. The easiest way to score a large entry field is to select either 16, 24, or 32 as the qualifying number of finishers, scoring one for the winner and so on down the line, with the lowest score winning; or scoring 32 for first place in a field of 32 runners, and so on down the line, with the highest team score winning. Informal, appropriate awards ceremonies can be organized to give special recognition to the prize winners. Some schools use donated prizes while others pay for all awards out of their funds. The prize list might include:

Champion	Intramural medal, certificate of merit, and a turkey
Second	Intramural medal, certificate of merit, and a goose
Third	Intramural medal, certificate of merit, and a duck
Fourth	Certificate of merit and a chicken
Fifth	Chicken

Sixth	Chicken
Seventh	Official University P. E. "T" Shirt
Eighth	Official University P. E. "T" Shirt
Ninth	Two pairs of sweat sox
Tenth	Two pairs of sweat sox
Last	An egg

The University of Georgia calls its cross-country event a Cake Race. It is open to all and is over a one-and-a-half-mile course. A minimum of four practice runs are required and five-man teams are entered. All the prizes are cakes, hence the name of the event.[2] At Brigham Young University this race is called a Turkey Trot.

Where a large entry field is anticipated it is well to plan carefully to avoid confusion and error at the finish line. If the distance is short, runners will bunch rapidly and make accurate tabulation very difficult. The use of a cross-country chute as diagrammed (Figure 19) will make the task easier. The race is fought out before the runners approach the finish chute, with

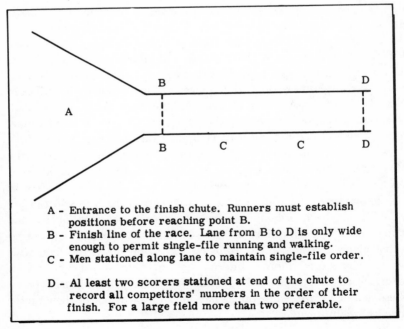

A - Entrance to the finish chute. Runners must establish positions before reaching point B.

B - Finish line of the race. Lane from B to D is only wide enough to permit single-file running and walking.

C - Men stationed along lane to maintain single-file order.

D - Al least two scorers stationed at end of the chute to record all competitors' numbers in the order of their finish. For a large field more than two preferable.

Fig. 19. Cross-country finish chute to facilitate scoring.

the finish line (B) near the front of the Y-shaped device. From there on down to the exit officials see to it that single-file order is maintained and the final checking is done at the end of the chute.

RIFLE SHOOTING

Institutions having military units experience no difficulty in promoting rifle competition. Both individual and team tourneys or leagues can be conducted with ease. Round-robin team matches will provide action throughout a longer season; the military department usually is willing to provide instructional and supervisory leadership without cost to the intramural department, after preliminary organization has been perfected. Many colleges and some high schools have interschool rifle shooting, at least on a postal or telegraphic basis. Intramural rifle shooting sets the machinery for school team tryouts. The following schools have strong intramural rifle programs: Cincinnati, Michigan, Nebraska, Louisville, and Minnesota.

Even the elementary schools are developing a rifle shooting program as a safety education device in addition to the competitive values of the sport. Others use air rifles for younger students. The high school at Sligo, Pennsylvania, developed a program in rifle shooting for both boys and girls; the government furnished free equipment. Rifle shooting is one of the most popular sports included in the annual calendar at the Harding Junior High School at Lakewood, Ohio. Here the shooting is done in the gymnasium, where specially built backstops and targets have been installed by the school shops.

Fig. 20. Elementary school children participating in a shooting match with Daisy air rifles.

SIGMA DELTA PSI

Although not all colleges and universities have chapters of Sigma Delta Psi, the events included in its list of requirements may be used effectively in any school. Some senior high schools have adopted a modified schedule of events and tests suited to boys and have set up an Honorary Athletic Club. Some junior high schools have made further modifications for such a testing program which fits very well into the intramural sports calendar. Certificates are granted to all who pass its requirements. This becomes an excellent competitive event, usually introduced in the fall, with tests given all year. Team competition can be organized easily through individual participation. Points could be given every man from each group passing each test, with final team standings established from these results. A similar athletic club with appropriate events could be set up for girls and college women and worked into the intramural schedule. The following table gives Sigma Delta Psi requirements together with a suggested modification for the high school honorary athletic club.

EVENTS	SIGMA DELTA PSI	H.S. HONORARY CLUB
100-yard dash	:11.6	:12
120-yard low hurdles	:16	:16.7
Running high jump	5 feet	4 feet 10 inches
Running broad jump	17 feet	16 feet 6 inches
16-pound shot*	30 feet	30 feet (12-pound shot)
20-foot rope climb	:12	:14
Baseball throw	250 feet	225 feet
Javelin throw	130 feet	105 feet
Football punt	120 feet	110 feet
100-yard swim	1:45	1:55
One-mile run	6:00	6:20
Front hand spring	Landing on feet	Same
Handstand	:10	Same
Fence vault	Chin high	Same
Good posture	Standard B(HBM)	Same
Scholarship	Varsity eligibility	Same

One varsity letter may be substituted for any one event above.

* If candidate is less than 160 pounds use the formula: 160 lbs.: candidate's weight: : 30': ×.

A modified Sigma Delta Psi testing program suitable for the junior high school club, with the following requirements, could be changed to fit the age level of the students:

EVENTS	JUNIOR H. S. REQUIREMENTS
50-yard dash	:06.8
100-yard dash	:13.9
Running high jump	4 feet

Running broad jump	12 feet 6 inches
8-pound shot	25 feet
Baseball throw	175 feet
Handstand	3 seconds
Rope climb	:10.1 second
Cross-country run	4:36
60-foot swim	:12.5

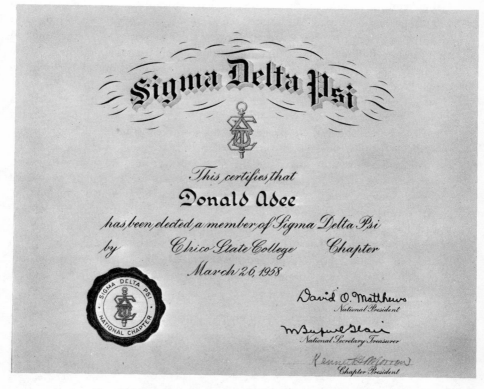

Fig. 21. Certificate Award—Sigma Delta Psi, Chico State College.

OTHER FALL SPORTS

Even though golf is discussed under spring sports, most well-balanced programs provide at least one type of golf competition in the fall with further events in the spring.

Archery is growing in favor, and school shops often develop handicraft work in making bows, arrows, and targets. Archery is an excellent carry-over sport, lending itself well to the beautiful outdoor fall season. It can be used as either team or individual competition. Archery golf is a very enjoyable variation which can be set up about the campus or school grounds, although every safety precaution must be taken. This sport is recognized for its postural value, and is equally fitting for both sexes. Ohio State, College of the City of New York, Michigan, Illinois, Knox, and Utah State all have well-organized intramural archery.

Some schools use softball and baseball as fall sports to relieve the crowded spring sports varsity and intramural schedule, or to supplement it. Bowling may well be started in the fall, and leagues and tournaments can then continue through the winter period. Horseshoes may be played in both fall and spring. Autumn is the time for the organized hiking and outing activities program to get underway; these activities will be resumed in the spring. Fall is the finest time for outdoor co-recreational activities, which usually reach their climax at the Halloween season. Many of these sports will be discussed in greater detail in later chapters.

Events centering around use of the bicycle are gaining in popularity in elementary, junior, and senior high schools. Several schools have included a Bicycle Rodeo in their program. This event consists of such specialties as circle riding, slow-speed riding, balancing, stopping, weaving, and U-turning. The event is staged on the school playground or a smooth street. Bicycles are all inspected, and judges decide on the recipients of special prizes. Various other cycling events are used by the schools of Kaukauna, Wisconsin; Long Beach, California; Winona and Rochester, Minnesota; and Greenwich, Connecticut. With a traffic problem facing cities and the schools, a program has been developed which increases interest in skillful and safe cycling. A level, hard-surfaced street is blocked off for the testing events. White street markings are used. The tests at Winona include

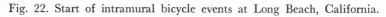

Fig. 22. Start of intramural bicycle events at Long Beach, California.

circling, balancing at slow speed, straight-line riding, weaving, riding between stanchions, and stopping on a spot. Leaders in Homewood, Florida, have recently promoted a great deal of bicycle activity and their city is now called the Bicycle City.

Pushball is used by a few schools as an intramural sport. There can be no doubt about the injury hazard of this game. It is a most strenuous and vigorous activity in every sense of the word. Careful experimentation should be undertaken before pushball is introduced competitively into the program.

Fig. 23. Intramural pushball at the Chicago City Schools.

Another hazardous sport that is finding its way into the recreational college program is mountain climbing. Western State Teachers College at Gunnison, Colorado, and Olympia College, Washington, give instruction to classes of men and women, followed by actual climbing in the mountains nearby. Several students have lost their lives in unofficial and daring climbing in some of the colleges of the Colorado area. Such an activity, if carefully supervised, might rightfully become a part of the outing and outdoor program of some colleges, but any attempt at organized competition in this direction might prove disastrous.

Winter Sports

Schools situated in the North often develop excellent outdoor programs of ice hockey, skiing, snow sculpturing, tobogganing, and ice skating. Outing clubs of mixed groups augment the winter program with enjoyable social activities. The unique and remarkable outdoor winter program at Dartmouth College stands as an example to all. Other schools carrying extensive ice and snow activities are Minnesota, Carleton, Wisconsin, Hamline, Lawrence, St. Olaf, Washington, Wesleyan, Middlebury, Cornell, Utah State, North Dakota, and Washington State. More detailed discussion of these phases of the modern program will be found in Chapters 12, 13, and 16.

BASKETBALL

This sport outranks all other everywhere in intramural interest and participation. Almost every conceivable type of league and tournament is employed. Some of these are: interfraternity and independent leagues and tournaments; interclass tournaments, single or double elimination; freshman, sophomore, junior, and senior jamborees; Saturday leagues and tournaments; noon-hour leagues; basketball golf and free throw tournaments; twenty-one, seven-up, and spot-shooting tournaments.

The cost of conducting basketball events is negligible, as regular gym suits are worn, and the floors and balls are always available. Good student officiating is one of the biggest problems. Many schools are attempting to meet this problem with regularly conducted officials' clinics and meetings where rules and interpretations are discussed and officials picked from those proving most competent. Many directors make the mistake of believing that, after organizing a single league for the year, they have properly included basketball in their program. This sport is so popular that many different types of basketball competition should be worked into the year's calendar so that all may enjoy a fair share of its pleasures.

BASKETBALL GOLF

This activity was first introduced in East High School, Green Bay, Wisconsin, in 1930, and is a fine individual competitive game, equally interesting to the novice or the varsity squad member as a change of pace from the daily practice grind. It is a good game to introduce in the fall before the gymnasium becomes crowded with winter play. It is easily administered and supervised. Scorecards should be used to stimulate and motivate play, making for better organization. One of the best methods of setting up competition is to provide two or three days for preliminary qualifying shooting over 18 or 36 holes by medal score. The best 16 or 32 men are then selected and seeded for match play to decide the eventual champion. Each match can be over 18 or more holes. Figure 24 gives a nine-hole layout for basketball golf, and Figure 25 gives a sample scorecard which can be mimeographed or printed.

Fig. 24. Diagram of playing chart for basketball golf competition.

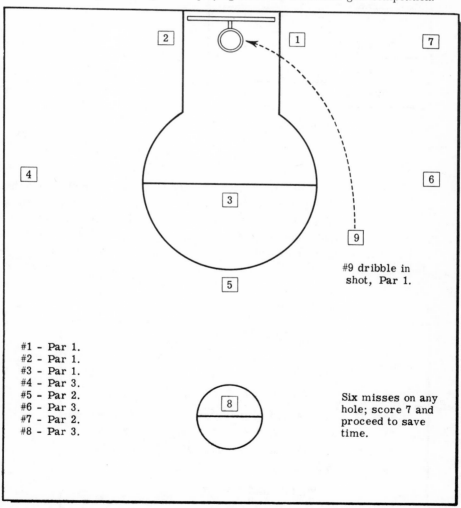

#9 dribble in shot, Par 1.

#1 – Par 1.
#2 – Par 1.
#3 – Par 1.
#4 – Par 3.
#5 – Par 2.
#6 – Par 3.
#7 – Par 2.
#8 – Par 3.

Six misses on any hole; score 7 and proceed to save time.

INTRAMURAL BASKET BALL - GOLF SCORE CARD			
Name..................... Score......			
Holes	Par	1st 9	2nd 9
Number One	1		
Number Two	1		
Number Three	1		
Number Four	3		
Number Five	2		
Number Six	3		
Number Seven	2		
Number Eight	3		
Number Nine	1		
TOTALS	17		

Fig. 25. Basketball golf scorecard.

BASKETBALL FREE THROWS

Free-throw tournaments are easily organized and conducted as either individual or team matches. It is not unusual to have over 500 participating in university tournaments. The best 32 scorers can be selected to continue in match play, and eight alternates chosen from the qualifying round to replace any of the best 32 who fail to appear for the matches. Figure 26 shows a sample scorecard which adds much to this kind of tournament.

Fig. 26. Free-throw scorecard.

INTRAMURALS
FREE THROW SCORE CARD

Name...

1	2	3	4	5	6	7	8	9	10	11
12	13	14	15	16	17	18	19	20	21	22
23	24	25	26	27	28	29	30	31	32	33
34	35	36	37	38	39	40	41	42	43	44
45	46	47	48	49	50 SCORE.................					

CIRCLE THROWS MADE ONLY

Signed.......................
(Score Keeper)

SWIMMING AND WATER SPORTS

Water activities should be central features of the winter sports calendar in all schools where facilities are available. Some schools without pools use nearby Y.M.C.A. or Y.W.C.A. pools where intramural competition can be scheduled even if interscholatic swimming is not possible. A new trend is for public schools to use nearby motel pools for school intramural events. Preliminary practice should precede all active competition. It is well to award as many places as possible in swimming meets to stimulate greater interest. It costs no more to award four, five, or six places in the meets, and more contestants then feel they have accomplished something in placing. Permanent record boards should be maintained at the swimming pool. These boards should include all-time records for intramurals, freshmen, varsity, and the pool.

Water polo ranks next in popularity among the water sports, and must be well officiated, with short playing time established. Water basketball has supplanted water polo in many schools, probably due to the great interest in basketball itself. Other water sports used in various schools are water ball, water baseball, bat polo, and various types of distance and endurance or marathon swims requiring several days for completion. Precautions must be taken to safeguard health in all these sports.

Bat polo is a good variation of water polo, especially suitable for junior and senior high schools. The game starts with the two teams lined up at the opposite ends of the pool. The ball is thrown into the center of the pool. On the whistle both sides dive in and race for the ball, which can be batted, slapped, or punched toward the opponents' wall. Whenever the ball is picked up or held it is awarded to the opponents by a throw-in. Balls batted out of bounds are also so awarded. To score a goal the ball must be batted, slapped, or punched against the short wall of the pool.

Fig. 27. Intramural water polo in action at the University of Texas. Note the use of quality equipment.

Balls hit above the wall are awarded to the opposite goalie. Opponents can be ducked but cannot be held down. Teams change goals after every point scored.

INNER-TUBE WATER POLO[3]

Robert E. Wear and Charles Arnold at the University of New Hampshire have developed a fun game that appeals to students with varied swimming abilities and endurance capacities. They briefly describe "Inner-Tube Polo" as follows:

> Equipment: One inner-tube for each player and a large rubber ball.
> Number of players: Two teams of three to six each.
> The teams line up on opposite sides of the pool, on their own goal line. The ball is placed in the center of the pool, with both teams dashing to get it. The main rule in this game is that no player may leave his inner tube, he must sit in it at all times and move by paddling his hands and feet. The ball may be thrown from one player to another, but to make a goal, a player must have the ball in his hand when the ball touches the opponent's goal. Each goal counts as one point. Two ten-minute halves are played.

More details on this sport may be obtainel by writing to Dr. Robert E. Wear, University of New Hampshire at Durham.

INDOOR TRACK

Many schools have some form of indoor track each year, even though adequate indoor track facilities are lacking. Schools having no complete indoor plant often improvise a series of physical achievement tests and modified track events, employing the gymnasium and often the school hallways. Such modifications as the standing broad jump rather than the running broad jump, the medicine-ball far-throw instead of the shot put, and the rope vault for the regular pole vault work out nicely. Such events as the tip-up balance for time, chinning the bar, rope climb, shuttle relays, and tumbling stunts can be added. Short dashes and hurdle races can be used in the gymnasium. A padded board wall can be constructed to take the shock of a fast finish. It is well to continue the indoor competition for several days, with only a few events scheduled each day, thus permitting wider participation and eliminating undue strain. Schools having proper indoor plants can establish a regular list of events without difficulty. Record boards should be permanently built and maintained for all intramural events in order arouse interest. Good varsity material is often uncovered in these early indoor meets. Here, as in swimming, points should be scattered liberally.

WRESTLING

More and more schools are adding wrestling to the intramural program. Entry deadlines should be set and all contestants required to work out a minimum number of times preceding matches. If these workouts can be arranged under the supervision and instruction of the wrestling coach, the program will profit. The day before competition begins all contestants should be weighed in and examined by a physician. Pairings can then be accurately made in the various weight divisions and doubtful entries eliminated. Three pounds overweight are usually allowed, and wrestlers should be required to make their weights each day they are scheduled for matches. One satisfactory plan is to conduct preliminary matches in the late afternoons, saving the final championship matches for the public. Several colleges and high schools conduct the finals each year immediately following one of home varsity basketball games, insuring a crowd of several thousand spectators for the competition. Awards are made as each match is concluded, while the taste of victory is still sweet. Official college weight classes are: 121 pounds, 128 pounds, 136 pounds, 145 pounds, 155 pounds, 165 pounds, 175 pounds, and the heavyweight or unlimited class. Junior and senior high schools can modify their weight divisions in any way necessary to insure a good spread of competitors in the various classes. Matches should

Fig. 28. Intramural wrestling is an excellent elementary school activity when properly conducted. Scene from program at Albuquerque, New Mexico.

be limited as to length, and regular wrestling rules should be observed. Use of the loudspeaker and good scoring and timing techniques will make the competition more enjoyable.

ICE HOCKEY

Schools attempting outdoor ice hockey with regular schedules are often disappointed at delayed and interrupted matches due to weather changes. Even with these occasional drawbacks, each fast and snappy game that does get played rewards the director for his willingness to sponsor the sport. Some schools, such as Colorado College, Michigan State, University of North Dakota, Dartmouth, Denver, Princeton, and Illinois, have indoor rinks at their disposal. Ice hockey is fast and furious and a wonderfully healthful sport. Outdoor hockey rinks at Carleton College, Rensselaer Polytechnic Institute, Harvard, and Minnesota are a beehive of activity and beauty during the winter season.

BROOMBALL[3]

This is the most popular sport at St. Francis Xavier University. There they call it The Great Equalizer. Simplified rules are:

Facility:	1. The ice surface should be identical to the ice surface for hockey.
	2. The keenest competition will be played on ice which has received a heavy skate prior to game time. A smooth surface will add to the comedy in the game.
Equipment:	1. All players must wear hockey helmets, gloves, and shin pads.
	2. Footwear must have a smooth sole or be a canvas running shoe.
	3. Regulation brooms and balls are supplied by the university.
Start of Play:	1. A face-off is conducted to start the play. This is similar to hockey with the exception that the ball lies on the ice before the whistle is sounded.
	2. The positions of the face-offs are identical to those in hockey.
Role of the Blue Lines:	1. Icing is called when a ball is shot from behind the defensive blue line to cross the attacking goal line.
	2. Offsides are identical to hockey with the exception that there is no two-line passing rule in broomball.
Penalties:	These and all other rules are similar to hockey.

VOLLEYBALL

The early growth of volleyball can be credited to the pioneer work of the Y.M.C.A. World War II again popularized the sport and today almost every school includes it among its team sports. Volleyball can be played for years after graduation and is popular with businessmen. It should not be omitted from the program of any elementary or secondary school or college. It is also one of the leading faculty sports. Lewis and Clark College of Portland, Oregon, uses two-man volleyball on its program. The regular game is more popular when rules are strictly enforced and team play is taught and stressed.

(Courtesy of Mankato State College.)

Fig. 29.

One variation of volleyball is volley-bounce. The game is played over a 7-foot net by teams of two men each. The ball may be hit twice by each team, either on the fly or after a bounce. The court is preferably 70 feet by 34 feet. Following the usual serve a player may elect to volley the ball or may allow it to bounce once. On receiving the ball the partner must play it over the net. Other rules are quite similar to regular volleyball.

Volley tennis, another variation of volleyball, has become popular in the Los Angeles and San Diego areas and is played on a regulation volleyball court. The top of the net is 3 feet high. Six players form a team and rotate as in volleyball. On the serve the ball must bounce once inside the server's court, whereupon it must be struck over the net by the center front player only. Balls may be volleyed or permitted to bounce once. Otherwise the game is much the same as regular volleyball, and similar to tennis.

HANDBALL

Handball is a "must" on every program. Few schools in America are without a suitable gym wall where one-wall courts can be laid out and competition established. It is a fallacy to assume that handball cannot be used without four-wall official courts, as the one-wall game is fascinating and popular. Both team and individual tourneys and leagues can be organized. Some schools conduct tourneys outdoors on specially constructed one-wall courts. Tournaments can be arranged for doubles as well as singles. It is often wise to substitute a softer and larger ball, such as a tennis ball, for younger players who may not have access to regulation handball gloves. Precaution should be observed where several rounds of matches are attempted in a single day, since too many matches will cause the hands to swell unless the player is hardened by constant play.

BOWLING

Since most schools do not have their own or enough alleys, the program must depend on local facilities. Very few communities in America today, including the smaller towns, are without at least one commercial alley, yet few junior and senior high schools conduct good bowling competitions. When we realize that bowling is one of the top adult recreational sports, it would seem that schools would meet this challenge with more planned student competition. The sport is usually inexpensive for the school, as most alleys are quite willing to provide the championship trophies, and students pay their own bowling fees, often reduced by arrangement. Bowling is particularly appropriate for older college men and faculty groups less anxious to engage in the more strenuous sports. It is also an excellent co-recreational activity. Many schools conduct several series of bowling leagues, making the sport almost continuous throughout most of the year. In addition Nebraska conducts intercollege faculty bowling and co-recreational duck-pin bowling on its own duck-pin alleys. Many schools use both round-robin leagues and individual championships. Others include postal or telegraphic competition with other schools. Competition may be from scratch or with handicaps. The latter plan will keep the weaker teams interested right down to the completion of each league.

While commercial alleys are usually willing to cooperate in promoting and stimulating bowling leagues for their own business purposes, it is well to maintain an active school administrative supervision over all such competition. One of the latest trends in school bowling is the Junior ABC intercollege bowling program, which seeks to take the best intramural bowlers from the various colleges and match then telegraphically over the nation.

BADMINTON

This sport is increasing rapidly in popularity in junior and senior high schools and colleges. It is a perfect co-recreational activity. Singles, doubles, and team match competition can be easily arranged. Schools in the South can conduct much of their competition outdoors. Team leagues are often organized with a number of singles and doubles matches played simultaneously.

TABLE TENNIS

Table tennis has enjoyed a phenomenal growth in late years. It is a favorite in club room, student union, fraternity house and dormitory, and everywhere that students congregate. Folding tables may be used where space is at a premium. It is a fine co-recreational activity or faculty game. Handicapped or restricted students find it one of their most enjoyable activities. Individual singles or doubles tourneys can be arranged with almost no faculty supervision other providing the facilities, accepting the entries, making the pairings, and posting the deadlines. Usually five-man teams are used between organizations, with line-ups seeded and five singles matches played to determine a team winner. Many junior and senior high schools in larger cities are playing extramural table tennis between schools, using their best intramural players.

One large high school climaxed its big annual table tennis tournament by having one night of remaining matches, and determining the school champion. All remaining competitors met in the school cafeteria. Chairs were moved around the walls for players and spectators. Heavy cafeteria tables were moved together, so that each pair of tables formed one table-tennis unit. A cardboard net was thumbtacked between the two tables. Thus seven or eight tables could be readied for simultaneous matches. Even though the tables were not quite official in size, they were close enough to provide excellent play. Following the competition all tables and chairs were replaced and the event was thus speedily concluded.

GYMNASTICS

Schools stressing gymnastics in the curriculum find it easy to draw a large entry field for an intramural meet. Best results are usually obtained by holding an all-school or open championship tournament, with team and

Fig. 30. Elementary school gymnastics and tumbling at the Dade
County Schools, Miami, Florida.

individual recognition possible. Intramural programs developed by some
universities have led to an annual state high school championship gymnastics meet. Junior and senior high schools should find the organization of
an intramural gymnastics meet easy following several weeks of instruction
in the physical education classes.

SQUASH

Schools having four-wall handball courts can adapt them readily for
squash competition. Many students prefer squash to handball if given an
opportunity to learn the game. Yale and Harvard are leaders in the nation
with their many courts in the dormitories where it is convenient for
hundreds to use them constantly. Squash will grow in favor only as rapidly
as skills of the sport are taught in the physical education classes.

OTHER WINTER SPORTS AND ACTIVITIES

Indoor baseball is still used by many schools as a winter organized
sport but is losing ground due to the popularity of softball in fall and
spring, and the great abundance of other winter sports vying for recognition
and attention. Tulane University has used indoor baseball in the gymnasium

as one of its regular sports. Basketball type games such as seven-up, twenty-one, spot shooting, goal-hi, and others are organized intramurally in several schools and used informally in many others. Winter is the best season for co-recreational sports parties where many activities are used, together with the ever-popular splash parties in the swimming pool. Bat ball in its many forms is an ideal winter sport for elementary, junior, and senior high schools. This game is excellent since it employs almost unlimited numbers on the teams, and has plenty of action and scoring. Paddleball and codeball are both used by some schools. Deck tennis, aerial tennis, and dart baseball are easily organized recreational favorites where the games have been properly introduced. Dart baseball lends itself admirably to faculty competition. Oregon State conducts tournaments in bridge, pinochle, and billiards. Many schools use tumbling and gymnastics as a co-recreational sport. Competition in weight lifting is increasing.

Denver University conducts intramural bridge tournaments following instruction open to all. Princeton includes billiards, pool, and cowboy pool. Minnesota and Iowa State schedule dual swimming meets between various organizations on the campus in addition to their regular swim meets. Minnesota features such unique events as bobsledding and the annual snow-trip by train for skiing and pleasure skating. Brooklyn College uses six-man football, chess, and roller skating in its program. Fencing is an old and well-established sport, but little used the country over. Many schools report fencing clubs where students enjoy their favorite sport on an informal basis as time permits. Roller skating events could be easily developed at all age levels.

For younger students cork ball is played using three-man teams, and fits nicely into the noon-hour program. Guard ball is another game that would fit well into the younger program. Shuffleboard and disco are somewhat similar games that can be used to great advantage indoors as well as outdoors, and fit well into the noon-hour program.

Snap-ball is a fast moving, inexpensive game that can be played almost anywhere and is a popular sport at the Technical High School at Erie, Pennsylvania. It crosses baseball, football, and under-leg, and requires no equipment except a football. It can be played indoors in the winter as well as outdoors. It can be played with nine-man teams using four bases, or with small groups using first base and home plate, the players moving up with each put-out. In the team game the players take positions much the same as in baseball, and there is no pitcher. The game is started with the snapper (batter) placing the football on home plate. Then, assuming the position of a football center, he snaps the ball in one continuous motion anywhere within the field of play. Following the snap, he races for first base. If he arrives before the ball he is safe. If not, he is out. Once he reaches base safely it is up to his teammates to drive (snap) him home.

PHYSICAL FITNESS PENTATHLON

Ronald Thompson at Nichols Junior High, Evanston, Illinois, started an intramural fitness pentathlon in 1961 which grew into a national telegraphic extramural event involving 50 junior high schools in each of the state capital cities. The AAHPER National Fitness Test of seven items was used. Similar interschool competition in fitness-centered events has become a trend in many areas, notably New York City.

Spring Sports

The spring season is the shortest and often the busiest intramural season of the year. If careful planning is not followed, the spring calendar is likely to get cluttered up with sports that started too late, sports that might better have been conducted in the fall, or with too many postponements due to weather. Yet the spring season is often one of the most enjoyable, especially in locations where winter activities demand indoor confinement. While some spring sports will not appeal to all students, there are as many more who look forward with anticipation to this season.

SOFTBALL

Softball is played almost universally as the number one spring sport in the nation. Its popularity has been due to several factors. Players need not be as expert as in regular baseball. Very little equipment is needed. Impromptu practices are easier to arrange, and less space is required. Softball is a popular adult public recreational sport.

Fortunately the earlier games of playground ball, diamond ball, kitten ball, and indoor baseball have all become standardized by the National Association. Softball is the most popular summer session team sport, and it ranks near the top whenever picnic planning suggests sports and games. Many schools have established the policy of loaning softball equipment for practice groups, picnics, and outings of all kinds. Some precautions which add to interest and safety should be observed in conducting softball leagues:

1. Have field and foul lines marked and flagged.
2. Have backstops built or placed behind home plates properly, and on all diamonds. The movable type of backstop is best.
3. Keep pitcher's box and batter's box smooth and in shape. A minimum of preparation, good texture of the soil, and occasional care will add much to the game.
4. Arrange players' benches on either side of the batters' box, but far enough back to guarantee safety.

5. Have small scoreboards placed near each diamond.
6. Prohibit the use of spiked shoes, since all players will not be able to furnish them.

ONE-PITCH SOFTBALL

This game has gained popularity in many California schools. It has been found that more than three times as many "at bats" are obtained than in regular softball; there is a great deal more running and fielding; a few expert players do not dominate the game. One-pitch softball is played like standard softball except for the following: (1) The batting team sends one of its players to the pitcher's box to do the pitching, but not the fielding of batted or thrown balls. (2) Each batter is allowed one pitched ball to hit; if he fails to hit a fair ball he is out. He is also out if he fails to swing at his one pitch, if he swings and misses, if he is thrown out or flies out. (3) The pitcher must take his regular turn at bat, someone else on the batting team replacing him on the pitching mound. (4) The regular pitcher on the fielding team performs all his regular fielding duties except pitching to the batters.

SLOW-PITCH SOFTBALL

The dominance of softball competition by the good pitcher has caused slow-pitch softball to gain in popularity. Some schools have conducted regular and slow-pitch softball leagues with the latter gradually supplanting the former. When both types are scheduled the teams with a good pitcher can elect fast-ball, and others the slow-pitch game. Slow-pitch softball predominates at Indiana University.[4]

At Ball State University slow-pitch softball attracted 89 teams and 1,047 participants in 1970 as compared to fast-pitch softball, which only enrolled 16 teams and 208 participants.

BASEBALL

This great national sport has been declining as an intramural activity for the masses of students. Softball has been replacing baseball on the calendar because of its minimum space and skill requirements, and ease of administration. Some schools do have special matched games to highlight their spring programs even though regular leagues have been eliminated. Shortened games can be used to facilitate play. The baseball field meet is an appropriate and popular event—practical for all age levels starting with the fourth grade.

OUTDOOR TRACK

Many schools use the indoor track meet as a way of getting acquainted with varsity potential, thus permitting the outdoor track events to be staged later in the spring when there is less danger of injury or harm to intramural competitors who are not finely conditioned. The outdoor meet can feature more relays, thus placing a premium on team organization and making the whole event more enjoyable. Double points should be awarded in all relays. Batons should be furnished; colored jerseys not only add much to the meet, but also make the judges' task easier. The use of scoreboards, loudspeaker and announcer, and all the usual varsity devices can easily make this meet one of the year's features. Care should be taken to require a limited number of practice sessions. Longer runs should be eliminated, with the 880-yard run perhaps the maximum distance for college men. Most schools have eliminated the javelin throw and have retained the shot put and discus throw. Many colleges use the high school 12-pound shot, with junior high schools using the 8-pound sphere. Permanent record boards should be maintained and kept up to date to enliven competition. Certificates or awards may be given to all who set new records in any event.

A novel team scoring method, which guarantees greater participation and interest, is worthy of consideration. Each group organization must have three or more entries in each event. No preliminaries are necessary. The plan prevents one group with two or three stars from winning the meet, and puts a premium on balanced performance, with the weaker entries often deciding the meet. In the field events the performance of all the participants is added together to determine final placing. In the track events the scoring is the same as for cross-country runs. Larger institutions could demand four or five entries from each group. Thus in the shot put, for example, three men might make a combined put of 98 feet 6 inches, and all other groups of three would arrive at various distances; all other events would be scored accordingly. A similar plan has been tried in intercollegiate track with splendid results, and as a result coaches have had to give more attention to the weaker members of the team in order to bring team balance to the front.

The track decathlon could be one of the intramural events. It might include the 100-yard dash, 440, 120-yard low hurdles, shot put, discus throw, high jump, pole vault, one-mile run, javelin, and broad jump. A special scoring could be used to determine the final rankings. This is a good secondary school event. In rural areas the extension of the intramural track idea has brought about much fine county grade school, and junior and senior high school competition.

An interesting event has been sponsored in the New Orleans area by the *Times-Picayune,* for children of all ages from Louisiana and Mississippi. This event is several years old and is considered by many school workers of that area a valuable contribution and incentive in starting many children on an ambitious program of physical development and health through sports. This program offers competition in classes for boys and girls. The athletic tests specify certain standards which the student must equal or better to earn recognition and awards. Most of the events are track and field in nature. The Nationwide Track and Field Project of Operation Fitness–USA (AAHPER) involved 10 million youth in 1960 and reached 20 million in mass-novice participation in 1961.[5]

Fig. 31. Elementary school track meets held in Lincoln, Nebraska, as part of Operation Fitness-USA.

Fig. 32. Start of cross-country run at Wilson Junior High School, Terre Haute, Indiana, as part of the program sponsored by Operation Fitness-USA in 1960.

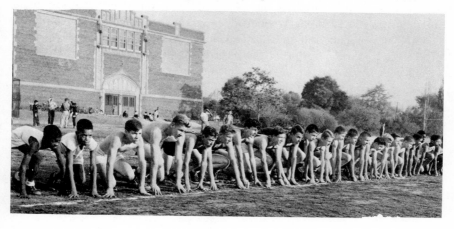

TENNIS

Competition in this great sport can be conducted in a number of ways, and no school program should be without tennis in some form. Some methods of organizing tennis competition are as follows:

1. Open singles tournament, single elimination.
2. Ladder tournament for singles; also for doubles.
3. Open doubles tournament by single elimination.
4. Double elimination tournaments in either singles or doubles.
5. Mixed co-recreational doubles tourney.
6. Team tourney, single elimination; three or five on a team.
7. Team round-robin leagues. Each team playing three or five singles or two singles and one doubles for each match.

Cement or asphalt and hard-surfaced courts are available for more constant play and demand very little upkeep. Some schools are adding lighting equipment to double the use of existing facilities by lengthening the playable day. Some schools use a novel plan for assuring good tennis balls for each intramural match. Each contestant must furnish three new tennis balls. The loser of each match keeps the three used balls, and the winner keeps the new balls. Thus each player buys only three new balls, and good balls are assured for each match.

GOLF

This sport needs little artificial stimulation as a natural intramural activity. Nearly all schools today have at least one golf course near enough to permit the organization of at least one annual tourney. Many schools use a one-day medal play tourney open to all students in the fall, and a spring tourney that starts as a one-day medal play event from which the best 32 medalists are selected to proceed toward the championship by match play. In the two tourneys any number of students may compete from each organization, with only the best four scores counted toward the team standings in the fall. A wonderful program can be worked out with facilities under school administrative control. Most schools furnish only the promotion and organization of the meet with competitors paying their own greens fees. A starter should have charge of each tourney, handling the scorecard and arranging all foursomes. Team matches are usually played according to the Nassau system of scoring. Handicap matches are usually difficult to arrange for schools without their own courses. Several co-recreational golf events may be planned, such as the mixed two-ball foursome. A faculty or faculty-student tournament near the close of the school year is always enjoyable. Oberlin College holds an annual factulty-alumni tournament each commencement season.

Almost any school can find a spot on its own or nearby grounds where a golf tee can be constructed or arranged. Daily practice in driving and pitching can continue here for months. Golf specialty meets are interesting and will be well received. To make the event more enjoyable and easily administered benches should be placed about the tee. Brightly painted tee markers can be built in the school shops and placed in the ground. Temporary distance signs can be placed out on the driving range, and a large scoreboard placed near the tee for recording length of drives and pitching scores. Helpers use wire or wooden markers to check each contestant's best drive, moving them forward as the mark is bettered, and only measuring when the competition is over. An improvised green can be arranged on the school grounds or athletic field for the golf pitching contest. Concentric circles are laid off and homemade flags add color to the event. Indoor putting contests can be arranged with homemade wooden inclines built. Holes can be cut in the putting platform; into these are placed tin cans to simulate regulation golf cups. A long strip of carpet is fastened over the framework, permitting a good putting surface and enough distance to make it interesting. Contestants are allowed a specified number of putts, and both individual and team scores can be easily set up in a variety of ways.

Goofy golf is another change-of-pace activity that might add spice to the outdoor program. The game is played with horseshoes. Golf scorecards are prepared and a number of pegs are set over varying distances in all kinds of places. Hazards are desirable, with pegs being set along a hillside, on a tree stump, near tree bases, and with numerous obstacles. The usual horseshoe pitching technique is mandatory. It is a good recreational game and unlimited numbers may participate.

Other interesting golf events are ringer tournaments, flag tournaments, and improvised comedy tourneys for pure relaxation and fun.

HORSESHOES

"Barnyard golf," or horseshoes, has increased in popularity. This is one sport that finds its way into any size or type of school. Its easy organization, demanding very little space and supervision, indicates top priority in large and small, rural or urban school programs. The director of the small school who complains of lack of time and facilities for intramurals could not exclude horseshoes with such an argument. Horseshoe competition attracts the active and physically handicapped participant alike. Tourneys may be organized in singles and doubles, or as team matches in either tourney elimination or round-robin league style. Some schools have large team leagues playing on a battery of lighted courts of their own or nearby city recreational areas. Some conduct co-recreational horseshoe tourneys.

Fig. 33. Intramural shuffleboard at Mitchell Park, Palo Alto, California.

SHUFFLEBOARD

Since shuffleboard has become so popular at summer and winter resorts from Florida to Minnesota, more schools are either providing informal recreational facilities or organizing competitive tournaments. Almost any school can improvise courts on gym floors, hallways, lobbies, sidewalks, or by constructing special concrete outdoor courts. Many of the schools' waxed concrete floors are ideal for one or more shuffleboard courts. It is a great noon-hour sport.

ADDITIONAL SPORTS SUGGESTIONS

Bait and fly casting tournaments are conducted at Ohio State, Pennsylvania State, Kansas State, Nebraska, and at Lincoln High School of Manitowoc, Wisconsin. It is an excellent event, with great leisure-time value, although best preceded by class instruction. Skish tournaments are growing in popularity, and employ bait casting techniques with the use of targets. Kalamazoo College, Ohio State University, and the Detroit Public Schools all have skish events.

Crew races are a great addition to any intramural program, and are annual sports at Wisconsin, Oregon State, Washington, Princeton, Pennsylvania, Navy, Boston, and Marietta College. Many girls' and women's schools make this event one of their highlights of the year. Rowing competition is provided at Cornell and Harvard. Sailing is featured at Dartmouth. Competitive rodeo events are now being staged at Utah State, Colorado A & M, Lewis and Clark College, and the University of Arizona. Archery in some of its competitive forms is used almost everywhere. Aerial darts is organized at Indiana University, and at Oklahoma A & M. An annual fox hunt is sponsored at the University of Tennessee. Syracuse University and College of the City of New York sponsor tournaments in chess and checkers, although these activities are usually organized in the various student unions. This type of event is well adapted to noon-hour planning. Billiards and pool are used intramurally at Purdue, Illinois, Chaffey, Princeton, Oregon State, Cincinnati, Chicago, and Lewis and Clark College. Contract bridge is sponsored at Oregon State, Syracuse, Nebraska, and Lewis and Clark College. Clock golf is another sport used at College of the City of New York.

Volley tennis would fit well in the broad sports program. Other events that could be popularized in various localities are horseback riding, codeball, necatos, pinochle, box lacrosse, cricket, cage ball, aerial tennis, quoits, deck tennis, paddleball, pushball, bicycling, polo, bowling on the green, tether ball, and zelball.

Wiskit is another fine game that has recently been developed on the West Coast. It is a combination of softball and jai-alai and is completely described by the author in another publication.[6]

At the elementary and junior high school levels dozens of games and sports can be added to those already mentioned. The top-spinning tournaments can be organized to include duration of spin, accuracy put, whip for distance, top dash, fancy looping contests, diabolo spinning, and pickups. Events using the yo-yo can be included. Events employing skates and scooters might include roller skate for distance, roller skating obstacle race, standing scooter race, speed races, one-legged races, relay races, and zigzag scooter races.

A "hash meet" has been held at Naperville, Illinois, for years, and, as the name implied, included all kinds of events for younger enthusiasts. Some of the events were running races, jumping, hop-step-jump, baseball throw, free throws, checkers, chess, ring-o-let, Ping-Pong, and other novelties, all worked together into a competitive point system.

Summer Events

Most junior and senior high school students enjoy competition during the summer in the city, county, or school district recreation program. The rapid expansion of the community-school idea, such as is used with very

Fig. 34. Intramural water activities of the army.

fine results at Rochester, Minnesota; Flint, Michigan; and Milwaukee, may cause even the intermediate and secondary schools to carry the intramural program into the summer months. Colleges and universities conducting summer school programs have found that students are older and prefer a more leisurely type of activity in the warm months. Softball has real appeal as a summer team game. Individual tournaments can be successfully organized in tennis, archery, golf, table tennis, horseshoes, badminton, handball, squash, shuffleboard, and similar events. More emphasis should be placed on providing necessary equipment for picnics and outings, and for voluntary recreation in all activities as desired informally by the students. Mixed splash parties and recreational swimming will be popular in the warm months.

Rules of All Sports

In recent years practically all sports have been given nationally standardized rules of play. These rules will not be given here, since they are easily obtained elsewhere. The University of Minnesota and the

University of Missouri both publish a handbook on rules of play of the various intramural sports. Many other schools include some rules material in their regular intramural handbook. Some place a complete book of rules for all sports in the hands of each unit manager, to be used as a constant source of reference. Best sources for rules, fundamentals, playing hints, and the history and background of all sports are listed in the bibliography at the end of this book.

Selection of the School Program of Activities

As the director introduces or rebuilds the intramural program, he must take into consideration the size of the school, its location, the age group to be served, available facilities, and possibilities for expansion. It is natural to assume that the smaller schools will have more limited programs, with larger junior and senior high schools and colleges offering the greatest variety of activities, since the cosmopolitan nature of the student body assures some interest in almost any conceivable activity. Yet some smaller schools can put their more fortunate brethren to shame in the extent and quality of their "sports for all" program. The success of any program will depend on the enthusiasm and ingenuity of the director, and he or she will be repaid amply for the expansion of the calendar by the deep satisfactions that revert to the larger segments of school and community. The program must not be static. It must reflect the ever-changing interests and desires of the student body. However, it should have certain basic program features that will not vacillate with temporary group whims and designs. It would be better to have a smaller number of well-conducted activities than a great hodgepodge of miscellaneous sports poorly organized and administered.

Programs having fewer than five events or sports during the school year are hardly worthy of comment. Such a program cannot possibly meet the needs and interests of youth. Otto Gullickson conducted a total of 74 different intramural activities during one college year at Marshall College, Huntington, West Virginia.[7]

All sports suggested in this chapter have been used successfully by schools of all types. In the succeeding pages are listed groupings of sports and activities for the various age levels, all tried and tested, from which any one school may build its program. Included also are annual calendar offerings of sports used successfully by various junior and senior high schools, colleges, and universities. These might be helpful in taking inventory of any specific school situation. The annual calendar of events should be well publicized in each school, so that all may plan well in advance of coming events.

Composite List of Adopted Sports
and Activities

Games and Activities for Grades 4-5-6

Bat ball	Hash meet	Pop the top
Bicycling	Hiking	Prisoner's base
Black and white	Hoc soc	Relays and stunts
Bombardment	Jacks	Roller skating
Cat and rat	Jump the shot	Scooter contests
Club snatch	Kite flying	Soak out
Cork ball	Kickball	Softball
Dart games	Marble tourneys	Spot shooting
Diabolo	Model aircraft	Three deep
Dodge ball	Paddle tennis	Track and field
Flicker ball	Pie in the sky	Yo-Yo
Free throws		

Junior and Senior High Schools

FALL	WINTER	SPRING
Archery	Badminton	Aerial darts
Baseball	Basketball	Aerial tennis
Basketball golf	Basket volley-ball	Archery
Bicycling	Bowling	Bait and fly casting
Clock golf	Boxing	Baseball
Cross-country runs	Dart baseball	Baseball field day
Deck tennis	Free throws	Bicycling
Flag football	Gymnastics	Checkers
Football field day	Handball	Chess
German bat ball	Ice hockey	Croquet
Golf	Ice skating	Dart games
Golf specialties	Indoor track	Decathlon
Hiking	Newcomb ball	Golf
Horseback riding	Physical tests	Golf specialties
Horseshoes	Roller skating	Handball, outdoors
Indian dodge ball	Seven-up	Handball, short court
Kick ball	Shuffleboard	Hiking
Pass ball	Skiing	Honorary athletic club
Rifle shooting	Spot shooting	Horseshoes
Skish	Swimming	Junior olympics
Soccer football	Table tennis	Marble tourneys
Soccer-Wilmette	Tumbling	Outdoor track and field
Softball	Twenty-one	Paddle tennis
Speedball	Volleyball	Rifle shooting
Tennis	Water baseball	Shuffleboard
Tether ball	Water basketball	Softball
Touch football	Water polo	Tennis
Zelball	Wrestling	Volley tennis
		Wiskit

Suggested Sports Activities for Grades 4-5-6-7-8

B—Boys' Sports   G—Girls' Sports   I—Individual Sports—Boys and Girls   C—Co-ed Sports

Grade		FIRST QUARTER	SECOND QUARTER	THIRD QUARTER	FOURTH QUARTER
4th Grade	B	Rotation soccer	Basketball hit pin	Track and field	Tee softball
	G	Rotation soccer	Basketball hit pin	Track and field	Tee softball
	I	Four square	Uno-goal golf	Tetherball	Hopscotch
	C	Rotation soccer	Basketball hit pin	Newcomb	Tee softball
5th Grade	B	Soccer	Basketball—9-ct.	Track and field	Softball
	G	Soccer	Basketball—9-ct.	Track and field	Softball
	I	Volley tennis	Basketball golf	Hand tennis	Jump rope
	C	Rotation soccer	Capt. basketball	Volleyball-one-bounce German bat ball	Tee softball
6th Grade	B	Football—6-man	Basketball	Track and field	Softball
	G	Soccer	Basketball—6-ct.	Track and field	Softball Fitness events
	I	Quoits	Rope jumping	Pateca	Paddle handball Hit pin softball Bike treks Bike race Bicycle rode
	C	Speedball German bat ball	Basketball Softball	Volleyball—unlimited Hit softball	
7th Grade	B	Flag football	Basketball	Track and field	Softball
	G	Speedball	Basketball—2-ct. girls	Track and field	Softball
	I	Deck tennis	Paddle ball or handball	Shuffleboard	Table tennis
	C	Volleyball	Hit pin basketball	Hit pin softball	5-4 softball
8th Grade	B	Touch football—8 Free throws	Basketball	Track and field	Softball Tennis
	G	Speed-a-way (G) Free throws	Basketball golf Basketball—2-ct.	Track and field	Softball Tennis
	I	Badminton	Paddle ball	Horseshoes	Paddle tennis
	C	Volleyball	Basketball (3G) (3B)	Hit pin softball	16-man softball Tennis

Colleges and Universities

FALL	WINTER	SPRING
Archery	Badminton	Aerial tennis
Archery golf	Basketball	Archery
Basketball golf	Billiards	Badminton
Bicycling	Bowling	Bait and fly casting
Bowling on the green	Bridge	Baseball
Clock golf	Checkers	Baseball specialties
Cross-country runs	Chess	Bicycling
Flag football	Codeball	Bowling
Football, regular	Dart baseball	Canoeing
Football, 6-man	Fencing	Crew
Fox hunt	Free throws	Cricket
Free throws	Golf putting	Croquet
Golf	Gymnastics	Fly tying
Golf specialties	Handball	Golf
Hiking	Ice hockey	Golf specialties
Horseback riding	Ice skating	Hiking
Horseshoes	Indoor track	Horseshoes
Lacrosse	Paddle ball	Necatos
Polo	Pinochle	Outdoor track
Rifle shooting	Pool	Paddle ball
Rowing	Rifle shooting	Paddle tennis
Sigma Delta Psi	Roller skating	Relay carnival
Skish	Seven-up	Rodeo events
Soccer	Skiing	Rowing
Softball	Squash	Sailing
Speedball	Swimming	Shuffleboard
Tennis	Table tennis	Sigma Delta Psi
Touch football	Tobogganing	Slow-pitch softball
	Tumbling	Softball
	Twenty-one	Tennis
	Volleyball	Volley tennis
	Water basketball	Wiskit
	Water polo	
	Wrestling	

Samples of Sports Calendars Over the Nation

Typical Good Junior High Programs

A. September   Pass ball, football specialties
   October   Pass ball, table tennis, golf, soccer, free throws
   November   Handball, badminton, basketball golf, free throws
   December   Basketball, gymnastics, bat ball, physical tests

January	Basketball, wrestling, twenty-one
February	Basketball, volleyball, boxing
March	Fitness test competition, volleyball, indoor track
April	Softball, tennis, outdoor track
May	Softball, golf, tennis, horseshoes

B. Fall   Touch football, football field day, soccer, tennis singles

      Winter   Basketball, free throws, table tennis, checkers, ice hockey, volleyball, ice frolic, swimming

      Spring   Softball, tennis doubles, outdoor track, golf, horseshoes singles and doubles

The intramural calendar at the junior high school in Lincoln, Rhode Island, includes cross-country and jogging for both boys and girls, soccer, badminton, basketball, swimming, bowling, tennis, gymnastics, volleyball, track and field, co-ed volleyball, co-ed softball, and co-ed gymnastics, and also horseback riding before the stables nearby burned down.

High school girls in Houston, Texas, are offered a balanced and diversified program, balancing team and individual activities in both instruction and competition.

Medium-Sized High Schools

A. Fall   Golf, horseshoes singles and doubles, soccer, table tennis singles and doubles, badminton singles and doubles, co-recreational badminton doubles, co-recreational volleyball, archery, co-recreational archery

      Winter   All-school basketball, sophomore basketball, junior basketball league, senior basketball league, bowling, swimming, recreational swimming, wrestling, free throws, co-recreational bowling, fitness test competition

      Spring   Handball singles and doubles, decathlon, track, softball, co-recreational tennis, water polo

B. Fall   Touch football, tennis singles, golf driving, golf, cross-country, basketball golf, bowling leagues, handball singles, horseshoes singles

      Winter   Handball doubles, table tennis singles, table tennis doubles, noon-hour basketball leagues, frosh basketball jamboree, sophomore basketball jamboree, junior basketball jamboree, senior basketball jamboree, Saturday morning basketball leagues, ice hockey, ice skating carnival, bat ball, wrestling, badminton, gymnastics and tumbling, indoor track modified

      Spring   Softball, outdoor track relays, horseback doubles, tennis doubles, baseball, golf, golf specialties, honorary athletic club, hiking

Large High School-Limited Facilities

The plan might consist of one medium-sized gymnasium, one large community room, and a small swimming pool. The community room can be used for stunts, relays, and tap and folk dances. In the gymnasium Ping-Pong tables are placed under the balcony along with four sets of ring toss. An improvised bowling alley can be arranged down one side of the gym, with Indian Clubs used for pins together with indoor baseballs. In the corridor outside the gym two shuffleboard courts can be designed and in constant use. The corridor can be used for fencing. There is no outside playground but it is possible to arrange competition and activity in hiking, roller skating, ice skating, and bicycling, using nearby facilities. All equipment can be constructed in the school shops.

Smaller College

Fall	Open golf tourney, touch football, basketball golf, tennis singles, mixed tennis doubles, free throws, cross-country turkey race, wrestling, bowling, handball singles, co-recreational swims and sports parties, hiking
Winter	Bowling, basketball leagues and tourneys, wrestling, handball doubles, swimming carnival, table tennis, ice skating carnival, co-recreational winter sports, snow sculpturing, water polo, individual bowling tourney, dart baseball, volleyball, fencing, indoor track
Spring	Volleyball, softball, outdoor track relays, golf, tennis doubles, badminton singles, archery, rowing, horseshoes, hiking, co-recreational golf and tennis, faculty-student golf, shuffleboard

University

Fall	Softball, tennis, golf, touch football, soccer football, badminton, cross-country turkey run
Winter	Basketball, bowling, free throws, table tennis, volleyball, water polo, handball, swimming, indoor track, wrestling, gymnastics, weightlifting
Spring	Softball, horseshoes, tennis, golf, Sigma Delta Psi, outdoor track

University of Maryland

FALL	WINTER	SPRING
Touch football	Boxing	Softball
Horseshoes	Wrestling	Open golf
Tennis singles	Bowling	Team golf
Cross-country	Badminton	Fraternity track
Open track	Volleyball	
	Basketball	

Table tennis
Foul shooting
Gymnastics
Skish
Weight lifting
Co-recreation volleyball
Swimming

University of Michigan

The University of Michigan has many divisions for various competitive units, and sports offered in each may vary. A·complete sports calendar for the year would include the following:

FALL	WINTER	SPRING
Volleyball	Badminton singles	Archery
Swimming	Badminton doubles	Baseball
Twenty-one	Paddle ball doubles	Rifle shooting
Cross-country	Table tennis singles	Lacrosse
Soccer	Squash racquets	Lifesaving
Handball doubles	Bowling singles	Tennis singles
Paddle ball singles	Codeball singles	Indoor track
Ice hockey	Codeball doubles	Softball
Touch football	Wrestling	Horseshoes singles
Outdoor track and field	Swimming	
	Ice hockey	
	Foul throwing	
	Diving	
	Boxing	
	Fencing	
	Gymnastics	
	Weight lifting	
	Sigma Delta Psi	
	Track relays	
	Basketball	
	Water polo	

University of Louisville[8]

FALL	WINTER	SPRING
Golf (medal play)	Basketball	Bowling
Touch football	Free throw	Track and field
Soccer	Handball singles	Tennis singles
Cross-country (turkey run)	Handball doubles	Tennis doubles
Swimming meet	Table tennis singles	Golf (team)
Sigma Delta Psi	Table tennis doubles	Softball
Horseshoes singles	Volleyball	Extramural Sports Day
Horseshoes doubles	Badminton	Co-recreation
Co-recreation	Co-recreation	

Fig. 35. Touch football under the lights at the University of Texas.

University of Nebraska

Fall	Touch football leagues, soccer football, tennis singles, free throws, cross-country turkey run, golf, co-recreational swim and sports parties, bowling leagues, table tennis team tourneys
Winter	Basketball leagues (A, B, and C, independent, intercollege, etc.), table tennis individual, bowling leagues, wrestling, swimming, handball, faculty bowling, water basketball, co-recreational swim and sports parties, rifle shooting, individual bowling, squash team and individual, gymnastics, weight lifting, indoor track, duck-pin bowling
Spring	Volleyball leagues, softball, golf, tennis doubles, mixed tennis doubles, mixed golf, outdoor track relays, co-recreational swim and sports nights, badminton team and individual, shuffleboard, horseshoes, faculty tennis and golf, water polo leagues, bowling, skish, skeet
Summer	Softball, golf, tennis, handball, squash, swimming, badminton, shuffleboard, table tennis, bridge

Brigham Young University

SPECIAL EVENTS:	ENTRIES CLOSE	PLAY BEGINS
Bicycle racing	Oct. 9	Oct. 19
Weight lifting meet	Nov. 6	Nov. 16
Turkey trot	Nov. 13	Nov. 23
Swimming and diving meet	Dec. 4	Dec. 10
Gymnastics meet	Jan. 8	Jan. 13
Fencing meet	Jan. 8	Jan. 14
Wrestling	Feb. 12	Feb. 22
Arm wrestling	Feb. 19	March 1

Fite night (obstacle course)	March 12	March 22
Kite flying	March 19	March 29
Track and field meet	April 16	April 28 & 29
Golf tournament	April 23	May 3
Road rally	April 30	May 10
Awards banquet	May 17	May 17

INDIVIDUAL EVENTS

Horseshoes	Oct. 2	Oct. 12
Tennis singles	Oct. 9	Oct. 19
Individual supremacy	Oct. 23	Oct. 23
Paddle ball singles	Oct. 16	Oct. 26
Badminton singles	Nov. 6	Nov. 16
Table tennis singles	Nov. 13	Nov. 23
Checkers	Nov. 20	Nov. 30
Handball singles	Jan. 8	Jan. 14
Paddle ball doubles	Feb. 12	Feb. 22
Table tennis doubles	Feb. 19	Feb. 29
Badminton doubles	Feb. 26	March 8
Squash	Feb. 26	March 8
Handball doubles	March 5	March 15
Chess	March 19	March 29
Horseshoes doubles	April 2	April 12
Tennis doubles	April 9	April 19

CO-ED ACTIVITIES

Tennis	Oct. 2	Oct. 12
Badminton	Oct. 2	Oct. 12
Golf (scotch doubles)	Oct. 9	Oct. 19
Bowling	Oct. 23	Nov. 2
Table tennis	Nov. 6	Nov. 16
Paddle ball	Nov. 13	Nov. 23
Darts	Feb. 12	Feb. 22
Skiing	Feb. 12	Feb. 23 & 24
Volleyball	March 5	March 15
Softball	March 12	March 22
Archery meet	April 9	April 19 & 21
Horseshoes	April 23	May 3 & 5

TEAM ACTIVITIES

Flag football	Oct. 2	Oct. 7
Volleyball and M-man	Oct. 2	Oct. 12
Rugby	Oct. 9	Oct. 19
Basketball and M-man	Nov. 6	Nov. 16
Water basketball	Feb. 12	Feb. 18
Softball (fast pitch)	March 12	March 22
Softball (slow pitch)	March 12	March 22
Soccer	March 19	March 29

North Carolina Central University[9]

FALL SPORTS	ENTRY DEADLINE	STARTING DATE
Flag football	Sept. 2nd week	Sept. 3rd week
Speedball (girls)	Sept. 2nd week	Sept. 3rd week
Archery	Oct. 1st week	Oct. 1st week
Pass–punt–kick	Oct. 3rd week	Nov. 1st week
Cross-country	Oct. 1st week	Oct. 2nd week
Free throw	Nov. 1st week	Nov. 1st week
WINTER SPORTS		
Bowling	Nov. 1st week	Nov. 2nd week
Wall ball	Nov. 1st week	Nov. 2nd week
Basketball	Nov. 2nd week	Nov. 3rd week
Badminton	Dec. 1st week	Dec. 2nd week
Volleyball	Feb. 1st week	Feb. 2nd week
(*Co-ed*)		
Physical fitness	Feb. 1st week	Feb. 2nd week
Extramural basketball tournament	March 1st week	Feb. 3rd week
Co-rec. night	Feb. 3rd week	Dec. 3rd week
SPRING SPORTS		
Table tennis	March 1st week	March 1st week
Golf	March 1st week	March 2nd week
Swimming	March 1st week	March 2nd week
Tennis	March 1st week	March 2nd week
Track	March 3rd week	March 4th week
Softball	April 1st week	April 2nd week
Pocket billiards	April 2nd week	April 2nd week
Horseshoes	April 2nd week	April 2nd week
All-Sports Day		May 1st week
Intramural dinner		May 2nd week

REFERENCES

1 Louis E. Means, "Post War College and University Intramural Athletics," *The Athletic Journal*, XXVIII, No. 9, May, 1948.

2 *Handbook of Intramural Sports*, University of Georgia, Athens, 1962.

3 National Intramural Association, *Twentieth Conference Proceedings*, 1969, pp. 217–19.

4 National Intramural Association, *Eleventh Conference Proceedings*, 1960, p. 6.

5 AAHPER-NEA Brochure—*Track and Field Project of Operation Fitness—USA*, 1960.

[6] Louis E. Means, *Physical Education Activities, Sports and Games* (Dubuque: William C. Brown Company, 1952, 1963).

[7] Otto Gullickson, *Marshall College Intramural Handbook*, Huntington, W. Va., 1960.

[8] Ellis Mendelsohn, *Men's Intramural Activities Handbook*, University of Louisville, 1962.

[9] Ross E. Townes, *Handbook for 1971*, North Carolina Central University at Durham.

7

POINT SYSTEMS: GROUP
AND INDIVIDUAL SCORING

Schools of all types will find that a good intramural program can be carried on without benefit of either awards or a carefully planned and administered point system. These same schools will also discover that a well-integrated point system will greatly increase student interest, entice more participants, increase the number of participations in a wider range of activities, and add zest and spice to competition.

The wise director is aware that other factors are basic to the program. First, he must organize a wide variety of team and individual sports; in this way, although not every student will be attracted to all sports, each will find several to his liking. Next, the director must organize the sports selected in a variety of ways. No one system of setting up leagues and tournaments will suffice. Some sports lend themselves to single elimination tourneys, others to double elimination or ladder play, others get far more participation and interest when set up in league form. But this is not enough. Leagues must be formed using every possible competitive unit. The newer college trend is to drive the organization deeper and wider in an effort to capture and maintain the interest of independent groups, scattered city residents, commuting students, and other special and often isolated segments of the student body.

The director will find that much participation is generated through pressure of the group on the individual; that is the fundamental reason why unorganized individuals show less interest in the program at the outset. Therefore methods should be devised to persuade more group participation. Individual and group point systems are the answer. Many colleges are now finding that the older supremacy point standings of interfraternity groups, so successful in the past, can also be employed to motivate independent groups, although more effort is necessary. Groups are well aware that a let-down anywhere along the line will permit rival organizations to move ahead. Without this urge to constant achievement, groups would concentrate on a few sports, deciding to forego entry in others. With the point system students are often induced to enjoy new sports which may later succeed in becoming leisure-time adult recreational favorites.

Robert Stumpner at Indiana University supports the opposite point of view:[1]

> We are concerned with free choice rather than compulsion of any sort. We have eased out our participation point system on the grounds that it is an artificial device which puts emphasis in the wrong place. We feel that numerical scales do not serve anyone's interest. We now depend upon the appeal of each sport on its own merits. This has eliminated the practice of dumping disinterested fraternity pledges into many activities only for points, and while it has lessened the push that some students seem to need to enter worthwhile activities, our total participation has picked up. Demoralization due to low point totals has been circumvented. We do not try to discourage excellence. We do try to provide sound incentives for everyone, including the lowest groups. Loading tournaments with lukewarm entries for the sake of point awards does not in itself provide meaningful experience. Consistent, spirited, and successful participation by any group carries its own stamp of quality and no arbitrary point scale is needed to prove it. We are now completely free to experiment with new ideas any time— before we were not.

The Universities of Kansas and Nebraska are two of the schools that no longer include a Sports Supremacy Race, after using such a plan for many years. Officials at both universities now feel they would not return to the supremacy plan.

Perhaps this point of view is gaining favor in colleges and universities. Perhaps the impact of point systems at this level may depend upon administrative practices. It is believed that junior and senior high schools and elementary schools may have much stronger reasons to employ a soundly conceived point system as a motivating device for quantity and quality participation. The recent decade has provided many nonschool activities of doubtful nature, each in competition for the recreational time of boys and girls. Directors may do well to try comparative methods to resolve this problem, and emerge with a workable plan.

There are almost as many scoring plans in existence as there are schools using them. Fundamentally, they follow certain patterns; individual features are easily adopted by any school. It is well agreed that such a plan motivates the total program, stimulates and invigorates constant and varied interest and participation in a wider choice of activities, and serves as a perfect basis for awards.

The good program will also have facilities and activities available for those who enjoy recreation informally and at their own desired time. It will offer an opportunity to participate in special features and events that do not always fit into the competitive point system, such as outing activities, co-recreational sports and swims, hiking, horseback riding, and winter sports events.

Group Scoring Suggestions

Most schools, in classifying sports, feel that team events should receive weighted credit over others arranged in single or double elimination style. The terms "major and minor sports" are often, and unfortunately, used in this classification. The practice should be abolished. Since the trend in interscholastic and intercollegiate athletics is to place all sports on an equal major basis, the same educational emphasis should follow for intramurals. Thus, sports could be classified as Group One, Group Two, Group Three; or Class A, Class B, Class C; or, in the point system, merely listed, with different point values for all sports and with descriptive differentiation avoided.

The following material presents practical scoring plans from which every director may get workable ideas.

SMALL JUNIOR AND SENIOR
HIGH SCHOOLS

Competition can be provided first by the intergroup plan. The entire school is divided into two groups, named after the school colors. Competition can also be divided on the interclass basis. The point system can include every phase of school activity, with 50 percent credit for athletics, 25 percent for citizenship, and 25 percent for all other school activities. The chart in Figure 36 gives suggestions for the scoring plan in detail. Further explanation of the system is as follows:

1. In intergroup games the number of points given for winning is divided by the number of games played. The result becomes the number of points awarded for each game won.
2. The same system is used in determining points in team leagues.

3. In team tournaments the number of points given for winning is divided by the number of games won by the champions. The result is the number of points awarded for each game won.

4. In individual tournaments the same system is used as in team tournaments. The individual scores as though he were a team by himself and is awarded points for the number of matches won.

5. In meets the number of points given for winning is divided by the total points made by the high individual scorer in the meet. The result gives the tabulating value for each point won in the meet.

6. Points for participation are added to the above points for games won.

7. One hundred points can be awarded for several noncompetitive athletic events such as:
   a. Hiking one unbroken mile each day for forty successive days.
   b. Five unbroken hikes of five miles each taken during a five-week period.

Fig. 36. A high school plan.

SCORING CHART				
JUNIOR OR SENIOR HIGH SCHOOL				
INTERGROUP GAMES	TEAM LEAGUES AND TOURNAMENTS	INDIVIDUAL TOURNAMENTS	MEETS	ATHLETICS
Baseball Basketball Football Football specialties Horseshoes Pentathlon Speedball Softball Soccer Tennis Volleyball	Baseball Basketball Football Football specialties Horseshoes Volleyball NOON HOUR Baseball Basketball	Foul Shoot Gymnastics Horseshoes Tennis Wrestling Shuffleboard Handball	Track Skating Swimming Skiing Bicycling	Basketball Tennis Track POINTS
POINTS Entrance −50 Additional − $\underline{100}$ 150	POINTS Entrance −50 Additional − $\underline{100}$ 150	POINTS Entrance −25 Additional − $\underline{100}$ 125	POINTS Entrance −25 Additional − $\underline{100}$ 125	Entrance −25 Squad −75 2nd- Letter −25 Letter −75 $\overline{200}$
Second team intergroup sports carried in TENNIS, HORSESHOES, BASKETBALL, VOLLEYBALL, AND FOOTBALL GOALS. 25 points given for entrance in these sports, with 35 additional possible.				

    c. A three-month period of daily early morning exercises worked out with the director and involving fifteen minutes each day.

    d. Three months of perfect attendance at all physical education class.

    e. Four trips of twelve miles each on a bicycle; and other trips of local interest.

  8. Points can be awarded for health practices, leadership, sportsmanship, and scholarship, with a definite basis worked out.

One of the finest high school intramural programs selects only four sports to be awarded group points on an interclass basis. They are pushball, swimming, basketball, and track. Boys on each winning team receive 25 points, with second-place winners getting 15 points. Over twenty other sports provide individual points only. A card index system is maintained and accurate records kept. More stress is placed on playing than on winning, with credit weighted for both. The ten highest scorers each year are presented special awards, based on the individual scoring race. The point system follows:

5 points	Sportsmanship and reliability
2 points	For participation in any intramural event
5 points	Member of a winning team in any sport
3 points	Member of any second-place team
5 points	Winner in any singles tournament
4 points	Second-place winner in any singles tournament
3 points	Third-place winner in any singles tournament
2 points	Fourth-place winner in any singles tournament
1 point	Fifth-place winner in any singles tournament
5 points	Completing AAHPER Fitness Tests
6 points	Completing the athletic tests (Delta Sigma Psi)
1 point	Bonus for first place in swim or track meet
$\frac{1}{2}$ point	Bonus for second place in swim or track meet
$\frac{1}{4}$ point	Bonus for third place in swim or track meet
$\frac{1}{2}$ point	For first hike. Each hike following first to be given $\frac{1}{2}$ point more
—2 points	Deducted for forfeiting a single match, or member of a forfeiting team

NEW TRIER HIGH SCHOOL, WINNETKA,
ILLINOIS

In addition to the usual points awarded for participation in sports at New Trier High School, Winnetka, Illinois, the point system adopted for service in the Sports Club is worthy of mention. The club seeks to sponsor, promote, and conduct as many intramural sports as possible; it improves methods of playing, officiating, and managing, and seeks to develop sportsmanship and a spirit of fair play in all interscholastic and intramural sports among spectators, officials, and players. The club has its own teams in many sports, but one of its principal duties is officiating. Members receive points for contributing service as follows:

Football	Referee, 10; umpire and timer, 8; head linesman, 6; linesman, 2; scorer or reporter, 4
Touch football	Referee, 10; umpire, 7; scorer or reporter, 8; timer, 5
Basketball	Referee, 10; umpire, 10; scorer or reporter, 8; timer, 5
Softball	Balls and strikes, 10; bases, 7; scorer or reporter, 8
Volleyball	Referee, 10; scorer or reporter, 8; linesman, 2

In all interclass contests 5 points are added to all above services regardless of assignment.

Scorers for football skills, free throws, track, floor and field managers receive 8 points per hour or any part of an hour. Members bringing in a new member receive 25 points.

LARGE HIGH SCHOOL

Another simple plan classifies all sports into three divisions, with points scaled down proportionately in each. The method of awarding points in the first division is presented here. All sports are organized on the home-room basis.

50 points	Entering a team
5 points	Winning each game
150 points	Winning school championship
125 points	Winning second place, school championships
100 points	Winning third place, school championships
75 points	Winning fourth place, school championships
50 points	Winning fifth place, school championships
25 points	Winning sixth place, school championships
5 points	For each boy participating
5 points	For every boy from group on varsity or "B" interscholastic squads

AMHERST COLLEGE

Amherst College developed a point system involving a final ranking system worthy of study. The sports are classified as major, submajor, and minor. The ranking team in a major sport receives for its score three times as many points as there are possible competing teams. The team in second place receives three less points than the winning team and so on down to three points for the team in last place. Submajor and minor points are scaled down in proportion, as the chart below indicates. Any team tied for a position but having on its record a game lost by forfeit or cancellation shall take the lesser rank. Any team failing to compete shall be scored 0 points.

To illustrate how the point system operates, the following is a specimen scoring chart for an activity in which fifteen teams could participate.

Rank	1	2	3	4	5	6	7	8	9	10	11	12	13	14	15
Major	45	42	39	36	33	30	27	24	21	18	15	12	9	6	3
Submajor	30	28	26	24	22	20	18	16	14	12	10	8	6	4	2
Minor	15	14	13	12	11	10	9	8	7	6	5	4	3	2	1

It should be noted that this chart would differ if there were more or fewer teams competing, but the gradations are the same. In swimming and track, groups having entered men and scored no points shall receive points behind the scorers in ratio to the number of men entered in the meet. Thus, two teams entering and scoring no points, while ten other groups did, will earn eleventh and twelfth places according to the number of men entered. Amherst College also includes academic ranks of all groups in the point system in addition to athletic competition.

RENSSELAER POLYTECHNIC INSTITUTE

Organizations at Rensselaer Polytechnic Institute compete for the Barker Supremacy Trophy on the following basis:

	TABLE 1	TABLE 2	TABLE 3	TABLE 4
Entering a team	$2\frac{1}{2}$	5	5	5
Group championship	5	5	10	10
Group second place	$2\frac{1}{2}$	$2\frac{1}{2}$	$2\frac{1}{2}$	0
League championship	$2\frac{1}{2}$	5	5	0
Second in each league	$1\frac{1}{2}$	3	3	5
Third in each league	1	2	2	4
Fourth in each league, meet	$\frac{1}{2}$	1	1	3
Fifth in each league, meet	0	0	0	2
Sixth in meets	0	0	0	1
Deducted for each forfeiture	$\frac{1}{2}$	1	1	0
Maximum points to champion	10	15	20	16
Maximum points to second	$7\frac{1}{2}$	$12\frac{1}{2}$	$17\frac{1}{2}$	

Sports classified under Table 1 are horseshoes, handball, table tennis, and tennis. Table 2 includes only bowling. Table 3 consists of volleyball, softball, basketball. Table 4 lists swimming and track.

NORTH CAROLINA CENTRAL UNIVERSITY

At NCCU, at Durham, teams and individuals are given points based upon the showing made in each sport. The individual and the team with the highest point total at year's end are awarded All-Sports trophies. The point system is as follows:

Team Points

30 points for entering tournament
5 points for each league win
15 points for league championship
20 points for activity championship
Loss of 5 points for each forfeit, cancellation, or postponement

All-Sports Day

The All-Sports Day is also a weekend of activities during which representatives from the Law School, Graduate School, Senior Class, Junior Class, Sophomore Class and Freshman Class compete for the Campus Wide Intramural Day Championship.

UNIVERSITY OF TENNESSEE

The University of Tennessee has used a scoring system that rewards organizations according to their size, thus tending to give smaller groups an equal chance with the larger and more powerful units.[2]

The scoring system is outlined as follows:

BASKETBALL, SOFTBALL, TENNIS, VOLLEYBALL

20 points for playing schedule through without forfeit; 10 points for each scheduled game won; 10 additional points for group champions; 5 additional points to runner-up. Also groups with a total membership of active chapter men and pledges within the following ranges will add points as follows:

Membership	5 to 29	25 points
	30 to 34	20 points
	35 to 40	15 points
	41 to 47	10 points
	48 and up	5 points

RELAY CARNIVAL

10 points for each relay team that competes; 5 points to winner of each heat; 10 additional points for winning either race. Groups with total

membership of active chapter men and pledges within the following ranges will add points as follows:

Membership	2-29	10 points
	30-34	5 points
	35 and up	3 points

SWIMMING AND TRACK

15 points for a team of six men competing; and 30-25-20-15-10-5 points are respectively awarded to those groups that score most points in the meets. Membership bonus points as follows:

Membership	5-29	15 points
	30-34	10 points
	35-40	8 points
	41-47	5 points
	48 and up	2 points

FOX HUNT

10 points for team of five men finishing the chase; and 25-20-15-10-5 points respectively to those finishing in that order, score being based on the total score of the order in which all competitors finish the race. Membership bonus points awarded as in swimming and track.

SHUFFLEBOARD, HORSESHOES

10 points for playing the schedule through; 5 points for each match won; and 5 additional points for the winner of the tourney. Membership points awarded as in relay carnival.

UNIVERSITY OF TEXAS

Organization All-Year Trophy Point System University of Texas

The system of scoring points toward the All-Year Trophy in all divisions shall be as indicated in the following table:

SPORT	MINIMUM NO. CONTESTANTS FOR PARTIC. PTS	PARTICI- PATION POINTS	POINTS FOR EACH VICTORY	ENTRIES LIMITED
Major Team Sports				
Basketball (Class A)	5	50	†20 and 35	1
Basketball (Class B)	5	50	†10 and 15	1
Softball (Class A)	9–10	50	†20 and 35	1
Softball (Class B)	10	50	†10 and 15	1
Touch Football (Class A)	7	50	†20 and 35	1
Touch Football (Class B)	7	50	†10 and 15	1
Volleyball (Class A)	6	50	†20 and 35	1

SPORT	MINIMUM NO. CONTESTANTS FOR PARTIC. PTS	PARTICIPATION POINTS	POINTS FOR EACH VICTORY	ENTRIES LIMITED
Volleyball (Class B)	6	50	†10 and 15	1
Track	4	50		2 men in
Division			5 for each point made in meet.	each event
Intramural Championship			3 for each point made in meet.	
Minor Team Sports				
Water Basketball	6	50	†15 and 25	1
Swimming	4	50		2 men in
Divisional			4 for each point made in meet.	each event
Intramural Championship			3 for each point made in meet.	
Bowling (Class A)	4	50	7 for each team point.	1
Bowling (Class B)	4	50	3 for each team point.	1
Individual Sports				8
Golf Singles	2	50	½ to 50–100 places	
Medal Play			6	
Match Play				
Golf Doubles	2	50		4
Medal Play			1 to 75–75 places	
Match Play			8	
Handball Singles (Class A)	2	50	5	8
Handball Singles (Class B)	2	50	2	4
Handball Doubles (Class A)	2	50	8	4
Handball Doubles (Class B)	2	50	4	2
Table Tennis Singles	2	50	5	8
Table Tennis Doubles	2	50	8	4
Tennis Singles (Class A)	2	50	5	8
Tennis Singles (Class B)	2	50	2	4
Tennis Doubles (Class A)	2	50	8	4
Tennis Doubles (Class B)	2	50	4	2
Wrestling	2	50	5	4

† In team sports conducted on double elimination basis, victories for the winning side of the tournament shall be given approximately twice as many points as victories on the losing side.

Fig. 37

UNIVERSITY OF NEBRASKA

The point system used for years at the University of Nebraska was devised on the group basis only. It is simple to administer, and gives credit for participation of all groups, with additional points awarded to at least six organizations in every type of sport. The system was used for inter-fraternity competition as well as separately for intercollege and interdepartmental divisions, the dormitory division, and the independent and denominational divisions. Each division had its own supremacy race, with appropriate awards in each. At the conclusion of each sport, champions from all the divisions met to decide the all-university championships. The sports accepted toward supremacy in each division were agreed upon in preliminary managers' meetings; therefore, some divisions include more sports than others. Sports were classified in the interfraternity division as follows:

Group One
Touch football, volleyball, water basketball or water polo, softball, bowling

Group Two
Basketball "B" leagues, outdoor track relays, indoor track meet, table tennis, wrestling, boxing, swimming, handball

Group Three
Tennis singles, tennis doubles, fall golf, spring golf, cross-country turkey race, rifle shooting, squash, horseshoes

Group Four
All sports that are not included in the point system, such as badminton, archery, shuffleboard, hiking, ice skating, Sigma Delta Psi, co-recreational events

Nebraska Group Scoring Plan

GROUP	PARTICI-PATION	FIRST	SECOND	THIRD	FOURTH	FIFTH	SIXTH
GROUP ONE	60	200	170	150	125	100	75
GROUP TWO	40	150	125	105	90	75	60
GROUP THREE	30	130	105	85	70	55	40
GROUP FOUR	No points awarded						

Forfeiting one game in Group One causes loss of 30 points; Group Two loses 20 points; Group Three loses 15 points. Forfeiture of more than one game, groups lose all participation points.

Whenever group standings are determined from an all-University individual tournament, the following plan is used to rank the groups for the points listed above:

Champion scores toward group standing	6 points
Runner-up scores toward group standing	4 points
Third place scores toward group standing	3 points
Fourth place scores	2 points
Next four quarter finalists score	1½ points
Next eight of final 16 score	1 point

Individual points are added to determine final group standings in the sport.

UNIVERSITY OF CALIFORNIA

The scoring plan used at the University of California at Berkeley is as follows:

American, Graduate, and National Leagues
Point System

	TYPE OF COMPETITION	CHAMPION- SHIP POINTS	MIN. PAR POINTS	ALL-UNIV. CHAMPION- SHIP
Touch football	Round-robin	200	50	25
Basketball	and Play-off	200	50	25
Softball	and Play-off	200	50	25
Soccer	and Play-off	200	50	25
Volleyball	Double elimination	150	30	25
Tennis	Double elimination	125	25	25
Table tennis	Double elimination	125	25	25
Bowling	Double elimination	125	25	25
Horseshoes	Double elimination	75	15	25
Handball	Double elimination	125	25	25
Badminton	Double elimination	75	15	25
Pocket billiards	Double elimination	75	15	25
Squash	Double elimination	125	25	25
Two-man volleyball	Double elimination	75	15	25

Places Determined by Time or Distance

Swimming	Meet—preliminaries and finals	100 (100–80–70–60–50–40–30–20–10)	10
Track	Meet—2 days	(100–80–70–60–50–40–30–20–10)	
Golf	4-day tournament	75 (75–65–60–55–50–45–40–35–30– 25–20–15–10)	10
Gymnastics*	Meet	50–40–30–20–10	
Weight lifting	Meet—preliminaries and finals	50–40–30–20–10	
Wrestling*	Meet—preliminaries and finals	150 (150–125–110–100–90–80–70–60– 50–40–30–20–15)	15

* American, Graduate, and National Leagues are combined in one league in these meet activities.

UNIVERSITY OF LOUISVILLE

The University of Louisville's point system[3] is a device to stimulate widespread participation in all phases of intramural activities by offering incentives beyond the immediate desire to excel in any particular activity. All points earned by an organization count toward the final intramural standings, and the All-Year Intramural Activities Participation Trophy. Entry points are offered in most activities and these are supplemented by additional points awards for successful performance. Full and spirited participation, rather than emphasis on a few winning teams, will best fulfill the objectives of the program. The employment of the point system has aided greatly in fostering such participation.

The All-Year competition is determined on a standard point basis which is furnished all organizations each Fall.

**Individual Scoring System
for Participation Trophy**

1 point for each match or contest participated in
1 point for each contest or match won
1 point for third place in any individual or dual sport
3 points for runner-up in any individual or dual sport
5 points for championship in any individual or dual sport

A separate card is filed for each individual who participates in the intramural activities program and a record of his play is posted on the card each time he takes part in any phase of the program. Intramural Units Managers as well as individuals are requested to examine the files for accuracy of record keeping and to keep posted on the current standings in the competition for the annual individual high point trophies.

TEMPLE UNIVERSITY

At Temple University the Interfraternity Sports Council has established a point system for intramurals. The fraternity having the highest point total for the year is awarded the All-Sports Trophy for one year. The point system follows:

Major	Football	First place, 60 points
Sports	Soccer	
	Basketball	Second place, 45 points
	Bowling	
	Softball	Third place, 30 points

PARTICIPATION RECORD

INTRAMURAL SPORTS

SYRACUSE UNIVERSITY

Name: _____ College: _____

19 ____ 19 ____

Class: _____

Total: [ ]   [ ]

	Mass Track	Horseshoe Pitching	Rifle	Soccer	Swimming	Touch Football	Basketball	Bowling	Boxing	Handball	Wrestling	Bridge	Dual Track	Foul Shooting	Gymnastics	Hockey	Ping Pong	Skiing	Volleyball	Baseball	Golf	Horseshoe Golf	Softball	Tennis							
Fraternity																															
Living Center																															
Independents																															
Class–College																															
Tournament																															

Fig. 38. Printed form used by Syracuse University to tabulate individual participation throughout the year's program.

Minor	Volleyball	First place, 75 points
Sports	Handball	Second place, 60 points
	Swimming	Third place, 50 points
	Track and field	Fourth place, 40 points
		Fifth place, 30 points
		Sixth place, 25 points
		Seventh place, 20 points
		Eighth place, 15 points
		Ninth place, 10 points
		Tenth place, 5 points

UNIVERSITY OF ILLINOIS

The University of Illinois scoring plan is adopted for both group and individual scoring. Illinois provides individual points in many different sports not shown on the table here, which includes only the group sports used in the supremacy race.[4]

Achievement Point System

A. Team Sports—playing or by forfeit
   1. League wins and play-off byes 5
   2. Play-off win 10
   3. Loss by forfeit .... −5
   4. League play-off 0

B. Meet Sports—total earned in meet
   1. Track—Places given 5–4–3–2–1
          Relay 10–8–6–4–2
   2. Swimming and Gymnastics
      Same places as track given for relays and same for individual events if 20 or more actually compete in the event.
      If 9 or less 3–2–1
      10 to 19 4–3–2–1

C. Individual Sports—beginning with winners of round four
   1. Singles ....c........................ 2
   2. Doubles 3

D. Bowling—(one night roll-off) championship
   1. Highest 3-game series 25
   2. Second highest 3-game series 15
   3. Third highest 3-game series 10
   4. Fourth highest 3-game series 5
   5. League Match Victory 5

E. Wrestling
   1. Win by bye 1
   2. Win by match or forfeit 2

OBERLIN COLLEGE PLAN

Point System for House and Class Sports

House

In order that a fair and equitable method of computation may be used in all intramural sports, the following method of awarding points has proven successful. First an equalization factor is calculated that is equal to:

$$\frac{\text{the number of men required times the number of contests}}{10}$$

e.g., Basketball ....32 teams

4 leagues of 8 teams

Therefore ....7 games each

5 men on a team

Equalization factor: $\dfrac{5 \times 7}{10} = 3.5$

Next determine the status of each team in the four leagues by the percentage or by the professional hockey method (in the case of touchball, water polo, or in any competition prone to ending in tie scores), and multiply the calculated equalization factor by the number which represents the inverse numerical order in which the teams finished in the league or leagues.

e.g., Final house points

Winner ....$32 \times 3.5 = 112.0$

Second place ....$31 \times 3.5 = 108.5$

Last place .... $1 \times 3.5 =$ 3.5

Number of Men Required for Team Sports

The number of men required for a track, swimming, or similar meet shall equal the total number of events including relays.

The number of men required for various team sports shall be the full team as specified by official rules except as these may be modified by the Intramural Division.

Number of Men Required for Individualistic Sports

Number of men required ....One for each man participating

Number of contests ....Number of contests engaged in by the individual player

Total number of entries ......Total number of houses that enter men

Basketball teams are divided into equally strong leagues (as nearly as can be estimated), with the exception that a second division shall be provided for all second teams and for those teams that do not desire to compete for house points. In computing the total number of teams entered, only those competing for points shall be awarded points although placement in ranking order is sometimes necessary for total team computation.

In the event that there are different numbers of teams in the various sport leagues:

1. If there are equal numbers of even and odd teams, the equalization factor shall be calculated on the basis of the larger number.
2. If there are unequal numbers of even and odd team leagues, the equalization factor is calculated on the basis of the leagues of which there are the greater number; e.g. six-, six-, and seven-team leagues—the equalization factor is calculated on the basis of six-team leagues.

Class

Class points are computed by the plan described above for house points. The class having the most points at the close of the year has its numerals engraved on the perpetual cup. Medals, ribbons, and class numerals may be awarded at the discretion of the intramural department.

One of the greatest needs in intramurals today is the further development of a point system that is successfully based on the amount of participation, and which also considers the number of players, size of the organization, wins and losses, and the members of the organization who are playing on varsity teams, thereby weakening their organization's chances in intramurals. Others feel that study should be made by intramural workers to arrive at a formula which would be applicable to programs at many institutions, with certain adjustments. The equalizing factor used at Oberlin College is a definite move in this direction. Perhaps the more scientific workers in the field will develop a carefully constructed point scoring formula embracing all the important factors meriting consideration.

WAYNE STATE UNIVERSITY

Loren F. Karnish at Wayne State University in Detroit suggests that a point scoring system is very necessary in the over-all promotional plan. He feels it is only a means to an end, the end being a quality program. At Wayne State the following scoring system is used for league sports:

15 points for league win and play-off win
4 points for league loss and play-off loss
40 points for team entry
20, 15, 10, 8 points for top positions in play-off
75, 60, 45, 30 points for top positions in league prior to play-off

S. S. & F. ------ Team ------ Team ------ Team

W. Trim. ------ Team ------ Team ------ Team

S. Trim. ------ Team ------ Team ------ Team

Last Name

Other Names

	SPORTS	Year	Year	Year	Year
INTRAMURAL	Badminton				
	Baseball				
	Basketball "A"				
	Basketball "B"				
	Fencing				
	Foul Throw				
	Golf Doubles				
	Golf Singles				
	Handball Doubles				
	Handball Singles				
	Horseshoe Doubles				
	Horseshoe Singles				
	Soccer				
	Softball (Summer)				
	Softball (Spring)				
	Swimming (Fall)				
	Swimming (Spring)				
	Table Tennis Doubles				
	Table Tennis Singles				
	Tennis Doubles				
	Tennis Singles (Summer)				
	Tennis Singles (Spring)				
	Touch Football				
	Track				
	Volley Ball				
	Water Polo				
	Wrestling				
	TOTAL				
INTERCOLLEGIATE	Baseball				
	Basketball				
	Cross Country				
	Fencing				
	Football				
	Golf				
	Swimming				
	Tennis				
	Track				
	Physical Training				

Health Grade

Fig. 39. Individual cumulative record participation, University of Texas.

A careful study of all the various types of group-scoring plans presented here, or found elsewhere in the nation, will reveal possible weaknesses when applied to any one situation. The wise director will carefully study his local problems and apply the most workable ideas to the local program. Nor should a point system be considered permanently set in any institution. New possibilities will arise with changes in enrollment, expansion of dormitories, and the perfection of new competitive units and bases for classification. This should demand constant evaluation of the point system, and every attempt should be made to employ it as a definite motivating force for the expansion of a truly great program.

M-Mixed S-Singles D-Doubles	University of Louisville-Division of Intramural Activities INDIVIDUAL RECORD OF PARTICIPATION				
Name _____ Last _____ First _____ Middle				Org. _____ Org. Phone _____ School _____	
Address _____ Home Phone _____					
ACTIVITIES	FRESHMAN 19	SOPHOMORE 19	JUNIOR 19	SENIOR 19	TOTAL
Touch Football					
Cross Country					
Swimming					
Basketball					
Volleyball M					
Bowling M					
Foul Shooting					
Track					
Tennis SDM					
Golf Team: Medal:					
Horseshoes SD					
Soccer					
Handball SD					
Table Tennis SDM					
Rifle					
Archery M					
Badminton SDM					
TOTALS					

Fig. 40. Individual record form, University of Louisville.

Individual Scoring Suggestions

Group scoring systems have been in operation almost as long as intramurals have been known. A more recent trend is the carefully devised plan of individual recognition which can operate in correlation with the group and unit type of program. A few schools recognized early the great value of individual point systems, but many institutions still do not. Large universities realize that such a plan will demand painstaking detail work and bookkeeping, yet several of the largest institutions in the nation testify to the great value of both group and individual point systems and have devised functional systems which undoubtedly have enhanced the quality and quantity of their total program.

Certainly the junior and senior high school level is perfectly keyed to the individual point scoring plan. Boys and girls at this age love to excel, enjoy self-testing events of all kinds, and seek to know how they rank with other students. Also at this age directors find no real problem in securing students who get real pleasure out of carrying on the clerical work demanded of such a plan. Preliminary apprehension of the detail necessary for such a plan will disappear after the efficient director gets his system routinized and in the hands of willing and enthusiastic students.

Several advantages become apparent in favor of the individual scoring plan, and might be summarized as follows:

1. An increased eagerness for group participation grows out of the system, since group play consistently adds to individual progress.
2. All individual tournaments and events will receive many more entries, and will include large numbers of students who are totally unfamiliar with the particular sport but are anxious to learn and to compete.
3. Greater interest is noted in the physical education classes, since they teach the skills through which a student may become more successful in the laboratory or intramural competitive period.
4. Much more interest is created in the noncompetitive aspects of the total program, since they, too, can be recognized in the individual point scoring plan.
5. The scoring system can be used to stimulate and promote better health and safety habits.
6. The student obtains a broader knowledge of many more recreational sports, some of which can be utilized in adult leisure-time living.
7. The plan offers a splendid basis for a progressive achievement awards system, easily adapted to the local situation.
8. All individuals are recognized in measure, not just the superior athlete who more often finds himself on the championship team.
9. The plan permits the combination of all school activities in the point system, recognizing accomplishment in athletics, debate, music, declamation, and other activities.

Some high schools have devised an awards system combining all athletic competition. Points are given for varsity squad participation, intramural competition, and other forms of recreation. Thus the student may progress from the school emblem to letters and the higher varsity honors, but the constant awarding of letters for each sport is abolished, and a more integrated awards system is possible.

Before setting up the individual point plan the director should take all possible precautions to avoid faulty administration. If the school offers several types of basketball leagues and tournaments, it would be well to limit the amount of basketball play any one student may elect, providing limitations in other sports as well. Sports should be organized in such a way that fairly uniform opportunities for play are maintained. To accomplish this, leagues must not permit some students to play more games than others before arriving at the championship play-offs. Again, the director must set up restrictions to prohibit some overzealous students from getting excessive competition to the detriment of health, studies, and other school and home affairs. Standards must be established so that awards are not too easily realized and thereby become more valued.

The department contemplating such a point system must set up proper machinery for a card index system, adequate printed forms to simplify the book work, and constant use of managers and student assistants. Several plans for individual scoring are presented here for study and examination.

INDIVIDUAL SCORING PLANS FOR
INTRAMURALS ONLY

The plan used for several years at East High School, Green Bay, Wisconsin, provided an award of the school emblem whenever 1,000 points were earned. Points were allowed to carry over to succeeding years, and interest was maintained throughout the four-year period. Points were given on the following basis:

LEAGUE AND TEAM SPORTS (MAXIMUM OF 150 POINTS PER SPORT)

20 points	For each game played
25 points	Bonus, member of championship team
20 points	Bonus, member of second-place team
15 points	Bonus, member of third-place team
10 points	Bonus, member of fourth-place team
5 points	Bonus, member of fifth-place team
—20 points	Deducted whenever team forfeits

TOURNAMENTS OF INDIVIDUAL NATURE
(MAXIMUM OF 125 POINTS PER SPORT)

15 points	For each match played or won by forfeit
20 points	Bonus to individual champion
15 points	Bonus to second-place individual
10 points	Bonus to third-place individual
5 points	Bonus to fourth-place individual
—15 points	Deducted for each match forfeited

MEETS OF INDIVIDUAL AND TEAM NATURE
(MAXIMUM OF 100 POINTS PER MEET)

20 points	Each event entered and competing
	(Number of events permissible always limited)
10 points	Bonus for winning each first place
5 points	Bonus for any record broken
8 points	Bonus for winning each second place
6 points	Bonus for winning each third place
4 points	Bonus for winning each fourth place
2 points	Bonus for winning each fifth place

This plan appears at first glance to be complicated, but actually it is very simple in operation. At the completion of each event the director or his assistant prepares a summary of the sport, tracing the progress of the tournament and building a composite point chart from which students may enter points on the individual record cards. This plan was a constant source of stimulation to hundreds of boys throughout each year.

The plan inaugurated some time ago by Grady Skillern of the Tulsa, Oklahoma, schools provided the award of numerals to a student acquiring 1,000 points. One might be inclined to question the weight given for a first place over the participation in all games. The Tulsa schedule is as follows:

BASKETBALL, WATER BASKETBALL,
WATER POLO, SOFTBALL,
SPEEDBALL, TOUCH FOOTBALL

500	First place
300	Second place
200	Third place
100	Fourth place
100	For competing in all scheduled contests in addition to winner's points

WRESTLING

500	First place
300	Second place
200	Third place
100	For competing in all scheduled matches in addition to winner's points

GOLF AND TRACK

250	First place
200	Second place
100	Third place
50	Fourth place
50	For competing in all scheduled meets in addition to winner's points

TENNIS AND SWIMMING

150	First place
100	Second place
75	Third place
50	Fourth place
50	For competing in all scheduled meets in addition to winner's points

The College of the City of New York does not award group points, preferring to give individual points only. This system is perhaps the most simple in the nation. Each time a student enters an intramural event, either as an individual or team member, his entry card is placed on file. For every game or match he plays he receives one point, which is scored on the entry card. Total points at the end of each event are recorded on master cards for each student. At the end of each semester the points are added. The student having the highest total has his name inscribed on a permanent plaque hanging in a prominent place in the gymnasium. This record is maintained for every year the student remains in college, standing as a measure of his participation and ability.

Purdue University maintains an individual point system in addition to the group awards. Three trophies are awarded each year to the ward or unorganized men accumulating the greatest number of points, as well as three trophies to the fraternity high-point men, the awards based on the following schedule:

1 point	For participating in a league, tournament, race, or event
2 points	For being the winner, or member of winning team
1 point	For runner-up, or being member of runner-up team

The maximum number of points allowed in any event is 3 points.

Wayne University of Detroit has used a simple scoring plan for individual ratings. A "Most Versatile Trophy" is awarded each year to the individual making the best all-around showing, computed by awarding 6 points for all first places, 5 points for second place, 4 points for third, 2 points for fourth, and 1 point for participation below that point. Whenever competition fails to decide the actual placement, intramural officials rate the teams or individuals accordingly.

Wheaton College of Illinois provides an easily administered individual point system:

FOR TEAM COMPETITION

25 points	Member of team winning championship
10 points	Participating and winning, each contest
5 points	Participating and losing, each contest

FOR MEET COMPETITION

6 points	Any first place
4 points	Any second place
3 points	Any third place
2 points	Any fourth place
5 points	Participating

Colorado State University at Fort Collins has used the point system shown in Fig. 41.

POINT SYSTEM
Intramural Sports

Team Sports	Minimum Number Contestants For Entry	Entry Points	League Points					Division Points				Campus Champion	First Minus	Total Possible
			1st	2nd	3rd	4th	5th	1st	2nd	3rd	4th			
Touch Football	10	60	30	24	18	12	6	40	32	24	16	50	20	180
Cage Ball	10	60	30	24	18	12	6	40	32	24	16	50	20	180
Basketball	8	48	24	20	15	10	5	32	25	19	13	40	16	144
Bowling	4	24	12	9	7	6	2	16	13	10	6	20	8	72
Softball	10	60	30	24	18	12	6	40	32	24	16	50	20	180
Volleyball	6	36	18	14	11	7	4	24	20	15	10	30	12	108

Open Meets and Tournaments	Individual Place				Team Place				
	1st.	2nd	3rd	4th	1st	2nd	3rd	4th	5th
*Tennis — Singles	10	6	4	2					
*Badminton									
*Handball									
*Horseshoes — Doubles	20	12	8	4					
Golf	10	6	4	2					
Skiing—Downhill, Slalom									
Combined	5	3	2	1	20	16	12	8	4
*Wrestling, each weight	5	3	2	1	20	16	12	8	4
**Swimming, each event	5	3	2	1	20	16	12	8	4
*Track, each event	5	3	2	1	20	16	12	8	4

*Entries per organization in each event limited to number places given.
Unit Representatives not present at official meetings lose 5 points.
**Scored by NCAA system for team standing, as above for All-Sports points.

[1]Ski Team points are determined on the combined times of the best three entries from a single organization.

Fig. 41. A point system devised in 1958 by Colorado State University, Fort Collins.

INDIVIDUAL POINT SYSTEMS WHICH
INCLUDE MANY TYPES OF ACTIVITIES

Another plan very popular in some schools, notably at the junior and senior high school level, is the point system that includes many types of school activities in addition to intramurals. We have already seen one plan earlier in this chapter, which gave point credit for intramurals, scholarship, leadership, health and hygiene, noncompetitive sports, and general recreation. We have also referred to the point system used at New Trier High School, Winnetka, Illinois, which rewards service rendered in officiating and recreational promotion through its sports club. The Sturgis, Michigan, High School has included activities such as debate and speech.

Southeastern State Teachers College, Durant, Oklahoma, has included such items as choir, band, debate, dramatic clubs, oratory, music, homecoming parade, as well as participation in varsity sports. Iowa State University awards points to intramural managers who attend regularly scheduled organization meetings of the department. The University of Cincinnati gives organizations credit for individual representation on varsity sport squads, as does Duke University. The trend among colleges and universities giving intramural credit for varsity representation has been to discontinue such a practice; instead, trophies and awards are given to organizations by the intercollegiate athletic department. Since this would appear to be an intercollegiate function instead of one the intramural department should sponsor, schools might well consider such a plan to increase motivation for greater varsity squad tryouts.

Special Scoring Features of Unusual Interest

The unique Michigan State University Sports Skills Championship is worthy of mention and emulation. The championships are open to every male student except letter winners, who may not compete in the activity in which they earned a letter. Twelve different contests have been used over the entire year, four contests in each quarter. In the events that require some training (turkey trot), contestants must complete the required training period before they are allowed to compete. Events are held from 4:00 to 6:00 P.M. for an entire week. The individual who totals the highest number of points for the year will be named Sports Skills Champion. Appropriate awards are given the four high-point men of the year. There are 425 possible points. The schedule of events is listed here with point credit:

FALL	WINTER	SPRING
Football pass 30 yards (accuracy) 15	Free throw (accuracy) 50 ½ point per basket	100-yard dash First 5 men 15

Rope climb (time)
First 5 men 15
Second 10 men 10
Third 15 men 5
Turkey trot (time)
First 5 men 20
Second 10 men 15
Third 15 men 10
Football punt
(distance) 60
½ pt. per foot

Swimming sprint
First 5 men 15
Second 10 men 10
Third 15 men 5
Dribble sprint
First 5 men 15
Second 10 men 10
Third 15 men 5
Swimming plunge
(distance) 50
1 pt. per foot

Second 10 men 10
Third 15 men 5
Baseball throw
(accuracy) 15
Shot put, 16 lb. 30
(according to
weight 1 pt. per
foot)
Baseball throw
(distance) 50
½ pt. per foot

Some of the sports skills listed above are also regular events in the tryouts for Sigma Delta Psi, and marks made here are counted in both.

West High School, of Rockford, Illinois, for many years combined varsity and intramural point scoring in the track and swimming decathlon, which annually stimulates much spirited competition in a number of events in both sports. This plan develops more varsity competitors as well as adding a spark to the intramurals.

Purdue University has used a unique plan which is a combination of varsity and intramural in cross-country each fall. An annual trophy is given under the following rules:

> Each group will enter not less than two freshmen (four preferred).
> These men run over the cross-country course 2½ miles not less than four times a week for a five-week period.
> Attendance is scored on a basis of 60 percent and winning on a basis of 40 percent. For instance, if a team of two men, running over the period of five weeks, ran the 2½-mile distance four times a week, they would earn 60 points for attendance. In the race the following points would be awarded:

1st place	40 points	5th place	20 points
2nd place	35 points	6th place	15 points
3rd place	30 points	7th place	10 points
4th place	25 points	8th place	5 points

> Each group scoring a total of 60 points or more receives 25 participation points for the campus supremacy trophy for the year. The final race is held the second week in November.

The University of California at Berkeley and several high schools in that area use a method of scoring track meets and giving subsequent point awards that holds much promise and guarantees good participation. Points are all scored by the aggregate system. No team is eligible for points in any event in which it has fewer than three men competing. No man may compete in more than two events exclusive of the relay. The system is complicated, but worthy of trial.

An example to show how running broad jump might be scored in this plan follows (Team E is given an extra point because it has the individual winner) :

TEAM	AVERAGE	PLACE	POINTS
Team A had three men who averaged 19 feet 3 inches		1st	10 points
Team B had three men who averaged 19 feet 1 inch		2nd	8 points
Team C had three men who averaged 18 feet 8 inches		3rd	6 points
Team D had three men who averaged 18 feet 6 inches		4th	4 points
Team E had three men who averaged 18 feet 3 inches		5th	3 points
Team F had three men who averaged 17 feet 9 inches		6th	1 point

In conclusion, it is apparent that many different types of point scoring systems are possible. The director may get much help and assistance from making a careful study of existing point systems and applying the best procedures for his own local situation. There is little doubt about the motivating force of a well-planned point system. If it is to achieve the desired results, plans must be worked out to keep standings up to date and on display in a prominent place and to maintain an efficient student staff of managers or assistants who can handle most of the detail work. It would also seem that colleges in the future will strive hard to work out practical scoring plans for independent and unorganized groups as they have so successfully done in the past for fraternity organizations.

REFERENCES

1 "Philosophy of Intramurals at Indiana University," *Eleventh Annual Conference Proceedings of the National Intramural Association,* 1960, p. 6.

2 *Handbook of Intramural Sports,* University of Tennessee, Knoxville, 1957.

3 Ellis Mendelsohn, *Men's Intramural Activities Handbook,* University of Louisville, 1969.

4 *Handbook of Intramural and Recreational Sports,* University of Illinois, Urbana, 1968.

8

AWARDS AND RECOGNITION

It is well agreed that the fun of play and competition should be the greatest incentive for the well-rounded intramural and recreational program in the schools. Some argue that awards in sports are objectionable, but it cannot be denied that awards are a great motivating force in intramural sports. Achievement is recognized in almost every other walk of life. Academically, we still recognize merit with grades, certificates, diplomas, and scholarships. We still select valedictorians and members of local and national honor societies. Retail business often uses similar devices to increase sales. The human desire for recognition is most natural.

A national conference report provides the following statement regarding awards:[1]

Every institution should establish a sound educational policy relative to awards.

1. Awards should not serve as the primary motive for participation.
2. Awards should have little intrinsic value.
3. Awards should be a symbol of recognition of achievement.
4. There should be a time and place for presenting the awards which will serve not only to recognize the winners, but also as a further means of publicizing the program. Awards may be presented at an appropriate assembly such as a banquet, convocation, or an intra-

mural carnival or festival. An invitation to faculty members representing other departments on the campus to attend the event serves to promote good relations with the faculty and administration as a whole.

In administering the program, awards should always be clearly differentiated from rewards. They should be a recognition of achievement at all times. They need not be expensive, and preferably should have little monetary value. Some of the finest awards in America today are the product of thoughtful minds and skillful hands in the school shops, art departments, and print shops.

Colleges and universities today are full of hundreds of capable athletes, most of whom cannot make the varsity teams. Intramural awards, therefore, become increasingly significant and highly valued. Quite often the effectiveness of an award is lost by tardy delivery. It is most highly prized at the moment victory is won. Wise planning would indicate that all awards for the year should be on hand before activity begins. Special display cases sharpen the desire of competitors in advance of the actual contests. Groups develop great *esprit de corps* when they can display their trophy immediately following the championship game.

Suitable display cases should be provided where all may see the cups, trophy plaques, and other types of team awards. Here also can be placed tropies designed to remain with the school permanently, carrying inscribed names of each year's champions. As school opens in the fall the awards should contain all the cases which will be presented during the year. For the display of individual medals a large, flat-type case can be secured to the lobby walls, with glass doors which can be kept locked. Small cardboard shields printed for each event that carries a medal award can be mounted artistically on the background of this case. A small nail or brad can be placed in each shield and the medal hung until won. At the completion of the event the medal can be taken from the hook and presented to the winner, and the name and home city of the recipient can then be placed where the medal once hung. The whole display can then become a roll of honor for the year's program. The motivating value of such a display cannot be disregarded; it is the little details that make an intramural program rise above mediocrity.

Consideration of awards naturally divides emphasis between individuals and groups. Organizations with any semblance of permanency prefer a trophy of some kind. Here, joy of accomplishment can be shared through all the school days, and relived later. Groups that are not permanent, or that continue only during that particular sport, should receive individual awards. Junior and senior high school home or session rooms often prefer a wall plaque or trophy, since their identity is maintained sufficiently long to develop group pride and loyalty. Semipermanent groups are sometimes given a very inexpensive team award, supplemented with individual awards. These can range from the most inexpensive paper ribbon or certificate to a more elaborate gold medal. Rotating trophies are well adapted to semipermanent group winners. Individual sports, such as track, swimming, and other similar events, often suggest medals, ribbons, or certificates to the athletes placing or winning each event, with the team trophy for the group. Most schools use at least one, and often more than one, trophy for the best all-around showing in all sports for the year. These items will be discussed in greater detail in the following pages.

Types of Awards and Recognition

SCHOOL EMBLEMS OR INSIGNIA

Junior and senior high schools use school emblems with great effectiveness. These are usually given individually, with a point system used to determine the award. Almost all schools have an athletic nickname such as Blue Devils, Tigers, Wildcats. Since interscholastic athletics awards block letters, and forensics, music, and other activities often award the Old English type of letters, an attractive emblem symbolic of the school nickname is perfect for intramurals. This can be prized when placed in the student's den at home, or may be worn with pride on a sweater in school colors. These emblems can be worked out in school colors in chenille or felt with embroidered artwork.

One system used for several years by a high school is a typical and workable plan where the individual emblem awards form the main structure of the whole recognition program. The school nickname was Red Devils. The individual intramural award was a 7-inch, felt-embroidered Red Devil head, suitable for sweater mounting. Cumulative record cards were maintained in the office by student managers. As each event was concluded, all points for all individuals were entered on the record cards. One thousand points were needed for the emblem. Points were accumulated and carried over from year to year. Thus, any boy might require one or more years before qualifying for the intramural emblem, or he might receive the recognition two or three times while in high school. Proof of the powerful motivating force of this plan was found in the constant crowds of students daily checking their record cards to study their progress, as well as the tremendous participation registered in some 35 annual organized sports.

Individual point systems are most easily used in smaller schools, and in junior and senior high schools, although many colleges and universities maintain individual point systems. This type of award, as well as numerals, or monogram letters, should represent the highest intramural honor the department can confer. It should be open to every student in the school and should place a premium on both individual and team participation.

MEDALS

Many schools present medals to individuals. Available finances more than any other factor regulate the extent of these awards. Many medal charms can be purchased reasonably, with appropriate sport figure panels inserted. Stock medals are the least expensive, and are very acceptable. Many schools have developed their own standard intramural medal which is more distinctive than the stock types.

The director should plan the year's program long in advance and have all medals ready as the year begins. By ordering in advance, considerable saving can be made if any engraving or lettering is to be contemplated on the back of the medals, since machine-engraved letters are less than one-half the cost of hand engraving. These medals are all made from one die, with interchangeable sports figure panels for each sport. Most schools provide a minimum of lettering, with individuals permitted the privilege of adding any further information desired at their own expense. Some colleges give medals to all deserving managers as well as to champions in all sports. Princeton and Oklahoma give gold, silver, and bronze medals to the first three places in every sport. College of the City of New York favors medals in all sports, awarding no team trophies. The University of Cincinnati gives a medal for every record-breaking performance. The University of Florida gives an intramural key award. Michigan presents champions with medals and gives ribbons to second-place winners. Ohio State gives many medals to its winners, but states in its handbook that all awards are not promised and are to be given if finances permit.

In the all-university track and swimming meets some schools give medals to the first three places in all events; some give medals only to first-place winners, some to record breakers only, while some present medals to the high-point winners only.

TEAM TROPHIES

Larger universities usually award a permanent plaque, trophy, or cup to the winning group in all regularly organized activities, particularly when groups involved are of the more permanent type. Other schools provide a larger and more elaborate trophy which travels each year until one group wins the award three times. Princeton places a larger trophy for each sport in the intramural trophy case, and each year engraves the winner's name, but also presents a smaller trophy to the winning group for permanent possession.

Some schools, like Williams College, have a larger trophy for each sport, presented and named in honor of an alumnus donor, which travels each year and is appropriately engraved. Some few schools have all or part of their trophies donated by sporting goods stores or other business houses. Many of Harvard's interhouse trophies are presented by alumni. Syracuse University presents trophies to first- and second-place winners each year. Nebraska and Michigan award first-place trophies only, allowing the organization the privilege of purchasing second-place trophies or additional official medals. Nebraska has presented the best unit managers with individual trophy gifts, properly engraved, to signify outstanding organizational leadership.

Illinois gives recognition to the team that has displayed the best sportsmanship during the previous sports season with a traveling trophy. To determine its award a poll is taken of all athletic managers, who rate organizations according to merit; all intramural officials give their judgment, and the staff and headquarters office also passes judgment. In making this selection all managers and officials might use the following criteria.

1. Honesty.
    a. Full regard for rules of the game and of the intramural program in general.
    b. Resorting to protest only under legitimate claim.
2. Cooperation with officials.
3. Lack of unnecessary roughness in contact sports.

Fig. 42. Chico State College Intramural group won the 1959 National Sigma Delta Psi Scoring Contest and was awarded trophies.

4. Control of temper during stress of competition.
5. Action displayed under the acceptable discipline of the rules and the judgment of the officials.
6. Winning without boasting.
7. Losing without alibis.
8. Eagerness to play the next game regardless of the outcome of the previous contest.
9. A sense of justice or fair play; "May the best man or team win."

Such a trophy could be permanently awarded to the group winning it most frequently in a two-year period. Usually, only team sports are taken into consideration. Some use a trophy that can be retained permanently by the group with the most "legs" or championships after three years competition in such sports as football, volleyball, water basketball, softball, basketball, wrestling, and track and field.

The following awards system is used at Washington State University as outlined in their 1970 Intramural Handbook:

The WSU Dad's Association allots funds to purchase the trophies awarded for intramural sports.

1. First- and second-place teams trophies are given for the following: All-University Intramural Championship (based on all sports except Turkey Trot)
   Basketball, Flag Football, Softball, Volleyball, and Track.
2. First-place team trophies are presented for intramural competition in all other sports sponsored by the Intramural Office.
3. An Improvement Trophy will be awarded to an independent living group and to a fraternal organization demonstrating the greatest improvement in intramural participation and achievement for the current year. The Improvement Awards will be based upon the following criteria:
   a. Increase in number of points scored in the point system.
   The Intramural Board will examine the records and determine the winners of the Improvement Award on the basis of the criteria stated above. First- and second-place winners in the All-University Intramural Championship shall not be eligible for this award. Only organized living groups shall be considered eligible for the Improvement Award.
4. A special award will be presented to the outstanding intramural manager of the year. A trophy will be given to this individual. Nominations for this award will be invited from each living group, and final determination will be made by the Intramural Board. Basis for this award shall be enthusiasm displayed for the program, *cooperation* with the Intramural Office, *dependability* with respect to his group and the Intramural Office, and *sportsmanship*.

The program at the University of Texas, administered by A.A. "Sonny" Rooker, provides increased participation motivation through a series of special annual awards:

1. A sportsmanship trophy presented by the Texas Cowboys, an honorary men's service organization, awarded to an Intramural organization at the Awards Banquet.

   This award is based on all-round team sportsmanship demonstrated by organizations while maintaining keen competitive spirit and the desire to win.

   The winner shall be selected by a Trophy Selection Committee, consisting of four Texas Cowboys and the full-time Assistant Director as chairman from the ratings of officials on each game scorecard. This trophy is to remain in the possession of the winning organization for one year.

2. Trophies are given each year to the first, second, and third-place organizations in the Fraternity. Independent, Club, and University Housing Divisions at the annual Intramural Awards Banquet. First, second, and third places are decided on the basis of total number of points accumulated over that school year. These points are earned in all sports—excluding Open Tournaments—by virtue of participations, wins, losses, bonuses for full entry competition, bonuses for championship play, and bonus points for service in the Student Managerial System.

3. An award presented annually in honor of Berry M. Whitaker, who founded Intramural Sports for Men at The University of Texas in 1961, to the individual student leader who displays the most outstanding leadership, in all phases of intramural participation and competition and awarded at the Award Banquet.

4. A sportsmanship award is presented by members of Alpha Phi Omega and dedicated in the honor of Dean Arno Nowotny, whose good sportsmanship, loyalty, energy, aggressiveness, and support contributed so much to the spirit of fair play in intramural sports.

   This award is presented to the individual who contributes most toward furthering sportsmanship, competitive spirit, team cooperation, and individual contribution to intramural sports. The winner is selected by a committee composed of the Intramural Council and the President of Alpha Phi Omega with the full-time assistant director serving as chairman.

5. Each year an award is presented to the Outstanding Intramural Official who has officiated three or more team sports during the year from football, basketball, volleyball, water basketball, or softball. Those men who qualify are submitted to a vote of team managers for consideration of ability, rule knowledge, mechanics, and attitude in working with teams and individuals. The award is presented at the Awards Banquet.

Wayne University of Detroit has given a plaque for the most versatile athlete of the year. Its supremacy trophy remains in the trophy case with new names added, and medals go to individuals. The University of Cincinnati demands that its supremacy trophy be won five times before retention by any group. Most schools using a traveling supremacy trophy require only three years. Some schools present a new supremacy trophy each year, with another trophy for second place in all sports, and a third trophy awarded the group with the most consistent participation.

Oregon State follows a unique plan worthy of mention.[2]

> The success of an intramural sports program is not dependent on awards. The Oregon State College intramural program, however, has for a long time maintained a policy of awarding trophies or medals to the champions in each sport. The department is guided in this respect by the wishes of the participating organizations (fraternity and campus dormitory club groups) who meet as a group in the fall. A vote is taken, and if trophies are desired, a fee is charged each group, based on the number of men in the group ($15 for organizations of 20 men or more; $10 for organizations with fewer than 20 men). Failure to pay the fee does not eliminate the group from competition, but it forfeits the right to the trophy in the event the championship is won.

A practice at the University of Washington at Seattle is also different.[3]

> A team trophy is awarded to the winning organization in all sports offered. Trophies will be released only to permanent organizations and into the custody of the organization's president upon receipt of a signed agreement to reimburse the Intramural Division for damage or loss. A trophy may be displayed only on the premises of the winning organization and must be returned to the Intramural Division for the summer period.

At Brigham Young University[4] points are given for all intramural activities based upon participation and winning. At the end of the school year the individual and organizations who accumulate the most points in the different divisions are awarded the supremacy trophy. There are fifteen supremacy trophies given each year; one for the supremacy ward in each stake, one for the supremacy floor in Helaman Halls, one for the supremacy floor in Deseret Towers, one for the supremacy club of the University, one for the independents group of the University, and one for the individual supremacy winner. The supremacy trophy must be won three consecutive years by an organization before permanent possession of it is gained by the group. The individual supremacy winner keeps his award permanently.

Certificates are given to each member of divisional winners (team and individual) and also to the second place team of all-school. Individual trophies are given to the members of the first-place team of all-school in

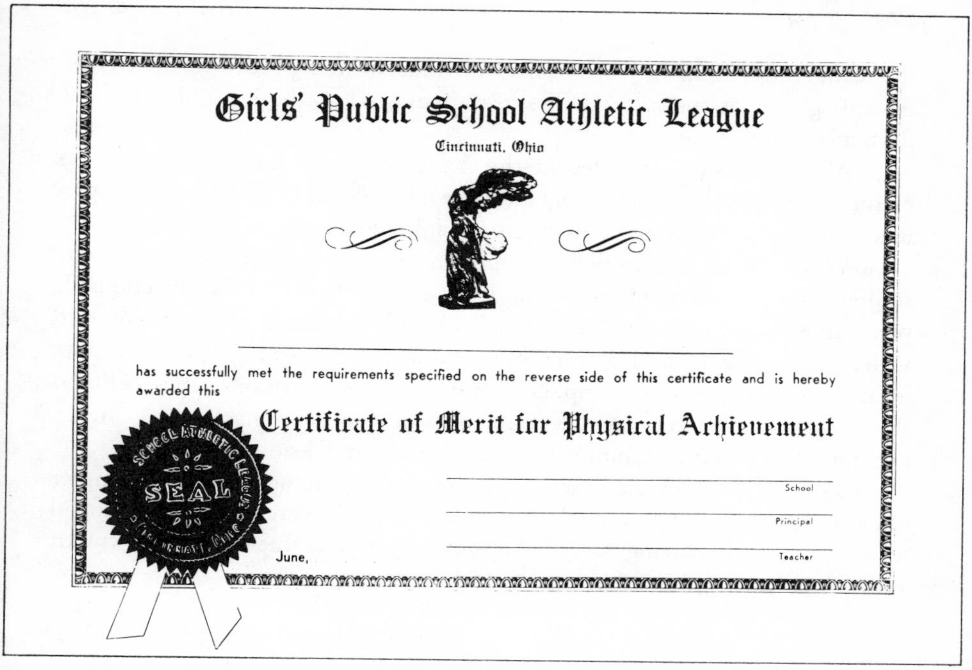

Girls' Public School Athletic League

Cincinnati, Ohio

has successfully met the requirements specified on the reverse side of this certificate and is hereby awarded this

Certificate of Merit for Physical Achievement

SCHOOL ATHLETIC LEAGUE SEAL CINCINNATI, OHIO

School

Principal

June,

Teacher

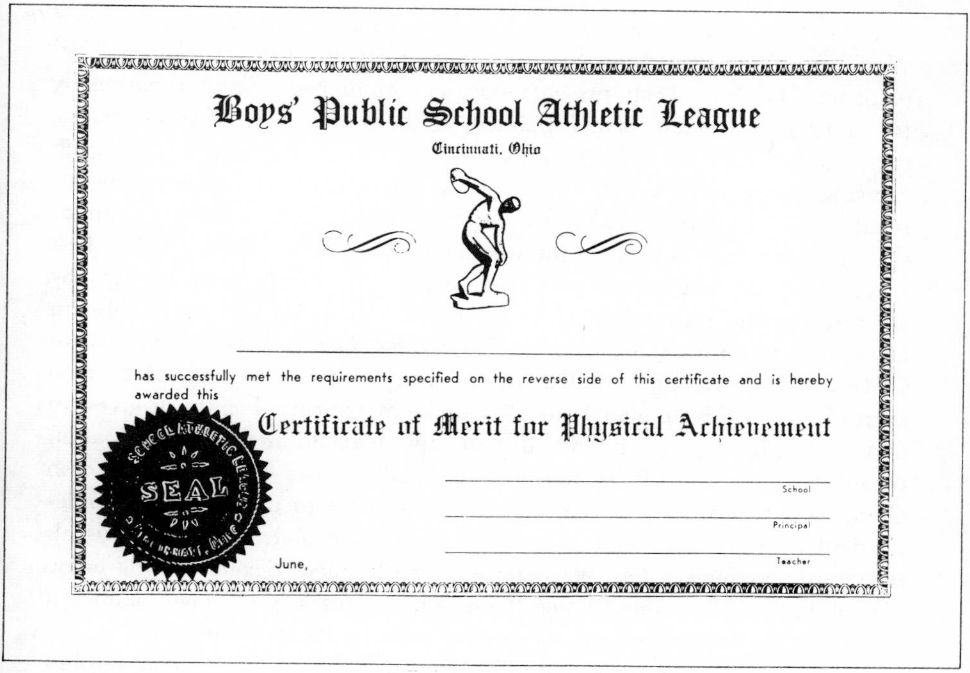

Boys' Public School Athletic League

Cincinnati, Ohio

has successfully met the requirements specified on the reverse side of this certificate and is hereby awarded this

Certificate of Merit for Physical Achievement

SCHOOL ATHLETIC LEAGUE SEAL CINCINNATI, OHIO

School

Principal

June,

Teacher

Fig. 43. Certificate awards given for achievement by Rudolph Memmel and staff in Cincinnati.

the team competition and also to the individual winning individual activities. Awards given for special activities are announced at the beginning of each particular activity.

All trophies are awarded at the Annual Awards Banquet, the climax of the year's program. All team, special events, coed, and individual supremacy winners are honored and given special recognition at that time.

While there is considerable opinion that an intramural year-round supremacy race often sharpens competitive zeal almost to an objectionable point, most schools give such an award. The advantages in increased interest, wider participation, and greater opportunities for learning sportsmanship, loyalty, and cooperation completely outweigh the objections. It is believed that any possible objectionable outcomes of the supremacy race can be alleviated by careful administrative safeguards and leadership.

Though much of the discussion presented here has dealt with the larger schools, the smaller high schools with imaginative leadership have developed awards systems involving school shop-made plaques, shields, ribbons, merit cards, certificates, and other effective ideas.

OTHER AWARDS SUGGESTIONS

DePauw, Illinois, Kentucky, Michigan, Florida, Oberlin, Purdue, and West Virginia have presented sweaters with intramural insignia to qualified managers. Georgia Tech presents sweaters to managers and occasionally to winners. Princeton places painted softballs, baseballs, hockey pucks, relay batons, and other sport symbols in the intramural trophy case, each carrying the colors, name, and year of the winners. Oklahoma awards regulation intramural sweaters to senior managers with a block O, junior managers receiving a lightweight sweater with a smaller block O. The best manager of the year is awarded a trophy, the recipient being selected by the director and his staff. Yale University has invited all its unit freshman champions to an annual outing at Cedar Crest Camp. Western Reserve of Cleveland gives ribbons to all first-place winners. Many schools give intramural belt buckles or medals to all individual winners. Kentucky gives an annual trophy to the individual with the best all-around participation record for the year. Princeton awards small bronze statues to all club champions. Many schools give all-around trophies to dormitory and independent champions as well as to fraternities. One high school rewards all intramural managers for their efficiency with guest tickets for all home varsity basketball games. Some high schools work with civic clubs in presenting merit cards or certificates for outstanding performances.

Chapter 18 describes and illustrates the use of wall championship plaques for the names of champions. This should be considered another form of the awards system, giving dignity and permanence to those who

NORFOLK CITY PUBLIC SCHOOLS

INTRAMURAL   **BTW**   CERTIFICATE

This is to certify that ❧

_____

HAS COMPLETED THE REQUIREMENTS OF THE PHYSICAL EDUCATION

DEPARTMENT AND IS AWARDED THIS CERTIFICATE FOR

PARTICIPATION IN_____ FOR THE YEAR_____

Greyson Daughtery

DIRECTOR, HEALTH AND PHYSICAL EDUCATION   PRINCIPAL

TEACHER   TEACHER

NORFOLK CITY PUBLIC SCHOOLS

INTRAMURAL   **R**   CERTIFICATE

This is to certify that ❧

_____

HAS COMPLETED THE REQUIREMENTS OF THE PHYSICAL EDUCATION

DEPARTMENT AND IS AWARDED THIS CERTIFICATE FOR

PARTICIPATION IN_____ FOR THE YEAR_____.

Greyson Daughtery

DIRECTOR, HEALTH AND PHYSICAL EDUCATION   PRINCIPAL

TEACHER   TEACHER

Fig. 44. Greyson Daughtery in Norfolk, Virginia, uses an appropriate award certificate at each school.

Fig. 45. Bill Heggen, Irving Junior High School Physical Education teacher, displays intramural championship plaques in Lincoln, Nebraska.

have won the championship. These plaques are usually wood, turned out as shields, panels, or in the shape of a football, basketball, or horseshoe, indicative of the sport. School colors can be employed, with each year's champions emblazoned for all to see.

Some schools award felt banners, various types of fobs, gold balls, track shoes, photographs, blazer jackets. Most high schools are wisely restricted by state athletic associations from awarding items valued at more than one dollar. Winners of girls' events are often awarded scarfs, pins, bracelets, and various jewelry-medal combinations. Instead of a school

Fig. 46. Felt blotter-type individual award used at New Trier High School, Winnetka, Illinois.

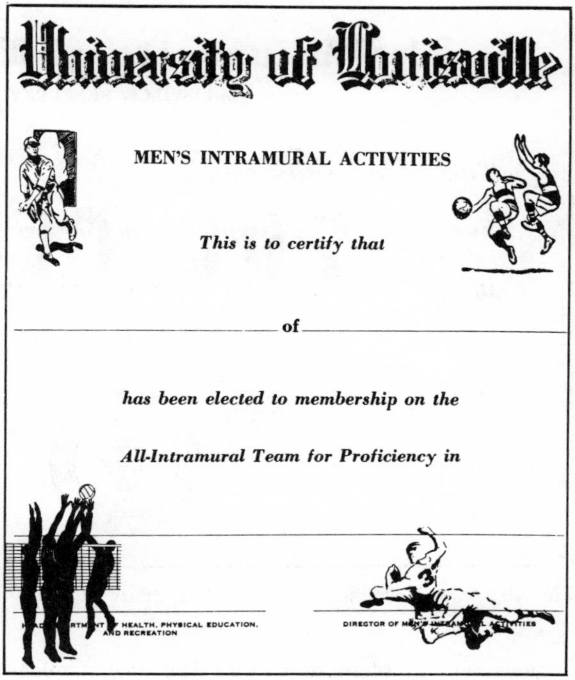

University of Louisville

MEN'S INTRAMURAL ACTIVITIES

This is to certify that

________________ of ________________

has been elected to membership on the

All-Intramural Team for Proficiency in

____

HEAD, DEPARTMENT OF HEALTH, PHYSICAL EDUCATION, AND RECREATION

DIRECTOR OF MEN'S INTRAMURAL ACTIVITIES

Fig. 47.

Fig. 48.

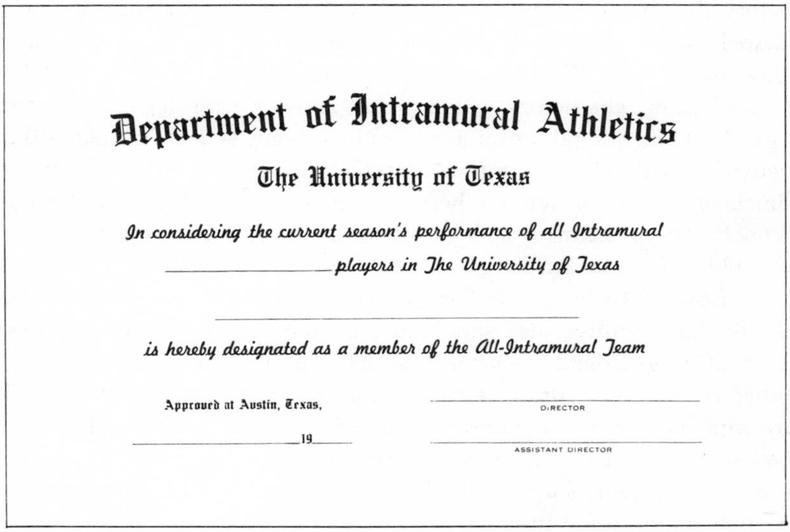

Department of Intramural Athletics

The University of Texas

In considering the current season's performance of all Intramural

________________ *players in The University of Texas*

____

is hereby designated as a member of the All-Intramural Team

Approved at Austin, Texas, ________________ 19____

________________ DIRECTOR

________________ ASSISTANT DIRECTOR

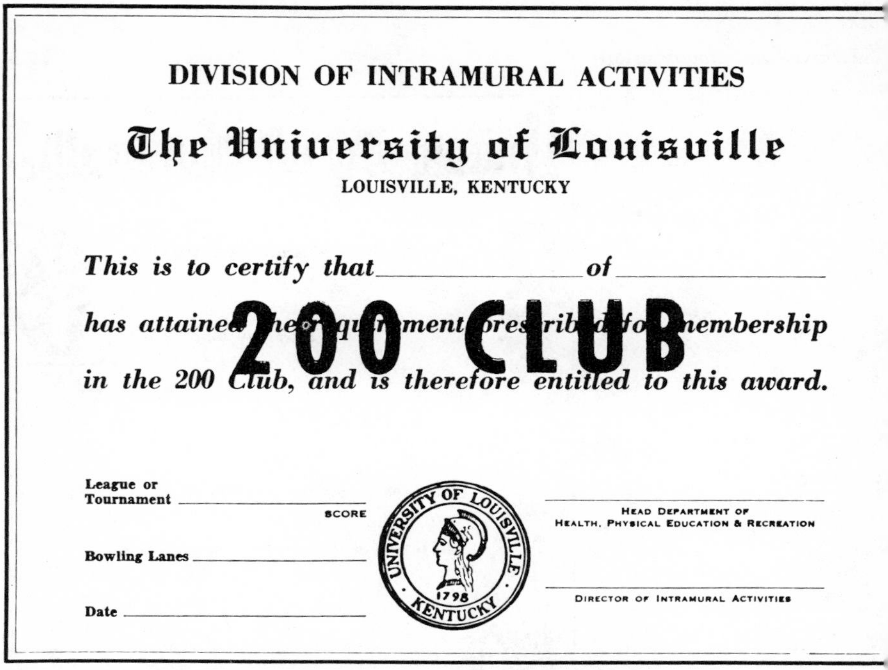

DIVISION OF INTRAMURAL ACTIVITIES

The University of Louisville

LOUISVILLE, KENTUCKY

This is to certify that ________________ of ________________

has attained the requirement prescribed for membership

200 CLUB

in the 200 Club, and is therefore entitled to this award.

League or Tournament ________________ SCORE

Bowling Lanes ________________

Date ________________

UNIVERSITY OF LOUISVILLE · 1798 · KENTUCKY

____
HEAD DEPARTMENT OF HEALTH, PHYSICAL EDUCATION & RECREATION

____
DIRECTOR OF INTRAMURAL ACTIVITIES

Fig. 49. Award certificate used at University of Louisville.

achievement emblem or medal, Wheaton College gives an attractive lapel button. Certificates of all types can be printed and presented in recognition of merit, and will be more highly cherished when signed by all staff members.

Other schools make awards more coveted and worth striving for by utilizing an appropriate presentation ceremony. The awards can be made before the student body at the annual Awards Convocation in the college chapel. Kansas University for years presented its awards at the annual All-Intramural Ball. Michigan often makes certain awards at special banquets honoring the champions. Ohio State and Oberlin have presented their awards at the annual Intramural Festival. Some schools conclude the year's activities with a faculty-student golf tournament, followed by a buffet luncheon at the golf club, where awards are made. Junior and senior high schools often arrange fitting programs with guest speakers in school assemblies for this purpose.

Edward Eichmann at Temple University feels that intramural awards should have utility; they should not be the type which usually become a part of a girlfriend's charm bracelet. He reports that colleagues from other schools have drawers full of medallions which are never called for by winners. Eichmann urges that imagination be used in selecting awards which really aid in the general acceptance of a program. He suggests the use of individual plaques, tie clasps, belt buckles, and similar items which carry a standardized insignia.

Administrative Problems

Financing the awards program is a problem that must be met in every school, large and small. Since it is given detailed attention in Chapter 14, it will be omitted here.

Limitations must be prearranged to prohibit promiscuous distribution, and to guarantee an esteemed value in the minds of students. If individual awards are made in the team sports, it is good practice to stipulate in advance the number to be presented in each sport. A good procedure is to specify one or two more than the required number for a team. Teams should be granted the privilege of purchasing additional medals for extra substitutes. Schools giving numerals or emblems should regulate how they may be worn, making official provision for the purchase of sweaters by the winners. The department should be willing to make all such purchases at reduced cost, being careful to collect in advance for such services. Some schools with elaborate point systems combining interscholastic and intramural achievement let the recognition through points suffice or give awards appropriate for the combination of activities.

Schools conducting the same sports more than once in a single year's program must set up restrictions to govern the awards. This is true where a sport, such as bowling, is conducted anew each quarter or semester. Many complications arise with the many basketball leagues and tournaments that are sponsored, and the administration of awards must be anticipated.

In conclusion, it can be said that a very satisfactory intramural program can be conducted entirely without awards. It will be found best, however, to carefully plan and administer a wise and appropriate awards system which is well-conceived, preannounced, and planned, and is a constant recognition of achievement in the truly American competitive fashion.

REFERENCES

[1] *Intramural Sports for College Men and Women,* National Conference Report, AAHPER, 1955, Washington, D.C. pp. 13-14.

[2] *Intramural Handbook,* Oregon State University, Corvallis, 1956-1957.

[3] *Intramural Sports Handbook,* University of Washington, Seattle, 1958-1959.

[4] *Intramural Handbook,* Brigham Young University, Provo, Utah, 1971.

9

INTRAMURAL RULES
AND REGULATIONS

The intramural program requires well-regulated rules to govern it, just as do all other school activities and interschool athletics. The program expansion, the addition of all kinds of competitive units, and the inclusion of more elaborate scoring and point systems all conspire to force at least a minimum of regulatory standards. A smooth-running program demands and expects mutually acknowledged standards which will govern participation. It has taken years to develop a set of regulations governing interscholastic or intercollegiate athletics. As a result of a confusion of differing regulations in the various states, the National Federation of High School Athletic Associations came into being and now has members from every state in the nation except one. The result has been more commonly accepted practices, a lowering of the high school age limit for competition, more acceptable eligibility rules, and other regulations attempting to safeguard the health of the participant. Some of these same objectives are equally important in the wisely conceived intramural program. In fact, the larger universities today serve almost as many potential competitors as does the state high school athletic association in some of our more thinly populated states. When one considers the wide variety of sports practiced, the great numbers and types of competitive units, and the many types of students affected on the large modern campus, one cannot but marvel at the progress made in providing simplified, workable regulations for this great competitive structure.

Progress in the development of rules to govern participation is the result of several years of experience. The school just starting its program will do well to study the best practices found in other institutions, thus eliminating the slow and unsatisfactory trial and error method. Of course there may be certain unique problems at any one institution, which may cause special rules to be formulated. Rules should be kept as simple as possible, and the fewer the better. Unless most of the administrative problems are anticipated and covered carefully in the adopted regulations, it is foolish to assume that difficulties will not arise.

Discussion of regulations falls naturally into three classifications. First, there must be rules to govern participation, involving such matters as eligibility, organization of teams and competitive units, protests, post-ponements, forfeits, etc. Second, special playing rules must be adopted to simplify and facilitate play in specific sports. Third, regulations are neces-sary in the matter of awards, recognition, point systems, and the like; these were discussed in the previous two chapters. The second group, dealing with specific sports, has also been covered in another chapter in part, but will receive some added attention here.

Rules that Govern Participation

THE GROUP ROSTER

The smaller schools using a more simple means of classifying students for competition will find it necessary to file a working list of the member-ship of each group, whether it be two chosen color groups, the various home rooms, or some other device. As the enrollment and the program of activities widen, the need for a roster of all eligible participants is more evident. Every attempt should be made to lessen the burden of secretarial duties. The roster placed on file becomes an aid for the department for statistical and record purposes. The burden of individual eligibility should be left to the students, who should be at all times responsible for their own status. When matters of protest arise or questions of eligibility are raised, the group rosters are invaluable. The use of the roster, added to as the rules permit from time to time, eliminates the necessity of eligibility certifications so common to interschool sports. There will be some activities that will require a special team eligibility list for the particular sport, but this is only true with loosely and temporarily organized playing units. Comparisons can then be made with the team roster and the score books of specific games to see that only eligible players represent the various teams.

One of the greatest needs for eligibility lists is created with the use of "A," "B," and "C" teams in any one sport from any one group. Here a check list is imperative so there will be no switching of players, thus destroying competitive balance and breeding ill will.

SCHOLASTIC ELIGIBILITY

Some schools and some teachers still feel that students should be deprived of the fun and pleasure of intramural competition when scholastic deficiencies are evident, as a prod to better academic achievement. They argue that students may not enjoy the thrill of interscholastic competition without maintaining a minimum academic average, and that the same idea should prevail in the intramural program. The last few years have seen considerable pressure developing for the elimination of individual academic eligibility, even in interscholastic sports. Certain large cities have gone a long way toward the elimination of many eligibility barriers for competition. The feeling is that wholesome recreation, properly administered, will contribute to a better attitude toward all school work, making substantial contributions to mental and moral outcomes, physical well-being, and a wise use of leisure time so often diverted to less wholesome pursuits. It is now common practice to allow intramural competition to any student permitted to enroll in the school. This has been a great boon to the intramural department, which might otherwise spend most of its time checking academic eligibility of a large student body. The department can now swing its weight into the problem of making the program accomplish the greatest good for the individuals who may or may not be properly adjusted academically, socially, and otherwise, and at the same time it can provide for the total student body a great motivating force for better school citizenship, school morale, and individual progress.

Some institutions occasionally find a student barred from intramurals, but this is only done by action of the Dean of Students, or some other authorized officer. Actually, discipline through elimination of wholesome recreation rarely if ever accomplishes its objective, merely driving the erring student to other places of amusement and activity. The argument has often been used that intramurals detract from academic progress since so much time is demanded for games and sports. This has not been the case, since no one student in the larger schools will find it possible to compete that often due to the usual lack of facilities and the limited playing time. Indeed, this argument could hardly be supported if the student were scheduled to compete for one hour every day of the week, since that much exercise and recreation is recommended by thinking educators today.

LETTER MEN

Most schools do not permit letter men from their own or other institutions to compete intramurally in the sport for which the letter was granted. Some universities support a rule that only letter men from other schools of equivalent athletic caliber cannot compete, thus permitting letter men transferring from smaller colleges the privilege of intramural competition. The theory here is that the larger university will have several intramural players who would easily have made letters at the smaller school. This rule often leads to difficulties, and perhaps the best plan is to bar all letter men in their particular sport, offering them plenty of opportunity in other sports.

Since intramural athletics are primarily designed for the great mass of students who are not of varsity caliber, it would seem best to safeguard intramural competition for the more unskilled, and to make workable rules prohibiting "stars" and semiprofessionals from taking the game away from the more strictly amateur students. It would seem also that schools should make adequate provision for the sometimes sizable group of men who would thus be barred from all forms of competitive activity in their favorite sport. This can often be done with special tournaments, matched games, and other similar devices to emphasize the fact that this program seeks to be as thoroughly democratic at possible, involving every student who expresses a desire to compete.

MEMBERS OF VARSITY, RESERVE, AND
FRESHMAN SQUADS

Satisfactory solution of the question of eligibility becomes difficult at times with the problem of squad members and intramural sports. Smaller colleges do not have as much trouble since the varsity program moves from one sport to another in season. Some of the larger universities have come to expect a varsity man to give his entire school year to one sport, thus practically eliminating him from all other forms of recreation. This is unfortunate when one considers that such an individual does not get the opportunity of learning skills and appreciations of the many sports and activities which can be enjoyed later in life. Certainly a coach would be wise to recommend to his players certain team and individual sports that could be enjoyed during the period of the year when intercollegiate schedules are not in progress. The football coach who demands that all squad members report in August, continue daily practice until Christmas, resume active daily practice in February and continue until late spring, has no place in the educational scheme unless he actively stimulates his men to participate in intramurals throughout much of that period when games are not being played.

While the bulk of the intramural competition will concern students not out for the varsity squads, the small segment of those who are will cause more difficulty when rivalries become sharpened. Perhaps track is the one sport where difficulties are most likely to arise. One commonly used procedure is to bar all letter and numeral men in track, allowing all others to compete in indoor and outdoor track until after the first intercollegiate meet. All men used on the varsity then become immediately ineligible for intramural track whenever intercollegiate competition is started. No system of varsity-intramural regulations will function smoothly unless the varsity coaches cooperate in setting up varsity squad rosters. It is primarily their responsibility to see to it that varsity participation is far more desirable to the individual, and that their stars are more concerned with competition for the team than with campus recreation. No intramural director desires to see men of varsity caliber competing on intramural teams, since there are always many more students in each group who can play when the skilled performers take their rightful place on the varsity. It is difficult to force students into going out for varsity sports by legislation. That must be done by wise and careful intercollegiate administration and leadership. It follows that varsity sports should attract the best players, with intramurals stepping in to absorb all the remaining students in its program. Both phases of the competitive program must be made constantly attractive, and neither can be accomplished without administrative attention to detail.

In other team sports, such as basketball, it is desirable to bar all squad members following the first, or not later than the second, varsity game. This permits the coach to maintain a large squad, giving each student a good tryout in preliminary practice sessions, seeing him in action in the first or second scheduled games, and then deciding with him his future varsity status. It is not good practice to continue to allow men from the varsity squad to drop and become eligible for intramural basketball. This disrupts the general level of league competition, injecting new and disturbing factors into a race which may have become interesting, and moving out other players who have been enjoying play up to that time. Each student must make his own decision with regard to varsity participation, and the rules must be set up to handle the movements from varsity to intramural squads.

While it is often common practice to allow more latitude with reserve and freshman squad members, the same rules should govern these men as the varsity. They are clearly of the varsity type, and are working toward ultimate varsity recognition. The best plan is to run intramural basketball simultaneously with varsity, reserve, and freshman seasons, with constant cooperation between leaders of each, so that the greatest number of students can enjoy basketball competition, each in his own area of ability. Squad lists should always be prominently on the bulletin boards and should not be subject to change without sanction of the coaches and director.

Most schools at some time face the problem of some athletes of varsity caliber deciding against varsity competition. For this case a rule is usually included permitting the coach to declare such a student ineligible for intramurals in the sport in which he would have made the varsity team. This prerogative is rarely, if ever, used but may be of some assistance merely by its presence.

ELIGIBILITY FOR INTERFRATERNITY SPORTS

Most schools demand that all fraternities file official roster membership rolls at intramural headquarters corresponding to the lists furnished to the dean's office. It is well to provide a rule that no student is eligible for play with his fraternity until his name has been thus filed for at least one week. Some schools bar all pledges on the following grounds:

1. The pledge may never become initiated or active.
2. New pledges may be quickly added just to give the group added strength in its quest for championships.
3. Upperclassmen should represent the fraternity since all freshmen and even sophomores are usually participating in the required physical education program.

Some schools bar freshmen from all interfraternity competition, opening up a series of sports for freshmen only. Certainly we must provide full competitive privileges for freshmen if we are to agree with the principle that physical education classes should teach skills, leaving the laboratory for their use to intramurals. Most institutions do permit all pledges and actives to compete for the fraternity, whether they be freshmen or upper classmen. It is advisable to set up a rule that no student may change to a fraternity team after having started that sport with an independent unit and having been pledged in the midst of play. He should be permitted to join his new affiliation as the next sport gets underway. Most schools having professional or honorary fraternities provide a separate competitive unit for such teams; thus, a student belonging to both a social and professional fraternity may compete with either and not cause significant problems. If both types of fraternities are placed in the same competitive leagues the practice of requiring the student to select only one according to his preference is often followed.

ELIGIBILITY FOR INTERCLASS GROUPS

It is foolish for the intramural department to set up standards to decide the class status of any student, since this is always done by the administration and may vary in different schools. If interclass activities are to be planned, the department should accept the existing regulations and use them in determining the status of all competitors. This is best done by announcing and printing the number of hours required for sophomore, junior, and senior standing, leaving the eligibility of each student to be determined by himself. Violations of this rule are then easily administered. Since interclass competition is giving way to many other methods of organizing competition, the problem has ceased to be very significant. In the junior and senior high schools for any size other factors such as height, weight, age, or grade classification are becoming more acceptable.

ELIGIBILITY FOR INTERCOLLEGE SPORTS

In this type of competition it is desirable to require that the student be actually registered in the particular college at the time the event begins (Medicine, Law, Education, Dentistry, Pharmacy, Engineering etc.). Since all freshmen and often upperclassmen are still taking a very general group of courses, taught, perhaps, by instructors in two or more colleges, some rule must be adopted to cover them. Even in this case they are a part of the Liberal Arts College, or can be grouped into one of the several departments which may enter teams in the sport. Since some colleges are extremely large, it is preferable to have teams entered from the various departments. An example would be the Engineering College with such large departments as Mechanical Engineering, Architecture, Agricultural Engineering, Engineering Mechanics, as well as the various engineering professional fraternities whose allegiances are so close to that college.

GRADUATE STUDENTS

Both graduate students and younger faculty members are often allowed to compete with their fraternities in many of the smaller colleges. The argument might be raised that their added age and experience would make competition unfair; but this is more than offset at the college age by more youthful enthusiasm plus the fact that graduate students rarely have enough time to make any profound contribution to team success in intramurals. Separate leagues should be created for graduate students whenever numbers make such a plan feasible. Graduate students will naturally select sports in which small numbers are needed and which are more purely recreational in nature. If a separate graduate unit is established, there should be no need to wonder whether the student is a candidate for the master's degree or the doctorate, or doing some other special type of work. Some schools provide recreational planning for a combined faculty and graduate student group which works out very satisfactorily. Adequate provision should be made for the graduate student to enjoy voluntary recreation whenever his time will permit.

RULES FOR INDEPENDENT COMPETITION

Since most of these groups are rarely permanent in nature, it is well to require team lists before competition begins in each sport. Rules should be clear on whether later team additions may be made. It would seem permissible to stipulate the official number that might comprise a team entry, with option of adding new members at any time before championship play-offs if the maximum number is not violated. This should be provided when it becomes necessary for team members to discontinue play. New additions should include only students who are not competing with other teams. A compromise plan might allow an independent group to file an entry team list which would contain more than enough players, to which could be made changes up or down before the second game is played. After that date the roster would have to stand without change.

Another complication might arise when independent teams are organized in a sport, followed by organization of independent players in several other types of competitive units in the same sport. An example of this would be the independent basketball leagues, interdenominational basketball leagues, interdepartmental basketball leagues, etc. Ruling would have to be made on whether an independent player could compete with just one basketball organization or whether he could then also join his other leagues.

CLASS "A," "B," "C" LEAGUES

Some of the more popular sports do not include all the interested fraternity members and much demand is created for Class B or C teams in the same sport. Some schools arrange the schedule so that the A games are played first. This automatically stamps certain of the group as A players. Play then begins in Class B and again eligibility is established which does not include any of the A players. If a C league is desired the same procedure can be followed. It would then be necessary to rule that no player could be demoted to a lower classification, but players could move up to the higher classification at any time, never to return. To stimulate competition in Class B and C leagues, additional awards can be made and the sport figured in the supremacy race with a reduced point system for each lower class. This practice need not be limited to fraternities.

EXTENT AND RESTRICTIONS

ON INDIVIDUAL PLAY

Many little problems develop which should be given attention as rules are adopted. Some players will be anxious to compete with as many teams as possible. This complicates schedule making, and becomes embarrassing when the championship play-offs are held. If allowed indiscriminate play some men would get too much competition, thus jeopardizing their academic progress, and at the same time they would take the place of other students not on any team. At most schools a student will be active on either a fraternity or independent team. It would then seem permissible to permit him to compete on at least one other team in another classification such as interdenominational, interdepartmental, or military. Perhaps the safest rule would be to allow participation on one team in only one sport. Many other miscellaneous regulations may be worthy of consideration here. The University of Illinois[1] provides that a man is not eligible for the championship play-offs of a sport unless he has competed in at least three contests in a round-robin league, or two contests in the double elimination tournament. Illinois also bars professional athletes, but only in the sport which professionalized them. Oberlin College specifies that no special permission may be given for the playing of an ineligible man by the manager of either team, the coach of either team, or the intramural manager or supervisor on duty. The University of Oklahoma provides that an intramural doubles champion must have a different partner in order to enter further competition in that same sport.[2] Cornell University requires that no student may compete in intramurals unless he has passed the University medical examination for athletes.[3] It is assumed this follows only for the active type of sports and activities, since many schools today are organizing events such as bait and fly casting, archery, billiards, bridge, checkers, chess, and similar events where even seriously handicapped students could participate.

Kansas University[4] demands that a man compete in at least 30 percent of the regularly scheduled games for his organization before he becomes eligible for play-offs in the championship series. Kansas also considers minor and major letters equally in determining intramural eligibility. Kansas also rules that any man who competes in one regularly scheduled intercollegiate game cannot compete in that same intramural sport until one full year has elapsed. The University of Washington at Seattle stipulates the regulations governing participation in every intramural sport separately. Conditions may vary in the various sports.

The University of Tennessee has the unusual rule that any man who has previously won the fox hunt, Ping-Pong, suffleboard, handball, free throw, golf, tennis, or horseshoes championships is then ineligible for that event thereafter.[5] The department at Tennessee also reserves the right to disqualify any individual or group for unsportsmanlike conduct. Most schools permanently bar any player who competes under an assumed name.

There has been a growing tendency in some high schools and colleges to establish a system which would regulate the number of activities any one student might select in any given year. The trend in this direction has been to develop a weighted point system of activities, usually including varsity athletics because of the great amount of time demanded, but excluding intramurals. This plan works to the advantage of the intramural program. Such a plan would include debate, band, chorus, school paper and annual, and other similar activities. Modern scoring charts and point systems can be so arranged and the sports calendar can be so well filled with events running simultaneously that no student would be able to overparticipate to the detriment of other school work. Even the most strenuous

Fig. 50. Card used at Syracuse University.

MEDICAL EXAMINATION

DIVISION OF INTRAMURAL SPORTS

-- College ------------- Year ---------

Has passed _____ failed _____ his medical examination..

He can participate in the following Intramural Sports:

_____ Touch Football	_____ Handball	_____ Baseball
_____ Swimming	_____ Skiing	_____ Softball
_____ Soccer	_____ Ice Hockey	_____ Horseshoe Golf
_____ Mass Track	_____ Ping Pong	_____ Tennis
_____ Rifle	_____ Indoor Track	_____ Golf
_____ Basketball	_____ Volleyball	_____ Boxing
_____ Bowling	_____ Bridge	_____ Wrestling
_____ Foul Shooting	_____ Gymnastics	

------------------------------- -------------------------------
Student's Signature   Examining Physician

and constant intramural competitor will never rival the varsity squad member in the total time spent in competition, nor in the mental and psychological strain constantly placed on him toward winning, game after game, through a long season.

Certain other limitations on competition are mentioned elsewhere in this book, and some of these restrictions might well be re-emphasized at this point. Certain sports require superior athletic ability and at least a minimum of physical conditioning before competition is permitted. Such sports as wrestling, cross-country, regular football, and some of the track events can be considered in this light. Every precaution must be made in the regulations covering these sports to safeguard the health of the individual and to guarantee that palpably unfair competition is impossible.

The University of Michigan uses an annual health card to guarantee that its prospective athletes will at least be physically qualified to participate in their chosen sport. The card illustrates a good way the health service can cooperate with the physical education department.

UNIVERSITY OF MICHIGAN

INTRAMURAL SPORTS DEPARTMENT

ANNUAL HEALTH CHECK-UP

I, the undersigned, acknowledge that I have been informed as to the vital importance of having an annual health check-up before participating in any intramural activity and especially the more strenuous sports. I understand that I, personally, shall assume the responsibility of having a physical examination which will determine my fitness for participation in these voluntary activities.

I further agree that for my own protection I shall, at the first opportunity, take advantage of the free examination offered by the University Health Service.

N.B. Advance notice has been submitted to the officers of the various organizations relative to the importance of having an annual health check-up before participating in intramural activities.

_____
NAME

_____
ORGANIZATION

_____
Date

Fig. 51. Annual health check-up card of the University of Michigan.

PROTESTS

Rules should be arranged to discourage protests as much as possible. Duke University provides that protests must be filed in writing within 24 hours after the contest. A fee of one dollar must be filed with the protest which is refunded only when the protest is upheld; otherwise it is forfeited. Claims and protests filed too late are not considered.[6] Protest boards should always stand behind officials' judgment, stepping in only when the official has not adhered to actual playing rules. Some schools empower the field or floor supervisor to attempt to settle disputes or protests as they occur, thus short-circuiting many formal protests that might later take much time for the Intramural Board to settle. Care should be taken in following this practice, as unpleasant differences of opinion often flare up which might disappear overnight in a cooling-off period. Naturally, protests will be less frequent if better officiating is developed. It would be better for the intramural staff to spend its time with officials' clinics, improving techniques of officiating, rather than to spend its time hearing protest cases. Protests often follow hastily granted permission for the use of an ineligible player; when a team regrets having given this favor, a fight will usually develop over the outcome. The best way to eliminate this friction is never to allow an ineligible player to compete under any circumstances when his ineligibility is known.

Some schools place final dispensation of all protests in the hands of the director. While it is true he will have to take the most active role in these matters, he will be wise to organize an Intramural Board. In the larger institution it would be more practical to have a small number of staff members on this board, since they can be more easily called together on short notice, and are more likely to be impartial. In smaller institutions the student representatives can act in this capacity, rendering their decisions by secret ballot. When fraternities are involved, this system too often reflects politics and is not best. When protests are reviewed the board should meet at a selected time, with representatives of the two groups present, as well as the officials who handled the contest. Statements should be made by the invited students, questions should be asked by the board, and the students should retire to permit the board to make a quiet decision. Letters should then be sent to all groups involved without delay. The department should constantly be alert to violations of eligibility, and it should not be necessary for a formal protest to appear before action is taken. Not infrequently an organization will ask that a game be replayed instead of being forfeited, and both teams will agree to this procedure. Permission could be granted in cases where there appears to be no intent to violate or deceive intentionally.

FORFEITS

Various institutions in the nation have slightly different regulations governing forfeitures, but they are all similar in nature. All provide a limited number of extra minutes beyond the scheduled starting time before a forfeit is declared, varying from five to fifteen minutes. Iowa State and Minnesota have adopted the practice of starting and ending all basketball games simultaneously, using but one timing device. Thus a team not ready to start must either forfeit or the other team is permitted to play against whatever opposition is on hand. Although it might be permissible for two teams to agree on a shortened playing time, it is unfair to ask one team to play a shorter game simply because the opponents failed to make an appearance on time. If both teams fail to have the required number present, it is sometimes satisfactory to play a shortened game when they do arrive. It should also follow that rules should be adopted to govern the number of players that can be used in cases where the complete team has not appeared on time. The usual practice is to demand full teams wherever two-man teams are involved; one less than the required number for three-four-, five-, and six-man teams; and perhaps two less for teams involving more men.

College of the City of New York declares a game forfeited when one team fails to appear after five minutes, eliminating a team or player from further competition automatically after one forfeit. Wisconsin collects a fee of one dollar which is sacrificed on the second forfeiture by any team. Syracuse University demands an annual fee of three dollars from each group, or one dollar for any one team sport, to eliminate forfeited games. Each forfeiture subtracts one dollar from this deposit. The deposit is returned following the sport season if the forfeiture rule is unviolated. In sports like bowling, where city commercial alleys are reserved, it would always be wise to have all teams post a forfeit fee which would protect the management when an alley becomes unused for any match. Western Reserve University deducts all participation points from any team guilty of nonappearance in any sport. Nebraska deducts one-half of the participation points for one forfeiture, and all points for the second offense. The University of Florida permits fifteen minutes' lateness before a contest is forfeited, and no appeal from this rule is possible. The University of Washington allows ten minutes for late starts. If both teams fail to appear both are charged with a loss and the game will not be rescheduled. It may be played by mutual agreement of the two teams but will not count in the standings and no facilities will be reserved by the department. Northwestern University declares that no forfeit can be claimed and one must not be posted except by consulting the Intramural Department. In individual events the player must report the forfeiture personally.

POSTPONEMENTS

The schools with large intramural programs issue schedules well in advance of the first day's play. Any appeal from the schedule, which is made up with all conflicts and special requests in mind, must be made well in advance of the date. Most of these schools then make no exceptions in the schedule time whatever, unless there are problems beyond control regarding facilities. Some schools permit an occasional game to be postponed provided both teams are agreeable and the department has been notified well in advance and has given consent. This agreement is often possible provided other teams may be substituted and no valuable facilities and time are wasted. Teams will often accept the schedule as a whole, later asking for postponement due to the illness or injury of some star players. This reason should not be sufficient and is just one of the breaks of the game. Other campus functions will occasionally loom as possible interference and the department must again decide whether postponement is allowable. A firm policy must be adopted if accusations of favoritism are not to be justly leveled at the director.

The guiding principle to be followed in avoiding postponements is to carefully clear all dates and times before arranging the schedule, asking each team to state preferences, possible conflicts, and dates that must be avoided. When the schedules are then published and accepted, they should be honored by all competing teams as religiously as for intercollegiate athletics. Teams with Jewish members should always be asked to specify any holidays on which competition for them should be avoided. Postponements due to inclement weather should be left to the jurisdiction of the department. Instructions should be clearly given that all games will be played, regardless of the appearance of bad weather, up until the headquarters office declares the contest postponed; this should be done prior to one hour before game time, if at all possible.

Illustrative Rules and Regulations of Three Schools

As possible assistance for schools in the process of adopting a set of rules and regulations, three typical programs are given here. They are not presented as an ideal or perfect set of rules, but rather as a guide from which a code can be built to suit the local school situation.

The University of Texas

Procedure for Participation in Organized Intramural Athletics

In order to encourage students to avail themselves of the excellent recreational facilities provided by the University, the Intramural Department conducts both organized competition and unorganized recreation in sports.

Organized Intramural Competition

Fraternity Division: A representative of a fraternity must be either an initiate member or a pledge of his organization and his name must appear on the official membership list in the Office of the Dean of Men.

Pledges who fail to make sufficient grade points at the end of the first semester will become ineligible to represent their fraternity the day on which grades are made available to the students by the Registrar.

Mica Division: This division is to consist of teams organized from men students residing or boarding (eating regularly at least two meals a day) within a defined area, the number of areas and boundaries of same to be determined by the Men's Inter-Community Association.

A student desiring to compete in individual sports without representing any of the organizations may compete in the Mica Division as an "Independent." Such students must, however, comply with the organization eligibility rules of their division.

Club Division: This division is to consist of teams organized from the membership of clubs, societies, and associations belonging to the Inter-Club Athletic Association.

Navy Division: This division shall consist of teams organized from the various companies in the Naval R.O.T.C. A man must be a member of the company he represents.

All organizations participating in intramurals shall be subject to the approval of the Intramural Council. The Council will not approve the entry of teams organized for the purpose of competing in one sport or unnatural units of superior ability.

Eligibility

(The Intramural Office cannot assume responsibility for the eligibility of players but will assist the organization managers and individuals with their problems of eligibility and interpretation of rules.)

All regularly enrolled men students in the University will be eligible to compete in intramural athletics except as provided later in this article.

Letter Men: Men students who have been recommended for a varsity letter (qualified or unqualified) from an acceptable senior college shall be ineligible to compete in the sport or associate sport in which they were recommended for a letter.

Men students who have represented The University of Texas in a varsity contest shall be ineligible to compete in that sport or associate sport for the remainder of that school year.

Associate Sports: Letter men in football shall be inegible to compete in touch football. Letter men in baseball shall not be eligible to compete in softball. Letter men in swimming shall not be eligible to compete in water polo.

Squad Men: Men whose names appear on an official intercollegiate squad list or are added to the squad list later shall be ineligible to compete in intramural athletics during the remainder of that sport season.

Should a man's name be removed from the squad list by the coach, he shall be eligible for *other* intramural sports.

Should an intramural sport be conducted after the close of the intercollegiate season (during the same scholastic year), all men whose names appear on the intercollegiate squad list for that season shall be ineligible to compete in that sport.

Health Grade: Only men who have a health grade of *A*, rated by the University Health Service, shall be eligible to compete in intramural athletics.

A veteran with a medical discharge is required to furnish to the Intramural Office a statement from the University Health Service that he is physically able to participate in intramural sports.

Professionals: A student barred from varsity athletics because of professionalism (according to the rules of the Southwest Conference) shall be barred from those branches of intramural athletics in which he broke his amateur standing.

Playing Under an Assumed Name: Should a player compete in an intramural activity at The University of Texas under an assumed name, his organization shall be disqualified for the remainder of that sport, losing all points scored in that sport toward the All-Year Trophy.

Eligibility for Championship Series: In team sports, a contestant must have played in at least one (1) regularly scheduled contest with the team he intends to represent, in order to be eligible for the divisional or intramural championship series, except that organizations may replace men who withdraw from the University, or men with health grade below *A,* with eligible men.

A student shall not compete with more than one organization in any one sport.

A student shall not compete in more than four (4) sports during any one of the three quarters (Fall, Winter, or Spring) or a total of ten (10) sports during a school year.

Organization Eligibility List

A student will not be eligible to represent an organization unless his name appears on the eligibility list of that organization. Names may be added to these lists at any time. *Eligible names on score cards or entries will satisfy this requirement.*

An organization's eligibility list shall be limited to a total of seventy-five (75) names. Any group may enter several separate eligibility lists. Each list, however, shall be considered as that of a separate organization, which shall be governed by all intramural rules.

An organization's eligibility list should be filed at the Intramural Office before their first contest.

A student's name may be dropped from the organization's eligibility list for good reasons by the Intramural Council.

Forfeits

Any established violation of the rules governing the eligibility of participants shall forfeit the contest in which the breach occurred.

The Intramural Office must have notice of the possibility of the ineligibility of a participant within forty-eight hours after the contest in question.

Should an ineligible participant in an individual sport be discovered before the All-Year Trophy points are tabulated, no points made by such individual shall be credited to him or his organization *in that sport*.

Defaults

Teams or individuals not ready to play within ten minutes after the scheduled time for a contest will constitute a default, subject to the approval of the official in charge.

Protests

If, during a contest, a disagreement should arise between players or between a player and an official concerning the rules or interpretation of the rules, a protest may be made to the official in charge of the contest. Such protest, however, must be made at the time a dispute arises and before play is resumed. The official in charge is to notify both teams that the game is being played under protest and so state on the score card.

In addition, a written protest must be submitted to the Intramural Director within twenty-four hours after the contest in question.

Appeals

A protesting team not satisfied with the decision of the Student's Advisory Committee may appeal to the Faculty Committee on Intramural Athletics. Such appeal must be presented in writing to the Director of Intramural Athletics within twenty-four hours after receiving notice from the Student's Advisory Committee of their decision.

Disqualification

An organization or individual may be disqualified from intramural competition by an act of the Students' Intramural Council approved by the Faculty Committee on Intramural Athletics.

Substitutes

Teams may substitute players in all contests with the following exceptions:

In sports where entries must be approved (boxing and wrestling).

In meets (track, swimming, etc.).

In tournaments (tennis, handball, etc.) each entrant is allowed a substitute for only one contest.

1. The substitute shall not be a student who was entered in the tournament.

2. Permanent substitutions may be made should an entrant withdraw from the University or receive a health grade below "A."

In sports where a qualifying round is required (golf).

Postponement

Organizations may postpone a scheduled team contest only with the unanimous consent of both teams' managers and the Director of Intramural Athletics. Postponement of contests shall be made at least one day before the regularly scheduled time.

In elimination tournaments (except boxing and wrestling) contests may be played ahead of time provided the score is turned in to the intramural office before the match is scheduled to be played.

Entries

In sports where entries are necessary, there shall be a definite time for closing the entry and no individual or organization shall be permitted to enter after that date.

A student competing in a tournament will not be permitted to change his position on the flight sheet.

Approval of Entries

The physical fitness and skill of all men desiring to enter such sports as boxing, wretling, etc., must be approved by a representative of the Intramural Office before the men will be allowed to participate.

Schedules

All schedules shall be made by the Director of Intramural Athletics for Men.

Bulletin Board

Intramural contestants and team managers will find important material on the bulletin board in the north hallway of the first floor of Gregory Gymnasium.

Important dates and the winners of each activity will appear on the bulletin board. We advise you to watch this board in order to be well informed upon the daily happenings in Intramural Athletics.

Oklahoma A & M

Rules for Independent and All-College Play
(Independent and all-college participation)

1. Competitor must be a bona fide student. (Exceptions are made in those events in which faculty members are eligible.)
2. Men who have won the varsity award at this institution or any other senior college are not eligible for competition in those sports in which the award was received.
3. Varsity and freshman squadsmen are not eligible in that particular sport. Men who have been issued equipment on varsity and fresh-

man squads are ineligible for competition in that particular sport. An exception to this rule is that men who have been dropped from or have quit varsity or freshman squads are eligible if they have been entered in that intramural sport before the deadline for acceptance of entries.

4. A student participating under an assumed name shall be barred from all intramural competition for the current year.

5. A man must have participated in at least one game in that specific sport for an organization before he is eligible to compete in the championship play-off.

6. A man may represent only one organization in any one sport. A student cannot play on both independent and fraternity teams in the same sport. Participation in scheduled games prevents a member from playing with any other team for the remainder of the period of competition in that sport.

7. Each organization must hand in a list of entries for any sport prior to the beginning of the schedule and additional names may not be added after two weeks of play unless approved by the Director of Intramural Sports. A man may not represent any organization and he may not compete until he has been officially entered at the intramural office.

8. A team playing an ineligible student shall forfeit all games in the sport in which the offense was committed.

9. Intramural schedules are posted on the bulletin board at the Old Gymnasium and in the Intramural office. These are the official schedules.

10. All students are supposed to have had a medical examination and to have been deemed fit for competition. The college and this Department disclaim any responsibility in case of injury.

11. The Intramural Director, Head of the Department of Health, Physical Education and Recreation, and the Varsity Coach of the sport in question, compose an advisory group to determine matter of policy.

12. Any team leaving the field of play before a contest is completed or called by the proper officials, will forfeit all future rights to compete in intramural competition.

13. Any team forfeiting two contests will automatically be eliminated from all further competition in the intramural program.

Inter-Fraternity Rules

Article I

ARTICLES OF INTER-FRATERNITY SPORTS

Section I—The power to make all interpretations and rulings of the following articles is to be vested in the Head of the Intramural Department of the College. His decision shall be considered as final. There is to be absolutely no rebuttal on decisions rendered by the Head of the Intramural Department.

Section II—Any changes or amendments to the following articles can be made only by a two-thirds vote of each approved fraternity of the Inter-fraternity Council present at the meeting at which the vote is taken.

Article II

ELIGIBILITY

Section I—Only those organizations approved by the Inter-fraternity Council will be permitted to enter a team in any contest or tournament recognized by this constitution.

Section II—All members and pledges of a fraternity organization will be permitted to participate in the particular organization's entry with the following exceptions:

(a) Any member of the pledge group who has not received varsity recognition, that is, has not received a letter in the individual sport in which he is competing at this or any other senior four-year college with the exception of men who receive varsity recognition while in service training institutions.

Interpretation: In the case of carry over skills in sports the men in question will be considered ineligible. Examples: Men who have earned the varsity football award may not participate in touch football; baseball lettermen may not participate in softball; track lettermen may not participate in any phase of the track meet, i.e., a varsity hurdler may not run the mile for his fraternity.

(b) A man who has received any degree from any four-year college or university will not be placed on the eligibility list.

(c) Any man who is enrolled in twelve or more college hours will not be placed on the eligibility list.

(d) Any man who has been out for the varsity sport in which the fraternities are participating but has not earned a varsity award and has not participated in any scheduled varsity or "B" squad ball games scheduled that sport year shall be eligible provided fourteen (14) days have elapsed from the time he quits varsity participation in an inter-fraternity contest.

(e) Has been listed as a member or pledge with the I. F. C. thirty (30) days prior to the first day of inter-fraternity competition in the sports event in which he is to participate, exception being made only by a majority vote of the I. F. C.

Section III—Prior to the first contest in any sport, an eligibility list containing the names of players to participate in the contest will be sent to the Head of the Intramural Department at a time designated by him.

(a) Failure to comply with this Section will cause the team violating this Section to be ruled ineligible for this sport only.

(b) Names may be added to this list after it has been prepared and sent to the Head of the Intramural Department, and must be added prior to participation in any contest.

(c) A full team according to standard regulations of sport concerned shall be required as stated in this constitution, or game shall be forfeited by team not having required number of players present. Ten (10) minutes after contest is scheduled to begin shall be the determining time for forfeiture.

(d) All rules, regulations, and methods of officiating inter-fraternity sports shall be left to the discretion of the Head of the Intramural Department.

Section IV—Violation of any part of Section II will result in a fine of twenty dollars ($20.00) per violation and the loss of the game in which the player participated. However, a team may be fined only once for the same player in the same sport. The violating team may continue to play in the contest or tourney after the violation. Fines gained from this section will be paid to the I. F. C.

Article III

PROTESTS

Section I—No protest shall be honored that questions the integrity of the referee, umpire, or field judge.

Section II—The only protest that will be honored is a protest that violates Article II of these governing articles.

(a) Any protest must be entered in writing within twenty-four (24) hours after the completion of the game or contest being protested; one copy of the protest will be given to the athletic representative of the organization being protested against, and one copy to the Head of the Intramural Department.

(b) This protest will contain reason of protest and evidence thereof.

The University of Toledo outlines their regulations in the *1960 Handbook of Intramural Sport and Recreational Activity* as follows:

Eligibility and Ineligibility

1. General Eligibility

a. All undergraduate students regularly enrolled for a minimum of 12 hours (Law-8) in any department or college shall automatically become eligible to enjoy all intramural privileges and shall retain that status until they withdraw, graduate, or until they fail to comply with the rules of eligibility.

b. The IMREC Board reserves the right to change any eligibility rule at any time. When any rule is changed or any exception made, the *Collegian* will announce the action, and the notice will be posted on the IM bulletin board.

c. Any questions concerning the eligibility rules are to be brought to the senior managers for interpretation.

d. Men who feel they have been unfairly made ineligible may appeal to the IMREC Board to have their eligibility reinstated.

e. *It is the duty of each team manager to check on the eligibility of any doubtful cases.* A strong policy toward violators will be followed. *Under no circumstances will ignorance be an excuse.*

f. Any man may switch from independent to fraternity or from fraternity to independent competition only once during the year. Fraternity men may compete as independents after participating for the house but may not return to fraternity competition for the remainder of the year. No man may switch in the middle of a tournament. Once having switched, the man must continue with the *second* team for the remainder of the school year.

g. A man is not eligible for interdivision playoffs of a sport unless he has competed in at least three contests. The same holds true in case of a tied league playoff.

2. Ineligibility

a. Membership on a varsity or freshman team *in the season of that sport* makes a man ineligible unless released by varsity coach and accepted by IMREC Board for other sports.

b. Freshman squad members shall be ineligible until they are placed on cut list by the coach.

c. A man who competes on a varsity team but who does not earn a letter is ineligible to compete in that sport or related sports during the following two semesters.

d. Any man who earns a varsity letter at the University of Toledo is ineligible to participate in that or related intramural sports.

e. A man who earns a letter at another school where the competition in that sport is of the caliber of that which the University of Toledo plays is ineligible. It is the duty of any man who has won a letter at another school to check on his eligibility.

f. A numeral winner will be ineligible for that and related sports for the following two semesters.

g. A man who competes professionally in a sport will be ineligible for that or related intramural sports.

h. Graduate and post-graduate students may not compete in any intramural sports. They may compete in recreational or co-recreational sports.

i. No fraternity team may compete in an independent league or vice versa.

j. Anyone found participating under an assumed name will be declared ineligible and banned for the remainder of the year.

3. Penalties for Violations

a. In individual sports, any man found to be ineligible after competition has begun will be dropped from the tournament. His next scheduled opponent will get a bye (unless it is discovered in time to place his last defeated opponent in the next round). All of the points won by the ineligible man will be lost. In doubles play the same penalties will apply. The ineligible man's partner may not continue to compete with a new partner.

b. In team competition all points won in games in which an ineligible man was used shall be forfeited.

c. If the use of the ineligible man is discovered before the inter-league playoffs all games in which the man participated shall be forfeited.

d. In case a tournament shall be conducted on a double-elimination basis the results of the last game only shall be reversed, provided the ineligible player was used in that game.

e. After the first game of the inter-division playoffs, the team using an ineligible man shall have the last game forfeited and the points lost. (Rule b, this section.)

4. Protests

All protests must be submitted orally to the supervisor on duty and submitted to the IMREC Office in writing by the team manager within 24 hours after the protest arises. A protest fee of $5.00 must accompany the protest. If the protest is granted the fee is refunded. If the litigants arrive at a favorable solution between themselves the IMREC Board may agree to the solution even though it may be in conflict with intramural rules.

In case of obvious violation of eligibility rules, the intramural senior manager may rule the contest forfeited without IMREC Board Action.

Protests will not be entertained in the recreational or co-recreational program.

No protest may be entered on any discretionary decision of an intramural official.

5. Forfeits

Two forfeits in a sport automatically drop a team from further competition in that sport for the remainder of the tournament. The remaining games will be forfeited.

It is important that the organization IM Manager check the schedules as soon as they are out to make certain there are no conflicts. Teams affected by special religious holidays should make it known to the IMREC Office when they enter a team.

Forfeit fee of $5.00 is refunded if no forfeits occur during the year. If a team forfeits, to re-enter another forfeit fee must be deposited in the IMREC Office. Forfeit fee accompanies the team's entry.

6. Entries and Deadlines

All entries must be in prior to the posted deadlines. Late entries will be accepted *only* to fill up a league where there is more than one league.

All deadlines in minor sports play are card deadlines and not match deadlines. The results must be turned in to the IMREC Office before the actual card deadline.

Rules and Regulations Governing
Specific Sports

Chapter 6 discussed specific rules and regulations covering the program
of activities. Various schools use different methods of presenting this
information to competing groups and individuals. The University of Minnesota has published an excellent booklet which is given to all organizations:
Rules of Selected Intramural Sports. It gives a very complete and useful
set of rules to be used in all intramurals conducted at that university. The
University of Missouri has also published a smaller rules edition for the
same purpose. Oregon State College includes all playing rules as part of the
intramural handbook. Other schools following this practice are Syracuse,
Illinois, Wisconsin, Louisville, College of the City of New York, Ohio
State, Cincinnati, and Kansas.

The University of Washington at Seattle devotes a full page of its
intramural handbook to each sport, and includes the following information:
team pictures of last year's champions, statistics of the last year's participation, and regulations covering participation in that specific sport.

MISCELLANEOUS RULES AND REGULATIONS

The New Trier High School at Winnetka, Illinois, requires a parental
approval card which is applicable to both interscholastic and intramural
participation. Since this procedure is sound, the form which is used there
is reproduced through the courtesy of W. L. Childs, Director, in Figure 52.

The University of Chicago rules that any player who commits an act
of flagrant unsportsmanlike conduct such as striking another player or an
official shall be immediately disqualified from that game and barred from
further competition in that sport for the year. Special rating systems for
sportsmanship displayed by teams representing organizations are used by
some colleges, such as the Universities of Nebraska and Washington.
Officials at Temple University adopt a "get tough" attitude with players
guilty of any unsportsmanlike conduct. They feel that one player expelled
from a game or even out of the league early in the schedule goes far in
creating exemplary conduct for others during the remainder of the schedule.

Northwestern University has a rule which demands that only nonbreak-
able glasses can be worn in touch football and basketball. Northwestern also
rules that there can be no change of entries after a sport has started. It
provides specifically that each man be limited to one weight in the wrestling
tournament.

Northwestern voices the prevailing practice concerning injuries in-
curred in intramurals: the department is not responsible for any injuries
received in the intramural program, but the university trainer and the

New Trier Township High School
Winnetka, Illinois

_____19_____

M—————————————————————————————

—————————————————————————————
(Street)   (Village)

Dear Sir:

Your son——————————————————————is interested in participating in athletics at New Trier.

We desire to know if this is in accordance with your wishes, and if he is doing this with your permission. In some cases there is parental objection to participation in certain types of games, and we desire to cooperate with the homes of students as far as possible.

We are operating our interscholastic sports program in conjunction with a comprehensive intramural sports program. This provides for a maximum participation on the part of students. Some sports are, however, more strenuous than others, and we desire to consult your wishes before we assign your boy to any particular group.

Will you please sign the form below and return at once.

Very sincerely yours,
W. L. CHILDS
Head of Physical Education Department

_____

Head of the Physical Education Department
New Trier High School,
Winnetka, Illinois.

Dear Sir:

I do hereby consent to allow my son to participate in the following Intramural and Interscholastic Athletic Activities for this school year and assume responsibility in case of accident or injury.

(Please draw a line through activities in which you prefer **NOT** to have your son participate.)

Interscholastic Sports
Baseball
Basketball (Varsity)
Basketball (Frosh-Soph)
Football (Varsity)
Football (Frosh-Soph)
Golf
Swimming (Sr. & Jr.)
Track (Indoor—Sr. & Jr.)
Track (Outdoor—Sr. & Jr.)
Tennis

Intramural Sports
Basketball
Football (Fall)
Football (Spring)
Football Skills
Free Throwing
Gymnastics
Golf (Fall)
Golf (Spring)
Hand Ball (Fall)
Hand Ball (Winter)
Horseshoes (Fall)
Horseshoes (Spring)
Ping Pong

Playground Ball
Life Saving
Soccer
Speed Ball
Swimming
Tennis (Fall)
Tennis (Spring)
Touch Football
Track (Indoor)
Track (Outdoor)
Tumbling
Volley Ball
Water Polo

Yours very truly,
(Signed)———————————————————

NAME (Last) (First) (Class) (Adviser)

1 | 2 | 3 | 4 | 5 | 6 | 7

Fig. 52.

training room with first aid are always available to intramural contestants. There is a growing feeling that intramural departments should arrive at some plan which would provide at least partial payment to a needy student who incurs an expense beyond the protection given him at the student health center. Perhaps only one or two such injuries will take place in the hundreds of games during the year. Such an unfortunate occurrence often strikes directly at the student least able financially to shoulder the whole load. The future program will endeavor to find some project annually which will provide a fund for just such an emergency.

Allegheny College adopted and put into use the following Code of Ethics for the conduct of its sports. It is reproduced here as a suggestion for other directors who are anxious to have their sports program yield the greatest possible sociological values.

Allegheny College Intramural Code of Ethics

The following code of ethics, adopted by the Intramural Council in the interests of fair play, will apply at all intramural contests and will govern the conduct of players and spectators alike:

1. All athletic opponents are to be treated as friends, with all courtesy due friends being accorded them.
2. All decisions of officials are to be accepted as final and without question.
3. No derogatory remarks shall be made at any time to players or officials.
4. Spectators and players shall not make abusive or irritating remarks from the sidelines.
5. Spectators and players will not attempt to rattle an opposing player, such as a pitcher in a baseball game, a free-thrower in a basketball game, etc.
6. Players will seek to win by fair and lawful means, living up to the spirit as well as to the letter of the rules.
7. Contestants will play the game for the sake of the game and not for what winning may bring.

Application of the Code

1. Officials at all contests are obliged to report all infractions of the code, as part of their officiation responsibilities. Officials may not waive this rule.
2. If a player or spectator commits an infraction of the code, the group to which he belongs will receive a warning notice. Two such warnings caused by undesirable behavior by members of a group will result in the group being asked to withdraw from that sport.
3. When a group has been asked to withdraw from two sports, it will be automatically dropped from further participation for that year, and will become ineligible for the intramural championship.

Note: Ignorance of the code will not be regarded as an excuse. An official has the right to report any offensive behavior on the part of players or spectators not covered in the code. The Intramural Council will act on all code infractions.

REFERENCES

1 *Handbook of Intramural and Recreational Sports,* University of Illinois, Urbana, 1960.

2 *Intramural Handbook,* University of Oklahoma, Norman, 1963.

3 *Handbook of Intramural Activities,* Cornell University, Ithaca, N.Y., 1956.

4 *Handbook of Intramural Sports for Men,* Kansas University, Lawrence, 1960.

5 *Handbook of Intramural Sports,* University of Tennessee, Department of Physical Education, Knoxville, 1963-1964, p. 8.

6 *Duke University Intramurals,* Handbook for 1968-1969, Durham, N.C.

10

THE NOON-HOUR PROGRAM

No intramural or recreational program in the elementary, junior or senior high school is complete without a good noon-hour program of activities. This period offers great possibilities for program development. The student who is compelled to work after school can enjoy the values of noon-hour participation. The rural-consolidated schools, so numerous in America, have their student body almost intact for this period. Carefully organized activities at noontime will practically eliminate the usual disciplinary problems, substituting something to do that is enjoyable, uses up surplus energy, provides added opportunities to maintain fitness, and eliminates harmful loitering.

One large city high school studied this problem for years, and became alarmed at the large numbers of students loafing and congregating in nearby candy stores daily. Their alarm was increased by the evidence of the sale of marijuana and liquor, gambling, sex problems, and all the accompanying evils of unorganized loafing time. This condition was later believed to have been relieved when an enterprising director of athletics introduced a large, well-planned noon-hour recreational program in the school. Faculty and students alike were enthusiastic about the new program. It is now a vital part of that school's educational scheme. It is interesting to note that the teachers who originated and administered this program

Fig. 53. Noon-hour activities at Wilmington, Delaware, Elementary School.

received salary increases, their indispensability became evident, and their efforts won them the warm affection of parents and community.

Dan Dasovic, former director at Toivola, Minnesota, wrote the following to the author after two years of his noon-hour program: "A well-balanced intramural program can successfully do away with all noon-hour problems, most disciplinary problems, and all problems of general nature that may not be serious but nevertheless are puzzling and a constant threat to the proper functioning of a school or group. Students are kept busy."

The noon-hour program does not lend itself as well to the college and university scene, although some institutions have made great progress with such a program. Many schools conduct some of the participation in free throws, table tennis, badminton, horseshoes, shuffleboard, and golf specialties during the noon period. Other schools make recreational opportunities available for their students without scheduling organized games.

There is much controversy over the use of strenuous activities during this period in the junior and senior high schools. This is not a serious problem in colleges since all students do not answer a 1:00 P.M. bell. Good health procedure would indicate that such sports as basketball, swimming, water polo, boxing, and track events should be avoided or carefully supervised. There is evidence to support the feeling that noon basketball is permissible if the game is properly administered. Some studies have been made on this subject, indicating no harmful effects from many of these sports. There are great numbers of sports and activities which can produce strong social experiences and outcomes that might be planned for the noon period, in addition to the purely physical sports.

After using short games of basketball and other active sports for years in the noon program, and carefully watching the reactions of students from a health and emotional point of view, the author would not advocate the elimination of such events from this program. Proper time must be provided for the shower and the lunch. One very practical solution is to arrange the scheduled games at the beginning of the lunch period. These are followed by the quick shower and lunch, with the time schedule rigidly enforced daily. Some schools allow a short free period following lunch. Such an arrangement would allow greater intramural planning throughout the luncheon period.

The noon hour provides one of the best possible times for co-recreational activities. Here boys and girls can be taught to play together more naturally than at any other time. Outdoor activities are to be preferred if weather permits. Many schools provide noon schedules which rotate the participants constantly, thus providing valuable spectator activity daily for the entire student body, all of whom become participants on regular schedule.

Kenosha High School, Wisconsin, developed a noon-hour program considered indispensable in the life and discipline of the school. Situated very near the business district of Kenosha, the school had found many problems to exist previously. It was discovered that 16 percent of the students brought lunches to school. Since there are no lunchrooms in the school building, students ate their lunches in parked automobiles, threw refuse everywhere, and spent the noon period riding about the city or hanging around in various places. It was felt a good program could aid materially in developing desirable individual qualities. Steps in the Kenosha Plan are:

1. A general assembly is held at the beginning of each school year. Tentative plans are discussed and student interests determined.
2. Activity questionnaires are passed out and information collected from all students.
3. A student committee is selected and meets to discuss plans.
4. Another general assembly is used to present all specific plans developed.
5. Student leaders are selected for specific activities, and for specific rooms to be utilized.
6. Students bring in quantities of donated recreational games and equipment from their homes.
7. Cooperation from the public recreation department is requested and obtained. This organization then furnishes additional games, equipment, and some supervisory help. Public recreation at Kenosha is administered by the schools.

Special rooms are set up to handle lotto, checkers, dominoes, Chinese checkers, chess, card games, reading magazines, books, dramatic club, dancing, etc. The gymnasium is set aside for basketball, volleyball, indoor baseball, basket shooting, and the more active sports. Ten minutes are provided for showers for those participating in the active games. Motion pictures are used once each week. A student selection committee arranges the choice of movies, both educational and purely entertaining, and student movie operators are trained. State university films are used constantly. All active games are organized on a competitive basis. Individual events are usually organized in ladder style. The outdoor program features archery, softball, volleyball, and horseshoes.

In the Kenosha Plan it soon became evident that the problem of distribution of students had to be solved. The principal listed all teachers alphabetically and each was assigned approximately one day per month for noon-hour duty. Individual differences in the students were quickly reflected in the same differences between teachers. The use of the noon-hour for study was discouraged unless chosen by the students, with a room set aside for them. It was soon evident that the areas with greatest possibilities for development were movies, use of the library, radio, and dancing. The total cost of this program for Kenosha has been less than $100 per year.

A similar program has been in operation in the junior high schools of Dubuque, Iowa. Here, students are selected to supervise each room, with a head supervisor who checks out equipment from a central office each day. The room supervisor is responsible for all equipment, as well as conduct in his room during the period. There have been very few rule violations. Trained student movie operators show selected motion pictures with a small admission fee charged.

In the Norfolk, Virginia, elementary schools an organized noon pupil activity program has been in operation for many years. Following the lunch period fifteen minutes are set aside daily for activities of nonstrenuous nature. Teachers arrange the schedule, rules for games, officials, duration of games, and other details. After a time the program is handled almost entirely by pupils. Complicated rules are eliminated as much as possible. The upper grades play volleyball, softball, newcomb, rubber-heel toss, O'Leary Ball, end ball, dodge ball, hopscotch, shuffleboard, and bat ball. The Parent Teachers Association awards banners to winning groups. Pupil officials are all trained.

The author has conducted a noon-hour program in past years in junior and senior high schools, with complete control and supervision in the physical education department. Tournaments and leagues were operated throughout the year, five days per week, in the following activities:

Badminton	Golf specialties tourneys
Basketball	Handball

Basketball golf	Horseshoes
Basketball free throws	Shuffleboard
Basket shooting	Softball
Bat ball	Table tennis
Checkers	Tennis
Dart baseball	Volleyball
Dart bowling	Zel-ball

With specific tourneys and leagues set up in many of these events at noon, the after-school program was not eliminated but greatly implemented and enlarged. Individual students were able to compete more than twice per week, but were usually on hand to see their rivals in action on other days. Members of the staff had their lunch time arranged before or after the activity period on a regular rotating schedule, which guaranteed the equalization of noon responsibility. Special games featuring mixed groups of boys and girls highlighted the program. Outdoor possibilities of the program were as unlimited as individual ingenuity indicated. Social and recreational values were stressed, with less emphasis on the purely physical.

Janesville High School, Wisconsin, has long been a leader in organized noon recreation. Big features of the program, in addition to the usual sports, are dances and movies. Roosevelt High School at Cedar Rapids, Iowa, operates four sports simultaneously at noon. The most popular events are shuffleboard, table tennis, deck tennis, volleyball, and Indian club bowling. The Theodore Ahrens Trade High School in Louisville, has been a leader in co-recreational activity planning. Activities are taught the girls in regular classes. Boys receive instruction just prior to the noon period. Every Monday through Thursday six tourneys are conducted in aerial tennis, basket end ball, paddle tennis, tenikoit, floor bowling, and volleyball. On Friday there is mixed social dancing. When special classes in social dancing for boys were organized at their own suggestion, participation in the noon program increased markedly. A brief luncheon period comes first, followed by the play period. Over 500 out of 800 students actively participated during the first year of this program. Girls learned lessons of sticking to the end; boys learned courtesies in the games. All acquired skills for later life.

The Monnessen, Pennsylvania, High School has used the noon-hour period almost exclusively for social dancing, thus eliminating the need for facilities at other times for dances, and permitting more after-school and evening athletics and intramural planning. The high school at Connellsville, Pennsylvania, conducts basketball leagues four days a week at noon, leaving every Friday exclusively for social dancing.

Teachers worked with the students of the Hackettstown, New Jersey, High School in developing a Recreation Club in a room just off the gymnasium. During the first year the room was used largely for billiards and table tennis; later it was expanded and facilities for other activities were added:

Badminton (paddles constructed)
Table tennis (bats made)
Shuffleboard (cues and discs made)
Bean bags (all made)
Paddle tennis (bats made)
Trophy shields and awards (all made)
Quoits (made with rope)
Tether ball (paddles and game made)
Discos (all equipment made)
Curling (all equipment made)
Volleyball and badminton standards also constructed

The Alexander Hamilton Junior High School of Oakland, California, has operated a unique noon program for years which attracts every one of over 1,600 girls daily in some sport or activity, either as a participant, official, or spectator. The schedule is arranged to permit rotation in these three capacities. The Lindbloom High School of Chicago offers proof that the lack of indoor facilities should never prohibit a fine noon recess program utilizing all available space, such as corridors, vestibules, gymnasium corners, classrooms, and other spaces. All kinds of competitive games can be planned to use particular spots that otherwise are wasted in most buildings.

Another fine program has been serving its large student body for many years at the John Marshall High School in Los Angeles, a six-year high school. Early in the school year each home room elects an athletic leader. Three athletic councils are formed from these leaders, one for the two lower grades, one for the two middle grades, and one for the two upper grades. As the time for each new activity approaches, these councils meet and discuss the organization and management of the sports. The athletic officers arrange the space assignment for their home room games, organize their room teams, check eligibility of all participants, see that captains are selected for all sports, run off any needed pretournament play-offs, and make themselves useful in any possible way to the faculty in the conduct of the competition. Games are scheduled for two lunch periods of 40 minutes each. The three grade sections operate independently of each other, arriving at championships without an ultimate all-school play-off series, thus equalizing competition throughout.

The program of activities for students at Garden Grove Union High School, California, is outstanding. Stimulation of student interest in extracurricular work has been the outstanding result since the 30-minute daily program has been operating.

At the University of Michigan, the varsity swimming coach has devoted five noon periods each week to swimming and water activity for the faculty for years. Tuesday and Thursday noons are given over to instruction to beginning faculty swimmers, with the other three days used for recreational swimming and water games. The most interesting noon-hour sport conducted at the University of Nebraska has been the annual golf pitching and driving tournaments. These events run for several noon periods, finally culminating in the championship final play-offs.

The noon program for elementary and junior high schools might well be centered around ladder and challenge tournaments in a great variety of activities. Weekly tournaments should be conducted in at least two activities. Following are several selected activities that are very appropriate at this level for noon-hour use:

Aerial darts	Checkers	Gym bowling	Roll-along
Aerial tennis	Chess	Halma	Rope quoits
Bean bag toss	Dart baseball	Handball	Shuffleboard
Bean drop	Dart bowling	Hole ball	Softball
Box hockey	Darts	Horseshoe golf	Spot shooting
Card games	Dominoes	Paddle ball	Table tennis
Checker pool	Free throws	Ring toss	Volley bounce

A broad noon-hour program in the junior or senior high school might yield the following results:

1. Provide boys and girls pleasurable use of their leisure time while at school.
2. Teach them a new way to use leisure time outside of school.
3. Make them eager to remain on the school premises rather than to frequent candy stores, drugstores, ice cream parlors, pool halls, and other less desirable places.
4. Eliminate crowded and noisy school halls.
5. By virtue of keeping the students occupied, aid in the elimination of mischevious pranks throughout the building.
6. Through the presentation of movies, provide a real educational experience and develop new appreciations.
7. Actually aid many students in healthful digestion.
8. Aid the classroom situation by eliminating unsanitary conditions of perspiring bodies, which is a previous evil generated from excessive free and unsupervised play.

Fine examples of student-teacher planning for noon-hour recreation are now to be found in many public schools across the nation. A status study of boys' intramural programs in Iowa high schools disclosed that the noon hour was the most frequently used time of day the program was offered. Some 44 percent of the state's high schools provide some form of noon-hour program.[1]

Industrial recreation has borrowed much from the school recreational program and incorporated many of its finest features. In turn, schools might well look to the great noon-hour industrial programs now being conducted in many plants and companies. These concerns have been quick to see the greatly increased working efficiency of their employees. Statistics of production prove conclusively that a happy and relaxing noon hour pays great dividends in accelerated output. Since the product of the schools is greater learning capacity and the assimilation of more knowledge plus the creation of a readiness for learning and thinking, might it not be equally important for all schools to begin giving attention to this vital phase of the educational curriculum? Many of the organizational techniques and the sports and events used could be duplicated easily in schools everywhere; a few ideas will be presented here as a possible source of assistance for school directors.

One of the most interesting events conducted by Stromberg-Carlson Company of Rochester, New York, is the Hole-in-One Tournament. Concentric circles are laid out and a tee established for golf pitching for accuracy. It is an event which will attract both the skilled golfer and the novice, who might well become an enthusiastic golfer from that experience.

The Ivorydale Plant of Proctor and Gamble Company organizes a large number of activities as clubs. Special recreation rooms are provided for some sports, while others carry on in all kinds of out-of-the-way places. Sports sponsored at Ivorydale are bowling, table tennis, chess, shuffleboard, checkers, pinochle, softball, darts, archery, bridge, volleyball, and the angler's club. The B. F. Goodrich Company has a very active chess club playing during every noon hour. The Miller-Paine Company of Lincoln, Nebraska, has a summer roof-garden recreational program for all employees which centers largely around the noon period. Here shuffleboard, quoits, deck tennis, card games, checkers, chess, and table tennis are organized competitively, with some merely enjoying the sport for restful relaxation and sunbathing.

The Sherwin-Williams Company of Chicago has a tremendous program of noon-hour softball competition. Games are held every day from 12:00 to 12:30 P.M., with each team playing once every five days. A competitive point system succeeds in motivating interest still further. Each noon approximately 400 employees play while 1,400 watch. Teams are mixed, with old and young employees. The management has noticed a great difference in the morale and noon group conversations after each softball season ends and activity decreases.

In conclusion, it should be emphasized that noon-hour athletics and recreation is not a new idea, but to most schools throughout the nation the period is still unused and undeveloped. It would seem that a well-planned program is not the unique opportunity of the large school, but is perhaps even more workable in the smaller unit. Better organized programs gradually utilize a maximum of student leadership with a minimum of faculty supervision, using a rotating schedule of responsibility. Reports everywhere indicate that the program is a powerful influence in school morale and discipline, affording the student body an opportunity for participation in a wide range of activities to meet individual interests. There is no question about its success in substituting worthwhile pursuits for the many questionable uses of the luncheon period. It affords the school's finest time for teaching boys and girls how to play together and enjoy each other's company in a wholesome way. New skills and leisure-time interests are developed which are valuable in later life.

For the busy director of athletics and physical education, always occupied with varsity teams after school, this time offers a grand opportunity for greater service to the rest of the student body. The discriminating school administrator cannot but appreciate the organization of such a program by the director. Great progress has been made by a few schools in the nation, but it is significant that most schools have not scratched the surface with noon-hour planning. It is a great medium for new attitudes and rich educational experiences.

This type of program is the best medium in which to introduce a great variety of activities that otherwise would be completely omitted from the program because of other use of facilities, preoccupation of faculty time, and outside student interests. The following recommended activities have been used in programs of this type with satisfying results. Each school must select activities best suited to its size, facilities, and ingenuity.

Archery	Dodgeball	Roller skating
Archery golf	Fencing	Shuffleboard
Badminton	Fly tying	Skeet shooting
Bait and fly casting	Golf driving	Skiing
Baseball	Golf pitching	Skish
Basketball	Golf putting	Snow sledding
Basketball golf	Gym bowling	Soccer
Bowling	Gymnastics	Softball
Bridge	Handball	Speedball
Cageball	Handicraft	Squash
Card games	Horseshoe golf	Table tennis
Checkers	Horseshoes	Tennis
Chess	Ice skating	Tether ball
Chinese checkers	Indoor baseball	Top spinning contests
Clock golf	Kick ball	Touch football
Croquet	Marble tourney	Twenty-one
Curling	Mass games	Volleyball
Cribbage	Necatos	Volley bounce
Dancing	Newcomb	Volley tennis
Dart baseball	Paddle ball	Wrestling
Dart bowling	Paddle tennis	Zel-ball
Deck tennis	Rifle shooting	

REFERENCE

1 Fred C. Beuttler, "Boys' Intramural Programs in Iowa Secondary Schools,"
    Eleventh Annual Proceedings of the National Intramural Association, 1960,
    p. 32.

11

ORGANIZATION FOR COMPETITION

It must be recognized that all intramural events in the year's calendar cannot be organized in the same way. Obviously, some sports lend themselves more to the elimination tournament plan with its many variations; other sports can be organized best in league style, while some events can be set up in a variety of ways. The plan to be selected must take into account the available facilities, time allotted, and possible number of competitors. The director should determine whether or not the plan selected will entice the greatest possible number of entrants, and after entry is secured, he must determine whether the plan will provide sufficient competitive experience. The well-organized program must include a variety of organizational techniques which will provide added motivation and interest throughout the year.

The Chillicothe, Ohio, and Bakersfield, California, High Schools have very fine athletic programs involving large numbers in some phase of the interscholastic activity. Here teams and schedules are maintained in several sports for the varsity, junior varsity, freshman, sophomore, and midget teams. Many smaller high schools in the nation have also attempted to solve the competitive athletic problem for most of their boys with varsity teams in as many sports as possible. Even though these plans are most commendable, it must be admitted that two factors are left unsolved in the process: first, there will always be many boys still unable to make these teams; second, even the boys who compete in from one to four sports per year in such a program will completely miss the opportunity to learn satisfying sports skills in the many other sports that could be provided on an intramural basis. In such a school situation many of these intramural activities would naturally fall into the elimination tournament pattern. It might be said safely that no school exists in America today where some form of intramural competition cannot be included.

This chapter will discuss briefly some of the more popular and basic methods of organization for competition, together with some practical hints for their use. The following techniques are included:

1. Meets involving group and individual events.
2. Single elimination tournaments.
3. Double elimination tournaments.
4. Leagues with round-robin schedules and combination plans involving:
   a. Leagues followed by single elimination play-offs.
   b. Leagues followed by double elimination play-offs.
   c. Leagues followed by championship play-off series.
5. Ladder and pyramid tournaments of perpetual nature.
6. Ringer tournaments.
7. Qualifying rounds followed by match play eliminations.
8. The quickly organized jamboree.
9. Team matches by single or double individual play.
10. Special events and miscellaneous competitive ideas.

Meets Involving Group and Individual Events

All kinds of individual events can be grouped together into a large team meet, involving a point scoring system, and possibly employing physical fitness or sports skills testing techniques. The more common sports organized in meet style are indoor and outdoor track and field, swimming, gymnastics, track relays, ice skating carnival and races, physical efficiency meets, baseball and football field days, golf specialties, and the jamboree involving faculty or students in a series of competitive and recreational events, all individual in nature. Some of these will be discussed in greater detail as an organizational guide and check list.

INDOOR TRACK AND FIELD MEET

Many junior and senior high schools do not have adequate indoor track facilities, and, therefore, never include track and field events in their indoor program. This is a remediable situation, as all kinds of special events can be organized interestingly into an indoor meet. This will be discussed in greater detail later in this chapter. The indoor track meet should include a sizable group of events, modified according to the size and extent of the indoor plant. The following are typical events where proper facilities are available:

25-yard dash	220-yard dash*	Running broad jump
40-yard dash	440-yard dash*	Four-lap relay (4 men)
50-yard dash	880-yard run*	Eight-lap relay (4 men)
60-yard dash	High jump	40-, 50-, or 60-yard low hurdles
One-lap run	Pole vault	40-, 50-, or 60-yard high hurdles
Two-lap run	Shot put	Standing broad jump
Three-lap run		

* Indoor distances depend upon indoor lap length and can be modified.

Many colleges and universities feature the more purely individual events in the indoor track meet, conducting the outdoor track meet on the relay pattern. This brings in more group and team rivalry and reduces to a minimum the number of individual running events.

The indoor track meet should be scheduled over a two- or three-day period, thus allowing a large field of competitors to enter each day. In this way organization becomes easier, and more time elapses between preliminaries, semifinal heats, and the finals in the lane events. It is excellent practice to provide as many winning places as possible in every event. Points are then scattered more liberally among the participants, and everyone has more opportunity to break into the scoring. Most meets of any size should provide at least six places for points. An ideal scoring plan for six places would be 7-5-4-3-2-1, giving more emphasis to the champion. It would be proper also to award an additional meet point to any winner breaking the existing intramural record for that event. When six places are given in the relays the usual plan is to score 13-10-8-6-4-2.

If the intramural meet is to be successful and significant it should have careful planning and organization. Officials should be selected to handle the meet as efficiently as any varsity meet. Usually there are a number of adults in any community who derive real pleasure from the assignment of track official and consider it a privilege to act whenever invited, be the game varsity or intramural. Judges should be posted on the curves, the clerk should know his job and work fast to observe the time schedule, and the starter should be experienced. All the refinements that go to make an intercollegiate track meet outstanding should be employed for the intramural meet. Colored jerseys should be provided for all competitors who do not have their own. The track should be conditioned and marked. The take-offs and weight areas should be prepared as for varsity meets. An announcer should be present, preferably with a loudspeaker, and should be provided in advance with all data concerning competitors, lanes, time schedule, announcements, track records of all kinds, and other pertinent information.

The department should provide all groups and individuals with entry blanks well in advance of the deadline. Entries should be arranged, lanes selected, heats drawn, and other details perfected before starting time. Care should be taken to keep all spectators in the stands and away from the competitors—a precaution commonly overlooked in many intramural track meets. A typical intramural indoor track meet time schedule is given here as a suggestion.

Indoor Track Meet Schedule of Events

MONDAY

4:30	Pole vault and shot put
5:00	Preliminaries, 50-yard dash (or 25-yard dash)
5:20	Preliminaries, 60-yard dash
5:40	Two-lap run. Three sections. All men timed.
5:55	Preliminaries, 60-yard low hurdles

WEDNESDAY

5:00	Running high jump
5:00	Semifinals, 50-yard dash
5:15	Semifinals, 60-yard dash
5:30	One-lap run. Three sections. All men timed.
5:45	Semifinals, 60-yard low hurdles

FRIDAY

5:00	Running broad jump
5:00	Finals, 50-yard dash
5:10	Finals, 60-yard dash
5:20	Finals, 60-yard low hurdles
5:30	Four-lap relay (each team of four men). Several heats with places all given on time.

In the above time schedule the meet rules prohibit any entrant's competing in both dashes, and both the one- and two-lap runs.

THE OUTDOOR TRACK AND FIELD MEET

Some schools use a complete list of events that corresponds to the varsity program. Care should be taken to limit the longest distance run to 440 yards for junior high schools or 880 yards for senior high schools, since the competitors are not well enough conditioned for the longer distances. A minimum number of practice workouts should be required regardless of the events selected. It might be more preferable to feature the purely individual events in the indoor meet, using almost nothing but relays and the field events for the outdoor meet. Relays suggested are:

> 440-yard relay (each man running 110 yards)
> 880-yard relay (each man running 220 yards)
> Sprint medley relay (440-220-220-880 yards)
> 330-yard shuttle low hurdle relay (three men running 110-yard low hurdles at high hurdle distance)
> Medley relay (110-220-440-880 yards)

Track meets designed for younger students must include events suitable for the age level. If no track is available, a very fine competitive event may be arranged at the county fair grounds, on the school playgrounds, in a well-graded, cinder alleyway, or wherever the director may find it necessary to improvise facilities.

JUNIOR AND SENIOR HIGH SCHOOL COMBINATION PHYSICAL EFFICIENCY MEETS

Schools lacking complete indoor track facilities can develop real competitive enthusiasm for a meet which would employ the school gymnasium, the school hallways, and other indoor areas. It is not impossible to use the school hallways late in the afternoon for such events as dashes, low hurdles, and high hurdles. For the latter two events, mats should be placed carefully beyond each hurdle for the landing to avoid bruised feet. The following events have been used by some schools:

25-yard dash	Tip-up balance for time
30-yard dash	Swinging rope vault for height
30-yard low hurdles	Tumbling stunts
Standing broad jump	Obstacle race around gymnasium on improvised course
Running high jump	Hallway dashes of any distance possible
Pull-ups	Shuttle relays of many types
Medicine ball far throw	Maze running for time
Rope climb for time	Jump reach

Any number of places can be scored in this type of meet, since most places are awarded by individual measurement or timing. Records for all events can be set up and maintained from year to year to give added motivation, with certificates given to all record breakers. In addition, separate records can be developed for the freshman, sophomore, junior, and senior classes. This type of meet often acquaints the varsity coach with many potential team candidates.

Fig. 54. Fitness testing, using AAHPER National Fitness Tests, are a part of the program at Inglewood, California, and many other schools.

THE INTRAMURAL SWIMMING MEET

All schools having swimming pools should have at least one big intramural swimming carnival each year. The event can feature a combination of competitive events together with comedy and special ideas, or it can be purely a swimming meet. Since only one event can be conducted at a time, it is well to have two or three days set aside for the running of the intramural meet as in track. Colleges frequently use the following events: 50-yard free style, 100-yard free style, 100-yard breast stroke, 100-yard back stroke, 200-yard free style, 200-yard free style relay, and 150-yard medley relay. Syracuse University uses only the 50-yard free style, 50-yard breast stroke, 50-yard back stroke, and the 200-yard free style relay. The University of North Carolina employs the metric system using the following events in its meet: 25-meter free style, 25-meter back stroke, 50-meter breast stroke, 50-meter free style, 100-meter free style, 50-meter backstroke, 150-meter medley relay, and the 200-meter free style relay, together with the diving event.

Some schools eliminate the diving because of difficulties encountered in equitable scoring, although it seems that diving could be as well scored for intramural meets as for varsity competition. Another event often used is the plunge for distance, but unless a long pool is available it will soon be found that some boys can reach the end of the pool, making further records impossible. All entrants in the swimming meet should be pre-examined by the health service and should be required to have a minimum number of conditioning workouts before competition is permitted.

OTHER SPORTS INVOLVING THE MEET
ORGANIZATION

Gymnastics meets are easily organized for competitive purposes. Judging can be done best by the varsity coaches or physical education instructors, with point scoring based on form and execution. The gymnastics meet can be a natural outgrowth of the class activity in mat and apparatus work, and is particularly fitted to the junior and senior high school level. Schools having intercollegiate gymnastics find it quite easy to develop meets intramurally.

The ice carnival should include intramural skating races and relays and should be conducted very much like a track meet. The same care and planning should be observed in selecting and organizing the officials, and in preparing the rink and course. Colored dye can be used effectively on the ice for starting and finish lines, as well as for lanes, if desired.

Single Elimination Tournaments

The shortest route to a team or individual championship is by a single elimination tournament. The very directness of this method of organization is its greatest weakness, since one defeat will eliminate each competitor from further enjoyment of competition. Some events on the year's calendar might well be organized on this basis to provide variation and interest in the "sudden death" procedure. Often, facilities and time will not permit more lengthy methods of organization and the single elimination technique will be found most applicable. Some schools conduct team leagues or tournaments in such sports as handball, badminton, squash, and horseshoes, followed by an individual, single elimination tourney in the same event to determine the all-school champion. Schools lacking adequate leadership and staff often find that many tournaments can be organized on this basis, with play proceeding without much further staff supervision. It should be remembered that there will always be one less match than there are original entrants. While it is better to have multiples of four in the draw (4-8-16-32-64), such a condition is not mandatory, as any odd number can be placed in the first round with eliminations which will provide the second round with a desired even number of competitors. All single elimination tourney drawings should be posted on the bulletin boards, attractively arranged, and with all names, telephone numbers, and deadline or scheduled dates listed. All deadlines should be strictly enforced. Any variation from this procedure will only get the director into difficulties as the program proceeds. A sample single elimination tourney drawing is shown in Figure 55. In this illustration the bracket is drawn for eight players. Larger

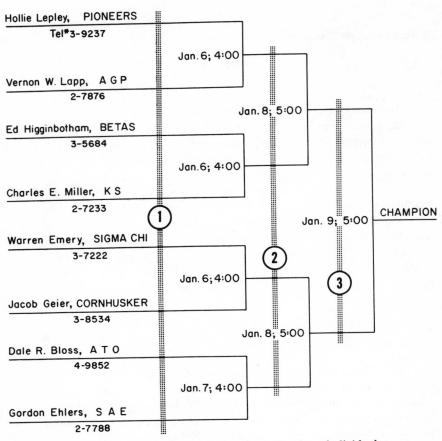

Fig. 55. A sample single elimination tournament bracket—individual sports.

tourneys could have as many such brackets as desired, with winners forming new single elimination play-off brackets for the championship.

In the single elimination style of play it is always desirable to seed individuals or teams according to known strength, thus avoiding early elimination of the stronger players because of a faulty draw. It is easy to determine third, fourth, fifth, and sixth places following the finals which always decide first and second place. The two losing semifinalists play for third and fourth place; and the four losing quarter-finalists play an elimination three-game tournament to determine fifth and sixth places, with one more game being played between the two losing teams if a determination of seventh and eighth place is necessary.

The consolation tournament is often added to the single elimination play since so many teams are eliminated early. Some states, such as Wisconsin, have consolation basketball tourneys for the high school interscholastic championships, but teams finding themselves in the consolation brackets are rarely happy, and the games in that bracket are usually not very popular. The same situation often exists in intramural tourneys. It might, therefore, be better to arrange a different style of tournament such as the double elimination, or some form of round-robin play. Diagram of a tourney draw using consolation championships is shown in Figure 56.

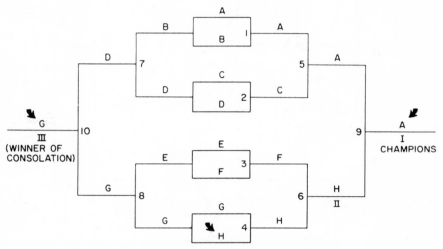

A, CHAMPION; H, RUNNER-UP; G, CONSOLATION WINNER

Fig. 56. Diagram of a tourney draw using consolation championship.

Double Elimination Tournaments

To prevent the possibility of teams being quickly eliminated by "off nights," and to provide additional competition, the double elimination tournament has been frequently used in recent years. In this tournament no team is eliminated until it has lost two games. Winners proceed to the right (see Figure 57) in the first eliminations; losers proceed to the left. If a winner of the first-round elimination flight loses to a winner of the second elimination flight, another game between the two teams must be played to determine the flight champion.

The double elimination tournament may also be set up in another form. Teams are drawn in the usual way with winners advancing into the second round. All teams losing first-round matches play off as in a consolation tournament. At this point the second-time losers are eliminated, but the losers who win their second game are allowed to return to competition with the original winners. To accomplish this an entirely new drawing must be made for the surviving teams, and play proceeds. Each team that loses twice drops out and each team that wins is placed in a new draw until a champion is finally declared.

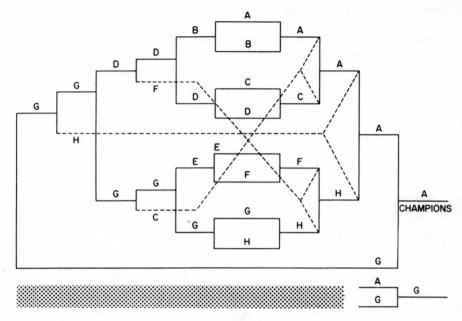

Fig. 57. Double elimination tournament bracket.

The University of Washington organizes swimming competition in double elimination tournament style. Meets are held daily between groups and teams in the late afternoons until a champion is declared.

Leagues With Round-Robin Schedules

The most satisfactory method of organization, if facilities and time permit, is the single or double round-robin schedule with all teams arranged in leagues. Most schools arrange the major team sports in this way. Every team is then privileged to meet every other team in its own league, eventually going on to play off with other league leaders for the all-school championship. When there is enough time it is desirable to play a double round-robin, thus permitting each team to meet every other team twice. If the year's calendar is composed of a large number of sports, it is usually better to have larger leagues of six, seven, or eight teams, with play-offs between leagues. This permits a fair number of contests in that sport during the regular league season, followed by the play-offs. It also allows each team to meet a greater number of teams instead of the same few teams more often. Organizations are then more willing to move on to the next sport in a crowded calendar instead of spending so much of the playing year in a single sport.

Every intramural director should have on hand a supply of printed or mimeographed league schedule sheets which are readily accessible for schedule making. These sheets should be made up for four-, five-, six-, seven-, and eight-team leagues and will save considerable time in office detail. Forms which can be used for two typical leagues are illustrated here. Play-offs following the termination of league schedules can be organized by single or double elimination play or by another round-robin schedule of the league champions. Assuming there have been four leagues formed in a sport, it is possible to arrange a play-off for only the four winners, thus settling the final four places. Then the four second-place winners compete in similar fashion for the fifth, sixth, seventh, and eighth places. Other schools might prefer to place all first- and second-place winners equally in the final play-off positions. Figure 58 shows a short-cut form which can be mimeographed and kept on hand for the quick drawing of a schedule where six teams are placed in round-robin competition. These forms can also be arranged for round-robin leagues of four- five-, seven-, eight-, and nine-team leagues. The form to be used for the round-robin league of seven teams is shown in Figure 59.

Fig. 58. Round-robin schedule for the league of six teams in any sport.

LEAGUE _____

1. _____   4. _____
2. _____   5. _____
3. _____   6. _____

DATE	TIME	PLACE	TEAM	vs.	TEAM
			1.	2.	
			3.	5.	
			4.	6.	
			1.	3.	
			2.	6.	
			4.	5.	
			1.	4.	
			2.	3.	
			5.	6.	
			1.	5.	
			2.	4.	
			3.	6.	
			1.	6.	
			2.	5.	
			3.	4.	

_____ League

	WON	LOST
1. _____	_____	_____
2. _____	_____	_____
3. _____	_____	_____
4. _____	_____	_____
5. _____	_____	_____
6. _____	_____	_____
7. _____	_____	_____

DATE	TIME	PLACE	TEAM	vs.	TEAM
			1.		2.
			3.		4.
			5.		6.
			1.		7.
			2.		3.
			4.		5.
			6.		7.
			1.		3.
			2.		4.
			5.		7.
			3.		6.
			1.		4.
			2.		5.
			3.		7.
			1.		6.
			4.		7.
			3.		5.
			2.		6.
			1.		5.
			2.		7.
			4.		6.

Fig. 59. Schedule for a seven-team league.

A very convenient form of organization of the round-robin league schedules together with elimination style of play-off is shown in Figure 60. This drawing gives the entire progress of the sport at a glance. By circling the number of each winning team in every game the record can be maintained on this one scorecard.

A good tournament for intramural purposes should provide for even and well-matched competition, should be neither too long nor too short, should exclude none from competition after only one or two games, should

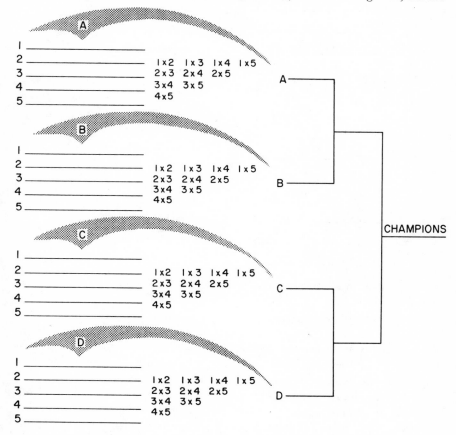

Fig. 60. Convenient organization form for round-robin leagues with the single elimination play-off series.

require few or no competitors to play a great many more games than other participants, and should produce a true champion. Figure 61 shows how twenty teams would be arranged under this plan. Two rounds of double elimination are played first to classify all teams into four leagues of five teams each. Teams are seeded as well as possible and a first round is played.

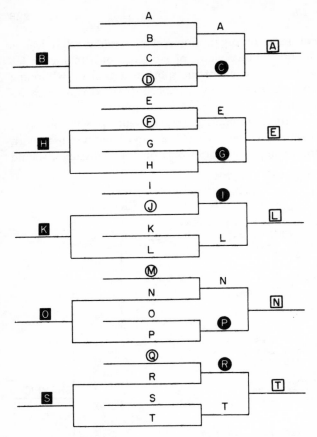

FIRST LEAGUE: A,E,L,N,T   THIRD LEAGUE: B,H,K,O,S
SECOND LEAGUE: C,G,I,P,R   FOURTH LEAGUE: D,F,J,M,Q

Fig. 61. Combination elimination round-robin tournament.

Then winners play winners and losers play losers. Teams winning twice are placed in the first league; teams winning once and losing once are placed in the second league and in a third; and teams losing twice are placed in the fourth league. This plan serves to classify all teams and play proceeds in round-robin style in each league. A final single elimination play-off settles the championship and gives everyone plenty of competition. This plan will discourage the practice of a team's losing the classifying rounds in order to gain a place in one of the weaker leagues.

    Schools using an elaborate individual or group point system may find it advantageous to arrange a play-off series for league winners of second, third, and fourth places as well as the champions of each league. This can be done easily, and all play-offs are scheduled to run simultaneously to avoid useless delays in completing the sport. Thus teams and individuals are given the opportunity to earn more points for participation even though they are not successful in pulling through to a championship play-off series. The point system should be arranged to permit play-off flight competition to be graded downward in cases of second-, third, and fourth-place winners, as they should not receive the same number of points as first-place winners.

Ladder Tournaments

Another form of competitive organization is the ladder tourney, often used by varsity coaches in the individual sports as a mechanism for constant competitive selection. The tournament is almost self-operative once it is organized. If a champion is to be declared it would be well to set a deadline date, giving all players ample opportunity to reach the top and stay there by virtue of their superiority. Contestants move up or down according to the results of their challenge matches. It is usually wise to seed the players of known ability and place them at the top. In this case any player in the ladder may challenge any of the first three. If the upper man loses the match he is moved to a place below his conqueror. Usually, however, the contestants are all placed in starting positions by lot, and each can only challenge the player above. If the lower one wins, the two exchange places on the ladder. Customarily, any player above who receives a challenge must play within a stipulated time or forfeit his position, unless he already is scheduled to meet another challenger. Once the contestants have met they cannot meet again until each has played with at least one other contestant. The ladder tournament is an excellent rating scale of ability for small groups, and would be best suited to smaller schools where the players are fairly well known to each other. Every program should experiment with this perpetual type of tournament in at least one sport as a change of pace.

Pyramid-Type Tournaments

A different form of ladder tournament, known as the pyramid, allows for more participation and challenging. A player may challenge any other player in his own horizontal row and if he is successful he may challenge anyone in the row above; if he is successful again, he changes places with his second opponents. This tournament plan is shown in Figure 62. Various methods may be used to portray the pyramid tournament on the bulletin board. A special board can be constructed with pegs or screw hooks placed in pyramid fashion. Cards bearing the names of all players are hung on the pegs, with cards being rearranged as matches are played.

Another form of the pyramid tournament is the bridge-type tourney. This type of competition is best adapted to games requiring courts, such as tennis, handball, or badminton. Courts are numbered, with one desig-

Fig. 62. Pyramid tournament.

nated as "head court" or Number One. The teams draw for original placing and play begins. Losers remain on the same courts and all winners advance one court closer to Number One. The winner at "head court" remains as long as he continues to win. The loser at "head court" drops back to the last court. Play continues for a predetermined number of rounds and the high percentage winner becomes the tournament champion when all matches are concluded.

Mabel Lee described another form of individual competitive organization known as the tombstone tournament.[1] The origin of this name is obscure but probably came into being since a marker is usually used to denote progress or scores. It can be used in a variety of activities. For competition in hiking the contestants maintain a record of their daily hikes over a prescribed period of time. On the closing day of the tournament the scores are totaled and comparisons made to determine places. It is an excellent motivation device and would be particularly popular at the junior and senior high school level. It is usually scored with a chart having start and finish markers and intermediate units indicating miles to be hiked, holes of golf to be played, or rounds of ammunition to be fired. The winner is the one who covers the distance in the shortest time, makes the highest total in rifle or archery, or has the lowest total in golf.

Another form of this tournament could be organized by setting a time limit of number of strokes in golf or swimming and ascertaining who covered the greatest distance in the allotted time. This can be arranged for teams as well as individuals. Another interesting variation is the progressive event in which a second teammate starts where the first left off and carries on to a certain point, giving way to the next team member, with each advancing or throwing as far as possible. There are many possible variations to this interesting and enjoyable type of competition.

The Ringer or Season's Low-Score Tournament

Another form of competition best used in golf, archery, free throws, and similar individual scoring events is the ringer tourney. In golf, as an example, the bulletin board might be arranged to accommodate all entrants,

228

allowing space for nine holes. All participants must compete on the same golf course throughout the tourney. During the season each player places his lowest and best score for each hole opposite the proper space on the card. At the end of the season the champion and all other ranking players are determined by the final medal total which is often below par. This is an excellent way to motivate varsity golf squads during the season of both practice and regular matches with other schools.

Qualifying Rounds Followed by Match Play Competition

The director in the larger school is often faced with the question of how to provide the best competitive method in some of the more individual events. He may elect to have each team and organization select its own small number of competitors, or he may open the event to all students. If the latter plan is used, a qualifying round is often the ideal solution to narrow a large field quickly to a perfect tournament number such as 16 or 32. In other words, the preliminary qualifying round is conducted by medal score with the best scorers selected to continue by match play elimination. In track and swimming this is done by time, by measurement of distance, or by preliminary elimination in heats. In such sports as golf, archery, rifle shooting, bowling, free throws, and basketball golf, the event can be wide open to all. At one school over 500 students participated in the qualifying round of basketball free throws with only the best 32 selected for the match play championship eliminations. It is also wise to select an additional six or eight low medalists to appear in case any of the low 32 fail to show for their matches at the appointed time, in which situation there would not have to be a single forfeit, with all matches played to the title. Another advantage of this plan is that the number of players selected are all in the process of self-seeding, and the arrangement of the final drawing can be completely seeded according to qualifying rank.

The Quickly-Organized Jamboree

This novel plan of organized competition is most popular at the junior and senior high school level. Announcement is made that all freshmen, for example, are invited to participate in a freshmen basketball jamboree. A time and place are indicated and no one knows what team selections will be made until the appointed time. Captains are chosen, and they in turn choose from the crowd present in rotation until all are organized. The tournament drawing is made on the spot by lot, and play proceeds immediately. Team allegiance at that age is often spontaneous and it becomes a great event for real fun and recreational pleasure. Short games can be played and often the entire tournament can be completed in a single day. Other jamborees can be scheduled for groups of similar age and ability whenever the time permits during the year. Any of these impromptu events can be worked into either the group or individual point systems as desired.

Team Matches by Single or Double Elimination

Most larger universities prefer to organize almost all sports on the league and round-robin basis. Sometimes a crowded calendar forces the use of an elimination tournament. Table tennis, handball, squash, badminton, horseshoes, tennis, golf, and similar sports can be set up in this fashion. Usually two singles and one doubles match constitute a team match, although three or five singles matches can be used as well. The team having the most individual wins moves on in the tournament, with the losers dropping by the wayside in single elimination or after the second loss in double elimination. Some schools conduct all these events in team style, following the entire tournament with an all-university individual tourney to decide the school champion. Another way to accomplish the same result without an entirely separate tournament is to keep individual standings of all matches played, to conduct the competition in league style so that all play the same number of matches, and then to rank individuals as well as teams on the basis of games won and lost. When this plan is used each match should always consist of three games instead of the best two out of three, so that games played would be equalized.

Special Events and Miscellaneous Competitive Ideas

No matter how the program is organized, the director should always be willing to arrange match games between special groups as the interest and need develop. Two or more teams from a particular college might normally have no chance to meet in regular league play and might desire to have a good friendly game. Perhaps fraternities will request the privilege of a game between their actives and pledges. Two Jewish fraternities may wish to square off for their own supremacy in each sport or two Agricultural College teams may want to have a game. Boys from one city may want to band themselves together to play a team from another city of the state. Whenever possible these games should be staged with proper leadership as a definite part of the total program.

Pennsylvania State University has conducted its annual swimming competition by a series of dual meets between groups arranged in double elimination style. The University of Minnesota and Iowa State have also used a series of dual meets to determine champions in some sports. Oregon State organizes its team swimming and track into dual meets, also conducting a larger all-university meet in both events.

Fig. 63. Start of the intramural cross-country run at the Citadel, Charleston, South Carolina.

The University of Washington organizes its cross-country competition somewhat like Purdue University. Three weeks of conditioning precede the competition. A series of time trial runs are then staged twice weekly for several weeks. Groups select the three best times of their own participants out of the entire series of runs, from which final places are scored.

Another event which must be staged in a single day is the high series championship tourney. In tennis, for example, all players would gather for the afternoon. Each man would be assigned three, four, or five different opponents and would play only a single set with each. His total score for the meet would be based on total games won and lost. Thus if his set scores were 6-0, 6-4, 6-3, 7-5, his record for the meet would be 25 games won and 12 games lost and percentages would be figured accordingly. This type of event could be employed in badminton, table tennis, horseshoes, squash, handball, and similar sports. One precaution should be observed in handball tournaments, especially when boys are competing who have not been playing frequently throughout the year. If too many games and matches are scheduled in one day, there is great danger of the participants' developing swollen hands and possible serious injuries.

Some schools provide special leagues and tournaments for the more

Fig. 64. Poster giving an idea of carnival activities at the University of Nebraska.

expert players in order to equalize competition. Often tourneys can be formed during the off season among members of the football squad and other varsity groups. Many California schools set up intramural tournaments by classification according to age, height, and weight. Many systems of testing classifications are employed and schools interested in a more scientific method of organizing competition will find much literature in the field. It is doubtful if the average school will find the detail connected with this type of organization worth the effort when many other more easily administered techniques bring such satisfying results.

Other forms of competition, such as the carnival, open house, and exhibition type of event, are described in Chapter 18 as motivating devices, also in Chapter 13 on financing the program. They offer a pleasing change from the usual leagues and tournaments. Ohio State University has conducted its annual intramural festival each year since 1914. The University of Nebraska has from time to time staged its Cornhusker Carnival. The poster for this event, shown in Figure 64, gives an idea of the scope of activity used on this occasion. The University of Chicago for years had its carnival; the University of California at Berkeley had its intramural carnival; and the University of Michigan has its annual open house. In most of these special programs a series of championship games are staged together with exhibitions and demonstrations by experts.

In conclusion, it should be repeated that every well-planned program will employ a variety of methods for organizing competition. Some techniques will fit certain sports better, others will permit the proper amount of time and promotional emphasis, and the combination of several techniques will give the program spice and interesting change.

A handy guide for the director is the chart shown in Figure 65. It is a quick index and aid in planning competition either in the elimination style or by round-robin schedules.

Number of Teams Entered	Single Elimination	Double Elimination		Round–Robin
	Number of Games	Number of Games Minimum	Number of Games Maximum	Number of Games
4	3	6	7	6
5	4	8	9	10
6	5	10	11	15
7	6	12	13	21
8	7	14	15	28
9	8	16	17	36
10	9	18	19	45
11	10	20	21	55
12	11	22	23	66
13	12	24	25	78
14	13	26	27	91
15	14	28	29	105

Fig. 65. Quick index guide in planning competition events.

REFERENCE

[1] *The Conduct of Physical Education* (New York: A. S. Barnes & Co., 1945), pp. 482, 483.

12

THE PROGRAM
FOR GIRLS AND WOMEN

Intramural sports and activities for girls have assumed a more significant role in education. The progress in this direction was not easy. Noneducational and professional influences have tried to fashion girls' sports to their own selfish ends. It is fortunate that education has had the assistance and leadership of so many capable and aggressive women physical educators who have recognized and courageously fought for desirable standards and practices in women's athletics. Intramurals play a dominant role in the best programs for girls' physical education.

The very nature of our changing society has emphasized the fact that girls are becoming more sports-minded. The last few years have seen a tremendous increase in feminine participation in outing activities and the winter ice and snow sports.

Educators have wisely held fast to the principle that the welfare of the participant is paramount. It is indeed commendable that the Women's Division of the National Amateur Athletic Federation adopted this as an underlying principle as early as 1923, and has never swerved from that ideal. Athletics for girls and women must be viewed in the light of the physical, social, and emotional welfare of the participant. Team victories and elaborate point systems to produce group pressure have been subordinated gradually to abundant play for the pure joy of healthful recreation.

234

Adult recreational interests for women are not built around team sports; this is one reason for the great increase in emphasis on the more individualized school athletic activities. However, it is well recognized that the greatest social values arise from group and team events during the school experience. This fact places a demand on the inclusion of both team and individual sports, and becomes more significant at the elementary, junior, and senior high school level.

Dorothy Ainsworth[1] found that some of the more competitive sports were noted quite early among women's colleges in this country. She states:

> From available information riding at Elmira in 1859 was the first sport mentioned. After this came boating at Vassar and Wells in 1879, swimming at Goucher in 1889, basketball at Smith in 1892, golf at Wells in 1894, fencing at Smith and track at Vassar in 1895, hockey at Goucher in 1898, lacrosse at Wellesley in 1901, volleyball at Smith in 1907, water polo and cricket at Bryn Mawr in 1919, and clogging at Barnard in 1920.

The more purely intramural sports emphasis for girls was not much in evidence before 1920, and the great increase in outing activities, outdoor winter sports, and co-recreational programs are of still more recent vintage.

A few years ago real co-recreational planning was still confined to only a minority portion of the colleges and universities of the nation. A study disclosed that only about 50 percent of the smaller colleges in America had thus far attempted organized co-recreational sports, and about half of those reported very few events. Among the larger universities only about 45 percent were carrying on such a program. It was noted also that the smaller colleges exceeded the larger universities in the extent and scope of mixed sports.[2] Since that date an increase in co-recreational activities has been observed. There is more participation in sports that can be played and enjoyed together. Chapter 13 is devoted exclusively to this phase of the program.

Statement of Policies and Procedures for Competition in Girls' and Women's Sports

by
The Division for Girls' and Women's Sports of AAHPER[3]

The Division for Girls' and Women's Sports of the American Association for Health, Physical Education, and Recreation believes the competitive element in sports activities can be used constructively for achievement of desirable educational and recreational objectives. Competition in and of itself does not automatically result in desirable outcomes, but competitive experiences may be wholesome and beneficial if they occur under favorable conditions and result in desirable conduct and attitudes.

The adoption of the best practices for the attainment of desirable outcomes is the responsibility of all associated with competitive events. Sponsoring agencies, players, coaches, officials, and spectators must share responsibility for valid practices in competitive sports if essential values are to be realized.

DGWS believes participation in sports competition is the privilege of all girls and women. Sports needs, interests, and abilities are best met through sports programs which offer a wide variety of activities and provide for varying degrees of skill. Limiting participation in competitive sports to the few highly skilled deprives others of the many different kinds of desirable experiences which are inherent in well-conducted sports programs. Development of all participants toward higher competencies and advanced skills is a major objective in all sports programs.

Where the needs of highly skilled girls and women are recognized and served, broad physical education intramural and informal extramural programs take precedence over an interscholastic program. The latter may be an outgrowth of such programs but is not a substitute.

DGWS presents the following policies and procedures through which desirable outcomes in competition may be achieved.

Forms of Competition

Competition is defined as the participation in a sport activity by two or more persons from which a winner can result. The outcomes of competition are determined by the quality of the participation. For the best results, organized competitive programs should offer equal opportunities to all in terms of individual ability, should be adapted to needs and interests of the participants, and should include a wide variety of activities rather than concentration on one or two.

Intramural Competition is defined as sports competition in which all participants are identified with a particular school, community center, club, organization, institution or industry, or are residents of a designated small neighborhood or community. This form of competition stresses the participation of the many. A well-rounded intramural program which offers a variety of activities, including co-recreational activities, at various skill levels should be sufficient to meet the needs and desires of the majority of girls and women.

For such an intramural program, it is the responsibility of the school or agency to provide the time, facilities, and competent, trained leadership with preference given to a woman if so qualified. Sound intramural programs are an outgrowth and complement of the school physical education program or the organized community recreation program.

Extramural Competition is defined as the plan of sports competition in which participants from two or more schools, community centers, clubs, organizations, institutions, industries, or neighborhoods compete. As conceived by DGWS, it also seeks to provide a broad base of competitive activities for participants of all levels of skill.

The informal and most desirable forms of extramural competition are *sports days* (school group participates as a unit), *play days* (representatives from each group are selected to play on play-day teams), *telegraphic meets* (results are compared by wire or mail), other *invitational events* (such as symposium, jamboree, game, or match).

The extramural program is planned and carried out to supplement the intramural program. For the best welfare of participants, it is essential that it be conducted by qualified leaders, be supported by organization funds, and be representative of approved objectives and standards for girls' and women's sports. This extension of the competitive sports program does not include rigid season-long schedules, intensive elimination leagues, or championships. However, it provides additional coaching by qualified staff members and affords group participation as a team in a series of games on appropriate tournament or schedule basis.

It is assumed the sponsoring organization recognizes its obligation to delegate responsibility for this program to the competent leadership of the women's department; and, likewise, recognizes that sponsorship entails forthright provision for funds, acceptable conditions of travel, protective insurance, appropriate facilities, equipment, and desirable practices in the conduct of the events.

Admission charges are not sanctioned, since such emphasis detracts from the real values and favorable welfare of the participants. Only in the proper budgeting for its proclaimed educational or recreational programs, can a sponsoring organization hope to establish a valid public concept of its functions.

A more formal and specialized form of extramural play commonly called *interscholastic* or *intercollegiate* may also have a place in the program. Such competition is characterized by selected groups trained and coached to play a series of scheduled games and/or tournaments with similar teams from other schools, cities, or institutions within a limited geographic area. It should be offered only when it does not interfere with the intramural and the informal extramural programs.

Adaptation of Competitive Sports for
Age-Level Groupings in School Programs

In *junior high school* it is desirable that intramural programs of competitive activities be closely integrated with the basic physical education program. Informal extramural events consistent with social needs and recreational interest of upper division groups may be planned occasionally. Interscholastic competition should not be offered under any circumstances for girls below senior high school level.

In *senior high school* a broadening program of intramural and informal extramural participation should be arranged as a complementary phase of a sound and inclusive instructional program in physical education, all conducted under qualified leadership and in a desirable environment. A school may consider arranging interscholastic competition provided the rest of the program is not jeopardized and the conditions listed under the extramural form of competition above are met.

Specifically, the following standards should prevail:

1. The health of the players is carefully supervised.
2. Girls and women are not exploited for the purpose of promotion.
3. The salary, retention, or promotion of an instructor is not dependent upon the outcome of the games.
4. Qualified women teach, coach, and officiate wherever and whenever possible, and in any case the professional training and experience of the leader meets established standards.
5. Approved, published DGWS rules are used.
6. Schedules are limited, not to exceed maximums set in DGWS standards for specific sports as defined in DGWS sports guides.
7. Games, where possible, are scheduled separately from the boys' games.
8. The program, including insurance for players, is financed by school funds and/or allocations of budget rather than gate receipts.
9. Provision is made by the school for safe transportation by bonded carriers with a chaperone responsible to the school accompanying each group.

Sound adaptations should be made for the high school too small to employ a qualified woman physical instructor, and/or too few girls enrolled to permit the organization of an intramural program. Intramural and informal extramural competition emphasizing individual and dual sports and/or activities organized for co-recreational play may be a partial solution. Play days, sports days, telegraphic meets, symposia, jamborees, invitational meets may be offered if the provisions listed above are incorporated. Only when the needs of the students cannot be met through intramural and/or informal extramural types of competition should interscholastic competition be considered. Only under the conditions listed above should interscholastic competition be provided.

In *Colleges and Universities*. The philosophy that a well-rounded intramural and informal extramural program offering a variety of activities is sufficient to fulfill the needs and desires of the majority of girls and women should also be applied to the programs of colleges and universities. If it is considered desirable that opportunities be provided for the highly skilled beyond the intramural and informal extramural programs, the amount and kind of intercollegiate competition should be determined by the women's physical education department in accord with administrative policy. Any institution which assumes responsibility for taking part in intercollegiate competition assumes:

1. Sponsorship of women participants as individuals or as members of teams who represent the institution and for whom part or all expenses may be paid.

2. Sponsorship of events in which:
   a. Colleges or universities organize and promote competitive events.
   b. Outside agencies use college or university facilities.

Furthermore, if an institution does assume the responsibility for any type of sponsorship the following principles should govern these intercollegiate events:

1. They should be conducted in conformance with DGWS standards of health, participation, leadership, and publicity.
2. They should not curtail the intramural and the informal extramural programs of the sponsoring institutions or the institutions entering participants.
3. They should not include events in which women participate:
   a. As members of men's intercollegiate athletic teams.
   b. In touch-football exhibition games, or any other activities of similar type.
   c. Either with or against men in activities not suitable to competition between men and women, such as basketball, touch football, speedball, soccer, hockey, or lacrosse.

If a college student wishes to go beyond the program offered by her institution, DGWS does not oppose participation by individuals in competitive events sponsored by other organizations, provided such events are conducted in accordance with the basic principles of DGWS. If a student contemplates entering events which appear to jeopardize her welfare, she should be given guidance which will help her to make wise decisions.

Adaptation of Competitive Sports for Age-Level Groupings in Public and Private Recreation Agency Programs

The Division recognizes that the sports programs of public and private recreation agencies make a valuable contribution to girls and women. Community sports competition is organized on the basis of neighborhood population, membership in an agency, religious or fraternal affiliation, or occupation of the participant.

However, the aims and objectives of community recreation agencies in their conduct of sports programs are similar to those of the schools. By using common rules and applying basic standards in organizing competition, many girls and women can be given the opportunity to develop skills and to enjoy a desirable kind of competition. If individuals are grouped according to age and skill-ability, the statements of policy outlined above can be applied by these agencies in organizing desirable forms of competition.

The formation of leagues is the organizational structure through which many recreation programs are conducted. The competition provided in public and private recreation may be comparable to school programs by the following interpretations.

Intramural competition: Competition in which the participants are from the same neighborhood, recreation center, playground, institution, or community.

Extramural competition: Competition in which the participants are from two or more neighborhoods, recreation centers, playgrounds, institutions, or local communities. It includes the informal forms of sports days, play days, telegraphic meets, invitational events.

It also includes the more highly organized form of extramurals which resemble interscholastic competition in that the participants come from different localities, towns or cities, districts or regions, and are coached to play a series of scheduled games and/or tournaments.

Modifications will be required in planning controls for competition depending upon the age level involved:

Girls under senior high school age: Competition should be limited to intramural games; that is, games with teams of the same age and ability from the same neighborhood, playground, recreation center, or league. Informal extramural events consistent with social needs and recreational interests of junior-high-school-age groups may be arranged with similar teams from other playgrounds, centers, or leagues.

Girls of senior high school age: Intramural and extramural competition as defined above may be arranged provided the standards listed above for senior high school, items 1-9, are upheld. A player should affiliate with only one team in one sport.

Girls over senior high school age: Competition defined as interscholastic competition may be arranged provided standards cited above are upheld.

Sponsorship by recreation agencies of the participation of women in tournaments and meets organized at successively higher levels (local, sectional, national) should be governed by the best practices for safeguarding the welfare of the participants. The organization, administration, and leadership of such competitive events should be conducted so that the basic policies of DGWS are upheld.

Departmental Relationships

Since interschool athletic competition for girls and women is very limited in this nation, the integration of the physical education program to include a carefully planned system of intramurals is of utmost importance. Since exploitation of the stars and the most skilled is not a factor, all personnel and facilities can be directed toward the well-rounded program. Directors of the girls' and women's program have had to do far too much battling for equal use of the school plant, and indications point to a rapid breakdown of any barriers between men's and women's physical education departments. School administrators are coming to safeguard a more equi-

(Courtesy of Theodore T. Abel.)

Fig. 66. Girls in the Pittsburgh, Pennsylvania, high schools participate in diversified intramural sports.

table use of the indoor and outdoor facilities, and to promote occasional opportunities for the boys and girls to participate together. Some colleges have combined the administration of men's and women's physical education, each with its separate chairmen, in an effort to achieve this desirable goal.

In the women's program there is frequently a closer cooperation between the required and voluntary classes and the recreational sports offered. Skills in a great variety of activities which can be enjoyed in the after-school intramural games are being taught. Separate and very complete facilities are being constructed for the women to make this expansion possible. It is absurd to suggest, however, that men and women must have separate tennis courts, golf courses, and bowling alleys, when it is evident that close cooperation between the two departments will guarantee the shared use of all these necessary but expensive play areas.

Organization of Competition

The methods used in organizing girls' and women's competition differ quite definitely from present practices for boys and men. The growth of the Girls' Athletic Association (G.A.A.), and the Women's Athletic Association (W.A.A.), has brought about more and more student leadership. It is common practice for the department to recognize, encourage, and stimulate these organizations to administer as broad a sports program as possible using sport clubs as its basis. It is the duty and function of the department to see that proper and energetic leadership provides adequate participation in organized form in each club activity. It is also a duty to sponsor open tournaments and leagues in all sports if closed club events are carried on by the various clubs, so that every student may participate. Usually the W.A.A. sponsors open tournaments which, if properly organized, will be sufficient to attract all interested students. Since many of the techniques used by girls in the organization of competition are similar to the boys', the material found in Chapters 4 and 11 need not be repeated here.

It is significant to note that the American Association for Health, Physical Education and Recreation added a special professional staff member in 1962 to assist in the development of G.A.A., W.A.A., W.R.A. (Women's Recreation Association), and all forms of campus recreation for girls and women.

The Program of Activities

Chapter 6 gives a more detailed discussion of the sports best suited for girls and women. Occasionally, playing rules will be slightly changed and local provisions made. Naturally, many of the sports listed previously in this book are not suitable for the girls' program, particularly those requiring unusual endurance, physical contact, and violent effort. Modifications must naturally be made in the selection of track and field events. The following selected events, sports, and activities have been successfully used in various schools. Specific rules for each of the activities can be found in greater detail in other publications.

THE ELEMENTARY SCHOOL PROGRAM

The earlier and primary grades should not have highly organized competitive events, but intramural and recreational activities can be arranged, especially for the upper elementary grades, during the noon hour and for a brief period after school. All of the activities listed below have been used for this age group:

Aerial darts	Field ball	Roller skating
Archery	Free throws	Shuffleboard
Basketball (modified)	Gymnastics (simple)	Skiing
Bat ball	Hiking	Snow games
Bean bag toss	Hit-pin-ball	Soccer (modified)
Bowling (improvised)	Horseshoes	Softball (modified)
Box hockey	Ice skating	Speedball (modified)
Captain ball	Kickball	Table tennis
Checkers	Kite flying	Tether ball
Chinese Checkers	Marble tournaments	Tether tennis

Croquet	Newcomb	Volleyball
Dart games	Paddle tennis	Zel-ball
Deck tennis	Relays and stunts	

JUNIOR-SENIOR HIGH SCHOOLS

The following activities are listed for use in the girls' program for the junior and senior high school. Some of these are best suited to the upper grades while others fit the natural interests of the younger girls. This list is not arranged by seasons, since some of the activities can be used at any time during the school year while others can be used in either fall or spring seasons, and the entire selection of events depends much on the geographical location of the particular school.

Archery	Field bombardment	Rebound ball
Archery golf	Field hockey	Rifle shooting
Badminton	File basketball	Ring toss
Ball throw	Floor hockey	Roll ball
Ball toss	Forward pass	Roller skating
Basketball	Four-team volleyball	Rounders
Basket speedball	Free throws	Seven-up
Bat ball	German bat ball	Shuffleboard
Battle ball	Goal Hi	Six passes and shoot
Beanbag toss	Golf	Skiing
Bicycling	Golf specialties	Soccer
Bombardment	Guards and forwards	Soccer dodge ball
Borden ball	Handball	Softball
Bounce ball	Hiking	Speedball
Boundary ball	Hit pin ball	Spot shooting
Bowling	Horseback riding	Swimming
Box basketball	Horseshoes	Table tennis
Box hockey	Ice skating	Team duck on rock
Captain ball	Indoor baseball	Team ten pins
Center ball	Indoor scoccer	Tennis
Checkers	Indoor speedball	Tether ball
Circle bounce ball	Kick ball	Throw and overtake ball
Coasting	Kick pin ball	Throw ball
Complete the circuit	Lifesaving	Tobogganing
Corner dodge ball	Line soccer	Touch and return
Croquet	Line volleyball	Track (modified)
Clock golf	Net ball	Volleyball
Dart games	Newcomb	Volleyball (giant)
Dodge ball	Norwegian ball	Volley ground ball
Double bombardment	Novice speedball	Volley Newcomb
Deck tennis	Paddle badminton	Volley tennis
Duck pin bowling	Prison dodge ball	Wall ball
Fencing	Progressive dodge ball	Zel-ball
Field ball	Punch ball	

THE PROGRAM OF ACTIVITIES FOR COLLEGE
AND UNIVERSITY WOMEN

Aerial darts	Duck pin bowling	Roller skating
Aerial tennis	Fencing	Shuffleboard
Archery	Field ball	Skiing
Archery golf	Field hockey	Snow sculpturing
Badminton	Golf	Soccer
Bicycling	Golf specialties	Softball
Boating	Gymnastics	Speedball
Bowling	Hiking	Swimming
Camping	Horseback riding	Table tennis
Canoeing	Ice skating	Tennis
Dancing	Lifesaving	Tobogganing
Dart games	Outing activities	Volleyball
Deck tennis	Rifle shooting	

Typical Programs in Various
Schools Throughout the Nation

THE CLIFTON PARK JUNIOR HIGH SCHOOL

The girls' intramural program used in the past at Clifton Park Junior High School, Baltimore, Maryland, has been supervised by women teachers for an enrollment of more than 1,000 girls. The boys and girls each have separate gymnasiums. The program is divided into four periods of eight

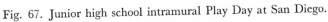

Fig. 67. Junior high school intramural Play Day at San Diego.

weeks each. Emphasis is placed upon participation of all in one or more activities, rather than on the students' earning places on a team or the instructors' devoting time and attention to a few skilled performers. According to one director of the program, "The span of interest in early adolescence is short, and the student's world is crowded with new ideas and projects to which she is subjected, which thereby demands a wide and large number of activities requiring a minimum of skill and perfection. This is the age concerned with doing and activity for the sheer joy derived from it. Since all girls are not alike, the program must be varied and elastic, both for individual and team activities."

The program of activities at Clifton Park has been arranged as follows:

	FIRST QUARTER	SECOND QUARTER	THIRD QUARTER	FOURTH QUARTER
	Badminton	Tumbling	Tumbling	Track and field
	Horseback riding	Horseback riding		
Mon.	Badminton (A)	Tumbling (A)	Tumbling (A)	Track and field (A)
		Bowling (B)		Softball (B)
Tues.	Horseback	Horseback	Bowling (B)	Horseback
	riding (A)	riding (A)	Volleyball (A)	riding (A)
	Soccer baseball (B)	Basketball (B)		Track and field (B)
Wed.	Table tennis (B)	Basketball (A)	Volleyball (B)	Volleyball (A)
				Softball (B)
Thurs.	Horseback	Horseback riding	Dance (B)	Horseback
	riding (A)	Dance (B)		riding (A)
				Hit ball (B)
Fri.	Roller skating*	Ice skating*	Ice skating*	
Sat.	Swimming (October 9 to December 17 and March 12 to May 25)			

Fig. 68. Girls Basketball Sports Day in the Dade County high schools at Miami, Florida.

Time: Activities in the gymnasium—2:45 to 4:30 P.M.

Bowling from 3:00 to 5:00 P.M., depending on number of games bowled.

Horseback riding; two classes at 3:15 to 4:15 and 4:30 to 5:30 P.M.

Pupils electing horseback riding are taken back and forth in a station wagon twice weekly to the Lakeside Riding Stable, which is five miles out.

Note: (A), Teacher, Miss "A"
(B), Teacher, Miss "B"
* Pupils on their own at one of the community rinks, with athletic cards punched by cashier and credit given toward awards.

Points are credited for athletic awards so that it is possible for the not-too-athletic girl to be accorded honors as well as those more skilled, since much weight is given attendance and participation as follows:

50 points for full-time participation
40 points for seven practice days
30 points for six practice days
25 points for four or five practice days
Team members on winning teams receive a bonus of 15 points for first place, 10 points for second place, and 5 points for participation in full-time games.

Awards are given according to the number of points earned:

150 points   Certificate signed by principal and athletic adviser
300 points   Felt school seal
600 points   Numerals
1,000 points   Sweater
1,200 points   Gold medal

Girls at Clifton Park have received honors by joining the various activities regardless of ability. Inferiority complexes are eliminated since it is not generally known by others whether points have been accumulated through victories won or by activities participation.

UNIVERSITY CITY SENIOR HIGH SCHOOL
ACTIVITIES AND AWARDS

The senior high school at University City, Missouri, has sponsored the following program of activities, with awards listed accordingly:

A certificate of award and the privilege of getting a five-inch chenille letter are awarded to each girl who has accomplished the following in Class A or B. After the first year, one inch will be added to the size of the letter for each additional year. No girl will be eligible to receive a certificate unless she evidences good sportsmanship in all situations.

Class A, Intramural.—Qualify in No. 1 and No. 2.

1. Member of good standing of three of the following group sport teams:

   Hockey   Volleyball   Basketball   Softball

2. Member of good standing of three of the following teams of individual sports:

   Archery   Badminton   Bowling   Golf
   Swimming   Tennis   Track   Table tennis
   Horseback riding   Semester's membership in Taberna

A second year's membership on a group sport intramural team may be substituted for one of the individual sports above. Three different five-mile hikes a semester, under school leadership, is considered an individual sport.

Class B, Interschool.—Choose either No. 1, 2, or 3:

Member of good standing of:

1. Four class varsity squads.
2. Two school varsity squads.
3. One school varsity squad and two class varsity squads.
4. Leader's Club.

Fig. 69. Roller skating opportunities are provided for all students at Flint, Michigan, both outdoors and in all gymnasiums.

GARY, INDIANA

In the Gary, Indiana, schools the girls' intramural program has a point system set up on a 100-point basis. In both organized and unorganized activities the completion of a specific unit of activity is required before credit is given. For each eight hours of participation 100 points are awarded. No credit is given for required physical education. Ample opportunity is given to each student to complete each activity unit. Each year that a girl earns 750 points she receives a chenille bar to be worn on a sweater. When she earns 1,500 points she receives a chenille school emblem, and for 3,000 points a felt banner.

Points are recorded on permanent individual record sheets. Various other methods can be used. Stamps may be given after a unit of activity is completed; these are pasted in special booklets. Or, a form may be prepared with the various units of activity listed, and as soon as a unit is completed it is initialed or checked by the faculty adviser.

The activities for which credit is given depend, of course, on the conditions existing within each school in the city. It may or may not be advisable to give credit for required physical education, for making a team, or for certain health activities. Each adviser decides for herself what plan is best for her association and school.

THE UNIVERSITY OF NORTH CAROLINA

The W.A.A. and the sports clubs play a dominant role in the program at the University of North Carolina.[4] The W.A.A. sponsors the following activities for competition:

Archery	Basketball	Softball	Tennis
Badminton	Hockey	Swimming	Volleyball

Sports clubs are organized to supervise and conduct tournaments in hockey, tennis, swimming, modern dance, basketball, and occasionally other sports. These clubs also participate in sports and play days with other North Carolina colleges. They also sponsor clinics and tournaments on the campus to stimulate additional interest. Membership in all clubs is through tryouts. Competitive units used are sororities, dormitories, and town girls. A supremacy trophy is given annually. All awards are based on the following point system of the W.A.A.:

Individual Awards for Participation

OFFICERS

President	50 points	Publicity Chairman	20 points
Vice-President	35 points	Awards Chairman	30 points
Secretary	30 points	Representatives	30 points
Treasurer	30 points		

CLUBS

Membership	15 points	Second varsity	5 points
Chairmanship	20 points	Tourney finalist	10 points
First varsity	10 points	Tourney semifinalist	5 points

DORMITORY AND SORORITY PARTICIPATION

Participation		Tourney finalist	10 points
(Membership)	10 points	Tourney semifinalist	5 points
Captains	5 points	Timers and scorers	3 points

Numerals are given for 75 points, monograms for 150, and a bracelet for 200 points. White blazers are awarded to the senior girls who have contributed the most to the W.A.A. program. These seniors are selected by the W.A.A. Council. All awards are presented by the president and awards chairman of the W.A.A. at a final banquet held near the end of the school year. All women students of the University may attend this annual banquet.

UNIVERSITY OF MINNESOTA

The Physical Education Department at the University of Minnesota works closely with the W.A.A. in sponsoring a fine program in intramural sports for women. During New Student Week each freshman is given an attractive four-page booklet which contains the W.A.A. activities schedule for the year. Excerpts from this booklet are reproduced here since they give an excellent picture of the scope and nature of the Minnesota program.[5]

Fig. 70. Girls line up their sights on the targets at the L. A. City Schools Youth Services Section, All-City Girls' High School Archery Tournament.

(Los Angeles City Schools Youth Services Section photo.)

Women's Athletic Association of the
Department of Physical Education
for Women

The Women's Athletic Association gives every coed the opportunity to take part in recreational activities and competitive sports, such as archery, badminton, basketball, bowling, dancing, golf, horseback riding, softball, swimming, tennis, and volleyball. The ninth hour daily and several evenings a week are devoted to W.A.A. activities at Norris Gymnasium. Belonging to W.A.A. gives you the chance to enjoy games familiar to you, to learn new play activities, to meet other students, and to engage in competitive sports.

The direction and leadership of the entire program depends upon the interest and initiative of students devoted to the service of the organization. The W.A.A. Board, including the officers and heads, meets weekly in the W.A.A. lounge to plan and direct the activities.

Make your headquarters at Norris Gym!!

W.A.A. Calendar
Activities at Norris Gymnasium for women

FALL QUARTER

September, Sports Shorts—A preview of the Physical Education Department and W.A.A. activities.

October, W.A.A. Mitten Mixer.

October, Tryouts for the honorary clubs—Orchesis, Aquatic League, Pegasus, and Tennis Club.

November, W.A.A. balloon sale, Homecoming game.

October-December, W.A.A. sports: recreational swimming daily, badminton, archery, bowling, volleyball tournament; honorary clubs: Orchesis, Aquatic League, Pegasus, Tennis Club.

WINTER QUARTER

January, Tryouts for honorary clubs.

January, W.A.A. Snow Week activity.

January-March, W.A.A. sports: recreational swimming daily, speed swimming, archery, basketball, bowling, and badminton tournaments.

SPRING QUARTER

April-May, Aquatic League Show, Orchesis Recital, Pegasus Horse Show.

April-May, State Play Days, Racket Day.

May, Aquatic League Canoe Trip, Pegasus House Party.

May, Award dinner.

April-June, W.A.A. sports: recreational swimming daily, speed swimming, archery, bowling, golf, softball, tennis, and badminton tournaments, honorary clubs.

The department also prints and distributes a larger W.A.A. handbook which is cleverly illustrated throughout with comic sport figures. The booklet includes information on standards, personal conduct, constitution of W.A.A., bylaws, dues, etc.

First award at Minnesota is the "M," given after eight quarters of W.A.A. activity, each quarter consisting of ten activity hours. The final award is the W.A.A. Seal, which is based on sportsmanship, a spirit of service to W.A.A. and to the University, scholarship, poise, and an interest in healthful living. This award is given by a committee consisting of the head of the department, faculty W.A.A. sponsor, newly elected president of W.A.A., two other members of the W.A.A. Board, and any other person deemed necessary. It is a secret committee appointed by the president at the beginning of the spring quarter. All students going out for any activity must pay an annual dues of 25 cents to W.A.A. Minnesota has had splendid results with its apprentice system whereby each girl on the Board appoints an assistant of her own choosing who may ultimately succeed her on the Board. Subsidiary organizations to W.A.A. are the Aquatic League, Junior Pegasus, Senior Pegasus, Junior Orchesis, Senior Orchesis, and Tennis Club. Special features are occasionally presented, such as Valentine Open House for women and the Shamrock Mixer for men and women. Another feature is the occasional canoe trip down the beautiful St. Croix River. The Honorary Modern Dance Society, Orchesis, presents a recital each spring. Membership in the society is gained through tryouts.

Fig. 71. Intramural hockey at Northeast High School, Lincoln, Nebraska.

The Aquatic League, women's honorary swimming society at Minnesota, presents a two-day swimming and aquatic show each year. Another feature is the annual Racket Day, which features a play day for women tennis players from several Minnesota colleges; this is usually held in Minneapolis. Social play nights are conducted, and occasional outing trips are taken to Lake Johanna and Minnehaha Park.

THE UNIVERSITY OF OKLAHOMA

The women's intramural program at the University of Oklahoma is unique in many of its features.[6] This is particularly true with certain phases of its organization and administration, its official's class, the high percentage of participation necessitating a limit to all entries, opportunities for co-recreation, qualifying scores for entering tournaments, and the separation from, but cooperation with, the women's recreation clubs.

Fig. 72. Finals of Girls' high jump in Nationwide Track and Field Project of OPERATION FITNESS-USA at Berea, Ohio. Girls enjoy participation and competition in appropriate track and field events.

The administration of the Oklahoma program is headed by a faculty director with faculty assistants in specialized sports. There is one student intramural manager, one student assistant intramural manager, one student sport head for each activity, one student intramural organizer for each competitive unit, and one student clerical secretary. The Intramural Council is made up of all the above and governs all policies pertaining to the program.

Competitive units are composed of sororities and independent zones, the latter being divided according to population distribution. With twenty competitive units (fourteen sorority and six independent zones), all competition is divided into two competitive brackets. The Red bracket and the Blue bracket are each composed of seven sororities and three independent zones. In every sport tournament the winners of both brackets play each other in the grand finals. Every season there is a shift of some units from one bracket to another. The program of activities used competitively includes:

FIRST SEASON (Sept.–Oct.)	SECOND SEASON (Nov.–Jan.)	THIRD SEASON (Feb.–March)	FOURTH SEASON (April–May)
Hockey	Volleyball	Basketball	Softball
Tennis	Swimming	Tennequoits	Badminton
Archery	Table tennis	Dance festival	Golf

In each sport season there is at least one team sport and one individual sport. An event is planned each season for the physically handicapped student, preceded by a medical examination. A student may enter only two out of three activities each season. Occasionally some of the following popular sports are substituted or added to the above schedule: shuffleboard, mass badminton, pool, and bowling. As a result of too many unskilled students entering the archery and golf tournaments, with its accompanying danger hazard and boredom element, the entrants must now qualify to enter both events.

The dance festival provides opportunity to select men as partners. Extramural tournaments are conducted in mixed tennis doubles and mixed bowling.

A large hand-carved intramural honor board stands in the intramural office. Recognition to the winners of each tournament is offered by placing their names on the honor board. The only other form of recognition is a cup awarded at the end of the year to the sorority or independent unit with the highest "percentage of participation winner." This figure is reached by a simple point system and formula which determine the ratio of activities entered and won to the number of persons in that unit who have participated. Oklahoma recently eliminated the point system and awards, but continued the recognition of the honor board for champions.

A voluntary "official's class" is conducted paralleling the intramural program. Physical education majors are encouraged to attend, and non-majors may also participate. The objectives of the class are to train officials to pass a W.N.O.R.C. (Women's National Official Rating Corps) test in all possible sports, and to furnish officials for all intramural games. Laboratory work in the professional course on intramurals requires conducting and officiating intramural tournaments.

In a great many universities the women's intramural programs are sponsored by and within the Women's Athletic Association. At the University of Oklahoma the W.R.A. and the women's intramural program are organized completely apart from each other. It is felt that they satisfy two different purposes. The W.R.A. serves the higher skilled student through its specialized clubs, and furnishes social parties, while intramurals are for the unskilled participant. Great cooperation is evident, however, between these two groups. The specialized sports clubs assist considerably with coaching and inspiring teams entering those particular intramural activities.

Oklahoma prints and distributes two very attractive handbooks each year. A folder entitled "Intramurals for Women" describes the program, discusses the awards system, gives a directory of all facilities and equipment available, presents the personnel organization, and gives a diagrammatical outline of the entire intramural administrative structure. The handbook distributed by W.R.A. is entitled *Women's Recreation Association and the Intramural Program*. It is replete with catchy descriptive material of great motivating design, together with clever sports sketches done by students to highlight each sport presented. Following is an excerpt from the page on Archery Club:

> Would you like to be another Robin Hood, or learn the skills of little cupid? Well, here's your chance right on the campus. Come out and enjoy this ever-popular sport. It's healthful, skillful, and an individual sport that can be played throughout the year. You can experience the thrill of sending your arrow straight to the target with true marksmanship.

The Badminton Club meets at least once a week to participate and increase skills. It puts on exhibitions, represents Oklahoma at sports days with other schools, and has its rackets furnished by the department. The Duck's Club offers the opportunity for swimming instruction and practice for later competition in intramurals and the telegraphic meet, and for the water pageant each spring. Membership is based on swimming and diving tests and lifesaving. The Dusty Travelers Club organizes and sponsors hikes, cook-outs, and weekend parties. Orchesis meets weekly throughout the year, has a series of lecture demonstrations, conducts two major programs annually, and stimulates interest in the dance. The Racket Club holds tryouts, conducts ladder tournaments, holds picnics with steaks over the grill, and competes in tournaments and meets on the campus. It also conducts an annual tennis exhibition and clinic.

The Swing Club promotes interest in golf, having matches with other schools as well as its own tournaments. It holds intraclub picnic tournaments, clinics, and mixed foursomes. The Timber Cruisers ride horseback. Seasonal sports clubs in hockey, softball, basketball, and volleyball provide weekly practice and instruction, as well as participation in Sports Days with other schools. W.R.A. parties highlight each semester's activities, with games, refreshments, and entertainment.

THE UNIVERSITY OF CALIFORNIA
AT BERKELEY

The University of California program is administered by interclass and intramural boards, each meeting weekly. Sports are sponsored by both groups. Academic eligibility is required of all participants. Through the W.A.A. a unique system of awards is conducted, which is described here in detail.[7]

Interclass

a. Certificates shall be awarded at the Field Week Banquets to every woman making a first team. All first teams shall be announced.
b. "All California" players having the qualifications of first team plus superior ability in a sport shall be chosen by the coach and shall be announced at the Field Week Banquet.
c. The Field Week Cup shall be awarded to the class which has been outstanding in the greater number of sports for that term.

Fig. 73.

UNIVERSITY OF CALIFORNIA W. A. A. RECORD CARD																							
Name ____ LAST NAME ____ GIVEN NAME ____ Class ____																							
SEASON:	F'		S'		F'		S'		F'		S'		F'		S'								
Participation:	1st Team	Int-Class	Int-Mural																				
Archery																							
Badminton																							
Basketball																							
Crop and Saddle																							
Fencing																							
Hockey																							
Riflery																							
Sailing																							
Softball																							
Swimming																							
Table Tennis																							
Tennis																							
Volleyball																							

Intramural

a. A certificate shall be awarded at the Field Week Banquet to every woman participating at least six times.
b. A certificate shall be awarded at the Field Week Banquet to each of the organizations receiving the greatest number of points for participation and winning in each sport.
c. The intramural plaque shall be awarded the organization receiving the greatest number of points for participation and winning.

Pennant "C"

A blue pennant with a yellow block "C" under the letters "W.A.A." shall be awarded at the Field Week Banquets to every woman who has participated for five semesters in at least two sports. Students transferring from another institution shall participate at least two semesters in at least two sports at the University of California and shall not receive the award before the end of the Junior year.

The Women's "C" Society

Membership to Women's "C" Society shall be granted on the basis of :
a. Active membership in the Women's Athletic Association.
b. Proficiency in two sports.
c. Correct posture and appearance.
d. Sportsmanship.
e. Scholarship average of 18 per cent more grade points than units for entire college course.
f. Service.
No freshman or first year transfer shall be eligible.
The insignia shall be a blue and gold block "C" presented on blazer.
The committee for granting the "C" shall consist of the coaches of the different sports, the active members of the "C" Society, and the Executive Officer of the Physical Education Department Division for Women. The chairman of this committee shall be the President of the Women's "C" Society.
This committee shall meet three times during each term before the Field Week Banquet to propose and decide upon candidates.
A majority of two-thirds of active members shall be necessary to elect to membership.
The Women's "C" shall be granted at the Field Week Banquet each term.

The W.A.A. at California publishes a very attractive intramural handbook each year. It gives the sports programs, uses a series of appropriate slogans, and is supplemented from time to time by mimeographed bulletins.

THE UNIVERSITY OF LOUISVILLE

The recreational and intramural program at the University of Louisville supports the standards and policies established by the National Section on Girls' and Women's Sports of AAHPER. The program is organized and managed by the Women's Recreation Association. Seven tournaments are scheduled in each of two leagues, one for the more highly skilled and the other for beginners and average players. The W.R.A. calendar also includes the following:

1. Annual square dance for the University students and faculty, including community friends.
2. Cooperation with physical education major students in planning a city and county High School Play Day.
3. Handling concessions at varsity sports events.
4. Participating on the Dean of Women's Leadership Committee.
5. Participating in the University Leadership Camp.
6. Publishing a handbook of activities annually.

Awards in the form of jewelry are given individuals through a merit system based largely on participation, although some weight is given to officiating and winning. Any group of women on the Lousville campus may enter a team in any event sponsored by the W.R.A.

THE UNIVERSITY OF MISSOURI

The program for women at the University of Missouri is also sponsored by close cooperative effort between the W.A.A. and the Department of Physical Education for Women. Students are encouraged to supply their own officials in most games. Pretournament practices are required in all events. The Missouri point system is presented here since it is somewhat different from other colleges:

Each group entered in an activity receives points unless the group defaults.

1. Points will be given as follows for Table tennis, Badminton, Tennis, Bowling, Archery, Pistol, Golf:

1st place	— 20 points	10th place	— 7 points
2nd place	— 18 points	11th place	— 6 points
3rd place	— 16 points	12th place	— 5 points
4th place	— 14 points	13th place	— 4 points
5th place	— 12 points	14th place	— 3 points
6th place	— 11 points	15th place	— 2 points
7th place	— 10 points	16th place	— 1 point
8th place	— 9 points	thru 32nd	
9th place	— 8 points	33rd place	— .5 point
		and on	

2. Points will be given as follows for Basketball, Softball, Swimming, Volleyball:

1st place — 40 points	9th place — 16 points
2nd place — 36 points	10th place — 14 points
3rd place — 32 points	11th place — 12 points
4th place — 28 points	12th place — 10 points
5th place — 24 points	13th place — 8 points
6th place — 22 points	14th place — 6 points
7th place — 20 points	15th place — 4 points
8th place — 18 points	16th place — 2 points
	and on

3. If teams tie for a place, the average is given to each team; for example, if there is a tie for 8th place by three teams, each team would receive the points ordinarily rated by 9th place, and no points would be given for 8th or 10th places.
4. Consolation tournaments will receive points as above, but based on 50 percent of the point value.

TEMPLE UNIVERSITY

At Temple University, Philadelphia, W.A.A. administers two programs, one intramural and the other varsity. The W.A.A. adviser is called the supervisor of women's athletics. The program is also partially supervised by a Women's Faculty Council on Athletics, consisting of the Dean of Women, a representative from each college in the day school, and the W.A.A. adviser. This group is a policy-setting body and assists greatly in determining standards. The Faculty Council, meeting monthly, hears reports from student representatives on their athletic activities. Any girl running for W.A.A. office must submit a petition signed by 100 members of the organization. Managers are selected by the Board, assisted by the adviser. Each manager is given a job-analysis sheet, which is helpful to her in executing her duties. Each student pays an annual activity fee which is used for athletics, dramatics, and other extracurricular activities. Most of the operating funds for the program come from this fee even though the budget is technically under the physical education department.

A point system is used and awards are presented as follows:

1. Individual bowling awards for first place.
2. Team awards for bowling and basketball. (Trophies)
3. W.A.A. plaque for 1,000 points.
4. W.A.A. blazer for 1,500 points
5. Team pins for four-year membership on a varsity squad.

Regular sports at Temple are basketball, archery, roller skating swimming, modern dance, golf, lifesaving, ice skating, hockey, skiing, bowling, horseback riding, and occasionally others. Temple has sponsored two-day co-recreational ski trips in the Pocono Mountains. Modern dance and golf are also arranged for both men and women.

THE UNIVERSITY OF NEBRASKA

Intramurals at Nebraska are governed by the W.A.A. Council, which is composed of a president, vice-president, secretary, treasurer, concessions manager, and the presidents of the various sports clubs as well as the faculty adviser. Administrative authority of this council covers four areas of activity:

1. Concessions. A special committee handles sale of refreshments at all varsity football games; the revenue permits a much wider expansion of activities and equipment.
2. Intramural sports, with its organization of sports heads and W.A.A. representatives, and the conducting of tournaments and leagues in most of the sports on the calendar.
3. Sports clubs sponsoring a number of activities for students at large as well as club members.
4. Cabin and bicycle. The committee has charge of the numerous weekend and overnight hikes and bicycle trips to the W.A.A. cabin 8 miles from the campus. Any group of University women may receive permission to use the cabin if properly chaperoned.

Fig. 74. Girls warming up for track events at the Flint Community Schools, Flint, Michigan.

W.A.A. actively sponsors competition in soccer-baseball, basketball, softball, volleyball, cage ball, bowling, and duck pin bowling as team sports; and badminton, table tennis, tennis, archery, deck tennis, golf, and swimming as individual and dual events. Sport clubs take the leadership in rifle shooting, Orchesis, horseback riding, and other sports as interest dictates. All student sport heads are given job-analysis sheets to assist in the carrying out of proper duties and responsibilities. Rules are often simplified in sports requiring skills that may be undeveloped. Competition is conducted in the dance. Health permits must be obtained and the annual complete examination is demanded. Practice sessions are compulsory in all the more strenuous sports.

Special Program Features
in Schools over the Nation

The marble tournaments are one of the highlights for the elementary and junior high girls of Philadelphia, with hundreds of girls participating. Duluth, Minnesota, features an elementary school Play Day annually for all girls in the city; the program includes a parade, ball games, running games and contests, singing games, and relays. Bicycling is one of the most popular activities at Roosevelt High School, Cedar Rapids, Iowa. Bicycling is also very popular in the San Diego, California, schools. Central High School at Trenton, New Jersey, conducts an annual Sports Night for high school girls; this program features games, songs, dances, music, pageantry, and skits, all produced, directed, and acted by the girls themselves. Its original purpose was to stimulate interest in the physical education program.

The Baltimore city schools have a large number of intramural sports organized by classes, years, colors, and every possible natural grouping, with extramurals climaxing the various sports seasons. Providence, Rhode Island, has used a similar program, with interschool play days ending each period. Many schools use tumbling and dancing in the girls' intramural program as a club activity. The elementary school program in Rochester, Minnesota, includes a series of sports and activities for girls of all grade levels. Competition is first conducted on a purely intramural basis, followed by extramural games between the city schools every Saturday. Rochester has one of the most extensive Saturday sports programs of any city in the nation, involving all grades and many sports.

At the University of Colorado ski classes for women are conducted each fall, with the first two weeks spent in straw skiing and conditioning gymnastics adapted to skiing. Then the large group of women continues activity on the smaller campus hills for four weeks. Buses later take them to all-day ski parties in the Loveland, Colorado, ski area. Here one hour is devoted to further ski instruction and review, followed by several hours of skiing for pleasure.

Fig. 75. Girls' high school volleyball at the St. Louis public schools.

At the Montana State Normal College at Dillon a Sports Night is held every Monday night, where all kinds of recreational sports are enjoyed. Special weekend student parties and trips are sponsored to Elkhorn Hot Springs, favorite Montana winter ski resort. Here the group enjoys skiing, dancing, group singing around the fireplace, and swimming in the outdoor hot-water pool surrounded by snow. A ski club has been organized to stimulate this activity.

The girls' intramural program at the Rufus King High School, Milwaukee, Wisconsin, utilizes the last period of each school day, plus additional after-school games. Sports in which competition is arranged are bowling, tennis, soccer, basketball, badminton, swimming, volleyball, softball, archery, and table tennis. Bowling is conducted on outside commercial alleys at reduced rates, supervised by a physical education teacher.

In the Kansas City, Missouri, high schools ice skating is an intramural sport. In addition, competition is arranged in softball, hockey, aerial darts, swimming, tennis, lifesaving, basketball, volleyball, soccer, bowling, golf, and horseback riding. In some instances where the school lacks facilities, community resources are used. A standard point and award system is in operation. A physical education, health, and intramural record is kept for each girl participating in an intramural program. Upon transfer of a pupil to another Kansas City school, the girl's record is sent to the new school. In this way girls do not lose credit for previous participation and they will receive the same award in any school for a like amount of achievement. The only difference in awards is the letter designating the school.

The University of Tennessee has one of the most active hiking clubs and outing groups, with from 50 to 100 taking each of the frequent trips. A favorite tour of the club is to the Great Smoky Mountains, which is indeed an inducement. Florida State has three housing units on a nearby lake with a boat house. Here, such events as boat races, canoe tilting, pageantry on the water, rowboat and canoe specialties, and riflery contests are staged each year.

Carol Harding of the M.S.U. faculty reported to the author in 1970 that some 2,500 to 3,500 women participate in regularly scheduled intramural events at Michigan State University. The growth of the "drop in" type of recreational program at Michigan State since the Women's Intramural Building was completed in 1963 is reflected in the following data:

YEAR	INFORMAL PARTICIPATIONS
1962–63	2,000
1963–64	7,270
1964–65	8,260
1965–66	8,400
1966–67	8,200
1967–68	13,480
1968–69	52,770

Fig. 76. Girls enjoy mixed hiking and outing activities in the mountains or anywhere. Events are easy to organize. Use buses or cars to transport them to scene of activities from urban areas.

It is noticeable that several colleges and universities are again stimulating activity on the water, with canoe and rowboat events conducted recreationally and competitively. Boating events were very popular from 1890 to about 1920, but the advent of the automobile seemed to dampen enthusiasm for this fine activity. Beloit College has again started boating activities for its women on the beautiful Rock River. A few miles farther south on the same river the Rockford College women are taking to the water. Women's colleges in the East have always continued to include these events, and schools of the West are now stimulating boating activities.

According to Luell Weed Guthrie, chairman for women's physical education, skiing is one of the most popular sports at Stanford University. Since snow does not abound near the Stanford campus, the department conducts classes, for both men and women, using straw instead of snow. These classes form the nucleus for the Ski Club which spends a number of weekends at famous Yosemite, some 200 miles away. The average number making these trips has been well over a hundred students. Other Pacific coast colleges are also using straw for ski instruction, later organizing ski and outdoor winter sports trips to the nearby mountains.

Mills College of Oakland, California, celebrated its centennial with its Twentieth Annual Horse Show. While this unique event is not the typical intramural event, it certainly is a highlight of a campus program which combines the outdoors with healthful competition and participation in horsemanship, trick riding, and judging. Over 200 women participated.

Middlebury College, Vermont, has long been a winter paradise for ice and snow sports. With the tremendous growth of ski events and growing interest in the New England area among private shools, junior and senior high schools, and colleges, Middlebury women have kept pace with a fine outdoor winter program. Here the women have their own toboggan slide and several toboggans, all of which are financed by the W.A.A. The organization is also the owner of an outing cabin for parties, which often take the form of a hare and hound chase. The Middlebury Mountain Club sponsors winter straw rides on sleighs, a Scavenger Party during Freshman Week for both men and women, autumn trips almost every week up to the mountains, and many overnight trips to the cabin for both men and women, with married faculty couples as chaperones. For the annual Ice Pageant the men build an ice throne, which is a lovely sight, electrically decorated, and equipped with loudspeaker. During the Winter Carnival the women have one full day of activity at Lake Dunmore which includes skiing, skijoring, skating, and a feast. As a part of the Ice Pageant several women's events are staged, such as downhill racing, downhill and uphill relays, obstacle and slalom races, broom hockey games, and skating races, followed by an informal get-together and tea.

One of the most recent activities to find its way into the intramural and competitive program is the dance. Grinnell College, Temple University, and the University of Nebraska are among those using the dance as a competitive part of their schedule.

Marjorie Larsen, Edison High School, Stockton, California, is the originator of Speed-A-Way, a field game which allows girls to run with the ball and combines elements from soccer, basketball, field ball, speedball, touch football, and field hockey. The game utilizes a field the size of a hockey field. A film was made at Redlands High School, Redlands, California, explaining and demonstrating Speed-A-Way.

Play Days and Special Sports Days

The play day has rapidly become a popular outlet for the more skilled participants at the conclusion of the intramural seasons. Delightful programs are now in existence all over the nation, with the keynote being a desire to have girls play together rather than against representatives from other schools. These events take a variety of forms, and are a combination of pleasurable play and social intermingling. Often they feature a single sport, such as an archery shoot, a tennis festival or "Racket Day," or a Ski Carnival. And again the students from many schools are brought together to enjoy recreation in a wide variety of sports. Highlights from several such play and sports days are mentioned here as suggestions to those directors anxious to get such a program started.

A College Women's Sports Day is sponsored at the University of Tennessee by the women physical education majors. Women from all state colleges are invited, and recreation is enjoyed in tennis, volleyball, swimming, badminton, and folk dancing. The Colorado Board of Women's Officials sponsors an all-day clinic in basketball at Boulder, Denver, Greeley, and Fort Collins, where coaches, officials, and physical educators are in attendance. Hockey sports days are held in several Colorado colleges. A Basketball Sports Day is held annually at Greeley, with nine colleges participating. An All-Day Swim Meet is sponsored at Colorado Women's College, with special events in racing, diving, and relays. Schools usually participating are Colorado Women's College, University of Colorado, Denver Bible College, Colorado College, Denver University, and Loretto Heights.

An annual Sports Contest is held each year for the high schools of northeast Missouri at Kirksville State Teachers College. In the morning, participation is conducted in volleyball, basketball, and softball. In the afternoon, dancing holds the spotlight. At the high school at Ferndale, Washington, a number of county play days have been conducted for all the high school girls of that county, using a number of sports and events. The Southwest High School in Kansas City, Missouri, introduced an Indian

Fig. 77. Sixteenth Annual Dade County Girls' Junior High School Volleyball Sport Day.

theme into its annual Sports Day Pow Wow. This event lasts all day, and includes the girls from many neighboring high schools, competing largely in field hockey. The play period is followed by a feast and is a memorable occasion for the girls of that area. The Senior High School at Mansfield, Ohio, has sponsored a play day which is outstanding. Other departments of the school cooperate in organizing and preparing for the event, which makes the entire school more conscious of the program. Included in this correlated planning are the departments of English, art, dramatics, public speaking, and journalism. Officials are recruited from recent alumni. The competition gets under way with competition for Mansfield girls only, later including students from other nearby high schools.

In the Kansas City, Missouri, high schools sports days are the culmination of skills and strategy learned in the instructional period, plus the development of these skills through the intramural program. The Advisory Council of the Physical Education Department determines the number and type of sports days to be held, and tentatively selects the host schools. Here no championship can be won because no team meets all eight high schools. This idea is impressed upon the girls before they attend such an occasion, and emphasis is placed upon sportsmanship, a knowledge of the rules, and satisfactory social practices, rather than upon winning a game. A clinic for both teachers and students is held a few days before the event to interpret rules, demonstrate officiating procédures, and discuss plans to be followed during the social hour and luncheon. The games are limited, with each team playing only three or four times during the Saturday forenoon, so that the girls who are not participating have time to rest, profit by watching the type of game played by other teams, and meet girls from other schools. At noon a luncheon is served in the school cafeteria. The luncheons provide the more formal part of the day. Board members, administrators, directors, supervisors, and guests are introduced; short programs are presented, and the girls have an opportunity to become better acquainted.

The Cincinnati, Ohio, public schools conduct Spring Sports Days, in which hundreds of girls participate in softball, badminton, tennis, shuffle-board, and table tennis.

At Bucyrus, Ohio, the half dozen nearby high schools gather together for an indoor play day. Volleyball is conducted in the gymnasium, shuffle-board along the gym sidelines, deck tennis in the school corridor, table tennis in the home economics room, peg ring in the corridor, tumbling and stunts on mats in the hallways, and challenges in the gymnasium and corridor. Frequent rest periods are called, at which time the girls get better acquainted and relax with songs and skits.

The Course of Study Syllabus for the State of Connecticut urges the high schools to engage in play days along the following patterns:

1. Interclass, with groups from one school in a certain class playing with a similar group from another school.
2. Interorganization, using several sports.
3. Seasonal play days within a single school with as many teams as possible organized in just one sport.
4. Rotary seasonal play days arranged between several schools each fall, winter, and spring, with the schools rotating the host privilege at least every two years.
5. City-wide play days in any number of sports.

One syllabus for the state of Florida urged its schools to promote play days and described the plan of organization of two of its cities as examples of this type of activity. At Winter Garden one school day has been set aside and school buses take all the girls to a central place. The event is for both boys and girls, who play separately in a large number of sports. From 500 to 750 students participate in this event annually. Here again the play day is not organized on an interschool competitive basis, but teams are mixed to avoid destruction of the ultimate aim of the competition. In the Jacksonville junior high schools the play day is for girls only, and is a miniature Olympics. Girls from all the junior high schools meet in a program which starts with a mixer or "ice-breaker" game. Color teams are chosen and school identities are sublimated to the general fun.

The Women's Department at the University of Washington has for years sponsored a play day which is a cooperative enterprise shared by the

W.A.A. and the Physical Education Department. A dozen girls from each of several towns in a radius of 100 miles are invited. They arrive on Saturday morning, register, pay a small fee for the luncheon, and receive programs. First comes a grand march, followed by a mass folk dancing session. Relay races precede the luncheon. After a short rest period the afternoon program begins, consisting of a series of games. Squads are rotated and all play each game. Special demonstrations are then given the group by skilled university women. All then proceed to the pool for a relaxing swim. A posture parade and contest concludes the day's festivities, and all leave feeling they have made many new friends.

Hundreds of girls participate in a St. Louis County hockey sports day held each year at Washington University, St. Louis. Following the games the players enjoy a recreational swim at the Wilson Pool. The Carlsbad, New Mexico, high school G.A.A. has hosted tennis sports days with girls from Alamagordo and Cloudcroft attending. The Carlsbad girls entertain their tennis guests in their homes on Friday night after taking them to a football game and to dance. The girls of Las Vegas, New Mexico, conduct similar tennis sports days with participants classified into three divisions, playing according to their experience and ability. Among the social features of this event have been a wiener roast in the canyon and a football game. Women of the University of Arizona, Tucson, entertain the women from Arizona State at Tempe in a semiannual sports day featuring hockey, volleyball, tennis, archery, golf, badminton, and dance composition.

Almost everywhere the play day has a social objective, and it must be planned to give large groups equal opportunity to play. This is possible only by presenting a variety of both low and high organization activities. Some of the play days start with parades or posture demonstrations, followed by social recreational mixers and folk dancing. Later come relays and games of higher organization, individual games and contests, and the social hour with songs, cheers, and refreshments.

In conclusion, it might be suggested that the girls and women have taken the lead in recreation and competition in its more purely amateur sense, and should be highly commended for the progress that has been made. Trends of the future point to a far greater expansion of the intramural and sports program for girls and women, with rapid growth predicted for the outing groups, and the increasing cooperation between men and women working in the field toward more pleasurable and frequent opportunities for co-recreation. Indications also point to the fact that the men's program will emulate the finer elements of the women's play days, retaining those features that are distinctly masculine, and planning more extramural competition. Here, winning will be secondary, and lasting friendships and social values will have an opportunity to supersede the fierce quest for victory.

REFERENCES

1 *The History of Physical Education in Colleges for Women* (New York: A. S. Barnes & Co., 1930), p. 29.

2 Louis E. Means, *"Post-War College and University Intramural Athletics,"* The *Athletic Journal,* XXVIII, No. 9, May, 1948.

3 Division for Girls' and Women's Sports, American Association for Health, Physical Education and Recreation, *Policies and Procedures for Competition in Girls' and Women's Sports,* Washington, D.C., 1969.

4 *Athletics, Intramurals, Physical Education,* Handbook of the University of North Carolina, Chapel Hill, 1964-1965. Material reproduced by courtesy of Oliver K. Cornwell, Director of Physical Education, and Walter Rabb, Director of Intramurals.

5 *W.A.A. Activities Schedule,* University of Minnesota, Minneapolis, 1957-1958. Reproduced through the courtesy of Dr. Gertrude M. Baker and Professor Sue Tinker of the Department of Physical Education.

6 From material submitted to the author by Professor Maurine Bowling, Department of Physical Education for Women, University of Oklahoma, Norman, May, 1956.

7 From material submitted to the author by Professor Pauline Hodgson, Department of Physical Education for Women, University of California, Berkeley, March, 1954.

13

CO-RECREATIONAL ACTIVITIES

The activities program for mixed groups bids for its rightful share of emphasis in every modern school. As the school prepares young people to enjoy academic pursuits and for vocational efficiency, so should it prepare them to make successful adjustments in social situations. An ability to adapt oneself easily and gracefully to constantly shifting circumstances entails the learning of certain accepted social customs and procedures which must be practiced frequently in order that they may be absorbed into the nervous system and so become a part of the personality of the individual.

Sensible association between the sexes is certainly essential to normal social life. Men and women meet in industry, on the streets, at dances, at parties, and in the professions. They build homes together, and work and play together. Later, as adults, they will be expected to get along with one another without difficulty or embarrassment. Their younger years should provide them with adequate opportunities to learn social customs and to adapt themselves, without self-consciousness, to life situations.

Co-education is now an established fact in American education. Yet, at one time women were barred from most educational institutions. The association together in the formality of the classroom does not guarantee real acquaintances. The leisure hours, when there is freedom to do things together, is the time for developing real fellowship. Yet we have been too prone to segregate boys and girls from each other in all physical and recreational activities, even though there are many activities common to the interests of both.

It is most unfortunate that organization for social-recreational activity has been untouched in too many schools, and has only recently been recognized as valuable in many others. Some experience indicates that the instruction in elementary fundamentals of activities should preferably be given in segregated classes, and that boys and girls then should be permitted to participate together in the intramural program after having mastered the preliminary essentials.

Another strong argument for school leadership in co-recreational activities is the competition coming from commercialized interests. People are becoming more dependent all the while on this type of recreation. Any type of organized school leadership which will minimize commercial recreation and provide wholesome, supervised social-recreational opportunity in schools and colleges will be a great step forward in happy, social adjustment of young people.

For the student's emotional well-being, a wholesome adjustment to the opposite sex is imperative. To enable more men and women to meet under wholesome conditions is one of the most important purposes of college life. Every college party, picnic, steak fry, breakfast hike, open house, tea, and the like, in reality constitutes a laboratory in which students can learn through doing to make happy and wholesome adjustments to the opposite sex. We are too often missing a basic drive of college students in denying, for the most part, an opportunity for them to get together in sports. Many activities, especially golf, tennis, badminton, bowling, and even swimming, could appropriately be organized co-recreationally on both an instructional and informal recreational basis.

At one National Recreation Congress meeting two leaders spoke convincingly on this subject. Miss Mabel Madden, of the Recreation Commission of Cincinnati, Ohio, stated that many lasting relationships have grown out of boy-girl play situations in that city. She added that these experiences which often result in marriage do not produce the frequent unhappy sequel of divorce. She further stated that "boys and girls who play together learn to understand each other and learn whether they have common interests. A boy who sees his glamour girl with her hair down and her makeup washed off after a swimming party will find out just how good a sport she really is." Marguerite Kehr of State Teachers College, Bloomsburg, Pennsylvania, stated:

> The ability to play is necessary for a democratic form of society. There is not much real recreation in the totalitarian countries. There is much truth in the theory that the dangerous people in the world are those who do not play. Men and women should learn to play together while in school.

An Intramural Handbook of Florida A & M University at Tallahassee emphasized the importance of co-recreational events and activities on that campus with the following comments:

> Many college intramural programs are too concerned with keeping men's and women's activities separate. At FAMU there is a strong feeling that there should be joint participation in activities whenever possible. Today, traditions have been dissolved to a point where many physical education classes are taught on a co-educational basis. Greater emphasis is being placed on recreation for mixed groups by numerous community groups such as churches, camps and social service centers.
>
> There are many opportunities in this phase of the program for students to know and understand the opposite sex. Frequently, through applications of adult standards, it is assumed that youth develop these associations naturally, when in reality there is a lack of opportunity to establish wholesome relationships.
>
> Much of an individual's life consists of sharing responsibilities, socializing, and working with members of the opposite sex. One of the major functions of education is to provide experiences which aid in solving personal problems and making social adjustments whether these situations arise at home or in the business world. A co-recreational program makes a very positive contribution to this educational process so we urge you wholeheartedly to take advantage of the opportunities offered to fulfill your individual needs of mutual understanding between men and women.

Aspects of Effective Administration

One of the most important considerations in the organization of a co-recreational program is the method of approach. Students and faculty alike must endorse its possibilities and be prepared for its administration. The calendar must be a product of student desire and expressed interests. It must be fitted without conflict into the social, academic, and athletic calendar for the year. In schools of small enrollment, where one individual assumes most of the leadership responsibility, students could be organized into advisory committees. In larger schools the director of men's physical education must be in harmony with the director for women. This must be a joint enterprise to be successful. Enthusiastic leadership is a prerequisite at the outset.

Many administrative problems confront enterprising leaders who would inaugurate this type of program. Most difficulties arise because of the traditional supposition that the sexes must be segregated until maturity. This tradition must be set aside, and a program of activities must be adapted to meet the needs of the particular group with the facilities at hand.

The school that desires a series of "splash parties" may have to make some adjustments regarding facilities. Dressing rooms must be so arranged that both sexes can be accommodated at the same time. Cloak and check rooms must be arranged for mixed dance programs. In situations where sex differences have been overemphasized it takes time to develop matter-of-factness in arrangements and accommodations. It also takes time to build the interest and skills which enable girls and men to enjoy participation in a variety of activities together.

Another problem of leadership is twofold. First, a way must be found to get young people to participate in a wider range of mixed activities so their joint recreational interests will not be as harrowly limited as they are today. Second, an environment must be created which is conducive to a normal social life between the sexes, and in which boy and girl friendships are approved and encouraged. It seems logical that new activities cannot be added until mixed participation has been enjoyed in activities girls and men do share. Then the list can be broadened. A dance or party is frequently the only way to introduce other mixed activities. One joint program might well lead to others. Going on a hike may lead to a mixed swimming party, a singing club, an outing club, discussion groups, or any number of activities. An International Relations Club might sponsor a costume dance with the participants dressed to represent various countries under discussion. This might later lead to other imaginatively planned parties and outings which gradually widen the sphere of mixed activity.

To maintain the interest and cooperation of boys and girls in this type of program they should be given a share in its planning and organization. Thus they have a better chance to be made comfortable and at ease in the group.

The "open house" is one of the best starting points for expansion. In this event the physical details of the gymnasium should be so arranged that newcomers will not feel like intruders. Nothing is more formidable to a young man entering the gymnasium than to see a lobby full of women or a severe-looking matron who seems full of questions. Appropriate signs might point the way to meeting rooms, dressing rooms, and gathering points. Pleasant hosts and hostesses could be on hand to answer questions and direct the way to desired places.

In addition to the main group events of the evening, which, perhaps, would be found on the gymnasium floor proper, rooms should be set aside for informal mixed activities. Here could be game rooms for cards, checkers, chess, darts, table tennis, and other table games. Other spots might be provided, as space permits, for tether ball, badminton, shuffleboard, and similar contests. Increased support for programs of this sort will be assured when faculty members are invited to join these mixed recreational programs. There is usually a nucleus of faculty families who would delight in this opportunity. Occasional parties for faculty people invariably meet with great approval.

The California State Department of Education has constantly urged that teachers in elementary, junior, and senior high schools organize an activity program in which boys and girls play together frequently. They have further recommended that students of the lower grades play together daily, with boys and girls of the upper grades getting together not less than once each week. In keeping with this suggestion, California schools have taken a lead in co-recreational activities. Quite early the high schools of Los Angeles developed a program, as did University High School of Oakland. Schools of the Los Angeles area have recently enlarged the mixed program to tremendous proportions as part of youth services and school recreation.

Fig. 78. Co-recreational cycling is excellent in providing a healthful outdoor activity yielding dividends in health and fitness.

A set of standards adopted by the California State Department of Education, together with the State Association for Health, Physical Education and Recreation, and other affiliated groups, defines the framework under which intramural, extramural, and special coeducational activities may become an outgrowth of school-student planning. Sports recommended for this purpose are archery, badminton, tennis, bowling, folk, square, and modern dance, golf, riding, swimming, volleyball, skiing, recreational games, and sports and play days. The standards as adopted are:

1. Play days and sports days may be held at any time during the school year.
2. Players should be grouped for practice and competitive play according to general level of skill.
3. Participants should have medical approval before participating. For girls, play during the menstrual period is subject to the approval of the woman in direct charge of the group.
4. Written permission of parent or guardian shall be required for all minors engaged in any extramural activities.
5. All practice periods and games shall be under the supervision of a certificated man and a certificated woman teacher.
6. Players shall be removed at once from a practice or a game if injured or excessively fatigued, or if they give any evidence of emotional overstrain.
7. Officials for games should be qualified, and women officials should be, if possible, those rated by the Women's National Officials Rating Committee.
8. Travel for games shall be limited to a small geographic area and a certificated man and woman shall accompany every traveling group. Wherever possible, transportation shall be by school bus or licensed common carrier. Overnight trips may be made in exceptional situations.
9. Admission fees shall not be charged for any event.
10. Awards shall be of a symbolic type, inexpensive, and should not be emphasized.
11. All publicity should stress the recreational and social values of play, and improvement in skill, as much as the winning of matches. Achievements of the squad should be stressed as much as those of individuals.

Under the leadership of Dr. John Merkley and Earl L. Harris, the Youth Activities program of the Los Angeles City Schools rapidly expanded. The program is geared to meet needs in both physical and social recreation for elementary, junior, and senior high, and junior college levels. The activities take place in the late afternoons, evenings, Saturdays and Sundays. The usual sports competition takes place daily after school, with the weekends leading directly to family and student group social recreation. Night events of coeducational nature include sport nights, dances, talent shows, and dramatic events. Schools exchange their talent and move about from school to school on occasion. Refreshments are often the finale of these night events. Los Angeles is also fortunate in being situated in the heart of the "show business" industry, and coeducational parties are often highlighted by visitations of celebrities.

Washington High School of Sioux Falls, South Dakota, several years ago started a program of mixed physical education classes, because of the feeling that the segregation of the sexes in play situations had been overstressed. Sports skills were taught in the classes. Many tourneys were started in the classes and completed outside.

Prior to 1946 such activities at Stanford University were sponsored by the W.A.A., a factor which seemed to discourage active male participation. Other groups and clubs sometimes existed through permission of the Associated Students of Stanford, but they were often handicapped financially, and interests too often were narrow and self-centered. More recently Stanford set up a Co-recreational Committee for the purpose of stimulating interest, acting as a clearing house in an advisory way to special groups,

(Courtesy of the Los Angeles City Schools Youth Services Section.)

Fig. 79. Roller skating in the Los Angeles city schools. All skates are supplied by the "traveling roller skating rink" operated by the Youth Services Section. Madison Junior High students take their turns on their own gym floor.

and seeing that all activities are carried on according to accepted Stanford policies. This move proved to be a wise step forward and was a hopeful force for the development of an excellent modern program, replete with good student leadership. Activities thus far developed are mixed archery, badminton, bowling, fencing, folk dancing, golf, hiking, riding, skiing, and polo.

The following points are worthy of consideration in building a co-recreational program in the schools:

1. Enlist the cooperation of other teachers. Form a committee from the faculty, students, and community leaders.
2. Start on a small scale and build gradually and sensibly.
3. Organize the program ahead of time and use techniques of advertising and publicity which will prepare the group in advance.
4. Use movies and visual aids to set the stage.
5. Discuss co-recreation in health and physical education classes.
6. Show the connection between the program and its utility for adult living.
7. Select popular teachers as sponsors. Pick those who are admired by the students.
8. Set the situation and utilize leaders so that courtesy and manners are in vogue with the group rather than teacher-imposed.
9. Let the students take responsibility for a code of ethics. Let them prepare decorations and an acceptable environment.
10. Forbid only when you have something more attractive to offer.
11. Instruction in skills should be given separately to the sexes, although it is sometimes feasible to let some of the boys instruct the girls.
12. Use a wide variety of activities including sports and games, hiking, stunts, dramatics, camping, discussion groups, clubs, music, crafts, special parties, and pageants.
13. Teach activities of a carry-over type whenever possible.
14. Parties must be happy and joyous. Eliminate the frigid and the conventional.
15. Use competitive elements whenever possible.
16. Try a little required co-recreation somewhere in the physical education program.
17. Open and supervise the playing courts and swimming pools over the weekend.

Activities for Social Recreation

There are many fine sports that lend themselves perfectly to the co-recreational calendar. Badminton ranks high in sociological value, since girls are perhaps more adept than men at the short, drop shot, which makes them admirable net players, while the men seem to get greater satisfaction out of the deeper court smashes and drives.

Bowling is a very sociable sport, and the tremendous increase in industrial bowling interest is mute testimony to the carry-over value of this type of competition, particularly for women. It is a game of skill, and is sufficiently intricate and intriguing to secure a lifetime of interest. It is a game that husbands, wives, and eventually children can all enjoy together. It is not a game of strength, and requires no extreme physical action. There is always time to talk, with opportunity for fellowship and mixing. Women often become equal to, or superior to men in accomplishment. Since most schools must work out plans with commercial alleys for their bowling program, it is just as easy to make room for at least a minimum of mixed bowling each year.

Archery is one of the few sports that can be enjoyed before real proficiency has been reached. It is adaptable for mixed groups, and is growing in popularity all over the nation. Orthopedically it is an excellent sport, involving good posture in the shooting positions. Archery can be used in almost any available space, indoors and outdoors. It is not expensive, and many schools have stimulated the development of archery clubs where the members construct their own equipment in the handicraft shop or school practical arts department. The roving archery classes at Knox College at Galesburg, Illinois, have attracted national attention. Knox men and women have taken the sport to the great outdoors, and have practiced their more difficult shots, together with actual competition, in the wooded and hilly areas of that vicinity.

Tennis is generally accepted as a suitable individual sport for mixed groups. Sports such as hiking, swimming, and ice and roller skating are unquestionably good. Other sports selected must be studied after consideration is given to the physical differences between men and women. The effect of physiological differences on men and women's performances in physical activities must be taken into account. The following observations are pertinent:

> The girl has relatively larger organs below the diaphragm and smaller ones above the diaphragm. The hips and thighs have more adipose tissue and less muscle. The center of gravity is thus lower. Metabolism is less rapid in women than in men, the ratio being 100 to 141. Women do better in exercises of moderate endurance than men. They fail to do as well in exercises of support on the hands or in exercises of speed. Because of their structure, women have less ability than men in heavy gymnastics and in those competitive games which require heart and lung power.

Therefore, games of skill are perhaps the best types of competition for mixed recreation. Some authorities will question the emotional spirit of the adolescent girl, and its relation to play and the desire to win. But with the greater emphasis on sports for sports' sake and the development of skill, lack of this trait should not be too great a handicap.

There seems to be considerable difference of opinion among recreational leaders regarding the advisability of mixed teams in active games. It would be safe to say that approval should be given for boys and girls to play together in the athletic games in which girls are not at a distinct disadvantage, and which do not involve physical contact. Competition between the sexes should be looked upon with disapproval. Rivalry in this case might eventually prevent the very relationships between the sexes which mixed activities are designed to develop. Several authorities have agreed upon the following table of activities for mixed groups:

Team Games

Volleyball, bat ball, deck tennis, three-pin ball, long ball, German bat ball, soccer baseball, softball, bowl club ball, bowling, base crick, hit-pin baseball, kick dodge ball, indoor baseball, rifle shooting, water dodge ball, cage ball, water volleyball, and water pageants.

Individual Games Involving Two or Four or More

Archery, aerial tennis dart, badminton, battle ball, bowling, curling, golf, hand tennis, paddle tennis, handball, horseshoes, lawn bowling, racket ball, skish, skeet, archery golf, roving archery, ring tennis, tether ball, shuffleboard, squash, tennis, ice and roller skating, snow sculpturing, bicycling, hiking, equitation, croquet, tap dancing classes, and many variations of the dance.

Games Suitable for Informal
Social-Recreational Programs in the Gymnasium
(Junior and Senior High School)

Dodge ball, run sheep run, last couple out, call ball, flying dutchman, bull in ring, spud, prisoner's base, slipper slap, duck on the rock, partner's tag, poison, hook on tag, hill-dill, and other similar games.

Card Games and Indoor Activities

Backgammon, Bagatelle, camelot, bridge, checkers, chess, cribbage, pinochle, rummy, caroms, dart baseball, dart bowling, Dodo, Halma, Monopoly, Parcheesi, Chinese checkers, Pit, Pegity, puzzles, Rook, table shuffleboard, table tennis, box hockey, dart variations, pool, billiards, gym bowling, and paddle badminton.

The list might be further augmented by an arrangement of special variations such as golf driving, pitching, and putting contests, clock golf, miniature golf, and target games.

Through the leadership of the physical education department at the State Teachers College at Kutztown, Pensylvania, every Monday night was set aside for a social-recreational party. This program grew to such proportions that several nearby churches were brought into it with similar events scheduled regularly. At the Florida State University at Tallahassee every Friday night was set aside as a mixed play night where the following events were used: swimming, dancing, darts, caroms, checkers, shuffleboard, badminton, table tennis, cards, and almost any game that was desired by the participants.

Every Monday night is mixed sports night at the University of Kentucky. This event is sponsored by the Physical Education Club, with all students invited without charge. Locker-room space is provided. Candy and soft drinks are sold. Majors are on hand to act as instructors for those who desire it and also to act as officials for the large variety of sports offered. In the high schools of Sioux City, Iowa, co-recreational events are planned in badminton, volleyball, ring tennis, golf, tennis, bowling, and hiking. At Ralph Waldo Emerson Junior High School in Los Angeles the girls' physical education department cooperates in sponsoring a program of mixed table games, volleyball, and other sports. Social attitudes and proper relationships are stimulated through folk and social dancing held frequently.

At the University of Texas the large staff of women's instructors, together with excellent facilities, provide an unusual and effective program for women as well as for mixed groups. Tournaments are constantly organized in a large number of sports. Hundreds of married student couples attend mixed sports and recreational parties each year. The evening is given over to contests in one gym, volleyball in another, table tennis in several places; badminton was organized in another gym space; the swimming pool is a center of activity for mixed swimming; and two small gymnasiums are given over to nurseries where the babies and small children of the married students are kept happy and occupied.

Fig. 80. Co-recreational tennis doubles tournament in operation at the Long Beach, California, high schools.

Outing Activities

Nature's boundless attractions constantly beckon those who would enjoy them. No month in the year is closed to those who love the great outdoors. Whether winter snows or summer sun reigns supreme, one never wants for things to do outside. Chapter 16 is given over exclusively to this great area of recreational opportunity; therefore, considerable detail is omitted here. By way of emphasis it should be remembered that winter offers the energetic director the ideal situation for such sports as skiing, winter hiking, tobogganing, coasting, snow sculpturing, and many features. Summer also brings a great and varied array of outdoor activities. There is one sport that knows no seasonal limitation, and that is hiking. Many people unfortunately assume that winter excludes all hiking. It is the most inexpensive of all school-sponsored activities. It can be enjoyed by small and large groups, and is unexcelled in its possibilities for companionship.

Mary Breen described some of the highlights of hiking as follows:[1]

> You can hike on the city streets or in the country; even the desert contains some spot worth hiking to. You can study people or houses while walking alone, or trees and bugs and birds and flowers. Overnight hiking is the best of teachers in the art of homemaking and, at the same time its most thorough examination. If you want to get acquainted with yourself or someone else, go on a hike. The heat or cold, the rain or snow and lonely hours of midnight; the time for frolic or work; the burned beans and cold coffee and mosquitoes; the glorious sunrise, the moon over the water, the tang of sage or pine and woodsmoke; will all tell you more about yourself and your friends than anything else in the world. And every hike is an experience to treasure.

Outings for mixed groups are easily organized in junior and senior high schools. However, there is little evidence to indicate that the schools are taking full advantage of their opportunities. Very fortunate indeed are those schools situated near points of great scenic interest. Yet there is no spot in the United States where opportunities do not abound for the enjoyment of nature's offerings. To most city dwellers with any spark of vitality, the opportunity to offset the deadening effects of urban routine by a trip into the country is gladly welcomed once they have had a taste of its rejuvenating powers. While the winter may offer more colorful and spectacular activities, the spring, fall, and summer offer greater variety.

By 1938 some 75 institutions of higher learning had organized outing or hiking clubs. Some 35 of these clubs, mainly in the eastern schools, were members of the Intercollegiate Outing Club Association. Membership in these clubs ranged from about thirty students to one thousand, the membership of the Dartmouth College Club.

This association was founded in 1932 with 24 colleges sending representatives to consider phases of this program. Three times a year a bulletin containing programs and plans of member clubs, trail gossip, and practical outing suggestions is issued. Two meetings are held each year, in spring and fall. The organization is greatly interested in the growth of this activity among the colleges. The Denison University Outing Club is a leader in Ohio, and the Alleghany Club has been of assistance to several Pennsylvania colleges. Since 1932 the list has steadily grown, but is still much too meager.

Union College (N.Y.S.)	Alleghany College	Dartmouth College
Vassar College	Brown University	Denison University
Wellesley College	Colby College	Massachusetts Tech
Williams College	Colby Junior College	Middlebury College
Yale University	University of Colorado	Pembroke College
Bowdoin College	Skidmore College	Pine Manor College
Harvard University	Smith College	Radcliffe College
Jackson College	Swarthmore College	Rutgers University
	Tusculum College	

In most cases outing clubs have been student-organized enterprises. In some, students and faculty joined efforts. In a few instances the faculty alone was responsible. Student initiative and responsibility seem to be dominant characteristics of all clubs. Many of these clubs collect small assessments with which equipment is gradually accumulated. The following events are usually of special interest to the student group:

Camping trips to state and national parks
General outing for the entire college
Picnic for freshmen during "Freshman Week"
Winter carnivals
Canoe trips
Skiing trips between semesters
Joint outings with other nearby college groups
Decoration Day beach parties
Ski competitive carnivals
Mountain climbing expeditions
Barn dances, and hay and sleigh rides
Supper trips; bicycle tours; skating parties

Some of the activities at various colleges have highlights that might be of interest to those active in this movement. The Alleghany College Club has planned and executed a picnic program for the entire freshman class. This consists of games, hiking, swimming, picnic supper, campfire, group songs, a short talk by the deans, and much comradeship. This club also sponsors annually an all-college outing with a program of winter sports, food, fun, and song for faculty and student nonmembers.

(Courtesy of the Los Angeles City Schools Youth Services Section.)

Fig. 81. A country dance at one of the Los Angeles City School District high schools.

Wellesley sponsors a barn dance for freshmen each fall. The square dance highlights this affair. Food is furnished by the college without cost. Yale has an inner circle of "Blue Shirts" in their club, which acts as the controlling body; admittance is gained by acting as a trip leader, and by unanimous vote of the society. The Swarthmore College Club holds "sleeping bag sews." The University of Colorado Club issues a printed schedule of hikes each semester. This club is the only unit on the campus without a faculty adviser. Massachusetts Tech gives a "dry course" for skiing every fall. Middlebury's hiking parties often have as many as 200 students. The Pine Manor Club thrives with practically no equipment whatever.

One cannot help but be impressed with the range and quality of the activities engaged in by these colleges. Particularly significant is the fact that choices are made and progress measured in the main by student leaders and student groups.

SUGGESTIONS FOR STARTING AN
OUTING CLUB OR ACTIVITY

Before complete plans for such a program should be laid out in any school, leaders should proceed carefully. It might be well to call in a few interested leaders and talk over the idea with them. The next meeting might include a larger representation of students. Saturday afternoon hikes might be one of the earlier activities. Out-of-the-ordinary meals might be planned, such as corn bakes, roasting leg of veal or lamb Indian fashion, or a mess of corned beef hash instead of the usual wieners or hamburgers. The procedure from that point should progress toward real camping and away from the usual cut and dried picnic. It should be kept in mind, however, that real discomfitures should be avoided in the initial activities.

Meetings on the campus, illustrated by movies of the outdoors or talks by faculty members who have had interesting experiences along this line, will provide stimulus. A small beginning in the fall and winter, followed by the campus meetings, will encourage student ingenuity for devising an increasingly interesting spring program. It is better to start with a small but enthusiastic student group and gradually expand than to attempt to start with a large and unwieldy group of semi-interested people. The next step might be the accumulation of permanent equipment, which does not have to be expensive or too plentiful. Each group will have needs peculiar to the local situation, and equipment must be modified to the possible program within that school.

Officials at Western Carolina College feel that outing activities contribute immeasurably to youth fitness. The Outdoor Club is a focal point, attracting students to camp-outs, cook-outs, and picnics. The Club mobilizes its members to construct nature trails, to plant rock, flower, and vegetable gardens, to build squirrel and bird boxes, zoological, botanical, and insect museums, and an arboretum. It also sponsors bird study; fishing, boating, skiing, casting, and spinning; riflery, pistol shooting, skeet, trap shooting; field and flight archery and archery golf; and such diverse studies as astronomy and bee culture.

The University of Chicago program has included several clubs which make a significant contribution to the co-recreational life of the campus. Each club has a faculty adviser. Some of these clubs are listed here as a possible guide to organization:

1. Badminton Club, which meets on Sunday afternoon from 3:30 to 6:00 P.M.
2. Fencing Club, which competes in meets of the Amateur Fencers League of America. Practices are held every Monday, Wednesday, and Friday nights.
3. Acrotheater, an acrobatic-adagio group for exhibitions and gymnastic group for competition. Open to men and women students, alumni, and friends. Practices every Monday, Wednesday, and Saturday.
4. Figure-Skating Club, which meets Tuesday and Thursday nights during the winter quarter on the rink under the stadium. Instruction and practice is provided in elementary school figures and ice dances.
5. Rifle Club, which competes in intercollegiate postal matches and in club shoulder-to-shoulder matches on Monday and Tuesday nights.
6. Outing Club, which sponsors hiking, cycling, camping, and skiing trips and square dances.
7. Yacht Club, which maintains sailing dinghies at the Burnham Park Lagoon.

HINTS FOR HIKING AND OUTINGS

Beginning hikers often like to add to their regalia several kinds of extra equipment, such as knives, canteens, axes, ropes, and similar items; this only adds to their discomfort later and hastens fatigue. It is well to keep in a unified group. A leisurely pace without hurry will assure best results. The problem of food should be carefully studied, with picnic lunch type at first, and real outdoor cooking later.

Hikes are a constant challenge to provide something different. The changing of seasons alone makes this task easy. Also, hikes may be held at sunrise, by moonlight, or they may be breakfast hikes or progressive supper hikes. New places to go, different times, and novelty menus will all make this type of activity more appreciated. Other interesting hikes might be planned along the following lines: bee-line hike, circuit hike, special evening and hike, gypsy patter-run, discovery hike, exploration hike, in-the-city hike, penny hike, and many others.

The State Teachers College at Wayne, Nebraska, has sponsored a Hiking Club in the co-recreational program which proved successful. The club enjoys cook-outs, map reading and camera trips, and miscellaneous hikes. Women at Russell Sage College join with women of nearby colleges for skiing, hiking, "spelunking," rock climbing, and canoe trips.

Swimming and Water Activities

Mixed swims and splash parties are always popular and should be a part of the intramural and physical education program in every school with a swimming pool. These parties might well be included by schools without pools if the weather permits beach parties. The question does not seem to be whether or not water sports are suitable for mixed groups, but how to provide more opportunities for their enjoyment. Informal swimming parties are often more successful than the carefully planned, semiformal type of program.

Girls and boys should not compete against each other because speed and endurance of boys is superior. However, mixed relays, stunt races, figure floating, and follow-the-leader might all be acceptable activities. Difficult stunts and fancy dives can be executed in burlesque, and many bits of nonsense will enliven a party. Sometimes a theme for an evening's activity can be planned successfully. Student committees often can work out a successful and pleasant program which will provide another opportunity for working and playing together.

Canoeing parties and trips are great experiences in the lives of the students if well done. Here many of the ideas of the hiking program can be utilized with good results. The Minnehikers of Minneapolis have a boat trip on a river barge followed by a hike on the river banks along the Mississippi. Groups in New York City plan supper dancing parties on boats to nearby points along the coast. In Los Angeles, canoe parties paddle to a nearby point for lunch, and return.

Many activities can be planned for these water programs, and some of these have been included in a previous list of activities. Water pageants can be developed easily with a minimum of effort on the part of student committees, and are a great experience in themselves.

Dance Mixers and Stunts

The usual formal and semiformal dance is such an ever-present part of the life of every college and university, and increasingly so in the junior and senior high schools, that a little thought and planning toward variety in this direction will captivate and interest the student body in surprising fashion. Perhaps the suggestions presented here might be a part of the "open house" program. Or again, special get-togethers might be provided for activities of a social-recreational nature.

Social and formal dances often fail to create a real opportunity for boys and girls to get acquainted with each other. Mixers and stunt affairs will help take care of this need. These events abound in good spirit and help overcome self-consciousness. They should lead to new acquaintances, conversation, and a genuine feeling of friendliness.

Elimination dances are stunts where fun and suspense add much to the enjoyment of the evening. A few might be listed: number elimination, balloon battles, paper-bag elimination, Tin Pan Alley, flower waltz, checkerboard, and lucky disc. The lemon dance is another bit of fun that will go over. Many of the Paul Jones features are good for mixing and good fellowship, with directions calling for walking or sliding around the circle. Here many types might be mentioned, such as: single circle, double circle, basket weave, carousel, circle reverse, grand left and right, rushes, and Cinderella's slippers. There are many types of the grand march that can be employed with good effect. Introduction games are also splendid get-acquainted maneuvers.

There is an increased interest in many parts of the country for folk dances, quadrilles, schottisches, and square dances. At Madison, Wisconsin, a director introduced a few square dances at a P.T.A. party, which was so successful that the group asked him to plan a later party with nothing else included. Soon, these events were held every two weeks.

The director of physical education at the high school at Antioch, Illinois, several years ago tried out a novel program with interesting results.

Two gymnasiums were provided for school dances, each with separate orchestras. One gymnasium attracted all the students who preferred modern social dancing, and the other gymnasium used the old-fashioned types of dance. It was interesting to note that Antioch students gradually shifted their interest more and more to the gymnasium where old-fashioned types held forth.

Snow and Ice Sports

The winter brings one of the most delightful opportunities of the entire year for outdoor recreational enjoyment. Hikes, with proper clothing, are often more enjoyable in this season. The campfire in some nearby shelter house always seems to cook the food more tastily. Not many schools and colleges can be so fortunate as Dartmouth College, with its fine chain of cabins in the nearby hills for winter outings, but any schools situated where snow or ice sports can be held have a rare opportunity.

City maintenance departments usually can be prevailed upon to flood areas for ice skating. Intramural ice carnivals can feature a winter program of mixed activities as well as the usual races and relays for boys and men only. James A. Cruikshank describes the winter carnival in the Spalding booklet, *Winter Sports,* thus:

> There seems to be some unique quality about the winter which stimulates people to merriment and enthusiasm. It is something more than the scientific fact that one-seventh more oxygen is found in the cold air of winter than the warm air of summer. The same group of young people will revel in winter depths of fun and prankish tendencies unsuspected by any actions of the summertime.
>
> All a winter carnival needs, given the right sort of weather, is a moving spirit. Let someone start the thing and the expression of interest will be immediate, and support will be generous. The very novelty of the affair will attract attention and draw people. And once it has been successfully carried out there will be demands for its repetition. There may be snowshoe races where start and finish are in front of the grandstand or in the center of the rink where folks can keep moving; ski races and ski coasting; skating races; couples skating in fancy movements or speed contests; fancy dancing on skates, double or individual; skating exhibitions; costume skating with prizes for the best costume representative of winter; parade of decorated sleighs, floats, sleds, or togobbans; parades on snowshoes, ski runners, and skaters in costume.
>
> Any number of most interesting events can be run off on an ice field, such as hoop races, wheelbarrow races, potato races, snow-shovel races, where the men drag the girls one half the distance and the girls drag the men the remaining distance; necktie races in similar fashion;

obstacle races, getting through a barrel or over a fence, or climbing
a rope ladder; toboggan races where two persons sit on the toboggan
and propel it by hands or feet over the ice; and lanterns of all kinds
everywhere, electric illumination, if it can be arranged; colored fire,
torches, toboggans rigged with tiny batteries and carrying individual
insignia and emblems (fraternity or sorority), topped off by the moonlight.

The author conducted a Winter Ice and Snow Carnival at Beloit
College, Wisconsin, for several years which combined the men's inter-
fraternity ice skating races with an evening of social-recreational outdoor
sport. This program cluminated a weekend of snow sculpturing, coasting,
and tobogganing, which served to get the whole campus outdoor-minded
and ready for the occasion. All campus organizations vied with one another
in building and exhibiting snow-sculptured models and displays in their
yards, with prizes awarded for the best exhibits.

The beautiful outdoor lagoon, with well-equipped warming house, had
a racing course laid out for competition, with colored flags and proper
starting and finishing lines. In the afternoon the men's races and relays
were run off, and competition was spirited. A loudspeaking system added
much to the occasion. Records were kept and distances remained uniform
each year. Relays formed one of the highlights of this meet, with a shuttle
relay offering variety from the usual types of relays for speed or distance.
Many of the students and faculty were attracted to this event, as well as
large numbers of spectators from the city.

In the evening, fraternity rivalry was pushed into the background.
Brightly colored lanterns, a loudspeaker, and a master of ceremonies set the
stage for one of the year's outstanding social and recreational events. The
program was attractively highlighted by medley relays for men and women,
special ice games and stunts, fancy skating demonstrations, and couple
skating with music. Follow-the-leader and maze skating offered pleasing
variety to the program. After the group began to tire somewhat from the
activity, the party adjourned to the nearby gymnasium, where coffee and
doughnuts followed a few warm-up novelty stunts of the mixer and square
dance variety. Faculty, students, and townspeople proclaimed this event
one of the most enjoyable of the year's calendar.

Dartmouth College, with its beautiful winter sports setting in New
Hampshire, has developed one of the outstanding ice and snow activity
programs found anywhere. Ripon College has also sponsored a program of
this type. Shorewood High School, in Milwaukee, has been a leader in ice
sports among Wisconsin high schools. Programs of this type offer unlimited
opportunities for ingenuity and enterprise which will pay big dividends in
student interest and appreciation. The University of Chicago annually
provides a fine skating rink, sheltered by the stadium walls from wintry

blasts, which is one of the most popular spots on the campus for outdoor recreation. The concrete also provides a roof over the rink. Many school district and recreation departments are making full use of this chance to sell their activities with success. When facilities are made available in some cities, there is no reason why schools so situated should not take advantage of this opportunity with organized events.

Highlights and Program Features
Throughout the Nation

The University of Michigan holds frequent Saturday night mixed recreational events, which are very popular with the student body. The co-recreational program offered at Aroostook State Normal School, at Presque Isle, Maine, is an example of what can be done by combining this phase of the program with Armistice Day activities.

University High School of Oakland, California, permits electives in cœducational physical education on Friday. Three choices are possible: archery or social dancing, in which boys and girls receive instruction together, or group games in divided groups. In the dancing group, identical numbers of boys and girls are assigned to the class. Many other California schools are having students work by two's and three's one day weekly, presenting activities they think would be enjoyable for party use.

The Randolph, Wisconsin, high school developed a fine co-recreational program which shows what can be done with limited facilities in the smaller schools. About twelve mixed parties headline the calendar each year. Some of these are strictly freshman affairs. Parents are invited and are usually on hand in good numbers. It has usually been found that the third freshman party finds most of the youthful bashfuls well adjusted socially, since only those of similar age have been present. This then makes interclass adjustment much easier. Equal numbers of boys and girls act as committees for each function, handling details connected with food, plans, features, and arrangements. The school activity ticket plan pays for most of the expenses of these "mixers." Different forms of dancing keep the gymnasium busy throughout the evening, while the typing room and another classroom are given over to games. The home economics room becomes the scene of table tennis activity, where heavy tables are moved together, forming excellent bounding surfaces. Cardboard nets are set between the table joints. The typing room is equipped with many kinds of card games. Students are free to move about from place to place at will.

At the University of North Carolina the Men's Intramural Department conducts jointly with the Women's Athletic Association an annual Intramural Sports Carnival. These activities are very popular on campus.

The program includes mixed team competition in track relays, foul shooting, archery, table tennis, Carnival games, badminton, volleyball, and bait casting.

A co-intramural program is conducted every Tuesday night at Arizona State University at Tempe. There are no eligibility requirements and all may come and participate. Sports usually utilized are volleyball, tennis, bowling, table tennis, badminton, golf, and softball.

The Division of Intramural and Recreational Sports at the University of Illinois sponsors a Co-Rec program to meet the demand for an informal competitive sports program in which both men and women can participate. All tournaments are played with teams composed of half men and half women. Adapted rules minimize any skill superiority of the men. Faculty and graduate students may participate. In different years literally hundreds of teams have been involved, especially in volleyball, bowling, softball, ice skating, tennis, and gymnastics.

Coeducational gymnastics, tumbling, and rebound tumbling are on the increase in the nation, in classes and in the recreational program. The latter may be through special clubs, or in classes or scheduled groups.

At the University of Colorado co-recreational volleyball competition was organized, using four men and four women on each team. Mixed bowling and skiing was also a feature of the program. Doane College, at Crete, Nebraska, introduced a Co-recreational Sports Night which included volleyball, table tennis, badminton, dart games, swimming, cards, and square dancing. It proved to be one of the outstanding events of each year's calendar. Certain days and special hours are set aside weekly at the University of Chicago for mixed recreation in bowling, dancing, roller skating, swimming, table tennis, cards, checkers, and chess. Special printed brochures are placed in the hands of all students concerning this program each year.

The junior colleges of the state of Illinois report the following co-recreational programs:

The Evanston Community College sponsors a Saddle Club, Bowling Club, All-School Athletic Banquet, and Beach Parties. La Salle-Peru Junior College conducts co-recreational seasonal activities. Every other week it has a Sports Date Night, and on the intervening weeks the girls invite their fathers to an evening of sports. It conducted a mixed ladder tournament in deck tennis, aerial darts, and badminton. Other sports and events included were square dancing, swimming, archery, tennis, and social dancing. Joliet Junior College has held play nights with sports in one gymnasium and dancing in the other. Sports in which competition is held are bowling, badminton, shuffleboard, volleyball, and table tennis. Joliet is planning roller skating parties, splash parties, hikes and picnics, and more school play nights. Morton Junior College has given co-recreational play days of an informal nature. It also sponsors a Kanter Klub and volleyball, swimming, and dancing. Wright Junior College operates its program totally through co-recreational sports clubs. It has swimming, horseback riding, bowling leagues, and table tennis. Wilson Junior College sponsors occasional weekend co-ed outing parties, and an all-school play night.

Minnie Maude Macaulay has developed an outstanding co-recreational program at Berea College, Kentucky. Al Lewis organized a mixed sports party for every Friday at the high school at Princeton. Illinois, The Oliver High Shcool at Pittsburgh has been conducting a co-recreational play day for years with splendid results. Friday nights are popular co-recreational sports nights at Iowa State. The George Williams College in Chicago conducts several mixed sports throughout each year. The John Adams High School in Cleveland uses table tennis, deck tennis, and social dancing in its program. Vassar College was one of the first women's colleges to recognize the need to invite male guests to sports participation events on Saturdays and Sundays. The North High School of Des Moines has a mixed sports program in swimming, diving, volleyball, cage ball, giant volleyball, golf, tennis, table tennis, deck tennis, badminton, and social dancing.

Co-recreational activities were introduced in the Wichita schools by Strong Hinman in 1936. They were started in six junior high schools and two senior high schools as a part of the compulsory physical education program. The high schools first had co-recreational classes every Friday, with the junior high schools using only two days each month. The program was very successful and gradually expanded into a voluntary activity. Augustana College at Sioux Falls, South Dakota, first started its mixed sports play nights with such sports as volleyball, cage ball, and badminton. It was found that the program had greater success after musical games, mixers, and dance features were included.

A Washington State University study of the colleges and universities in the Northwest indicated that all the seventeen institutions reporting co-recreational programs had a purely recreational objective, giving no credit in physical education. Swimming was found to be the most popular sport. Skiing was found in thirteen schools. Nine institutions had their own outing cabins, others rented suitable buildings, and all expressed a great interest in the outing activities. One school reported an All-College Horseback Ride, another held a Salmon Bake at the school cabin, others held all-college picnics, and another had an all-college dance outdoors on an outing trip, followed by group singing. Some reported sailing, camping, and weekend hikes.

Other colleges reporting outstanding co-recreational programs are Hamline, Lawrence, Tarkio, Emporia, Wheaton, Valley City, Wittenberg, Simpson, Milwaukee State, Sterling, Knox, and College of the Pacific.

Universities reported placing increased emphasis on this type of program are Denver, North Carolina State, Idaho, Wake Forest, Auburn, Butler, San Diego State, Tennessee, Alabama, Minnesota, and Nebraska. The University of Illinois has started an increased promotion of co-recreational sports, both competitive and noncompetitive. The men's department coordinates closely with the W.A.A. in developing this program.

Implications of the Social Recreational Program

One thought must be kept constantly in mind in the development of social-recreational activities in the school and college program. No school should be without this valuable part of the complete and modern program, yet the enthusiasm and student interest developed must not be allowed to overwhelm the rest of a valuable and balanced offering. It is evident that there are too many indispensable parts to the total intramural activities program to permit any one phase of physical education experience to dominate or overshadow the many student needs which must be served through many types of approach. Co-recreational sports offer just one more valuable method of effecting and approximating the socially, mentally, and physically adjusted individual who will be better prepared to meet his adult responsibilities.

REFERENCE

1 *Partners in Play* (New York: A. S. Barnes & Co., 1936).

14

FINANCING THE PROGRAM

A few years ago the problem of budgeting and finance for the intramural program required ingenuity, sometimes proving a stubborn barrier for expansion and maintenance. Many plans for raising sufficient funds were used, some of them questionable. This was necessary since intramurals were considered purely extracurricular and brought little or no revenue. Fortunately, both educators and the public have become aware of the great values of a good program which reaches the total student body, and regularized revenue is now the rule rather than the exception in most schools; but directors still find it necessary to plan carefully in order to expand the program properly.

Boards of education in the future will see to it that adequate funds are available for equipment, leadership, and facilities. In some cases laws will not permit the use of public funds for such items as awards and special features. In other situations the budget allocated for intramurals will have to be supplemented by special fund-raising projects. This chapter will attempt to assist those who must find additional cash to maintain a satisfactory program. In every case the director will be wise to sell the program on its own merits, and constant effort should be made to secure adequate budgets through regular channels, even though temporary plans must be perfected to supplement income.

One large, prominent American university, nationally famous for its intercollegiate teams, recently asked an intramural director to operate his entire program for men on a total budget of $200. The same university, through its athletic director, spent an average of $7 per meal for every man on a varsity football team of over forty men, sparing no expense to make each trip enjoyable and interesting. This startling fact serves to indicate that wise directors often can rearrange emphases and expenditures for the total program without stifling any one varsity sport, thereby providing adequate funds for all sports as well as for intramurals. The application of good business procedures in the care and use of equipment also often results in sufficient savings to finance much of the intramurals.

H. Carroll King, city director of physical education at Raleigh, North Carolina, reports a plan which is gaining acceptance in many cities. The school board was reluctant to allocate sufficient funds for a diversified program of intramurals. Joint school-community planning saved the situation. Joint planning and financing of facilities had been done effectively in past years. In this case, school officials worked out a plan with city recreation leaders so that all junior high school students could have intramurals. The school board furnishes facilities, equipment, and supervisory-operational personnel. The recreation department provides the funds to pay this personnel. Activities were planned for after school, evenings, and weekends. After two years this program was so successful, and so mutually acceptable to both jurisdictions, that recreation leaders asked the school board to broaden the plan to include the senior high schools.

The policy of attempting at least one or two annual projects to augment conservative budgets is strongly recommended. A double objective can be attained with such a plan: added motivation and public appreciation of the program can be stimulated simultaneously with the raising of needed finances. One or two major projects will also eliminate the necessity of holding several rather questionable money-raising schemes each year. Care should be exercised in the choice of projects, to avoid bringing any trace of disrepute or disfavor on the total program.

The University of California at Berkeley formerly conducted an annual carnival, which financed intramural costs and awards. The carnival began at noon and ended at midnight with the "jitney dance" as the concluding attraction. The event was a combination of three-ring circus and state fair, giving outsiders a "bird's eye" view of the complete intramural program. Held in the men's gymnasium and on adjoining fields, this yearly festival lacked only a tent to make the circus illusion complete. There were the usual side shows of magicians, fortune tellers, bunco games, peanuts and popcorn. Regular intramural competition in basketball, swimming, squash, badminton, table tennis, soccer, softball, basket shooting, and football passing and punting contests were held continuously during the afternoon.

The famous baby buggy race between the fraternities added to the color and noise of the show. Following an afternoon of such hubbub the evening's attractions offered welcome relief. Finals in wrestling, fencing, and gymnastics occupied the gymnasium. Following the last contests the floor was cleared and dancing closed the carnival. Sales from concessions added considerable revenue to the venture.

The University of Nebraska for years conducted one or two major projects for purposes of money-raising as well as to assist in better public relations. One project has varied from a championship intramural carnival, to presentation of the National Danish Gymnastics Team on tour, to a carnival and fair somewhat similar to the California Plan. While the annual budgets at Nebraska provide substantial maintenance funds, these special projects have enabled the department to procure many pieces of more expensive equipment for intramurals, such as electric scoreboards for all basketball floors, canvas partitions between the sections of the larger playing area, and expanded outdoor facilities and night-lighted fields.

The Gymkana at the University of Illinois and more recently at Florida State have been so well developed, and are so full of unique and daring ideas, that they cannot help but add spice to the program. West Virginia University conducts an annual intramural carnival with great success. Sports championship nights have been conducted by Ohio State University and the University of Michigan, and are masterpieces of organization and effectiveness. Chicago University has been featuring an annual carnival, combining all kinds of campus activities, ever since the earlier days of Alonzo A. Stagg, Sr.

The high school at Mt. Vernon, Iowa, conducts a carnival for the purpose of raising funds, and it includes movies, floor show, dancing, contests, games of skill, and other carnival attractions. Novelties, needlework, handicraft items, and refreshments are all on sale. A carnival queen is crowned. The school circus at Ironwood, Michigan, has been outstanding. The affair is replete with all kinds of tumbling and apparatus stunts, as well as the usual sale of refreshments. Funds are raised which make possible a more diverse and extended school recreation program.

As a fund-raising project, the schools at King City, Missouri, conduct a sale of felt banners and pennants which are designed with the names and colors of the competing high schools in some of the basketball tournaments. Maryville College at Maryville, Tennessee, finances all its intramurals through the college Y.M.C.A. This organization arranges special events to bring in needed revenue for this program. The University of Tennessee and Louisiana State University are examples of schools that finance intramural sports through varsity gate receipts, supplemented by private donations.

The policy of charging admission for intramural competition generally is not recommended, as it defeats the democratic purpose of participation for all. Estimated attendance during a year's running of the large university intramural program of today is astonishing where admission is not charged. However, having one or two major projects each year with an admission charge seems perfectly justifiable; it will be well received by the student body and public at large, and can be made to produce considerable revenue as well as recognition for the program.

Prior to 1937 only Michigan, Oberlin, Ohio State, and Rutgers used entry fees to purchase awards. Many other schools now do so. West Virginia receives many of its trophies from sporting goods companies without charge.

Kentucky uses receipts from wrestling and boxing tourneys for intramurals. Wisconsin derives proceeds from concessions at intercollegiate events. Only a few larger schools such as Illinois, Kentucky, and Penn State charge individual and team entry fees for each individual and team intramural event. De Pauw and Wisconsin make assessments for team entries only. Purdue has charged an annual fee for each award independent player, good for all sports. At Minnesota, West Virginia, Nebraska, Kansas, Beloit, and others, an annual small fee is charged each organization, which does not seek to finance the entire program, but can be used to partially pay for awards and officials' fees.

The University of Kansas has used the following schedule of entrance fees:

Entry fees will be charged for each sport in order to acquire funds to buy trophies and awards. **Fees must accompany entry.** The following schedule has been adopted:

SPORT	MAX. NO. PLAYERS	FEE PER INDIVIDUAL
Touch football "A"	No Limit	25c
Touch football "B"	″ ″	25c
Handball	″ ″	25c
Horseshoes	″ ″	25c
Tennis	″ ″	25c
Golf	″ ″	25c
Basketball	″ ″	25c
Softball	″ ″	25c
Track	″ ″	25c
Swimming Meet	″ ″	25c
Badminton	″ ″	25c
Bowling	″ ″	25c

Any other activities' fee will be determined at the time the entry blanks are sent out.

At Duke University entrance fees must be paid at the time of entry as follows:

	INDIVIDUAL	TEAM
Badminton	$1.00	
Basketball		$10.00
Bowling		10.00
Cross-country	Free	
Golf	1.00	5.00
Handball	1.00	
Horseshoes	1.00	
Softball		10.00
Swimming	1.00	
Table tennis	1.00	
Tennis	1.00	
Touch football		10.00
Track	1.00	
Volleyball		10.00
Wrestling	1.00	

At the University of New Hampshire emphasis is placed on forfeiture fees. Each team must deposit a $25 forfeiture fee at the Intramural Office at the start of the college year. Independent teams deposit $5 when entering each sport. Deductions are made from these deposits on the following basis: Each game or match forfeited deducts $2.50 in:

touch football	tennis	basketball
handball	volleyball	badminton
water polo	wrestling	soccer
	softball	squash

Five dollars is deducted in swimming, bowling, golf, indoor track, and ski meet when forfeits occur. Ten dollars is charged for forfeits in ice hockey. When the entire $25 deposit is exhausted, another $25 fee is required. Refunds of deposit money remaining are made at the end of the year.

The University of Toronto publishes an annual rate sheet for the payment of officials in all sports, with revenue for this purpose provided through regular budgets. Illinois, Michigan, Minnesota, Colorado, and Wisconsin are dependent in part on varsity athletic incomes. Many of the smaller endowed colleges like Carleton, Beloit, Swarthmore, Haverford, Lawrence, Colorado College, and Oberlin receive, through their regular budgets, a portion of the student activity fee every student pays each semester. This is also true at the University of Texas.

A study of most college intramural departments would indicate a tendency to use student activity fees to finance all or a part of the intramural and recreational program. This would appear to be more defensible than the practice of charging a special fee for each sport entry. With this plan all students share in the financing, can feel responsible for the success of the program, and, therefore, might want to participate more actively.

Leo G. Staley of Ohio State described the financing plan used by the university, which should be of help to some institutions: [1]

> Up until 1932 intramural sports at Ohio State were almost entirely financed out of athletic gate receipts. With the depression years it became increasingly more difficult for intramurals to receive adequate support. In the face of increasing student enrollment the program was in danger of curtailment.
>
> In 1932 the athletic and intramural directors proposed a plan to add fifty cents to the charges levied all students which consisted of $1.00 for Student Health, $1.00 to support the Student Union, and $1.00 for library support. The proposal was accepted and $12,000 was realized for intramurals the first year.
>
> In 1934 all fees were thrown together and raised to $4.00 per student per quarter. In 1939 the fee was raised to $5.00 per quarter and now embraces support for some twenty student services. Since 1934 no attempt has been made to apportion funds to beneficiary groups on a percentage basis. The President allocates funds according to budget requests, modified by necessary adjustments. [Other changes in fees have been made at Ohio State since that time.]

The Intramural Division at Ohio State has fared well under this plan. The major advantages are as follows:

1. Fairly stable funds are made available for intramurals without concern for uncertain athletic receipts.
2. Funds are proportional to number of students.
3. Planning is simplified and improved, and budgets can be arranged according to anticipated enrollment.
4. By embracing several services besides intramurals, the student is more apt to be served in one way or another and to support the plan.
5. By having paid the activity fee, the students may enter all tournaments and activities without additional charges and fees. This eliminates much bookkeeping and financing worries.

One disadvantage of the plan is the restriction in use of funds. They may not be used for capital investment. For instance, canoes may be purchased but a boat house may not be built. However, it can be seen that this provision is a safeguard against misuse of funds for projects other than for student use.

Miller found that over 50 percent of the universities he surveyed in 1938 derived all their intramural funds from the physical education budget.[2] He found only 26 percent of these schools still receiving all funds and income from varsity gate receipts. Later studies indicate a greater percentage financed by regular budget.

Wood found that the practice of financing intramurals from sources other than varsity gate receipts was used as early as 1935.[3] Good administrative practice would indicate that all schools should develop financing plans which have no dependency whatever on varsity gate receipts, and that all funds if possible should be derived from regularly budgeted school or university income. Plant and play fields can then be expanded properly with the help of the intercollegiate department.

Some years ago several large city high schools in the East collected five- and ten-cent fees from players for each sport. It is hoped the schools in question have long since eliminated such an unsound practice. When one considers the great number of students who ought to be participating, the cost per capita is, after all, exceptionally small. School administrators and boards of education will probably realize more actual benefits to pupils per dollar invested in a well-planned and well-directed intramural program of sports than in almost any other activity in which students participate.

The cost in the junior and senior high schools per student is usually very low. Students can be required to furnish most of their playing equipment, and other items can be borrowed from physical education or varsity athletic supplies. It should be noted that whenever the financing of the

Fig. 82. Volleyball league play at Florida State University. Note use of official intramural jerseys for participants.

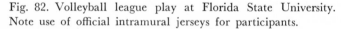

intramural program must depend on assessments and fees from student sources, much of the equality of opportunity is destroyed and the program is curtailed.

At Amherst College all major trophies are donated by graduating classes and alumni. Amherst has a large Sportsmanship Trophy which is also donated by the alumni. Civil clubs in many cities have often assisted financially in the project of recreation for all. As a general policy it would seem wise to eliminate the subscription of donations, prizes, and awards from local businesses and to shift the emphasis toward a permanent educational budgetary arrangement whereby intramurals are treated as any other department of the school. There would appear to be no reason why much-interested alumni foundations or groups could not finance specific awards, since their interest in the institution is more sentimental and educational than pecuniary. Trophies for such sports as bowling, where all competition takes place in commercial recreation halls, could be furnished by the management, and often are in many cities, since they receive a substantial income from student participation.

Lloyd G. Blakely of Southwest Baptist College at Bolivar, Missouri, suggested a novel method by which $6,114 was netted in a two-day "Old Fashioned County Fair"; it is worthy of study for the director who is searching for fund-raising ideas.[4]

The following ideas have all been used by schools and are listed here as a check list only. Some of them might be used to provide temporary funds until such time as school administrators could observe the value and worth of the program.

1. Receipts from plays and variety shows using local talent.
2. Candy, cake, pastry, and novelty sales at school or in city.
3. Rummage sales conducted by students, with all items for sale donated.
4. School and community dances.
5. Special movies during school day or at night for general public.
6. Sale of special tickets to downtown movies with a percentage of the advance ticket sale going to intramural athletics.
7. The school circus or gymnasium exhibit.
8. Scrap paper drives. One high school in Wisconsin raised over $4,000 in one year by this method. City trucks donated services for hauling and pick-ups.
9. Split of profit from professional traveling entertainers.
10. Beauty contests. Votes sold on favorite contestants.
11. Box socials or pie and cake socials.
12. Sale of food and refreshment concessions at varsity games and school functions.
13. Magazine subscription campaigns.
14. Cookbook and recipe contest campaign.

15. Staging Sunday School or church basketball tournaments in the local community, using school facilities.
16. Egg and farm produce sales days, with items donated by students.
17. Special feature basketball games between student and faculty.
18. Games and stunts night followed by school dance.
19. The school activity fee from which a percentage of receipts are apportioned to intramurals. The Ten-Cent-A-Week Plan originated many years ago at Tech High School, Omaha, Nebraska, and variations of this plan have become increasingly popular over the nation in financing all types of school activities.
20. The annual carnival, where all kinds of special money-raising ideas can be arranged, some of which are:
    a. Baby doll rack.
    b. Basketball free throw pitching contest with prizes.
    c. Fortune teller.
    d. Freak side shows.
    e. Style show.
    f. Magician side show.
    g. Bean bag throw for prizes.
    h. Fish ponds with prizes.
    i. Bingo games with prizes.
    j. Refreshment stands.
    k. Miniature bowling alley.
    l. Barrel toss.
    m. Grab bag and grocery counter.

It would be safe to say that the intramural program is worthy of community or institutional support. As its value becomes more apparent to the public the question of finance is usually speedily solved. The trend is unquestionably toward complete subsidization by school boards, student body funds, or college budget, and not dependent on gate receipts or other kinds of money-raising schemes.

REFERENCES

1 *"Intramural Finance Plan at Ohio State University,"* Proceedings, College Physical Education Association, 1946.
2 Charles E. Miller, *"Intramural Athletics for Men in Large Colleges and Universities,"* Unpublished Thesis, University of Nebraska, Lincoln, 1938.
3 Harold S. Wood, *"New Developments in the Administration of Intramural Athletics in Colleges,"* Proceedings, College Physical Education Association, 1935, p. 45.
4 "Financial Worries? Try This," *School Activities,* XXIII, No. 1 (September, 1951), 27.

15

EXTRAMURAL ATHLETICS

With the expansion of intramural activities and the desire of many directors to broaden and deepen the interschool competitive program as far as possible, a new phase of recreational activity in America has been evolving. Extramural athletics might be defined simply as the expansion of intramural competition between schools without the complex problems that necessarily characterize interscholastic or intercollegiate sport. Two or more schools make arrangements to match their intramural champions in an informal and recreational series of contests. The extramural idea is not new and unique, but its expansion has been very slow, and it remains untried in many schools. Extramurals are a variation on the girls' play day idea started several years ago by the women of Stanford University, Mills College, and the University of California, and successfully adopted by the women in many schools since that time.

Extramural athletics offers a splendid medium for the greater expansion of competitive values to large sections of the student body not usually proficient enough to make the varsity teams. Students with above-average skills who find it impossible to spend the time necessary for varsity participation can fulfill many of their needs and interests through occasional opportunities in extramurals. It also permits inclusion of many sports and activities not usually found in the varsity program. Boys lacking size and maturity of the "athlete" may absorb some of the benefits we claim for outside competition. Extramurals offer one of the finest mediums for attaining the objective of democracy in sports.

Extramurals are most practical for areas where schools are situated close together and travel is at a minimum. Long schedules are eliminated. Perhaps only one or two extramural meets per year should be featured on the program, and only neighboring schools scheduled. With the present doubtful emphasis on interscholastic junior high school athletics, extramurals offer an excellent substitute for competition with outside teams at this age level, eliminating many of the objectionable problems of strenuous game preparation, premature publicity, awards, and the pressure of winning over a long season. Cities having two or more junior high schools would do well to expand their intramurals into a workable extramural program, as could city high schools unable to provide complete varsity sports programs in enough sports.

Fig. 83. Junior high schools of Miami in a mass volleyball sports day at Miami University.

Several years ago the author added an extramural program to a school's already extensive intramural program. This school maintained twelve interscholastic sports and over thirty intramural events per year. The rival high school in the city was invited to participate with very stimulating competition in such intramural sports as handball, volleyball, basketball, free throws, badminton, table tennis, horseshoes, and bowling. Almost without exception the boys representing the host school were nonvarsity athletes. Boys of both schools had a memorable experience on each occasion. As an outgrowth of the program, repeated between the two high schools for three years, two new interscholastic sports were added to the program: intramural bowling champions were scheduled to compete with several nearby schools, finally emerging into a regular annual interscholastic schedule in bowling; extramural ice skating races and ice hockey similarly grew from an informal event into the Fox River Valley Ice Skating Carnival for competing high schools in Wisconsin.

Extramural days were also arranged between the men of Beloit and Carroll Colleges in Wisconsin, events that proved very popular on both campuses. Champions from the two institutions met in volleyball, water polo, table tennis, basketball, handball, horseshoes, free throws, badminton, and shuffleboard. A large busload of students made the trip together, with the event being scheduled the following year on the other campus.

Similar events have been held between Lawrence College, the University of Wisconsin, and Milwaukee State Teachers College with pleasing results. The University of Illinois inaugurated a program very similar in nature, between the four branches of the University (Galesburg, Navy Pier, Medical School, and Champaign). Eight sports were used by Illinois: touch football, intramural basketball, all-star basketball, handball, volleyball, table tennis, badminton, and softball. Illinois was sufficiently impressed with the program to suggest that it might set a pattern for other schools.[1]

The University of Illinois, Purdue University, and DePaul University have on various occasions enjoyed extramural competition in such sports as tennis, golf, and softball. Three Pennsylvania colleges, Gettysburg, Dickinson, and Franklin and Marshall, report very interesting and successful extramural competition between their student groups in basketball, and have enlarged the idea to include touch football and softball, as well as other possible sports.

The Women's Club of the College of Physical Education, Health and Recreation at the University of Maryland hosts an annual play day for Maryland high school seniors. Girls from a dozen schools participate in mixed team competition, square and round dancing, volleyball, relays, and swimming. The affair is student-organized with the majors taking full responsibility for its planning.

The University of Louisville and Bellarmine College annually conduct an Extramural Sports Weekend. These events include competition in bowling, horseshoes, table tennis, tennis, golf, softball, and volleyball. A rotating extramural trophy is retained each year by the winner of the most events.[2]

Harold Haskins reported on the extramural program in Florida junior colleges in 1969:[3]

The Florida Junior College Conference was organized in 1964 by action of the Council of Presidents of the Florida Public Junior College. Its purpose was "to promote and regulate *intercollegiate activities* as an integral part of the educational program of the member institutions."

The State is divided geographically into four divisions, each with its secretary, to promote regional activities and competition. State-wide activities are coordinated by Standing Committees in the several activities who make their recommendations to the Executive Committee.

...our main interest is with intramurals and extramurals....

Division IV is an organizational example, involving seven junior colleges. Each college appoints an Extramural Director. The seven directors choose one of their group to act as an Extramural Chairman for the Division. The responsibilities of this chairman are:

1. To organize and chair meetings at the three Extramural Sports Days.
2. To appoint committees for re-evaluation of the Division IV Extramural handbook as needed.
3. To serve as an advisor on any problems which may arise with the extramural program.
4. To aid in resolving problems which may arise on Extramural Sports Days.
5. To work with the other three Division Chairmen in organizing state-wide competition.

Division IV Extramural Directors have developed a Division IV handbook which includes:

1. Philosophy and objectives.
2. Eligibility rules.
3. Activities and events.
4. Type of tournaments for activities.
   a. number of players per tournament.
   b. rules governing tournaments.
5. Point system for each activity.
   a. entry points.
   b. place points.
6. Awards and certificates.
7. General policies and procedures.

Description of Intramural program. Whenever possible the competition will consist of a men's team, women's team, and co-ed teams. In activities in which we are restricted as to time and as to space available, preference is given to co-ed activity.

Three Divisional Sports Days are scheduled each year. In addition, an Invitational Bowling Tournament is hosted each year by Palm Beach Junior College.

Activities for these Sports Days vary according to the host school. Generally one team sport plus two individual competitions are scheduled. Team sports may include volleyball (men's, women's, and co-ed's) and/or slow-pitched softball (coed). Supplemental rules governing this type of softball designate that a team must be composed of five men and five women; women cannot play as catcher, pitcher, or third base; sliding isn't allowed.

Individual competitions include archery, badminton, bowling, table tennis, and tennis.

Points are awarded on the basis of activities entered. Additional points are awarded for placing 1st, 2nd, 3rd, or 4th in each event. At the completion of the day, points are totaled, and the school receiving the highest number of points is declared winner. Trophies are awarded for 1st and 2nd place.

On this point a problem has developed. One of the primary objectives of the Sports Day was to provide an opportunity to come together and enjoy the experience of competing on a physical, emotional, social, and moral basis. Currently the emphasis seems to be on "winning" and the over-all value became over-shadowed. In order to correct this situation, the awarding of trophies was later eliminated. Instead, certificates are awarded to first and second place teams in each activity, and teams can be made up of players from different schools.

Augustana College, of Sioux Falls, South Dakota, has conducted a number of extramural events with the local Y.M.C.A. and with Gustavus Adolphus College of St. Peter, Minnesota. Sports used in this series have been handball, table tennis, volleyball, and badminton. In the East four colleges have often enjoyed extramurals in many sports: Wesleyan University, Harvard, Massachusetts State College, and Lafayette College. Mass tennis meets have been organized for the students of Duke and North Carolina University, where as many as 100 players from each school have enjoyed competition. Twenty to thirty men have often met in various sports from Wesleyan University and Amherst College.

At the University of California at Berkeley, Kooman Boycheff discontinued the annual Intramural championships which had evolved from the earlier sports carnivals. A series of Intramural Sports Festivals was started in 1963 with competition for both men and women intramural champions in several sports. The first event of this type was held at the University of California at Santa Barbara with 300 men and women from six University of California branches participating. The event has continued in popularity with events held at Berkeley, Davis, UCLA, and Santa Barbara.

In addition to all the "so-called" major sports, the Baltimore schools have held annual competition in table tennis, bowling, handball, and several other sports usually considered more intramural in nature. This was an outgrowth of earlier extramural competition which grew into permanent activity.

In all the junior and senior high schools of Providence, Rhode Island, an unusual intramural and extramural program exists.[4] All sports are divided into seasons, and dates are set in advance for the length of season. Three-fourths of each sport season is devoted exclusively to intramural competition. The final fourth is given over to extramural and interschool play, with the best intramural players selected to represent each school. No coach or director may start team practice until ten days prior to the scheduled start. School teams are all the result of earlier intramural play in the following sports:

JUNIOR HIGH SCHOOLS

Touch football	Basketball	Outdoor track relays
Indoor track	Handball	Swimming
	Baseball	

SENIOR HIGH SCHOOLS

Badminton	Gymnastics	Tennis
Handball	Indoor track	Swimming
	Baseball	

Over 400 basketball teams, representing all the Denver high schools, have played an extensive extramural schedule of games for years, thus carrying their basketball competition out of the realm of intramural play and into a kind of interschool rivalry for thousands of youngsters.

Fig. 84. Elementary School Volleyball Field Day involves six thousand boys and girls from many schools in Norfolk, Virginia.

Extramurals in the form of an annual Big Four Sports Day feature competition of nonvarsity nature are held between intramural teams from Duke, Wake Forest, North Carolina State, and the University of North Carolina. Host responsibilities are rotated.

It has been frequently said that this occasion does more to establish and perpetuate good rapport among the four colleges than does any other association.

The winners and runner-up of every intramural team and individual activity at Duke are automatically selected to participate in Big Four Day. Other interested students are also encouraged to sign up for participation.

The activities and numbers of entrants in each event are as follows:

1. Badminton—5 players (2 doubles and 1 singles)
2. Handball—5 players (2 doubles and 1 singles)
3. Horseshoes—5 players (2 doubles and 1 singles)
4. Tennis—5 players (2 doubles and 1 singles)
5. Table tennis—4 players (2 singles and 1 doubles)
6. Bowling—4 players
7. Golf—4 players
8. Volleyball—10 players plus 1 official
9. Softball—12 players plus 1 official

Similarly, Pomona, Claremont, University of Redlands, and the University of California at Riverside hold an annual Sports Day for men and women. Sports involved are basketball, softball, volleyball, archery, and tennis. In the latter sport competition is provided in men's and women's singles, men's doubles, and mixed doubles.

The extramural movement has been much more prominent in the eastern area, with Syracuse University and Colgate receiving credit for initiating this type of competition many years ago. While some critics have maintained the idea would result in intramural neglect, there has been no such result in the following schools, all of which have occasionally sponsored extramural athletics: Princeton, Columbia, New York University, Lehigh, Brown, Bucknell, Penn State, Connecticut State, Swarthmore, Antioch, Catholic University, University of Vermont, Washington and Jefferson, Syracuse, Colgate, Amherst, Harvard, Yale, Lafayette, Wesleyan, and Massachusetts State.

One of the most colorful and traditional extramural series of contests is that of the Yale colleges and the Harvard houses. This fine relationship was interrupted by World War II, but again quickly renewed as one of the outstanding features of their annual program. Each year, on the day preceding the varsity clash between the old rivals in football, the several houses meet the many colleges of Yale in extramural football. In the winter the same groups again meet in basketball, squash rackets, and swimming. They also meet in tennis, rowing, golf, baseball, hockey, and touch football.

Intramural champions from St. Ambrose, St. Norbert College of West DePere, Wisconsin, St. Joseph's College of Collegeville, Indiana, and Loras College of Dubuque, Iowa, meet to enjoy competition in bowling, basketball, table tennis, and volleyball. Each college becomes host by rotation each spring at the time of the annual conference meeting.

Henry Shenk at Kansas University reports that the biggest change in recent years in their intramural program has been the addition of many sports clubs which compete on an extramural basis. Recently sponsored clubs are in fencing, soccer, rifle shooting, volleyball, and cricket. Kansas women's clubs participate in tennis, badminton, swimming, field hockey, volleyball, basketball, softball, and gymnastics on an extramural basis with students of other institutions.

"Sonny" Rooker, at the University of Texas, is expanding club extramurals rapidly. Figure 85 shows the Texas Soccer Club, which emerged from intramural schedules to compete on a club basis with students in other colleges. This group was undefeated in 42 consecutive contests.

Another practice that seems to be gaining favor in some areas is the challenge games in touch football, basketball, softball, and a few other sports between the fraternity of one college and the same fraternity of rival college. Usually a home-and-home arrangement is worked out over a two-year period, with the game preceding a dinner for the visitors. The date agreed upon usually coincides with the varsity games between the schools. It is significant to note that such a series was tried over a four-year period between groups of two long-standing rival colleges, with remarkable good

Fig. 85. Texas Soccer Club.

fellowship and sportsmanship exhibited in spite of the fact that the varsity football teams of the two colleges seemed constantly to have difficulties. It would seem to be good administrative procedure to cooperate in making such events successful rather than frowning on the practice, even though the idea has both good and bad implications. If properly conducted, informal challenge games can provide enjoyable experiences, develop sportsmanship, and increase interest in the total program of physical education and competitive sports.

Some have objected to the extramural idea largely on two counts. They have felt that objections might be raised by the director of intercollegiate athletics as to possible encroachment on his program. There has also been feeling that the intramural director could object to extramurals for constituting an improper emphasis which might lead the way to the destruction of the whole intramural idea. It would seem that these feelings are unwarranted, since each of these programs complements the others in the ideal organization. Wide gaps which often exist between the two departments can be cemented over by this type of program, if handled with wisdom and careful planning, and not repeated too often.

The problem of awards and team uniforms need not embarrass the extramural program. These games will be played solely for the fun and enjoyment of the participants, with no undue premium placed on victory. Great loyalties can be developed through such a program, since students have ample proof that the director and his staff are vitally interested in all the students and not just the varsity star. These events can be staged

Fig. 86. Intramural stars in table tennis from Flint, Michigan, and Hamilton, Ontario, enjoy their part in the broad extramural program featured each year.

Fig. 87. Boys from all high schools in Lincoln, Nebraska, participating in an extramural volleyball event.

without great preparation, without admission charge, and attended by favorable public opinion. No coaching time is required. No tedious and lengthy practice sessions are necessary. Extramurals are not suggested as a substitute for a broad and extensive varsity program, which should always stand at the apex of the competitive pyramid. Neither are they the substitute for a good and steadily working intramural program that consistently reaches more and more of the student body throughout the year. Rather, they are simply an occasional highlight of the year's activity, adding interest to student participation.

Although play days and sports days have been discussed in an earlier chapter in some detail, a few selected illustrations of excellent events of this type over the nation are presented here. The sports day is actually an extramural event which extends the intramural participation between schools, eliminating the pressure usually associated with highly coached varsity sports.

Arizona State at Temple plays host to neighboring high schools in a Volleyball Sports Day which has been highly successful. The University of Nebraska women conduct a gala sports day involving soccer, badminton, duck pin bowling, soccer-baseball, Nebraska Ball, tennis, and baseball. Colleges participating are Doane, Luther, Nebraska Wesleyan, Omaha University, Hastings, Kearney and Wayne State Teachers Colleges, York, and the University of Nebraska.

Five hundred boys and girls had a touch football and volleyball field day at Anaheim, California. The children were brought by bus from seventh and eighth grades of elementary schools. When the boys and girls arrived, lots were drawn to make pairing for games. A score of some kind was kept—eastern against western parts of the county—but it was unimportant, as everyone won by having a grand time and a fine experience in meeting and playing with children from other parts of the county.

Bret Harte Junior High School entertains girls from Hamilton and Oakland Junior Highs in California at annual play days. The unique feature is a committee of students from all the schools, advised by a faculty member from each, which plans the event in advance. Each girl pays for ice cream served, thus relieving the hostess school of the financial burden.

A Field Hockey Sports Day has been sponsored by the Deering High School in Maine, for the Portland area. Demonstration games start off the activities between teams of the Boston Field Hockey Association. Schools participating usually are Thornton Academy, Sanford High, Wayneflete School, Cony High, Westbrook Junior College, Gould Academy, Kent's Hill, Edward Little High, Wilton Academy, and Fryeburg Academy.

In the Livonia Public Schools of suburban Detroit, George Calkins and his staff have developed an annual series of elementary school Field Days for fifth- and sixth-grade boys and girls. About five thousand children each year have participated in these several Field Days since they were started. School administrators and teachers, as well as parents, are all unanimous in their praise for this activity, which is carried out with much preplanning, attention to detail, pupil planning involvement, and motivation toward individual excellence.

Fig. 88. Even rain did not dilute the joy of participating boys and girls in this extramural event which is typical of many at Richmond, California.

Events used in these Field Days are:

Running broad jump	Standing broad jump
Softball throw for distance	600-yard run-walk
Softball throw for accuracy	Pull-ups for boys
Bent arm hang for girls	50-yard dash
Shuttle relay	Running high jump
Tug-O-War	Volleyball

Anderson Valley High School in northern California plays host to Potter Valley and Hopland High Schools, demonstrating the worth of play days as opposed to interschool varsity sports for girls. All facilities are turned over for play in softball, basketball, and volleyball. The hostess school provides luncheon at noon. Principals and teachers attend. The G.A.A. president and her assistants are in charge of the program of sports, and a special kitchen committee handles the luncheon.

In Tulare County, California, volleyball play days have been held with great success at Sunnyside Union and Grand View, with hundreds of boys and girls participating. Strathmore Union Elementary holds a touch football play day for girls. Many other areas hold successful fall play days, and the spirit of good sportsmanship exhibited throughout the county has been highly commendatory.

Fig. 89. Extramurals in the Richmond, California, schools even feature this Folk Dance Festival. Note the large group of cerebral palsied children on stage serving as Festival Kings and Queens.

The Mariposa County Schools in California report a wonderful play day program for county elementary schools each year. Much preplanning goes into the event; students are polled on interests and activities. School buses transport all children to the central location. Boys and girls are classified into many groups for all activities mixed together. Children of ages 6-7-8-9 enjoy rhythm games, stunts and relays, and story telling, while the upper-grade children enjoy track events, relays, folk and square dances, amateur hour, and team games. Pupils are tagged with identification cards. The ceremonies open with registration, followed by an assembly featured by presentation of colors, singing, and salute to the flag, together with announcements of activities details. Luncheon is served, and high school students sell other refreshments during the day. Motion pictures are taken of all the events. This program is indeed a highlight for the more mountainous areas of California.

The following activities are outlined as a tentative guide for selection, and all lend themselves to the junior or senior high school or college extramural program. Lull periods in the usual varsity sports can be used to avoid congestion during the busy periods of the year.

Selected Outdoor Extramural Sports

Archery	Horseshoes	Lacrosse	Softball
Bait and fly casting	Ice hockey	Rowing	Speedball
Golf specialty contests	Ice skating races	Soccer	Tennis

Selected Indoor Extramural Sports and Activities

Badminton	Checkers	Handball	Table tennis
Basketball	Chess	Paddle tennis	Tug-o-war
Basketball golf	Cribbage	Pool	Volleyball
Billiards	Dart bowling	Rifle shooting	Water basketball
Bowling	Duck pin bowling	Shuffleboard	Water polo
Bridge	Free throws	Squash	

A national conference report on intramurals for college men and women produced the following statement.[5]

> Extramural activities should be organized and conducted when there is a demand for them, provided they meet the needs and standards of health, participation, and leadership of the intramural department... when certain requirements are met such as accident insurance, insured transportation, limited travel, approved facilities, proper supervision, and competent officials, extramural events may be used to enrich and complement the intramural program. . . .

Women's intramural activities and sports day petition conducted on an informal basis should be meet the AAHPER Division of Girl's and Women health, participation, leadership, and publicity.

REFERENCES

1 Hartley Price, *"New Trends at the University of Illinois,"* Proc Physical Education Association, 1947, p. 115.

2 Ellis Mendelsohn, *Men's Intramural Activities Handbook,* University o 1961-1962, p. 36.

3 National Intramural Association, *Twentieth Conference Proceedings,* 19 24-27.

4 Information submitted to the author by correspondence from John H. Osterbe Supervisor of Boys' Athletics, City Schools, Providence, R. I., 1954.

5 National Conference Report, *Intramural Sports for College Men and Women,* Washington, D.C., AAHPER, 1955, pp. 12, 23, 24.

16

EXPANDING
THE OUTDOOR PROGRAM

The traditional pattern of school recreational and intramural sports for the outdoors has been largely centered around a very few sports for fall and spring seasons. The United States and Canada are glorious outdoor countries, replete with all kinds of natural beauty which varies with each geographical location. Every school faces the constant problem of a crowded indoor program in a crowded indoor plant which is often inadequate for the complete modern program of activities. The result has been that many directors take the path of least resistance and permit a minimum of sports without much stimulation and promotion.

The program of the future will take advantage of the tremendous possibilities of the outdoors for healthful and invigorating play and of the ease with which facilities can be developed there. Ideas for the expansion of outdoor activities are as numerous as the ingenuity and inventiveness of the director. Every school holds a challenge for this type of leadership. Possibilities are unlimited. The economic structure of our society indicates that an increasing premium will be placed on leisure-time recreation in coming years. It is the responsibility of the schools to provide early experiences that will make for satisfying adult life. The director of intramurals and recreation can meet this challenge four-square with an ever-increasing outdoor program featuring a great variety of activities that will "stick" with the student all through life.

Not every school can develop *all* of the ideas and facilities suggested in this chapter. Some of these are limited to certain geographical locations. It is believed, however, that the enterprising director entering a new position can lay out a one-three-five-year program which gradually can achieve many of the program features that will make possible a new direction in the school and community recreational program.

This chapter will attempt to give practical suggestions, from which some ideas may be found, applicable to various school situations. It is intended to implement the many suggestions made in previous discussions. All of these ideas have been used in actual school situations. First, a brief presentation of outdoor activities will be given. Second, the expansion of outdoor facilities will be quickly reviewed. There is much new literature on details of facility construction and standards, eliminating the need for specific plans in this brief treatment. Third, suggestions will be made for the preparation of teachers and leaders who must form the nucleus for the more variegated recreational program of the future.

New Emphases in Activities
for the Outdoor Program

Brief suggestions are presented here for a great variety of sports and activities that fit perfectly into the outdoor intramural program. Many different methods of organizing competition will be given. Some activities are clearly intramural competitive sports, while others might be considered purely recreational in nature, yet all fit definitely into the modern school schedule of experiences that contribute much to the total educational scheme.

The simplest of all sport from an organizational standpoint, requiring a very modest outlay of equipment and space, is horseshoes. Yet few schools organize competition in this fine outdoor activity. Elimination tournaments, round-robin leagues, ladder and pyramid tourneys, and co-recreational events will make horseshoes a welcome addition to the year's calendar. School leagues and annual tournaments provide competition for scores of young players who will continue this activity into city league competition after graduation. Schools having city parks nearby often find it possible to work out plans with city recreation department to install night-lighted horseshoe courts which can be used in the daytime by students and at night by the adult leagues. Some schools have installed a simple and inexpensive lighting arrangement on their own grounds. This idea would be very practical for colleges and universities having late laboratories and crowded academic schedules.

Handball and paddleball are fine sports when played outdoors. A provision for outdoor handball courts opens up possibilities for continuous play by youngsters of all ages every day in the week. One-wall concrete courts will be found most practical, and a series of courts can be arranged along a single wall on the school grounds. This wall can also be used for tennis practice. One of the criticisms usually made of handball is that it is played deep in the recesses of many school basement areas with poor or no ventilation and artificial lighting. Since so many school gymnasiums are overcrowded during the winter season, handball is often completely eliminated from the program. It is a game that can be played outdoors by children of all ages, and is one of our most energetic and healthful games contributing greatly to fitness.

Tennis courts have been, and perhaps will continue to be, a serious problem at many colleges and universities. During World War II hundreds of tennis court sites were taken over for post-war housing projects which were supposed to be temporary but which remained. Some universities are situated in crowded metropolitan areas where play field and tennis court expansion is almost too costly to be considered. The ideal solution would then seem to be the installation of tennis court lighting so that available courts would practically double their usefulness. Lighting for tennis areas is not excessively expensive, and can be self-supporting after installation by use of slot-coin devices which require that players insert a coin for every half hour of play. Tennis courts placed between two buildings make the most of available space and provide the two vantage points from which lights

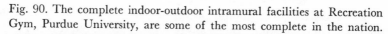

Fig. 90. The complete indoor-outdoor intramural facilities at Recreation Gym, Purdue University, are some of the most complete in the nation.

can be installed without the use of poles. Some of the methods for organizing tennis competition are as follows:

Mixed doubles tournaments

Team matches of singles players between groups

Team matches of doubles and singles matches between groups

Ladder or perpetual tournaments

Ringer tournament for the season, involving one-set matches with several opponents, with scores of all matches added, or best scores computed

Pyramid tournaments

All-school singles or doubles tournaments of single or double elimination

Faculty-student tournaments

Tournaments involving all kinds of competitive units

Two outdoor autumn sports that have not yet received popular promotion are speedball and soccer. A rather meager number of universities conduct regular intramural competition in these sports. In the larger schools touch football can be supplemented with these two vigorous sports, thus including another large segment of the student body. The number of play fields again looms as a major problem all over the nation. Here again the enterprising director will want to give considerable thought to the possibility of lighted play fields. If the indoor intramural sports can be scheduled at night there is no reason to assume that the fall and spring sports cannot also be so scheduled if lights are available.

Some public recreation departments have shown schools how to expand their softball competition by means of lighted areas. Quite often it is possible for the school district and city to cooperate in developing lighted facilities which can be used exclusively by the school program in the spring, and by the city during the summer months.

Very few schools make the most of golf as an outdoor sport. One small tournament often comprises the total program in many places. Interesting competition can be arranged in the following ways:

Medal play individual tournaments from which team standings can be determined

Medal play qualifying rounds, from which a select field can proceed to the championship with match play eliminations

Team round-robin leagues playing a large number of matches

Co-recreational mixed two-ball foursomes

Flag tournaments and all kinds of specialty and novelty meets

Golf driving and golf pitching or putting contests

Ladder and pyramid tournaments

Ringer golf tournament, using season scores for championship

Special holiday feature recreational tournaments

The success with which commercial golf interests have developed golf driving ranges, miniature golf courses, and other types of golf specialties would seem to indicate that school administrators could just as easily stimulate and organize similar school facilities that would attract hundreds of students throughout the year. Many schools would find it practical to build a golf driving range with lights on the campus where students could enjoy the activity at their leisure.

The popularity of basketball, along with the lack of an adequate number of indoor courts, would indicate that many schools could plan some outdoor facilities where games could be played part of the year and students could shoot baskets at any time. The same could be said for volleyball, badminton, deck tennis, and similar games. An ideal outdoor arrangement would be a hard surfaced area, equipped with lights, which would include basketball courts, additional basketball goals, volleyball lines and courts interchangeable with the basketball courts, and room for badminton, horseshoes. goal-hi, and handball.

School rifle and skeet clubs may be provided for by either working out arrangements with private clubs or by building their own range in a safe outdoor place. The National Rifle Association and many manufacturers of firearms now offer to schools many informative booklets that are helpful in the stimulation and organization of these various types of shooting activities.[1]

Fig. 91. Elementary school children of Troy, New York, are taken to the outdoors away from the city to learn shooting skills and participate in intramural shooting using the air rifle.

(Courtesy of the National Park Service)

Fig. 92. What a fitting setting for students situated not too far from the High Sierras or the Rockies—a spot for riding treks, camp-outs, cook-outs, outing retreats, and the like.

Archery is a fine fall and spring outdoor sport. Equipment and facilities should be made available to more students. One of the most fascinating and enjoyable events on the year's calendar could be archery golf. If the campus is spacious, a series of targets could be placed about it with competition arranged over the course in cross-country and target-to-target style. Roving archery clubs and groups are growing in popularity. Many schools have handicraft shops, and students could be encouraged to make their own bows and arrows.

Fig. 93. Men's archery competition at Mankato State College, Minnesota.

In line with archery tournaments a new type of shooting competition should be mentioned, since the idea could be used in the intramural program. Clout shoots are a pleasing departure from the usual target style. In this competition the arrows fly a considerably longer distance than in target shooting, and are shot into the air, coming down well over a hundred yards away on a target which is indicated on the turf. Scores are tabulated according to markings on a ground target.

Shuffleboard courts arranged in a pleasant outdoor spot on the campus offer great possibilities. The fine outdoor, lighted shuffleboard courts in the state of Florida are examples of what can be done on school grounds all over the nation. Floodlights can be provided for shuffleboard at very little cost since the area involved is small. These areas would prove to be extremely popular during the summer sessions at most universities.

Fig. 94. Adult shuffleboard participation in Pasadena, California. Why not utilize such school or community facilities for school intramural shuffleboard tournaments and leagues?

Fortunate indeed is the school situated near areas where winter sports can be enjoyed fully, yet how few schools in the great northland carry on extensive intramural programs featuring these sports. Special events of all kinds can be arranged for the winter outdoor season. Small and large ski jumps can be constructed for the beginner and the expert. Slalom ski courses can be set up. Ski trails and lifts to facilitate more concentrated action can be developed. Middlebury College has a large ski jump at its Bread Loaf Snow Bowl area in Vermont. Here beginners can learn how to jump on part of the layout while the experts have one of the best jumps in the nation. Middlebury has also provided a 700-foot tow service on a wide-open slope for beginners and co-recreational skiing. This tow carries the students to any desired height on a 3,200-foot slope. At the top of this area numerous trails have been layed out for cross-country skiing and winter hiking. Middlebury is fortunate in having a northern exposure for the ski area, guaranteeing plenty of snow from early fall to late spring.

The University of Wisconsin has long provided recreational ski jumping and tobogganing on the campus. The former ice and snow sculpturing program at Wisconsin featured contests all over the campus, with each group making an aesthetic contribution in its own yards. In 1948 Wisconsin modified this program, having a gigantic ice sculpturing contest arranged on the central campus on one mall, with all exhibits arranged side-by-side up the hill in one big display.

Every northern campus should have its own outdoor ice skating and ice hockey rink for competitive races and games as well as recreational winter-long activity for both men and women. Many football fields are converted into winter ice rinks, which seem to do no damage to stadium sod. Some schools have arranged concrete tennis courts in series, with a slight curb around the total enclosure for winter flooding and skating, and with some lighting for night activity. One precaution which should be observed in this plan is to see that the concrete is in one large slab. Otherwise water seeps down around the edges of the courts and freezes, later cracking the courts through expansion and contraction.

Ice hockey goals are easily made in the school shop. Lines can be made quickly on the ice for races by use of colored dyes, and flags installed for skating events. Hockey rinks can be made with the wooden retaining walls, or a substitute rink can be made merely with snow banked around the edges and frozen as desired. Ice rinks should receive continued care and maintenance. Spraying and freezing should be done at night, and scrapers should be used to keep the ice surface smooth during the day.

Marilyn Christlieb[2] suggests several splendid ideas for the organization of ski events in the school program. She suggests the formation of clubs or instruction classes out of which will grow races and intramural events adapted to the various levels of ability. Her suggestions follow:

I. Games.
  A. Relays using the herringbone, sidestep, walking, etc.
  B. Tag games confined to an area and giving the person who is tagged a few seconds' head start.
  C. Follow the leader.
  D. Hunting games: scavenger, treasure, Easter egg hunt, etc.
  E. Throwing games.
  F. Ski songs and yodeling contests.
  G. Novelty races, barrel staves, dishpan, or snow shovel, etc.

II. Adapted races (boys and girls, men and women, classified according to ability).
A. Slalom: vary the number and width of gates.
B. Downhill: vary distance and terrain.
C. Jumping: vary the height of the jump from a few inches to
several feet.
D. Cross-country: vary the distance or the ruggedness of the
course.
E. Other variations:
1. Tandem race in which a man's and woman's times are
added for the winning time. Very appropriate for husband
and wife competition.
2. Obstacle races. The Association of Women Skiers of Oregon held a slalom race on Mt. Hood for officials who had
helped them during the season. Cource included such gates
as a toll gate where each skier had to pay to pass; a teeter
totter (ski up, balance, and ski down); a hurdle made with
saw horses; a pup tent which filled the gate, forcing the
skier to crawl through; rope mesh between trees; a flush
on the flat; a milk and tea bar where each had to drink his
portion before going on.
3. Such handicaps as sealskin climbers attached to skis; only
one ski; a heavy back pack; towing a first-aid toboggan, or
carrying four pairs of ski poles. Each runner is timed and
novel awards are presented.
III. Form or style competition.
A. Judges choose techniques to suit the group participating.
IV. Demonstrations by experts. Skilled skiers demonstrating turns and
skills.
V. Ski classification tests. National Ski Association, local, or club ski
ability tests. Two of most popular tests are the slalom, consisting
of running a course of set gates in the proper order against time,
and downhill, which is a longer race over a course which has only
a few wide gates set to control speed. This is a test of speed and
endurance.

Special ski schools have been sponsored for the women of Mount
Holyoke College and Wellesley. Women students of Smith College are
first taught skiing on level terrain, and are then taken to the hills for practice
and further instruction. Then comes the big Winter Carnival, which
includes a Ski Play Day, to which women of other schools are invited. At
the Abbot Academy at Andover, Massachusetts, every girl has skis, poles,
and boots. This paraphernalia is stored in a special ski room in the
basement of a classroom building where racks are built to handle all equipment. Work benches are provided where each girl can wax her own skis
and repair equipment as needed.

The New England Intercollegiate Ski Conference has done much to stimulate winter sports in that area. Several competitive events are staged each year, bringing together students from Tufts College, Boston University, Massachusetts State, Boston College, Worcester Tech, and Brown University. One of their features is the Down-Hill Slalom Meet. Williams College held its first post-war carnival in 1948 and invited Bowdoin, Yale, Norwich, Rensselaer Polytechnic, Syracuse, and Amherst to participate in ski jumping, slalom racing, and downhill skiing; the event is now an annual one. The Hus-Skiers Club of Northeastern University holds several co-recreational competitive events, including the following: ski chase, ski lessons for members and guests, intraclub downhill slalom, dancing, and songfests.

The Dartmouth College ski tramway reported that 400 skiers an hour were carried to the top of their slopes. The construction of this tramway increased popularity and participation in skiing over 100 percent in one year. Dartmouth holds a giant slalom for both men and women on Mt. Moosilauke's Little Dipper Trail. The Outing Club at the high school at Amherst has been extremely active in developing hundreds of outdoor winter enthusiasts. Skiing is a great sport among the private schools and academies of the East. Private schools at Eaglebrook, Deerfield, Cushing, Mt. Hermon, Kimball Union, Northwood, and New Hampton all feature a very active ice and snow program every winter for the younger students.

The Eaglebrook School at Deerfield, Massachusetts, celebrates an Annual Winter Carnival each year, which includes all kinds of events for students, parents, faculty, and alumni, many of whom come back year after year to enjoy the fun. Eaglebrook boys range from the fourth through the ninth grade, and are seldom over 15 years of age; every Eaglebrook boy skis well. For the Carnival all boys are divided into four groups for equal competition. The program consists of cross-country skiing, slalom with ten gates and two runs, and ski jumping. A hilarious interlude of obstacle races through barrels, over tennis nets, and around benches highlights the festivities. Special awards are presented for carnival helpfulness, sportsmanship, excellence in winter sports, and the most improvement during the year. The event was started in 1922. All 135 boys, the total enrollment of the school, competed in 1948. The Eaglebrook fathers compete in a three-legged Keep-in-Step Race, while the mothers compete in the mothers-and-sons Dressing Race. There is a Ladies' Downhill Race, "Mystery" Race, Carnival Ball, Tug-O-War, and the annual alumni banquet.

Those interested in securing additional information concerning the organization and promotion of winter sports and outdoor recreation may write the National Park Service, Merchandise Mart, Chicago. This organization has considerable literature and a splendid bibliography of practical value to schools. The Massachusetts State Department of Education has compiled a great deal of material on skiing and skating which would be helpful for those planning expansion of facilities and teaching techniques. The American Ski Annual is published at Hanover, New Hampshire, for the National Ski Association of America, located at Barre, Massachusetts. The National Ski Patrol System has headquarters at 415 Lexington Avenue, New York City, and is interested in supplying schools with information on ski safety layouts of courses, tows, trails, and the like.

Ski clubs are very popular in the California high schools. Carmel High School's Ski Club enjoys annual ski trips to Yosemite, with instruction in fundamentals carried on regularly on its own beautiful campus near the ocean. The St. Helena High School Ski Club of California offers positive proof that the smaller high schools are capable of developing excellent programs of this nature.

Coasting has also rightfully taken its place among interesting winter outdoor activities, and is rapidly becoming a school-sponsored sport. Safety is of utmost importance in coasting, and it might be well to point out what some cities and schools have done to safeguard this fine sport for both young and old enthusiasts. Oswego, New York, has a supervised coasting program in the winter from 3:00 to 10:00 P.M. daily. The city provides a starter at the top of every hill that is used, to prevent sled collisions. Barriers are set up at all street intersections to make the sport safe. Portland, Maine, has provided coasting facilities on all school and park grounds to keep students from using dangerous city streets. On the few streets that are used, a 50-foot belt of sand is placed at the foot of the hill to prevent sleds from running into traffic. Streets are set aside for school coasters in Montclair, New Jersey, and police are assigned to see that no cars are allowed on these streets during coasting hours. The students themselves have been organized at Ely, Minnesota, to supervise coasting. They act as starters, divert traffic, enforce safety precautions, and learn to accept leadership responsibilities. East Orange, New Jersey, provides coasting on its playgrounds, together with a specially constructed slide that is supervised. Elementary schools at Beloit, Wisconsin, have coasting slides constructed on the grounds—a source of constant healthful outdoor exercise for the students.

An annual series of skating parties is conducted in the schools of Rutland, Vermont. These events feature games such as hill-dill, jump the barrel, snap the whip, spud, prisoner's base, and ice hockey, as well as figure and fancy skating. Prizes are awarded for the most graceful couples, the king and queen are crowned, and refreshments always top off the activities. Ice skating is a great winter sport for both men and women at the University of New Hampshire. The Central High School at Sheboygan, Wisconsin, conducts an Annual Ice Carnival which includes a grand march, crowning of the king and queen, fancy and figure skating, couple skating to music, and refreshments.

Fig. 95. Intramural ice skating races as part of the Winter Sports Festival at Beloit College, Wisconsin. Other features include skating to music under the lights in mixed groups, fancy and figure skating exhibitions, and social activities.

A winter sports festival or carnival that would be ideally suited for junior high school might include the following:

Dog derby	Snowman contest	Figure skating contests
Sled parade	Snowshoe race	Speed skating contests
Barrel stave ski jump		

Lloyd W. Roberts organized the Winter Sports Club at West Hartford, Connecticut, at the William Hall High School. Its membership soon included one-half of the student body, and it has continued to be popular. Parties are organized for Halloween, Thanksgiving, and Christmas; a ski trip is arranged to the Bousquets in Pittsfield, Massachusetts, and to Pico Peak and Mount Washington. The club sponsors horseback riding, swimming, roller skating, and ice skating.

Unquestionably one of the most popular organized developments in the last few years in the schools is the outing movement. Some schools direct this program in the regular administrative channels, while others stimulate its progress through student clubs. Recently some schools, particularly the colleges, have appointed a supervisor of recreation, and much of this type of activity is his responsibility. In some schools the intramural director assumes full charge. The Outdoor Education Project of the American Association for Health, Physical Education and Recreation has been giving a much needed impetus to leadership development in activities of the great outdoors. Dr. Julian W. Smith, its director, has organized leadership clinics all over the nation, and the next several years will see more of these opportunities provided by AAHPER-NEA. Certain schools have already made significant progress in this area: others will soon be awake to the great educational possibilities in a fine outing and hiking program. Before leaving the subject a few unique developments should be mentioned.

Syracuse University has tried to meet this challenge by a fourfold program which (1) provides a ski school for all students, (2) sponsors an annual winter carnival, (3) keeps outing clubs functioning and active, (4) and provides outdoor leadership training. The Amherst High School Outing Club at Amherst, Massachusetts, made a film on skiing.

The California colleges annually sponsor student-faculty treks to the high Sierras, and many of them have their own facilities such as cabins, lounges, and warming rooms, plus ski lifts. Among these is the excellent camp of the University of California at Berkeley, nestled high in the Rockies west of Reno; hundreds of students spend weekends there. In addition, the "Lair Of The Bear" is a fine mountain camp devoted to alumni families of the University as well as students. This mile- high camp is complete with swimming pool, boating, sailing, power boating, fishing, and horseback riding. Hiking trails wind into the beautiful outdoors. There is a nightly camp fire, family style meals, and organized sports such as softball, tennis, volleyball, badminton, horseshoes, and swimming are held in tournament style each week during season. In addition, younger members of the university family groups have facilities for crafts, art work, and nature study.

The Middlebury College Mountain and Outing Club has developed one of the most extensive and unique programs in the nation. Middlebury is essentially an out-of-doors college, and in view of this the Mountain Club was organized in 1931 as an extracurricular body to take advantage of the incomparable 31,000-acre mountain campus, and to sponsor and encourage outdoor activities not provided for by the Athletic Council. In the past several years this organization has grown into one of the largest and most active clubs of its type in America, numbering hundreds of undergraduates. Membership is open to the entire student body. Members are entitled to participate in all hikes and other activities, and to use any of the club's equipment.

In addition to sponsoring day and overnight hikes and winter ski parties, the Mountain Club is affiliated with the Intercollegiate Outing Club Association. As a member of this group the Club participates in several joint hikes and ski weekends, as well as a three-day conference in the spring and the Adirondack's College Week each fall. Another feature of the Mountain Club program is the Winter Carnival, which was initiated in 1932 and which has enlarged each year, now being one of the finest in the country.

The management and the execution of the activities of the Club rest with the Governing Board and a Junior Body of Skyline. Organized in 1935, Skyline became the legislative group, consisting of twelve members from each of the three upper classes. Elections to it from the freshman class each spring are based on interest in the Club, potential qualities of leadership, and contribution to the Club. From within this body, nine members are chosen to comprise the Governing Board, in which the executive and motivating powers are vested.

The Middlebury Mountain Club conducts weekly student hiking parties to points of interest in the Green Mountains during the college year. Among the destinations for these Sunday trips are Pleiad Lake, Bread Loaf, Lincoln Mountain, Moosalmoo, Snake Mountain, Brandon Gap, and Camel's Hump. Students are urged to join the club early in the freshman year for an early start in mass hiking. The *Middlebury College Handbook* gives detailed information on a large number of planned hiking trips, including points of interest, distance, time required, and precautions to be taken. A series of trails and hikes for fall and spring are also listed, some of which are undertaken on horseback, or with skis in winter.

The Hiking Club of the high school at Knoxville, Tennessee, sponsors hikes on Saturday into the nearby Great Smoky Mountains. Membership

Fig. 96. Part of a group of 950 boys and girls who are taken by train to an outdoor setting for diversified outing activities. This recreation program is administered by the Cleveland, Ohio, city schools.

grew so fast that this club soon became the largest and most popular club in school. Each hike was also used for the intimate study of geography, nature study, birds, natural history, and botany. Among the smaller high schools the program at Spring Arbor, Michigan, high school is different. Class meetings are first held each fall, and committees are appointed to make arrangements for the series of autumn hikes which are highlights of the entire school year. The high school coach at Waldron High School, Indiana, organized a number of after-school and weekend hikes. Not satisfied with this fine start, he later conducted a number of hikes for the grade school students as well. Waldron is a town of less than 1,000 people.

School-sponsored camping is another phase of the recreational program that is fast growing into an important and forward looking trend in the nation. In the type most usually called Conservation and Natural Science Education through Outdoor Education every boy and girl in the fifth or sixth grades is given an opportunity to spend one week during the year at camp with his own group and teacher. The feeling of educators in this country is that this program can rejuvenate student interest in the school curriculum by taking education into the open whenever and wherever the outdoors can make educational experience more real and vital. Greatest expansion of this fine program has taken place in California, Michigan, New York, Missouri, New Jersey, and in other scattered areas. Every child in the sixth grade spends one week at camp in San Diego and Long Beach, California. At Indiana State Teachers College of Terre Haute the personnel from home economics, physical education, and science cooperate with the college camp committee in planning the activities. The Laboratory School of Ohio University at Athens has also introduced a camping program for school children. Similar developments have been noted at Central College of Education, Ellensburg, Washington, schools in Catskill and Roslyn, New York, the Los Angeles City Schools, Newark Valley, New York, and Atlanta, Georgia. The Battle Creek schools operate a school farm. Baltimore schools have made use of the Highwood Day Camp School for Boys. The Clear Lake Camp is conducted by Western Michigan University at Kalamazoo. Schools of Frederick County, Maryland, are taken to a camp in the nearby Catoctin Mountains.

California has set the pace among states developing school camping experiences for students, followed by Michigan. It will be interesting to watch the gradual progress of this fine outdoor program in years to come. California elementary schools customarily provide camping and outdoor education opportunities throughout the entire school year to sixth grade students, accompanied by their teachers. Leaders in this program have been San Diego, Los Angeles County and City, Long Beach, Garvey, Carmel, Coalinga, Santa Clara and Tulare Counties, and more than 200 school districts. A few provide similar experiences for secondary school students. While school camps do not build their programs around the recreation program, activities of this nature are so natural and spontaneous that they cannot be omitted.

Fishing and bait and fly casting are growing in popularity each year. The University of Pittsburgh and Pennsylvania State have gone far in the stimulation of fly tying, and casting. Growing out of the classes, the intramural tournaments in casting are interesting and different. Classes at Pennsylvania State have proved so popular that the physical education department is now conducting extension courses for adults all over the state. Certainly this move to take recreation to the great outdoors is commendable and within the reach of every high school, college, and university in the nation.

Canoe and boat racing is another sport that is destined for a comeback. Canoe races are held at Yonkers, New York, where over 3,000 spectators are reported to have watched the annual school regatta on the Hudson. The Red Cross has been working with many high schools and colleges in an effort to provide a canoe for every indoor swimming pool, so that students may be taught water safety and proper use of a canoe in water.

Fig. 97. Angling and casting clinics such as those sponsored by the Outdoor Education Project of AAHPER are a possibility for schools at every level. Instruction can be combined with intramural competition in skish, followed by cook-outs and other activities.

Fig. 98. Children from the Frederick County, Maryland, schools are taken to nearby water areas where fishing and casting are among the many outdoor activities provided.

The following suggestions are worthy of mention and should provide food for thought to the director who plans to enlarge this phase of outdoor recreation:

1. Several student gatherings and meetings could be the first step in organization.
2. Motion pictures on outdoor recreation could be shown to large groups of students at varsity athletic events.
3. Illustrated lectures of descriptive nature would stimulate interest.
4. A series of Saturday hikes could then be planned.
5. Sunday afternoon could be given over to bus hikes, the students traveling out to a given spot on foot, being picked up for the return trip by bus.
6. Ski parties could be planned on the weekends, with transportation out by bus.
7. Skating parties could be arranged, with the students being transported to the rink in faculty cars.
8. Class instruction could be given in fly tying and casting.
9. Student groups could be organized to repair existing cabins and build new ones.
10. Facilities could be used for roller skating parties.
11. The department could be set up to furnish two-man camping kits to be rented at a modest fee.
12. Trail maps and descriptive trail literature could be prepared for distribution to students.

13. The director could plan an all-college Outing Club and move forward with plans for the building of a large lodge in the mountains as headquarters.
14. He could start a drive to acquire a campus recreation activity building which would house a myriad of indoor activities and hobby clubs.
15. An additional budget could be developed to permit the payment of modest sums to various faculty personnel for the part-time supervision of recreational activities.

If we are to realize a maximum use of the great outdoors in the modern school recreational program, it naturally follows that new leadership must be taught and trained to stimulate and sponsor these many activities. In the smaller schools the coach, the athletic director, or one of the staff is usually weighed down with varsity and detail assignments and cannot give adequate time and attention to this project. It also follows that the busy coach might easily gain many staunch friends by diverting at least a portion of his energy to promotion of these areas, an emphasis that will make him far more indispensable to the educational system. One suggestion for the larger university would be to conduct annual training institutes to which faculty people in the surrounding area could come and receive instruction and motivation, thus enlisting a whole new group of teachers who might never be induced to give time and energy to the coaching of varsity sports, but who might develop an interest in the more purely recreational activities. Such a plan might produce, in time, much needed faculty supervision and sponsorship.

St. Lawrence University conducts an Annual Winter Sports School, which has been sponsored by the New York Public High School Association. High school students, coaches, intramural directors, and community recreation leaders attend a four-day session of training in skiing, winter camping, and winter recreational sports. A standard system of instruction and practice is followed. Talks, informal discussions, movies, and actual participation outdoors form the basis of the meetings. Representatives of the State Department of Education are in attendance. Another instructional institute very similar in nature is held at Syracuse University. It is evident that if faculty members all over the nation could be induced to attend training institutes to learn techniques of leadership in outdoor activities through a brief period of self-participation, it would not be long before organized outdoor sports would show appreciable gains in many schools and communities.

Another way to stimulate outdoor recreation for school students without much supervision is the plan of providing picnic and recreation kits for all kinds of school picnics and private parties. Some departments have already risen to the occasion and have widely publicized the availability of this service to the student body. Intramural handbooks of many institutions carry invitations for all student groups to avail themselves of these free kits. Usually a deposit is required when the kit is checked out.

Other schools are solving the shortage in faculty personnel by sponsoring sport clubs in many different sports. Purdue University has helped organize sport clubs in archery, bait casting, boxing, rifle, gymnastics, hiking, skating, skiing, soccer, squash, fencing, volleyball, table tennis, and badminton. After these clubs are organized they are able to carry on a number of organized activities without too much faculty control and supervision.

The program at Western Carolina College at Cullowhee, North Carolina, features many outing activities for men, women, and co-recreational groups. It also provides for the faculty, their families, and their friends. Lakes and mountains attract most of the activities, which are mainly hiking, fishing and casting, shooting, cook-outs, hikes, and the like.

Clubs composed of physical education majors often "set the pace" for other clubs and groups of colleges in outing activities. The Club at Bemidji (Minnesota) State College has many winter activities, and the big annual event is an all-day fishing trip followed by a fish fry. The Olympian Club at the University of Florida enters teams in all intramural

Fig. 99. Take your clubs and groups out to rural roads and trails for a bike hike and cook-out.

sports, but also conducts splash parties, camp cook-outs, square dances, wiener roasts, movies, and occasionally presents demonstrations in dance and sports skills.

We are likely to think that some schools are more fortunately situated than others, being nearer the mountains, snow-covered hills, lakes and streams, and other attractive features. These resources are tremendous assets, but one can hardly deny that every locality has a natural outdoor area that will lend itself to some kind of organized program. It is significant to note that boating and water activities are on the way back, following a prolonged period of desertion with the advent of the automobile and the craze to get out on the highways. Some schools are increasing their rental and available facilities for student use. Boat houses are being constructed. The outing movement is gaining momentum. Recent growing awareness of problems of Ecology and the misuse of our natural resources is helping to take both youth and adults into the great outdoors. Students are becoming better organized to take a more active leadership role in their own activities. Physical education workers are becoming more conscious of the wide scope of their influence, and the early and more narrow concept of physical education is undergoing transformation. It is safe to say that the next few years will see a great trend forward in the expansion of the outdoor program.

Fig. 100. Start of the Boys Quarter Mile Rough Water Swim from the shores of the Pacific Ocean at Manhattan Beach, California. This event is part of the International Paddleboard and National Beach Volleyball Championships conducted by the school-city coordinated recreation department of Manhattan Beach.

In conclusion it might be said that the great American outdoors is available for recreational exploitation in every community, to the end that worthwhile recreational interests may be taught to each generation of students. The success and extent of such a program depend purely and simply on the interest and enthusiasm of school directors and physical education staff members.

REFERENCES

1 Three valuable sources of information on gun club and rifle organization are:
  (1) *Rifle and Pistol Shooting,* National Rifle Association, 1600 Rhode Island Avenue, N.W., Washington, D.C.
  (2) *Handbook on Gun Club Organization,* Trap and Skeet Section, Remington Arms Company, Inc., Bridgeport, Conn.
  (3) *Handbook on Shotgun Shooting,* Committee on Promotional Activities, Sporting Arms and Ammunition Manufacturer's Institute, 343 Lexington Avenue, New York 10016, N.Y.
2 "Planning and Organizing Ski Events," *Journal of Health and Physical Education,* XIX, No. 2, February, 1948. Also information sent the author by Marilyn Christlieb Wade by letter from Fairbanks, Alaska.

17

COMMUNITY RELATIONSHIPS
AND PARTICIPATION

Realizing that many junior and senior high schools, elementary schools, and even colleges and universities are still conducting rather meager intramural and recreational programs, it might seem presumptuous to suggest a still greater expansion of personnel and facilities to include the total school community. We must face the fact that the nation is on the threshold of a wide-sweeping trend in recreation that will look to the schools for leadership and administration, and will eventually combine the total community resources of facilities, staff, and equipment, so that people of all ages and interests may be served better in the years that lie ahead. The community-school idea is no longer a remote objective, an ideal worth thinking about but still out of reach. It is now a reality in hundreds of American communities and the movement is spreading as it should.

We must not lose sight of the fact that a diversified school program of physical education and recreation is often seriously handicapped for want of proper facilities, trained leadership, and adequate financial support. We must then turn to the adult community for assistance. Perhaps more attention to the recreational needs of the school families, the faculty, and the total community might bring the needed understanding and support that is so vital to the educational scheme.

Irwin[1] makes the following comments on this subject:

Schools are coming to be recognized more and more as community centers. This is particularly true in smaller communities where school facilities are usually the most pretentious of the public buildings in the community. Also the school personnel holds a position of leadership which is conducive to making the school a community center. Although the trend is toward making the school the community center for all phases of activity, it is particularly true of the curriculum in physical education, which should include some responsibility for community recreation. . . . It is relatively safe to say that as time goes on the schools will assume greater and greater responsibility for the leadership activities within a community.

The report of the proceedings of the Council of Chief State School Officers at its meeting in Baltimore stated: "The council believes that school and community recreation is appropriately an integral part of a comprehensive education program." The Chief State School Officers and the Society of State Directors of Health, Physical Education and Recreation have made a series of statements through the years backing this point of view and giving the community-school concept their constant support.

One of the most significant documents ever to appear on the American scene relating to the role of the public schools in recreation and community services is the publication in California on *The Roles of Public Education in Recreation*. A few quotations are here appropriate:[2]

Leadership of the schools should be in evidence at the community level in all activities that have educational significance. A basic responsibility is to help the community develop awareness and understanding of the recreational needs of its children, youth, and adults. The school is a logical agency to assist in the organization and development of all community resources that can be used to meet these needs. This concept of the role of the school should be developed during the preservice preparation of school personnel.

Responsibilities

1. The community-school concept should be supported and strengthened.

The community-school concept offers a great potential to sound community recreation development. In this concept, public schools become a focal point around which the entire community can organize and operate. Teachers and administrators are catalytic agents in the community to marshal resources, initiate action, and activate programs. Schools and school people provide a basis for co-ordination and co-operation, so essential to effective functioning in a democracy. In practice, the community-school is a mechanism for developing understanding, co-ordinated thinking, and co-ordinated action.

The corollary concept of the education-centered community or the community-centered school is that every resource within a community is needed and used to meet the educational and recreational needs of all people in the community. This does not mean that all facets of community education are a monopoly of the school. By bringing people together inside the school plant, and by full utilization, both for academic and for recreational pursuits, of the resources outside the school, individuals are encouraged to give of themselves in the development of their community.

In our complex society it becomes more difficult for each citizen to take care of his own leisure. Therefore, in the community-school concept this means that, when not used for instructional purposes, the public schools are needed to serve the leisure needs of citizens 365 days of each year, 12 to 15 hours per day.

2. The school should be a community service agency.

The schools have accepted as one of their objectives, the strengthening of community life. The school can become the natural center of the community's civic, cultural, and recreational activities, augmented by other community resources.

The school is one of our basic social institutions, and should serve as a center for the organization and operation of many community activities. School leaders should use school facilities for such activities, and provide the leadership which guarantees opportunities for all to meet their needs and desires. School officials may give leadership to program features on nonschool facilities as needed and available, just as nonschool community agencies will need to use school facilities.

One of the great needs today is to re-unite and revive intimate family relationships through recreation. A multitude of program features and opportunities are possible when home and school are brought close together. The community-school should provide a splendid opportunity to bring about this ideal.

It is apparent from this point of view that joint planning and close cooperation are imperative in the future. Programs of education and recreation are broad programs which complement and supplement each other, and both require similar facilities. Why should we then have thousands of school buildings tightly locked after school hours, throughout weekends, and during all holidays? The cooperative efforts of city, county, and school interests in this forward-looking type of program have accomplished remarkable results in hundreds of American communities, where all kinds of new sport programs are now being developed twelve months of the year.

On July 31, 1946, the mayor of San Francisco signed an ordinance calling for the preparation of a comprehensive master plan for youth to be prepared by a representative group of citizens to be appointed by the mayor. After careful studies were completed, the report of the committee gave a number of specific recommendations for action as follows:

1. The submission of a bond issue for $12 million was needed to carry out the post-war development program of the recreation department.
2. The recreation department should be consulted by school officials in all phases of new building construction.
3. The schools should make available all school indoor and outdoor athletic facilities when they are not in use by the school program.
4. The park department should develop additional park areas for general recreational use.

One of the finest examples in the nation of joint city-school administration and planning of program and facilities exists in Long Beach, California. The total program of school physical education, athletics, and recreation, together with all municipal recreation for people of all ages, is unified under the leadership of one director and his staff. A few years ago this group split into subcommittees, studied and planned every phase of new recreation and physical education buildings, came up with recommen-

Fig. 101. Senior citizens bowling on the green in the school-city coordinated recreation program at Richmond, California. An ideal setting for the expansion of school-centered opportunities for youth and citizens of all ages.

dations which were almost all accepted by architects, and then proceeded with the construction of well over $22 million in new gymnasiums and playgrounds. Every new school gymnasium, regardless of its grade level, was equipped with kitchenette, toilets, and washrooms adjacent to and opening out toward the playfield, and many other features were designed to provide for community recreation at all hours of the day. Nineteen gymnasiums were built in this tremendous program; more have been built since. All school cafeterias are also combination auditoriums. Special game rooms and dance studios provide additional areas for community use. These fine facilities were the subject of a mass visitation by authorities from all over the nation during an AAHPER Convention at Los Angeles.

The program in the Rochester, Minnesota, schools will go far toward making the community school a reality in that progressive city. Every teacher in the city system is required to serve eleven months a year. Each teacher must become a part of the all-day Saturday program of intramurals and recreation which has been enlarged extensively for both boys and girls, involving every playground, school play field, and gymnasium in the city. Each teacher must serve for at least six weeks during the summer vacation period in one of the following options:

1. Teach in the summer school classes for all ages.
2. Provide leadership for the summer workshops in education.
3. Assume active recreational leadership in the summer program.
4. Return to the universities for additional professional preparation if the B.S. or A.B. degree has not been attained.
5. Travel one summer in five (if allowed).

In the Rochester Plan summer assignments may be rotated. Newly contracted teachers must start their duty on August 1 in this program, and resigning teachers must continue their duties until June 30 or receive a salary reduction pro-rated accordingly.

All teachers in Glencoe, Illinois, are employed on a twelve-month basis, with one month vacation with pay. The schools operate the year round, giving special attention to recreational activities during the summer months. During the regular year teachers are expected to carry on these recreational activities after school, in the evenings, and on Saturdays.

The Board of Education of the Los Angeles City School District operates a program of youth activities which is being watched with interest and envy all over the nation. The plan provides for a youth supervisor in each school who relates curricular and extracurricular activities of youth playground, youth center activities, and the programs of nongovernmental youth agencies. Emphasis is given to expanding the activities available for youth so that as complete coverage as possible may be obtained. The program is under the direction of a Supervisor of the Youth Service Section of the Board of Education. The program provides youth activities leading to good citizenship and wholesome character. The principal components of this broad service include the following features:

1. Provide consultant service to principals and teachers.
2. Make surveys and study needs of the total program.
3. Help each school set up a youth activities coordinator, a faculty youth activities committee, a student committee.
4. Seek to effect coordinated youth activities, and start the promotion of many new activities.
5. Place a full-time recreational director in every school.
6. Develop play days, G.A.A., intramural sports, special sports interest clubs, and all types of recreation.
7. Attempt to eliminate duplication of efforts of all agencies.
8. Provide leadership for the rapid expansion of facilities.
9. Attempt to give direction and purpose to out-of-school youth in recreational activities.
10. Obtain youth-minded citizens to sponsor and guide youth.
11. Supplement the work of outside youth-interested agencies.
12. Stimulate students to work on worthy community youth projects.
13. Develop and use student talent through orchestras, photograph clubs, etc.
14. Utilize talented adult leadership of the community, capitalizing on a hobby, or recruiting and training classes.
15. Expand off-campus activities which often originate on the school campus, including such activities as hiking, camping, excursions, skating, student canteens, noon-hour recreational programs, bowling, co-recreational events, etc.
16. Stimulate and sponsor clubs such as Hi-Y, Tri-Y, and all the various sports which lend themselves to club formation.
17. Play a major role in the planning and staging of school social functions, dances, socials, mixers, jam sessions, pep assemblies, booster parties, and the like.

Some of the finest school-community coordinated and school district operated recreation programs in the nation are found in Pasadena, Monterey, Fresno, Long Beach, Los Angeles, and El Monte, California; Roslyn, Huntington Station, Niagara Falls, and Great Neck, New York; Cleveland, Cleveland Heights, Parma, Hamilton, and Cincinnati, Ohio; Milwaukee, Madison, Beloit, Kenosha, Sheboygan and Janesville, Wisconsin; Fairfax County, Virginia; Erie, Lancaster, and Harrisburg, Pennsylvania; Gary, Terre Haute, Columbus, and Muncie, Indiana; Flint, Monroe, Plymouth, Detroit, Alpena, and Escanaba, Michigan; Newark, New Jersey; and in the Summer Enrichment School Program in the State of Florida, which reaches many school districts and counties.

In Madison, Wisconsin, the Annual City Cribbage Championship Tournament is one of the feature events. These oldsters play cribbage in organized leagues all winter, which finally culminate in a championship series.

(Courtesy of George Seedhouse.)

Fig. 102. Instruction and participation in bridge in the community schools of Cleveland, Ohio.

It is apparent that rapid progress is being made in a vast expansion of the combined and cooperative services of school and community. Lasting and friendly relationships between school and community take up a large part of the planning and thinking of all physical educators and athletic leaders today. Often it becomes necessary to study new ways of obtaining parental cooperation and interest in the immediate school program and a closer understanding of the real and vital objectives of physical education, recreation, and athletics in each community. It will be found that no one specific plan or idea will completely develop the desired close harmony and understanding. Each community has individual problems. Perhaps a combination of many different ideas, with much initiative on the part of school authorities, will be necessary to create and maintain good school-community relationships.

After the school program itself has been developed as carefully and extensively as possible, the next consideration might well be the inclusion of the school family and faculty. In previous chapters some suggestions were presented on faculty recreation. Too many schools have completely neglected this responsibility. Fine programs are in operation at Amherst College, Oberlin, Michigan, Purdue, West Virginia, and Illinois. At the University of Georgia the gymnasium is reserved every Friday night for faculty recreation which includes the following calendar of events.

Fall: Tennis singles, golf, volleyball
Winter: Badminton and bowling
Spring: Tennis singles and doubles, softball, and golf

Indoor facilities are always available at Georgia for faculty swimming, volleyball, badminton, and miscellaneous games. Special family swimming parties are occasionally scheduled.

Faculty bowling, for both men and women organized in leagues on an interdepartmental and intercollege basis, seems to be the most popular sport. Leagues can be operated throughout the academic year. Private dressing rooms for the faculty increase recreation for this group appreciably.

Teachers of the Rigler School in Portland, Oregon, bowl together once a week, an event which proved to be very popular. Faculty men of the Riverside High School, Milwaukee, spend 45 minutes every noon playing dart baseball and other light activities. These men have exhibited a keen interest in the program and have received complete relaxation from school problems which makes a significant contribution to the mental and physical health of the faculty family.

In an article by the faculty of the Ohio State University School, in *Childhood Education,* the value of play in personal growth of teachers is effectively brought out. The following description of faculty recreation at the University School is evidence that the faculty believes what it preaches:

> If teachers are to be happy and well adjusted individuals, there must be a balance between work and play. The staff of University School has the opportunity to participate in many different kinds of recreational activities. There is "shop nite" where some work in wood, jewelry, paint or clay. Others enjoy weaving. The faculty chorus proved to be very popular and participated in the spring music festival. Horseback riding, tennis, badminton, archery, bowling, square dancing, and swimming are other activities in which staff members assist, or participate in with students. A social committee plans parties to provide maximum participation and fun for all. Many campus groups provide cultural opportunities—concerts, movies, hobby lectures, flower shows and plays.

Western Carolina College officials feel that the example of "oldsters" is a great motivator to get young people to participate. Individual tourneys are conducted for the faculty in tennis and handball. Team events include volleyball and basketball. College bowling alleys are open each evening for faculty and staff bowling.

After expanding the program to include at least a minimum of faculty recreation, the next obvious expansion would include the immediate families of the students. Included in this category could be a Father-Son Night, or Mother-Daughter Night, with any number of recreational events planned, with both competitive and noncompetitive ideas. The evening could be preceded by a banquet, or followed by a "Dutch-lunch," buffet luncheon, or "pitch-in" eat-fest, with all the food brought from the homes for the occasion. Another feature might be a Family Fun Night to which all fathers, brothers, mothers, sisters, and relatives would be invited. Here the more purely social-recreational activities would be appropriate. Another possibility could be a Family Movie Night, which might include some movies on sports and recreation. A Family Swim Party also could be scheduled occasionally during the year. The Annual Open House program also would attract more parents and families if real effort were given to their invitation.

Fathers have much fun with their boys at the Callahan Junior High School at Des Moines.[3] The boys bring their fathers or brothers to "Dad's Night," where a program of athletic stunts, sports exhibitions, and games are carried on from 7:30 until 9:00 P.M. Following these activities refreshments are served in the school cafeteria.

The next step in community expansion would offer some events each year open to everyone. Morris Roth, in the Cook, Minnesota, schools has conducted community nights twice weekly, where adults take part in a wide variety of activities with real enjoyment and ethusiasm. Tourneys are arranged in cribbage, bridge, disco, free throws, table tennis, shuffleboard, checkers, badminton, volleyball, basketball, tether-ball, and whist. Men and women are both welcome at these frequent events at the Cook High School.

Occasional special nights and scheduled match games are arranged for local businessmen of the community in the gymnasiums at Oberlin and Amherst Colleges. Sports used in these programs are badminton, volleyball, and squash.

The Inter-Civic Club Recreational Jamboree

The author has conducted a series of recreational jamborees at Beloit College and the University of Nebraska.[4] The primary objective of these events is to establish a program that will bring to the school gymnasium, at least once a year, every man in the community representing any civic or service club. The whole program is built around a competitive framework, augmented with plenty of opportunity for good fellowship and relaxation. Many of the busy men who will attend will be in the gymnasium for the first time in their lives. They may have had no prior interest in athletics or things recreational. Perhaps they never had the opportunity to learn how to play. Others will be "old timers" in recreational experience and will make natural leaders. It is a program appropriate for young and old alike. Activities must be selected to appeal to all types of men. Old friends will welcome this opportunity to get together again. It is a wonderful chance for new friendships and acquaintances under the most ideal conditions. It may be one of the few times in the life of many communities when members of all the civic clubs rub elbows together. It affords the director and all his staff a fine opportunity to get acquainted with the men who influence thinking most in the community. It can be done with a minimum of work and effort, but must not be approached too lightly, as much is demanded in organization, planning, preparation, and cleanup of the plant and facilities.

PRELIMINARY PLANNING

The first step in organizing the jamboree is to sound out a few leaders of the various clubs to see if the program might seem inviting to them. The next step is to invite each club, through its president, to send one or more representatives to a meeting to discuss preliminary plans and details. A luncheon meeting is best, if possible. The director would want to have all details well in mind, and all plans carefully worked out. New suggestions from the group could then be accepted if feasible, but the men will be there to hear suggestions and plans and not to formulate them. Each club must appoint a Jamboree Chairman who will be interested enough to organize his entries carefully and follow up to see that each man is present and active. Each club chairman should, in turn, appoint captains in each team activity, so that responsibility can be passed down the membership roster, and to insure the presence of each team entered by each club. The director should have mimeographed bulletins ready for the first meeting. Matters of finance must be worked out and approved at this meeting. Approval of the point system, the events to be used, and the actual date should all be agreed upon.

ORGANIZATION OF THE JAMBOREE

After years of trying out different activities, it has been found that the following events lend themselves best to limited space and will meet the age and interest of the major part of those present. All lend themselves to competitive organization.

Bowling	Dart bowling	Shuffleboard
Bridge	Dart baseball	Table tennis
Cribbage	Badminton	Ping-Pong shot put
Checkers	Free throws	Golf putting contest
Pinochle		Barbershop quartette singing

One or two comedy-type events could be included, such as the Ping-Pong shot put and barbershop quartette contest. Basketball, zel-ball, tether ball, competitive swimming, and similar active games are not appropriate for heated competition without conditioning, and will cause too many sore muscles and aching after-effects if used. Other activities could be provided and not included in the competitive program of the evening so all present can keep interested and busy. Among these items might be:

Recreational swimming	Ring toss
Golf driving cage	Tether ball
Extra table tennis tables	Deck tennis
Zel-ball	Whist
Miscellaneous dart games	Basket shooting
Miscellaneous card games	

Champions should be determined in the events selected for competition, with single elimination method used in most of the tournaments. The bowling competition could be organized as a part of the jamboree but with

Fig. 103.

LINCOLN INTER–CIVIC CLUB RECREATIONAL JAMBOREE														
CLUBS	DART BOWLING	DART BASEBALL	BRIDGE	CRIBBAGE	CHECKERS	GOLF PUTTING	P.P. SHOT	FREE THROWS	VOLLEY BALL	BADMINTON	PINOCHLE	SHUFFLEBOARD	QUARTET SINGING	BOWLING
LIONS	210	50	50	210	175	75	75	75	150	40	150	75	50	75
ROTARY	50	75	210	50	150	50	50	100	125	40	75	50	75	210
KIWANIS	50	150	50	50	50	100	50	125	75	180	50	50	100	175
CO–OP	175	210	50	75	125	125	50	50	50	150	125		50	150
OPTIMIST	50		150	100	100	50	100	150	180	125			125	50
COSMOPOLITAN	50	125	175	50	75	50			50	50	50	50		50
KNIFE & FORK	50	175	125	50	50		50	50	50		50		150	100
UNI–PLACE LIONS	150	50	50	175	50	150	150	175		100		100	180	125
BETHANY LIONS	125	50	75		50	180	180	50	100	75	180		50	50
COLLEGE V–LIONS	100	100	50	150	50	50			50	50			50	50
Y'S MENS' CLUB	50		50		50	50	50	50			50	50		
J. S. C.	75	50	100	125	50	50	125	50	50	50		50	50	50
HAVELOCK LIONS	50	50	50		50		50	50		50	50		50	

actual bowling preceding the major event by about one week. One or two five-man teams from each club would compete, with total net scores determining the final placing. As the jamboree gets under way, the points scored in bowling would be posted on the large scoreboard in advance (see Figure 103).

In arranging the jamboree time schedule, it is best to have all events except volleyball running simultaneously. This prohibits men from competing in several events and insures a large entry list from each club. Some events may be organized to accommodate unlimited entries, such as the free throws and golf putting. In this way men who are eliminated from one tournament early will still be able to compete in other activities. Playoffs must not only decide the champion and second place, but also third and fourth places. The volleyball competition can form the exercise climax of the evening with short games used, since the winners must play several games and will wear out quickly.

THE POINT SYSTEM

A point system must be worked out carefully, as competition will be keen. Competitors will want to know how every point is determined as they begin to "catch" the competitive spirit. The following schedule of points is workable:

GROUP ONE ACTIVITIES		GROUP TWO EVENTS	
Bowling	Bridge	Free throws	Checkers
Volleyball	Cribbage	Ping-Pong shot put	Badminton
Dart baseball	Dart bowling	Shuffleboard	Golf putting
Pinochle		Barbershop quartette	

Points should be scored as follows:

PLACE	GROUP ONE	GROUP TWO
First Place	210	180
Second Place	175	150
Third Place	150	125
Fourth Place	125	100
Fifth Place	100	75
Sixth Place	75	50
Participating	50	40

It is well to award almost as many places as there are clubs, entered so that all will be happy in winning some points in every event.

If the individual sports are staged on a single elimination basis a system must be worked out to determine how the clubs will rank in the event. The following plan is workable:

Lose first round match	20 points
Win first round match	25 points
Play each additional match	15 points
Bonus to losing finalist	10 points
Bonus to the champion	15 points

The addition of all these points in any event will determine team rank for that event.

CLUB ENTRIES

Proper entry blanks must be prepared in sufficient quantity to permit each club chairman to have copies, with one official copy due in the director's office well in advance of the jamboree. Each club must be restricted to two bridge teams, two cribbage and pinochle teams, and not more than three or four entries in such events as checkers, table tennis, free throws, etc. Each club would have one team in dart baseball and bowling and in volleyball.

SPECIAL EQUIPMENT

Much interest will be aroused if a large scoreboard can be placed where all can follow the progress of competition during the evening. A scorer should be on hand to record results as they come in. A scoreboard is usually used as an aid in preparing for the event. A loudspeaking system and announcer should be provided. It will be valuable at the start of the jamboree to get all captains and their teams to the proper places, and to give calls throughout the evening for matches and games scheduled. The announcer might have an assistant who goes from place to place, gathering results, winners, best marks and scores, etc. Other interesting comments from the announcer will further enliven the evening.

OFFICIALS

Several faculty members and older students should be organized to supervise the various events and to see that they move smoothly. Each dart game will need umpires and scorers, and other events will demand various types of supervision. It gives faculty men who might not otherwise belong to the civic groups a chance to get acquainted and join in the fun.

Universities can use the jamboree as a laboratory for major students who will receive practical experience in conducting a community recreational event of major importance.

Following the preliminary meeting, proper local publicity in the newspapers should be planned. Advance schedules and pairings should be published. Newspapers almost invariably will have photographers on hand to catch the "city fathers" off guard during the evening. These photos will also help motivate the program in future years. Final results should be published in detail.

It has been the author's experience that all civic clubs will demand the right to pay their share of the total expense. When three to fourteen clubs split the expenses of such a party, the cost of the evening's fun and refreshments is almost insignificant. The school should furnish the gymnasium without cost. It is better to have each club make advance reservations and then pay its pro-rata share of the cost after all accounts are in. This will eliminate the possible embarrassment of individual collections at the door or assessments on the night of the event, and makes the affair more like a party. Some men will want to come and go as they please, others will compete and leave early before refreshments are served, while others will come late just for the "eats." It will also be found practical to have the various club chairmen sell tickets in advance. Local merchants usually can be found who will lend playing cards, tables, additional chairs, smoking trays and pedestals, and other needed paraphernalia. The director must be sure to have plenty of ash trays everywhere, as the air will be blue with smoke, and he should not forget to purchase the little things that make the evening a success, such as bridge score pads, pencils, and accessories.

A checkroom should be available for coats and hats. One or two students can set up this room and maintain it throughout the evening, being assured of adequate compensation through tips. An equipment cage attendant should be on duty to furnish towels, soap, and equipment to all who desire it. The swimming pool should have an attendant ready at all times for those who want to enjoy a short swim. A special committee should be on hand early near the entrance to make everyone welcome, and to show the men where to find the various competitive areas, checkroom, etc. Quiet rooms should be arranged for such games as checkers, cribbage, bridge, pinochle, and miscellaneous card games.

SPECIAL FEATURES OF THE JAMBOREE

A buffet should be served at the conclusion of the volleyball games. Tables that have been used for cards and table tennis can quickly be arranged in "night-club" style. Special program stunts or features can be worked in at this stage, but care should be exercised not to have too much in the way of entertainment since the evening will be too long. This is the appropriate time for the barbershop quartette singing contest, which will climax the night's activities on a pleasant note. The announcer can make constant reference during the repast as to results, new champions, and program highlights. Special music novelties can be worked in at this time also. Group singing is very appropriate as the party begins to break up and some of the participants start for home, bringing to a close one of the most interesting and enjoyable events of the year in any community.

The director who is willing to try out this plan of community recreation will find plenty of work for two days connected with all necessary arrangements, but every minute of it will be well spent and will pay big dividends in community appreciation of the school program, future good will, and genuine mental hygiene and relaxation for a large cross-section of the community that needs it greatly. It is well worth the effort. The aftermath of this winter jamboree might be a spring or summer golf and horseshoe tournament followed by dinner.

University Faculty Recreational Jamboree

Larger schools would have little difficulty transplanting the idea of the Inter-Civic Recreational Jamboree onto the campus for their faculty. The event could be staged similarly between the various colleges or departments. The Dean of the Faculties should be interested in such a project early in the academic year because of its potentialities in getting the large and unwieldy faculty together under pleasant and enjoyable circumstances. New staff additions would welcome the opportunity to meet their associates on an informal and friendly basis.

The faculty jamboree, at least at its inception, should not strictly emphasize the competitive side of the evening but should stress the other aspects more. It might lack some of the rivalry of the civic clubs, but in time could develop some *esprit de corps* in the various faculty units.

The Kansas City, Missouri, schools have made it a practice to invite civic women's groups to the school Volleyball Sports Days for Girls, while men of the civic clubs are invited to boys' Softball Sports Days. The department and staff there feel that these leaders, who often address groups of men and women, will thus be prepared to give a more accurate picture of what is being accomplished in the physical education program.

Civic Club Contributions
to the School-Community Program

We have given some space to the idea that it is purely "good business" to occasionally sponsor and initiate various recreational activities for the civic and business groups of the community. It might also be well to discuss briefly some of the tangible returns that such a program can bring to the school itself. Most civic and service clubs are just what the name implies, and are constantly on the lookout for worthy recipients for their educational and community betterment funds. It is encouraging, in looking over the many worthwhile activities of such organizations as Lions, Rotary, Kiwanis, Cooperative, Junior Chamber of Commerce, Optimist, and others, to see the recent rapid trend to support school and community recreation and sports. Fine improvements in each local community have not been attributed to any one club program.

The Community Sports and Recreation Show

Another plan for bringing the community and school closer together is the sports and recreation show. This is a fine opportunity to develop an appreciation for the entire field of recreation among the adult and outside groups of the community, as well as to stimulate the students to a broader concept of the whole field of recreation, so often neglected in the modern race for superior varsity football and basketball teams. The sports show idea has been growing rapidly in the large cities as a semiprofessional pageant. Industries have been recognizing the great value of such a program for their employees. The program developed by the Bucyrus Club of South Milwaukee is typical of what can be done by industry, and could be used easily by the enterprising school director who is anxious to interest the public and the student body in recreation. The Bucyrus Club has a series of monthly features such as dances, parties, card clubs, and sports competitions. In their search for new ways to reach the community and club people, the sports show was originated. A notice was sent to all club members requesting that they bring their favorite fly rod, golf clubs, tennis rackets, etc., to the club house for display. In fact they were urged to bring anything of a sports nature, such as mounted fish, deer heads, trophies. The response was great. In came loads of fancy homemade flies, bait, plugs, boats, rods, and sports hobby items. Some brought all their equipment, which included tents, stools, dishes for camping, sleeping bags, guns, and trophies of the hunt. Several cleverly arranged photo displays of outdoor recreation were offered. The gymnasium was filled and the lobby overflowed with exhibits.

The afternoon was given over to inspection of the exhibits. Fir trees and pine decorations gave the area a camping atmosphere. Some of the fishermen were making flies and plugs and giving them away. Persons who brought the exhibits were on hand to explain their hobbies and answer questions. At six o'clock a venison dinner was served; there were speakers from the game conservation department. After dinner the crowd assembled in the gymnasium, where a stage had been prepared as an outdoor scene. Demonstrations were offered in archery and rifle shooting. Hunting dogs working out of a blind constructed on the stage demonstrated their retriev-ing abilities. The program continued with duck calls, fly casting and fishing techniques, followed by movies in color from the conservation department. Since the introduction of this sports show, the club at South Milwaukee has found it to be the most popular annual event sponsored in their re-creational program. Insurance should be carried on exhibits brought in, since some of them are priceless to the owners. Any school could work out a similar program for the community once a year, and the ideas and fea-tures of such a program are as unlimited as the ingenuity of the director and his staff.

Fig. 104. Family Sports Night in one elementary school in Alameda, California.

The Community College

Another trend in education in the United States is the development of community colleges. Many universities have featured night classes and special courses for years. Now several of the smaller colleges have developed the community college. These differ from the traditional adult educational organization in three respects. First, they offer courses in general education, not in vocation. Second, they appeal to people not previously reached by the college or university. Third, a majority of the people served are not interested in credit. They take the courses just for pleasure, mental stimulus, and a desire to broaden their culture and knowledge. The California junior colleges have made a tremendous impact on community life and culture.

To date, the community college has overlooked or only partially served one of its finest possibilities, the field of recreation. While many communities have recreation programs that serve this need, the fact still remains that many recreational features could be brought to the adult population through the medium of special groups and courses of the community college, or simply as an offering to the public from the recreation director of the school. Such activities as bait and fly casting and fly handicraft would be extremely popular and well received. Golf instruction, and techniques in many adult recreational sports could be taught and followed by competition. Courses planned to meet fitness needs would be popular. Such a program could have no other result than to stimulate a closer harmony and appreciation of the school student program in intramural sports and recreation. This could be the stepping stone to an enlargement of staff personnel, better sports facilities, and understanding of the total program.

Some schools have developed noon-hour classes for business and professional men and women. In addition to physical fitness and health for these groups, many games could be arranged, such as chess, checkers, badminton, shuffleboard, and dozens of others. These programs can be financed by fees charged the participants. Thus additional income becomes available to staff members.

Emory University has cooperated with the Northside Atlanta Kiwanis Club in sponsoring the famous "Havalanta Fiesta," which brought adults together from Atlanta and Havana, Cuba, in a project worthy of special notice. Flint, Michigan, and Hamilton, Ontario, conduct similar annual intercity events full of interesting sports competition. These serve as fine examples of cooperative planning and use of facilities.

The School Serves its Alumni

For the past several years the Eaglebrook School at Deerfield, Massachusetts, has had events for alumni as a part of its Winter Carnival. The program has grown until alumni of all ages, anxious to relive their earlier winter sports experiences, return and participate in the various ice and snow events each year. Directors of athletics in any school would do well to plan some events during the year to let their own graduates know they have not been forgotten. Perhaps it would only be occasional challenge basketball games with intramural teams. It could take a variety of forms, each bringing back to the school gymnasium and play fields some enthusiastic alumni who will appreciate the consideration given them and in turn repay the courtesy with support and much needed cooperation. Some universities provide special recreational opportunities for returning alumni at each commencement season. The high school has a unique opportunity of enlisting alumni cooperation through this medium since most of its alumni group remain in the local community. It is fundamental to assume that harmony and understanding between the school and its alumni can be nurtured best in an atmosphere of play and friendly recreation that does not exclude the student as soon as his diploma has been presented.

Fig. 105. Three generations out for roller skating at Potter Community School, Flint, Michigan. All Flint school gymnasiums have regularly scheduled roller skating activities.

Enterprising directors of intramural sports and campus recreation are taking advantage of many of the program features of the national physical fitness movement and modifying their own programs accordingly. The program provides awards and recognition for achievement, has scientifically developed national fitness tests with norms for all ages in physical fitness components and in sports skills, and will gradually enlarge this type of service. Use of fitness testing as part of intramurals has become significant.

A word of caution is appropriate here in the matter of sports sponsorship for very young children especially when endorsed and promoted by noneducational groups. Competitive sports are neither good nor bad because of being competitive or of being sports. They are either good or bad depending on the atmosphere that surrounds them and the leadership given to them. Real zeal and interest in "kids'" sports are commendable, but organizations attempting to sponsor and direct such sports should be guided by standards that are acceptable to education and recreational leadership, based upon generations of good practices and known facts about the growth and development of children. Programs of this sort should be coordinated with existing recreational leadership in every community.

Conclusions

It is apparent that any comprehensive program that seeks to attract all the students of a school or community needs all the support it can get from every possible source. The fine physical education and intramural program in the schools of Norfolk, Virginia, owes much of its success to popular support generated in the community through an active campaign carried on for some years in the following ways:[5]

1. Constant radio broadcasts about the program.
2. Constant writing of articles for all newspapers.
3. Inviting the public to attend numbers of demonstrations.
4. Actual movies made of the total program from day to day during one whole year. These movies then shown constantly to civic clubs, parent-teacher groups, elementary schools, and other groups interested in education.
5. A constantly studied and active program of public information and interpretation.

The enterprising director will not overlook any technique which will legitimately weld the total community closer together. His tool is recreation in its many unlimited possibilities. He will strive to make democracy in sports a reality for his own student body. He will also realize that the doors should not be kept closed to outside opinion, which is influential in every community and which, when unfavorable, can undermine and destroy the good work he has already done. The director should constantly encourage cooperation by initiating it whenever possible, thereby setting the example.

REFERENCES

1 Leslie W. Irwin, *The Curriculum in Health and Physical Education* (St. Louis: The C. V. Mosby Company, 1960).

2 *The Roles of Public Education in Recreation,* A joint project of CAHPER and the California State Department of Education, Burlingame, Calif.; CAHPER, 1960.

3 "Dad's Night Is a Good Project," *School Activities Magazine,* April, 1947, p. 256.

4 Louis E. Means, "Inter-Civic Club Recreational Jamboree," *Recreation Magazine,* XL, No. 10, January, 1947; and *The Athletic Journal,* XXVII, No. 2, October, 1946.

5 From materials supplied by City Schools Director Greyson Daughtrey of Norfolk, Va., in 1962.

18

MOTIVATION AND
PROMOTION OF THE PROGRAM

In the early stages of intramural sports it was necessary to use many devices to sell the merits of the program and to stimulate student participation. In the modern school intramurals have proved their worth and stand solidly on their own merits. The problem now becomes one of utilizing every legitimate method of promotion to reach the smaller segments of the student body, particularly the unorganized individuals and the reticent and unskilled students who are often amazed to find that the program is for them. There also remains the need for raising the level and quality of intramural participation, creating greater administrative efficiency, and giving the entire program added character and significance, together with the educational emphasis it deserves.

Several ideas are presented here which can be used with telling effectiveness. Employed wisely and constantly, they make intramurals an integral part of the total physical education and athletic program of any school, no longer allowing them to be considered a poorly administered orphan of the interschool program.

The Bulletin Service

Larger schools are coming more and more to use a colorful bulletin service to announce coming events, give results of completed activities, supply entry blanks, and give complete details of upcoming programs. Figure 106 is a sample of a bulletin head used to disseminate information. These bulletins are printed in advance with a stock heading on which mimeographed details of each event will be printed later. By being printed on different colors of paper, each bulletin will attract more attention, proclaiming each time that something new has been added.

The Universities of Nebraska and Louisville circulate bulletins to all groups and interested individuals on every phase of the program throughout the year. A standard heading sheet is printed in quantity. Appropriate sports cartoons catch the eye and give special significance to each particular sport. To make the promotion still more effective the director could give a series of orientation lectures to all incoming freshmen each semester. The talk could present recreational and physical education opportunities. Interest-finding questionnaires could be passed out, filled in, and collected, thus providing a mailing list of all freshmen for future bulletin distribution covering their indicated sports interest. This is an excellent system for

Fig. 106. One of many sports bulletins used to motivate interest at the University of Louisville. (Bulletin heads are imprinted on 8½" by 11" mimeo stock.)

reaching unorganized students and the large group of married veterans.

Sequoia High School, Redwood City, California, has made use of a number of bulletin boards. A stock bulletin sheet printed in various colors carries the bold type heading of "What's Doing?"; at the bottom is printed, "Feature Event," with space for daily highlights. The day's activities are posted every morning on all bulletin boards.

Junior and senior high schools can develop bulletins to be sent to home rooms, and for better bulletin board display. These need not be elaborate or expensive, can often be printed in the school print shop, and are always effective.

The bulletins should give accurate data as to deadline of entries, time, place, special rules and regulations, past winners, all-time records, and other information to arouse interest. Bulletins may also be used as publicity material from which news stories are built and radio programs developed. Copies of all bulletins should be sent to boards of education, administrators, and others who are called upon for support.

Howard Ploessel of Huntington Park, California, sends out a continual stream of bulletins and printed materials, each cleverly illustrated, motivating his fine swimming and water safety program. The very intensity of this project cannot help but secure added interest and possible support from administrative sources.

Fig. 107. Attractive announcement bulletins add much to student motivation and interest. Some items can be purchased; others can be designed by students.

(Courtesy of Program Aids, Inc.; Mt. Vernon, N.Y.)

Emory University uses an attractive stock bulletin form. Nebraska and Louisville not only have blank bulletin sheets with appropriate headings, but also print bulletin headings with specific sports cartoons, to be used for particular emphasis from time to time. Iowa State, University of Texas, and Cincinnati use mimeographed bulletins with heading and sports figures mimeographed also. This requires more time in the preparation of each bulletin, but may be worthwhile if a good artist is available. Mimeographed bulletins at Texas employ clever eye-catching cartoons for the various sports. Students at the University of Illinois publish the Intramural-Rec Bulletin, which contains all kinds of news items and program highlights, in addition to the Daily Illini school newspaper coverage. Many high schools have developed interesting bulletins which can be mimeographed in the high school departments just as easily as in the largest university. These are posted on bulletin boards and distributed to all students in the home rooms.

The Bulletin Board

No single motivating device is so mistreated and poorly utilized today in all too many schools as the bulletin board. Every school should have at least one bulletin board for interschool athletics and separate boards for intramurals. A bulletin board that is unique, attractive, and constantly changed will attract a constant crowd of students. At one large university visited it was observed that the only bulletin board in the physical education building was dirty and small, and carried only two tattered typewritten notices, one on the varsity baseball squad and the other on varsity track practice, both outdated. One need not go further to know that intramurals in that institution were suffering from dry rot. Interest cannot be aroused without stimulation and salesmanship. Advertising techniques are as effective in sports and recreation as in business and industry, and just as essential to promotion.

Items on the bulletin board must be kept up to date. Devices must be used to catch the eye. Standings of leagues must be changed constantly. Smaller schools can get splendid cooperation from the art department in printing and painting lettered headings. The enterprising director will watch magazines for catchy printed headings, brightly colored sports figures, comic sport cartoons, and other items that will make the board sparkle and tell a never-ending tale of activity. Sports stores are always willing to donate cardboard sports figure displays, which often can be used with fine effect. Dress up the department and new interest and participation will result.

The bulletin boards should be conspicuously placed, well lighted, and available to the greatest number of students and the public. Orderliness should be observed in the placement of materials. School print shops often can give valuable assistance in the preparation of materials. An additional spot announcement board mounted on wheels could be placed where all may pass and observe.

Several schools have a large photo display mounted in the lobby of the gymnasium, where photographs are annually mounted, forming a permanent and progressive record of winning teams and individuals. This display can be mounted on the Multiplex type of leaf-style cabinet, and scenes from each year's program arranged on each leaf.

The Intramural Handbook

Most larger colleges and universities develop and circulate a handbook of intramural athletics. These are usually republished annually, although some schools economize by producing a better handbook every two years. The handbook is definitely an advertising and promotional medium and should be attractive and constantly useful. To invite attention and closer inspection the cover should be unique and colorful. Certainly the cover is not the most vital part of the booklet, but it is often the element which will cause people either to give it closer examination or to lay it aside with a yawn.

The handbook should have photos and illustrations. Pictures of facilities, championship teams, staff, comic sports illustrations, and intramural action are all highly desirable. Nor must good handbooks be the exclusive tool of the college or university. Many high schools have developed outstanding handbooks that are highly prized by students.

One feature that makes the handbook valuable and adds motivation to the program is a section devoted to individual and group champions in every sport and activity all through the years. Records, best marks, and outstanding achievements should have a prominent place.

MINIMUM ESSENTIALS OF THE WELL-PLANNED HANDBOOK

Attractive cover	Organization of the program
Activities and program	Objectives of intramurals
Awards	Postponements
Bulletin board	Point system and scoring
Champions of all years	All-time Records
Calendar of events	Recreational services
Equipment and facilities	Equipment for picnics and parties
Fees, forfeits, protests	Co-recreational program
Greetings from school officials	Supremacy race information
First aid and injury information	Swimming permits, foot hygiene
Units of competition	Locker and towel regulations
Independent organizations	Staff and administration
Instruction in activities	Action photographs
League play-off regulations	General information

Rules and regulations	Entry instructions
Officials, managers	Practice possibilities
Participation statistics	Health examinations
Special features	Rules of various sports, if desired

The above list covers most ingredients in a good handbook. The list is not arranged as to format, degree of importance, and nature of the item. The enterprising director will make this arrangement.

Fig. 108. Illustrations of cover design for intramural handbooks from selected universities.

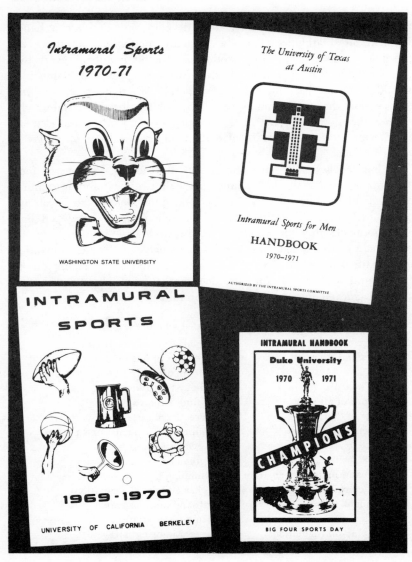

109. Attractive cover illustrations from selected college and university intramural handbooks.

Schools can modify the nature of their handbook to suit the local situation. Some schools use a mimeographed or lithographed handbook. It would seem that while the book is primarily a source of detail information, some ingenuity and salesmanship can be injected into its editing. When such a policy is followed it is safe to assume greater motivation and administrative weight is given to the whole program.

Intramural Publicity

Securing good publicity for intramural athletics is a difficult task in city and state newspapers. Patience, hard work, and diplomacy are needed in abundance to gradually break down traditional press lethargy toward recreational events. When the varsity coaches are active in the administra-

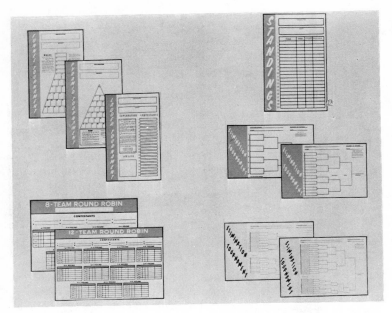

Fig. 110. Types of permanent-type charts for drawings, standings, league schedules, etc.

tion of intramurals this task becomes much easier. Publicity material must be studied, laborious details omitted, and special features emphasized to claim press attention. One high school in Wisconsin a few years ago started a student staff of sportswriters, handling both interscholastic and intramural sports events. Boys from all classes were selected and a regular press managerial staff developed. The first year or two most of the releases found their way into the wastebasket in the larger newspapers. Slowly and gradually this high school began to secure more and more local and state and interstate newspaper space until it was actually consistently getting more good, legitimate publicity than any four or five combined high schools

or colleges outside of the state university. In later years three boys from this staff became well-known sports editors and radio announcers as a result of this early experience.

The school paper is the best source of good, constant publicity. Some intramural departments have their own photographic equipment and take action photos which sooner or later find their way into the printed page. In order to obtain press space the enterprising director must look for items of unusual interest and unique program features, emphasize new sports and events, recognize outstanding individual feats, give statistical records of significance, make varsity sport correlations, and bring out many high-lights. Special stories sent to home-town papers concerning the exploits of local boys should always find a welcome reception.

In publicizing the high school program an abundance of names should be used, since more families are affected, all of whom are daily subscribers to the newspapers.

A number of suggestions for schools desiring adequate and increased publicity from the newspapers are as follows:

1. Organize the school staff to handle all news to the papers constantly when it is news.
2. Send in news; not just propaganda.
3. The school public relations program should be a continuous and centralized responsibility.
4. Release features whenever possible.
5. Do not feel hesitant or reluctant to send news items to the papers; they need news of all kinds.
6. There is no harm in getting well acquainted with the members of the press. Do not try to persuade them that "you should get a break."
7. You do not need to call the editor to tell him you are sending a story; just send it, and keep on sending them.
8. Prepare copy carefully. Type all stories double-spaced, and on one side of paper only. Be brief and concise.
9. Be sure that you know what news is. Names make local news.
10. Send in news constantly. This does not eliminate the possibility of inviting reporters to the school for something "big," or occasionally to social functions. Also honor them occasionally.

Orientation Lectures—Assemblies—Meetings

Many colleges and universities have a series of orientation sessions for freshmen on various subjects. These offer the director an excellent opportunity for the presentation of recreational information, using interest-finding questionnaires, passing out handbooks, and creating interest in general.

School assemblies offer an opportunity for spot announcements, clinical demonstrations, and the chance to honor champions publicly. Some schools have an interroom communication system which is ideal for intramural announcements.

Frequent meetings with managers, special councils, and other student groups can be used for more effective administration and promotion. New events can be introduced in the democratic fashion in this way, making them more effective.

Championship Plaques

Another great motivation idea is the series of championship plaques placed in a permanent and conspicuous location. Each sport should have a plaque on which is emblazoned the sport and each year's team and individual winners. Thousands of students and visitors walk along the corridors, greatly interested in looking at the plaques hung there. Alumni come back and point with pride at their own achievements.

Schools of all sizes can build and maintain plaques with help from the industrial arts shops, the art department, and others. This one motivating device helps create and maintain as much or more interest in intramurals as any other medium. It is a permanent roll of honor for all to see. Newly entering students develop a desire to see their own name placed there before they leave.

Record Boards

Special permanent boards should be built for all-time records in many sports, such as the following:

Indoor track	Physical achievement tests
Outdoor track	Swimming meet
Track relay events	Cross-country run
Specialty events in golf and football	
Record scores in bowling, rifle shooting, golf, free throws, etc.	

Boards should be constructed to permit easy insertion of new names and records. Intramural records should have a prominent place beside varsity records in all sports.

Sports Clinics

New interest always can be aroused with the use of sports and skills clinics. Outstanding players of local or national skill can demonstrate techniques. Students often develop a curiosity and desire to play these games after watching experts. Even a few minutes of skills instruction in some sport by a varsity coach or outstanding performer will create unbounded interest and enthusiasm. More prominent in recent motivation is the use of visual aids for students. Motion pictures, film strips, and colored slides all motivate participation, appreciation, and skills development.

Special Features

Many other novel methods are used by some schools to add motivation to their program. Utah State and the University of Michigan hold annual victory banquets near the end of the year, at which time awards for all events are presented. Kansas University does this at the annual Intramural Ball. Utah State presents qualified intramural managers with sweaters. Wayne University, Louisville, Nebraska, CCNY, and Texas make constant use of comic sports cartoons in bulletins, handbooks, and bulletin boards to catch the eye. Emory University makes frequent use of motion pictures to stimulate sports. Illinois presents a Sportsmanship Trophy to

Fig. 111. The Flint Olympian Games act as a motivation for year-round conditioning and preparation. Here, three high schoolers near the finish line in one of a series of early summer road races sponsored by Cook Community School Teen Club.

stimulate better attitudes, and sports clinics to create greater interest and skill.

Ed Hubbert, Monterey, California, has conducted a series of dinners and banquets to which parents, sportswriters, recreation leaders, and teachers are invited. These are arranged to motivate and stimulate participation in school-community recreation. Most of these are "potluck" with families bringing the food. At one such event, to which many were invited, the cost was paid out of school district funds. He felt the money spent for this one banquet was well worth the effort and productive of great enthusiasm, cooperation, and new ideas for the rapidly expanding program.

Some schools make constant use of the radio to promote intramurals. Others have secured the cooperation of the art department in producing murals on school walls depicting all sports with emphasis on the broad program. A carefully maintained card index of the participants' point totals, compiled by student workers, will always attract a crowd of students eager to find out where they stand.

Baylor University prides itself on the annual All-University Day for mass intramural interest and competition. Michigan and Ohio State have conducted Open House or Intramural Festivals highlighting their program for over thirty years. Carnivals and big intramural events are conducted annually by many schools, school districts, and colleges.

The University of Michigan's annual Open House brings to a climax the winter sports program with championship matches in:

Badminton	Handball
Basketball	Paddleball
Bowling	Squash
Boxing	Swimming
Diving	Tennis
Gymnastics	Volleyball

Championship basketball games in six divisions highlight the program. Exhibitions are staged in various sports.

The Ralph Waldo Emerson Junior High School at Los Angeles climaxes each semester with an Intramural Sports Club Banquet which has become a fine tradition. It includes a fine feed, an entertaining program, several "big names" as guest speakers, and other features.

The New Trier High School at Winnetka, Illinois, has organized and operated a Sports Club for years which is a powerful motivating force in this school's fine intramural program. One of the objects of this club is to sponsor, promote, and conduct as many intramural sports as possible each year. Meetings are held once every week. Appropriate awards are given club members who have contributed unselfish service to the program and the school. In addition, their names are emblazoned on permanent Sports Club Plaques which are mounted in a public place.

Illinois has an honorary sports group called Imrec, representing the combination of service to intramurals and the recreational program. The purpose of this club is to:

1. Stimulate interest in intramural and recreational sports.
2. Strive for sound sportsmanship within and without the program.
3. Show the advantage of the noncompetitive as well as the competitive part of the program.
4. Improve relationships between fraternities and independent groups.

Each member receives a charm. No dues are assessed for membership. This honorary group adds to the motivation of the program, giving it dignity and quality. Illinois strives hard to place maximum responsibility and leadership in the hands of student leaders.

Crane Tech High School, Chicago, has used the following ideas to stimulate and motivate the program at that school:

1. A new type of intramural medal is presented each year.
2. Large signs are posted on all school and gymnasium bulletin boards, featuring a liberal use of sports pictures, to attract attention to coming events.
3. Each school hall is used for a location to post the "street car" type of poster on all coming events. Stapled to each of these posters is a quantity of entry blanks, with a large notice inviting every student to take one. A box is placed conveniently near for entry blanks. When the supply is exhausted, more are stapled on the poster.
4. A list is sent to all home rooms showing all students who are already entered in each coming event. The effect is to stimulate further additional entries, and to increase interest in the coming event for those already entered.

At least one special Field Day event each year is a powerful motivating force for the usual sports offered each season. The event can include novelty events, special features, and relays and track events. Among the novelties are shoe scrambles, egg toss, melee, greased pole contests, greased pig chase, chariot races, football push contests, stilt races, potato races, and similar numbers. Among the special features could be the tug-of-war over water and dry hazards, and bicycle relays and races. Relay events are arranged with an eye to the comic and fun aspects, as well as the physical outcomes.

Even the use of bright-colored paint is cited by some schools as a motivating device. The "gayest playground in Orange County" characterizes the grounds at Capistrano Beach School, California, where all playground equipment and apparatus, and the fences, have been painted in circus colors—red, yellow, green, and blue. The whole thing gives an atmosphere of carefree fun. School officials paint the equipment in bright colors as new pieces are added. Sequoia High School at Redwood City, California, has bright red, white, and blue colors on the obstacle course, designating the degrees of difficulty for their three levels of physical achievement. The bright coloring certainly makes the devices more inviting to the participant, and adds much to their lovely campus among the huge trees.

Some schools have large collections of activity and championship photos, permanently framed and hung to attract interest. Others build up a framed collection of intramural highlights for the year, consisting of head-lines clipped from the newspapers and pasted over each other to make an attractive display.

Other schools are convinced that the presentation of adequate medals, trophies, plaques, and certificates add much to the program. Smaller schools substitute printed heavy paper ribbons for more expensive medals or rib-bons. Other schools maintain attractive and up-to-date scrapbooks con-taining all intramural news stories, and placed in the offices where students and guests may see them at all times. Most businesslike departments pre-serve bound copies of each year's collection of intramural bulletins, results of all events, and a complete history of each year's program.

Some excellent high school programs combine achievement in sports and physical education efficiency into many novel ideas of award and moti-

Fig. 112. The hiking group en route back to camp for a cook-out. Part of the intramural program at the University of Pittsburgh.

vation. Chief among these is the awarding of satin trunks to special honor boys. Physical education classes are grouped according to physical ability. Beginners wear white trunks. After certain achievement levels are reached, the boy becomes a "red" and wears red trunks. Then comes graduation to advanced wearing of the "blues." Boys must furnish these trunks for daily activities. The school then provides satin purple trunks for the next honorary group; a step still higher is the award of gold trunks, and the final or top is the silver. Boys may also earn stars which are sewn on these trunks, depending on the number of times tests are met and sports honors deserved. If the boy fails to continue to meet these standards he loses the right to wear his satin honor trunks. It is a badge of great distinction in these schools to be able to wear these tokens of superior achievement.

The wise administrator will provide superior contest arrangements to give "caste" and character to intramural games, thus creating greater desire to participate in them. Fields can be well marked, flags used on the goal or foul lines, good nets kept on all baskets, and loudspeakers used whenever appropriate. Officials can be dressed properly in officials' shirts, score books or sheets can be prepared in advance, scoreboards can be operating for each game, and the other simple arrangements that make any game important to the competitor and the spectator can be made.

One feature often neglected is the inclusion of the intramural program and other varsity sports and schedules in the football, basketball, and track official programs. Here is an opportunity to sell the broad "sports for all" program philosophy to thousands of patrons of the school, and to win more friends for an educationally sound athletic program.

Other items worthy of mention as motivating and promotional aids are tours of inspection, addresses before student and civic groups, and the broadening of the program to include fathers and civic leaders at least once a year in a big Recreational Jamboree, designed just for them.

Robert Mott, at California Polytechnic College, uses many unique program features to add motivation to that splendid intramural program. One of the Cal Poly highlights is the annual track and field outdoor carnival, which is featured by an unusual sprint between the leading campus sprinter and a good riding horse. The sprinter wins in the shorter distance, but is soon overtaken by the horse. (Figure 113.)

Another unusual event is shown in Figure 114. Here students at Mankato State College, Minnesota, participate under the lights in such events as stilt races and wheelbarrow races. These are features of all-college events and add much local color and humor.

In conclusion, it is safe to say that the best programs in the nation are succeeding because leaders have vision, are not afraid to promote and sell the total activities at every opportunity, and use every legitimate stimulus possible to make their program interesting, stimulating, and satisfying.

Fig. 113. California Polytechnic College adds features for motivation like this "race" between the best college dash man and a purebred quarter horse. Here 1,500 spectators watch the event, which saw (top) the start of the race; (center) both man and animal getting off to a fast start; and (lower) the horse running away from the sprinter after 25 yards. Ideas like this help stage intramurals on an attractive basis — with real participation appeal.

(Courtesy of Robert Mott of California Polytechnic College.)

Fig. 114. Stilt and wheelbarrow races under the lights are special features at Mankato State College, Minnesota.

19

CHALLENGING IDEAS
FOR INTRAMURALS

The preceding chapters have stressed many factors that determine whether a program of intramurals and school recreation will be inadequate, successful, or outstanding. The reader has been taken from philosophy and background of the movement to actual "how to do it" details step by step. Preferred methods of administering the program were given; organizational details outlined; solutions for finding time for the program cited; and a broad complement of activities listed and prescribed for use by children and youth of all age levels. One more word of emphasis should be stated. Every single activity and plan presented has been successfully utilized by actual programs administered by busy teachers and school leaders; these ideas are not a galaxy of ideas from which selections can be made, but are attainable in almost any school or college by people who are dedicated and who believe in the concepts developed.

Factors that help to motivate participation—such as point systems, awards, promotion, publicity, attention to detail, and unique program features—were all pointed out, supplemented, and reinforced with actual recent techniques used in various elementary schools, junior colleges, and college and university programs over the nation and in Canada. References have been made to promising trends and practices in industrial recreation that have direct application to the school setting.

This chapter will take the reader into an atmosphere of creative thinking; it will take a brief look at some promising and rather new trends, and then touch on future directions that may well reshape traditional programs. It makes no attempt to scour total possibilities, or to pronounce the final word on the future. Perhaps a few comments on what appear to be substantial and sound changes that are taking place will be helpful as leaders strive for the kind of program that attracts and involves major portions of the student body, the faculty, and others. Above all, it hopes to set the stage for local staff ideation and exploration of ideas that could change programs from mediocrity into islands of excellence.

Trends in Co-Recreational Sports

Organized sports and recreational activities bringing males and female together in a cooperative or competitive situation can hardly be classified as new. Chapter 13 is devoted exclusively to this subject. However, there is a trend developing over the nation to promote and stimulate more opportunities for mixed groups to enjoy together a great variety of appropriate sports and activities. A study of college and university intramural handbooks discloses much greater emphasis in this direction than in years past: more space is devoted to the idea; more events are being planned in this way; more opportunities for informal or unorganized play together are being provided; facilities are being reserved more and more for mixed group activities. The subject is being given greater prominence in local, state, and national conventions and conferences. If we are to educate for leisure and for a lifetime, it becomes more important that all forms of school and campus recreation reflect those individual and dual sports that can be carried on throughout life. Young men and women need to share together those experiences that are wholesome and healthful and which can contribute much to adjusted and happy family life. It does appear that intramural directors over the nation are moving from a narrowly circumscribed field of fraternity or sorority events into a service to the entire school community more nearly based upon the true recreation concept of leadership.

At Purdue University[1] a co-recreational program is organized and conducted by the Men's Intramural Department separate from the women's intramural program, which is handled by the Women's Recreation Association. It is designed to supplement the existing men's and women's intramural programs. Here, both an organized competitive cluster of events is sponsored, and a free play activity program also provides many social and physical activities. Emphasis is not on winning each contest, but rather upon enjoyment and understanding as a result of participation.

All league play activities in the co-recreational program at Purdue are organized on an all-campus basis with entries accepted from an organization, combination of organizations, or any student interested in entering a team. In the single elimination tournaments the students sign entry blanks posted on bulletin boards provided on campus for that purpose.

All tournaments and league games are played with mixed teams with equal numbers of men and women on each team. Rules limit the advantage of the men. Each unit is asked to select a "co-rec" chairman for its group to keep members informed and to voice opinions on the possible improvement of the program.

The co-recreational sports program at Purdue is designed to be as complete and far-reaching as students desire. The program is for their own personal enjoyment and satisfaction. Sports are added at students' suggestion.

The co-recreational free-play activity program gives every student an opportunity to participate in a varied program of physical and social activities such as riflery, golf, swimming, roller skating, volleyball, badminton, different types of dancing, shuffleboard, table tennis, bocci ball, gymnastics, softball, and archery. Some of the intramural sports clubs are co-recreational in membership.

The Purdue Co-Recreational
Sports Calendar

FALL	WINTER	SPRING
Volleyball	Swimming	Softball
Badminton	Team table tennis	Tennis
Archery	Riflery	Golf
Golf	Bowling	Outdoor volleyball
Tennis		Outdoor archery
Turkey run		

NONCOMPETITIVE ACTIVITIES AT PURDUE

Among the noncompetitive activities are swimming, trampoline, gymnastics, ice skating, and classes in judo and calisthenics. In the Recreational Gymnasium opportunities are provided for mixed participation in fencing, darts, riflery, handball, shuffleboard, bocci ball, archery, golf, badminton, squash, basketball, and table games. In most of these sports instructors are ready to help as needed.

SOCIAL ACTIVITIES FOR MIXED
GROUPS AT PURDUE

The management of the Recreational Gymnasium places much emphasis on social utilization given the facility by Purdue men and women. Students with dates can use any of the facilities.

Square dancing is offered on a scheduled basis. Roller skating or swimming with a date can be a great deal of fun. All of these combine to make up a variety of social activities for students and their dates at Purdue. If a recognized student group of men and women wish to reserve the pool, roller skating rink, social room, or the kitchen, the management is happy to accommodate them. Trade parties are always given full attention. If a group wishes to have a special theme for its trade party, management helps with plans and decor. All such reservations must be made on a co-recreational basis.

The program at Purdue is not unique. Many other schools and colleges provide similar opportunities. It is given emphasis here because it does represent a shift to greater co-recreational emphasis now taking place across the nation.

Changing Administrative Emphasis

Another favorable trend is a shift toward the recreational concept of intramural and campus activities rather than a purely physical education emphasis which so often characterized programs in the past. Keynote of this trend is the acknowledgment that the elementary school, the junior or senior high school, and the college or university are each in effect a community composed of students, faculty, and staff and their families. Especially is this evident in schools with larger enrollments. In such a community everyone should have the benefit of physical sports participation, and of social and less competitive forms of recreation during school years. Too often in the past leaders have failed to support the concept of "community" by keeping programs separate and distinct. They are now finding that it is so easy to involve everyone in a sharing of the values of school-community recreation.

Implementation of this concept in a broader concept of intramurals suggests new organizational ideas, new administrative patterns, and new objectives. This concept demands the employment of trained or professional leadership rather than the haphazard use of students or others so often added temporarily to a staff because of budgetal limitations. Intramural leadership in this connotation must have a recreational philosophy as well as the typical physical education concept of exclusiveness. Such a concept demands that skills be taught that can be used over a life span. Thus education for leisure becomes a reality.

In the public schools various federally financed projects have given impetus to the provision of staff leaders for intramurals with no other major diversions to detract from genuine leadership. An example of this recently was in Fort Worth, Texas, where the city director, working with his superintendent and the Board of Education, has been able to add a trained intramural coordinator at each of the district's middle schools and senior high schools. These teachers are paid out of a special budget arranged for just this purpose.

Encouragement of Sports Clubs

In Chapter 1 we discussed the early evolution of intramurals, largely an evolution from informal sports clubs developed by the students themselves into the modern, well-organized program of sports—both intramural and interschool.

Sports clubs at some universities date back a long time. The Crew Association at Stanford dates back to 1905, and the Rifle and Pistol Marksmanship Team began in 1918.[2] Purdue University has been providing facilities, financial support, and professional guidance for years. In many schools, sports clubs impetus began as late as the 1960's.[3]

The growth and popularity of sports clubs may be attributed to several factors: younger people in graduate schools; more single students; more scholarship assistance giving students more "free" time; more students with athletic backgrounds in high school who are not selected for intercollegiate varsity teams or who themselves choose not to participate in intercollegiate programs; more overseas study where students are exposed to foreign clubs and bring back ideas to their own campuses; desire for "outside" competition not offered by intramurals; dissatisfaction with existing intramural programs; exchange programs in which foreign students implement their club sports on our campus.

In 1968 a sports club survey,[4] 78 United States colleges and university campuses were sent questionnaires. Sixty-four (82 percent) responded with information, in the most comprehensive study on club sports yet made. The number of sports clubs per institution ranged from 0 to 38 with an average of 7. Soccer, karate, sailing, skiing (water and snow), judo, fencing, gymnastics, and rugby were the most frequently mentioned.

Administrative policies governing sports clubs vary greatly. In February of 1968 this same questionnaire was mailed to athletic directors in all four-year American colleges and universities. Five hundred and ninety directors responded. In answer to the question, "What administrative unit is responsible for the administration of sports club activities in your institution?" 176 (41 percent) answered—physical education department; 107 (25 percent) answered—student union; 96 (23 percent) answered—athletic department; 40 (9 percent) answered—other, such as student activity office; and 9 (2 percent) answered—an autonomous intramural department.

About half of the schools returning questionnaires had requirements for membership such as academic status, health clearance, eligibility rules, and the like. Club members pay any travel costs in a majority of cases;

members themselves assume legal responsibility; the majority travel free of any regulation, and are expected to maintain the same quality of conduct as for intercollegiate teams; the majority require a faculty representative; class absences for trips are not granted in most instances; in half the schools the clubs officially represent their institutions; about half have no priority in use of facilities; most receive no physical education credit; and a majority assume that club team members should not have awards.

From all available information, club sports most probably will increase in scope and numbers during future years. At Stanford alone, the number of affiliated clubs has grown from two to fifteen within a five-year period, with more to come in the very near future. This trend will apply to most of the colleges and universities in the United States.

Early affiliation between sports clubs and a single responsible school unit is most desirable. The department of physical education is the most logical choice for official attachment, as most sports clubs are dependent upon facilities, qualified guidance in instruction, scheduling, provision for officials, eligibility, and other related matters. In most institutions the director of intramurals, with the cooperation of the dean of students and/or other official representatives, is the most qualified person to assist in the supervision and direction of club sports programs. The club members themselves should strive to promote, finance, and conduct and continue their programs with the assistance and guidance of the intramural director.

Club membership should include only affiliated students, faculty, staff, and their immediate families. They should establish controls over eligibility, medical and liability requirements, faculty or staff advisors, instruction, etc., in line with the policy of their respective institutions. Thoughtful planning should be given to: the development of local leagues to minimize travel expenses and time away from classes; female club members and their desires to participate actively in their clubs' activities; more alumni interest and support; more and better publicity for club sport activities; representatives from each of the club sports on campus to advise the director in policy-making matters; criteria, for those who desire it, for sports clubs to become intercollegiate sports; criteria for awards—if any—how selected and how financed.

Sports clubs are a natural outlet for college men and women. Under proper guidance and control they should be encouraged within bounds. In many cases they are the intermediate step between an intramural sport and a full-fledged varsity-administered program. In these years of unusual costs for the operation of each varsity sport, the sport club which grows out of genuine student interest may be a way to meet competitive needs without the expensive budget allocations.

Below the college level there is no reason why groups of highly motivated boys and girls should not be able to develop sports clubs where further opportunities for participation would be possible.

Fig. 115. Gymnastics Sports Club, University of Texas.

The positive results from desirable and fair competition are many. Students, staff, and faculty will continue to look to directors of physical education and intramural directors for guidance, direction, and support. This challenge should be met.

There is the possibility that interschool athletic officials may balk at this extension of intramurals as a threat to their traditional program. It is likewise a possibility that state high school athletic association and college athletic conference officials may see a need to curtail interest in this direction. Such a move does not need to take place if sports clubs are properly controlled and administered.

Faculty-Staff Recreational Programs

Another very desirable trend is the increase of sports participation opportunities in the intramural framework for faculty, faculty families, and staff members. If the recreation concept of "community" is supported, there is no reason why portions of the program, the facilities, and the equipment should not be available to this group. Illustrative of this trend is the University of Texas, which publishes and distributes an annual handbook titled, *Handbook for Faculty and Staff Program*. At Texas a group of 150 staff persons started activity several years ago. The figure mounted steadily and now each year sees from 1,500 to 2,000 staff members participating. The faculty program is shown below to guide those thinking of starting such a program.

University of Texas
Faculty and Staff Program

Tuesdays and Thursdays, 11:45 a.m. to 1:30 p.m. most gym areas reserved for Faculty-Staff Program.

Instruction: (starting Tues. after Labor Day)

A. Physical Fitness & Conditioning (limit 40 per class)
   Sec. 1—MWF   12 noon—Tom Martine
   Sec. 2—TTS   7 a.m.—Stan Burnham
   Sec. 3—T & T   12 noon—Frank Medina
   Sec. 4—T & T   4 p.m.—Bob Smith
   (Another section at 4 p.m.—MWF will be added after the others are filled.)

B. Sports Sections with Instruction
   Sec. 5—Handball—TT noon—Sonny Rooker
   Sec. 6—Squash—TT noon—E. H. Saulson
   Sec. 7—Badminton—TT noon—Darrell Williams
   Sec. 8—Golf—TT noon—Spring Semester only, 5 weeks

Supervised Free Periods:

A. Swimming	—MWF		—12:50–1:30 p.m.
	—Weekdays		—5–6 p.m.
	—Sat.—Sun.		—2–3 p.m.
B. Gymnastics	—MWF		—5–6 p.m.
C. Weight Training	—Weekdays		—7–8 p.m.
D. Faculty-Staff	MWF after 4 p.m.		
Gym	TTS&S all times available		

Massage Service: (by Carl Pavick, IM Trainer)
Hours: Mon. through Fri.—10 a.m.–2 p.m. and 3–7 p.m.
Fee: $1.00 to be paid masseur for 20-minute massage, no tipping

Gym Schedule: (September through May)
Weekdays: 6 a.m.–10 p.m. *Saturdays:* 6 a.m.–6 p.m .
Sundays: 2–6 p.m.
Special holiday and summer schedules to be posted.

Reservations: Start at 2 or 3 p.m. daily, except at 11 a.m. Saturdays. Call *before 2 p.m.* or one day in advance for reservations in badminton, basketball, handball, squash, volleyball, and seasonal outdoor sports.

Identification Card: Gym Privilege Identification Cards must be available at all times to present for identification upon request of an institutional representative acting in the performance of his duties.

Guest Privilege Card: May be obtained at the Intramural Office for one day for an out of town guest. Please do not bring guests into gym without a card.

This excerpt from the University of Texas Handbook indicates the scope of faculty family recreation there.

Family Recreation

At the present time the Family Recreation Program is limited to FAMILY NIGHTS when facilities of both gyms are open to all members and their families. During Family Night all facilities may be used by every member of your family. Extra equipment that may be needed for participation of any member of your family is furnished except swimming suits.

ACTIVITIES AVAILABLE

Swimming	Golf
Ping-Pong	Handball
Weight lifting	Volleyball
Trampoline	Gymnastics
Basketball	Steam room (men only)
Squash	Badminton
Kiddie korner	Movies

DRESSING FACILITIES FURNISHED
MEN—Check out basket at gym store
WOMEN—Use visiting team locker room

DATES FOR EACH FAMILY NIGHT ARE POSTED
ON THE BULLETIN BOARDS

"THE FAMILY THAT PLAYS TOGETHER......STAYS TO-GETHER"!

The program at Purdue University is reflected in the description given below, taken from their handbook:[1]

Faculty Intramural Sports Program

All male faculty members, administrative staff, teaching fellows, and research assistants are cordially invited to participate in the organized program of competitive recreational activities. The sports program is designed to afford excellent opportunities for faculty members to relax from their many academic pressures and to become better acquainted with fellow staff members. A player may represent only one team in a sport in a given season (after entering one contest with a given team, a player may not transfer to another team in that sport).

In the faculty individual and double tournaments, the men interested may enter by: (1) calling in their entry to the Intramural Office, or (2) submitting by mail their entries to the Intramural Office, Recreational Gymnasium. Entries will be accepted any time prior to the entry deadline given by the Intramural Office.

In the faculty sports conducted on a league basis, the departmental athletic manager may enter his team by submitting to the Intramural Office an official entry blank (supplied by the Intramural Office). Each department should elect or appoint an athletic manager to represent them in the faculty sports program. The Intramural Office should be provided with the following information: the name of the athletic manager, his address, his home telephone number, and his office telephone number.

The following summary gives some idea of the amount of faculty participation at Minnesota:

**University of Minnesota Faculty
Participation Summary 1967-1968**

ACTIVITY	TEAMS	GAMES	PARTICIPATIONS
BASKETBALL	12	30	430
BOWLING	42	1,120	2,180
CURLING	1	—	54
GOLF	—	—	2,540
HANDBALL	—	—	850
JOGGING	—	—	2,000
SOFTBALL	20	50	1,033
SQUASH	2	583	248
STAFF FAMILY	—	—	9,435
SWIMMING	—	—	800
TOUCH-FOOTBALL	11	30	507
VOLLEYBALL	6	80	1,415
TOTAL	94	1,893	21,492

New Program Features

An examination of rather new or unique program features across the nation reveals some that are more unique than practical or desirable, such as:

Pie-eating contests   Hamburger endurance jamborees
Parachute jumps   Horse and man team relays
Skate-athon   One-man volleyball
  Basketball endurance games

Some ideas are presented below to stimulate greater program width and depth. Some are most appropriate for elementary and secondary school youth. Others are better for college men or women or adults, but may be used at almost all age levels.

Floor hockey	Gym bowling	
Team handball	Sacket	Trampoline
Three-man volleyball	Splashketball	Space ball

The intramural program at Ball State University includes three-man volleyball and splashketball. Sacket is a relatively new game, originating in California, very appropriate for upper elementary and junior high boys and

Fig. 116.

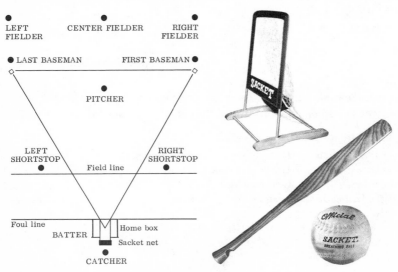

girls. A "breathing" ball is used. Sacket is inexpensive and exciting, with plenty of action, and it can be played indoors or outside. It is played with five to nine players on each team, with the special ball and a flat bat, with an "automatic umpire" sacket net, which eliminates arguments or judgment decisions. The playing area, equipment, and an action scene are pictured on previous page.

BASIC OLYMPICS

Thomas P. Sattler of the University of Illinois at Chicago reports the use of basic olympics in the intramural program thus:[5]

The name was coined from the *basic* course of instruction for incoming freshmen and *olympics* from the nature of the games selected for that particular activity. There were three objectives. The first objective of the special intramural activity was to incorporate competitive activities of a vigorous nature that would be harmonious with the components of physical fitness, such as agility, flexibility, strength, power and endurance. Secondly, since the participants were incoming freshmen it provided an initial exposure to the intramural program. Lastly, it provided an activity that appealed to those poorly skilled kids that any intramural program would normally lose. The events consist of a mile relay or obstacle relay depending on the season, rope climb, standing broad jump, parallel bar hand walk, tug-of-war, and a modified version of the jump reach. The students in each class are divided into the various events according to their interests and become representatives for their section. The activity initially drew 8 or 10 class sections, depending on the freshment enrollment, with a total of approximately 100 participants. (Remember, as a commuter college, interclass activities have a useful role in our total program.)

The winning team of each event is determined by the best average of the top two competitors for that particular team. This applies to events 1 through 5. The sixth event is an individual attempt, which in reality is nothing more than a motor fitness test. The winning section is determined by the students of that section who score highest in all six events. Awards are presented to the top individual in each event, to the best team in each event, and to all members of the winning section.

PHYSICAL FITTNESS THROUGH INTRAMURALS

We have now added "Physical Fitness Through Intramurals." This activity includes the events of "Fitness, Strength, and Endurance." In "Physical Fitness Through Intramurals" we will appeal to every male student during each quarter of the school year, drawing from fraternities, independents, physical education classes, and including every male student interested enough to self-evaluate his fitness level.

The activity consists of two phases; Phase I is termed the "timed circuit" and Phase II the "individual event."

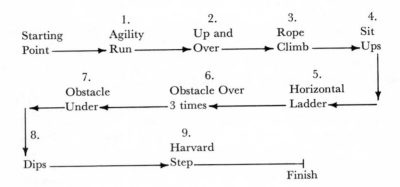

The purpose of Phase I is twofold: it serves as a physical conditioner that will motivate an individual to compete against a clock, and it serves as a screening device to determine who will compete in Phase II. The procedure for running the circuit is as follows:

On signal, the participant starts with the agility run (a 10 yard course with four fixed standards 10 feet apart). He runs down and back; on the second trip he weaves in and around the four standards down and back; the last trip is the same as the first. Sixteen seconds is considered excellent for this activity. Upon completion, he runs to station two, a horizontal bar 8 feet from the ground. He gets over the bar any way he can manage. He then sprints to a 13-foot rope and climbs up until he touches the ceiling and slides down using the feet. (If he jumps down from any height over 3 feet from the floor, he will be disqualified on that trial.) Station four consists of fifteen bent knee sit-ups with feet anchored by the spotter; the butt must remain within a prescribed 24 inches measured from the anchored toe. Next, to the horizontal ladder that he will "walk" hand by hand for 15 feet. Station six consists of three 4-foot matted objects that the individual must hurdle. Station seven is a 30-inch arch that the individual must go under. At station eight the participant does five dips. (The elbows must completely lock on the upstroke and the arm must pass a 90 degree angle at the bottom of the exercise.) The last station consists of thirty repetitions of the Harvard Step Test on a 20-inch box. (The exercise will be counted "up-two-down-*one,* up-two-down-*two,*" etc.) As he sprints to the finish, this concludes the Phase I circuit.

The amount of time it takes an individual to complete the circuit determines his competition level in Phase II. A participant is allowed three attempts at improving his time during physical fitness week. After all the times are recorded they are ranked numerically. The top 25 become the "A Level" competitors, the next 25 the "B Level," and the last 25 the "C Level."

New Directions in Facilities

So often in the past the intramural department had to be satisfied with leftovers in facilities, supplies, and equipment from interschool athletics. That era should now be a thing of the past. Intramurals has long since come of age and is now recognized as a vital part of the total program. It is not inconceivable that creative and energetic leadership in intramurals can, in the future, avail itself of all kinds of new and exciting equipment and facilities.

In recent years, as the scope of intramurals became broadened, and as school or campus recreation became important and highly desirable, many colleges and universities have succeeded in planning and building new fields, courts, and recreation buildings designed for mass participation instead of vested interest and gate appeal. The Recreational Gymnasium at Purdue University is a prime example of such a broadly conceived facility. Others are adding extra units to existing buildings devoted exclusively to intramurals and class instruction. Some enterprising directors in state-supported institutions have even gone to their state legislatures and requested that buildings be funded and constructed with legal restrictions placed upon them so they will be used exclusively for student and faculty recreation, and not as an extension of intercollegiate athletics.

In a more practical vein, a few facilities developments are mentioned here as suggestive of future trends. At the University of California at Berkeley, with an already crowded and fully built area, recreational and intramural facilities have been built on the top decks of parking structures, thus making dual use of expensive land space. They now have one turfed field, 251 X 336 feet, as well as 21 tennis courts, 2 volleyball courts, and a basketball court, all above two levels of parking. Other similar facilities are planned for the immediate future.

At Washington University in St. Louis they have a two-way radio hook-up from the intramural fields to the head trainer's office in case of injuries or other problems. This equipment cost about $400. A cheaper walkie-talkie might be satisfactory in other situations. They also mark their playing fields by spraying on a water paint. The paint is purchased by the gallon at local paint stores.

Another promising development is the creation of mobile equipment units. These are especially valuable in larger city school systems where it would be impossible to finance complete sets of apparatus, sufficient mats, special weight training equipment, physical fitness laboratory equipment, and so on. Special truck chassis units are purchased and mobile units built to meet special needs. Such units can drive from school to school in a few minutes and be ready for the day's instructional or intramural activity. These are especially practical in hauling complete sets of roller skates, ice skates, fly and bait casting equipment, and the like.

In Los Angeles and Memphis, among other cities, numbers of portable swimming pools have been purchased and are used for intervals at any school in the city. This is a trend that is growing rapidly.

The following facilities and equipment innovations may seem now to be fantastic or impossible, but each has been advanced and tested by the Educational Facilities Laboratories and may be obtainable and usable in the years immediately ahead.

1. Geodesic or dome-shaped gymnasiums have been constructed and may be an even more important part of future facilities construction. It is also possible that smaller units will be portable, even to the extent of rolling on wheels to a new location.

2. Locker rooms will have an "athletic club" atmosphere. In place of the usual musty, odoriferous, uninviting atmosphere, these areas will contain carpeted floors, steam and dry heat rooms, sun and heat lamps, whirlpool baths, scented-climate-controlled air, and a masseur.

3. Outdoor fields and swimming pools will be completely enclosed in a plastic dome, thereby making the facility available on a year-round basis. It is also conceivable that rather than any structure, walls of forced air will keep the cold air out and the warm air in or vice versa, depending on the environmental conditions.

4. Instead of lighting fields with many different lights perched on several different poles, the lighting system of the future may be one lamp strategically placed to light the entire area. This type of lamp may not only produce light, but heat as well. In other words, it will imitate the sun.

5. In the future it may not be necessary to arrange for track and swimming judges and timers for intramural meets. Computerized totalization boards have been devised for swimming and are in the development stages for track, not only to select the final places but to time each lane to a small fraction of a second.

6. Electronic automated umpires are being developed to identify the strike zone and "call" balls and strikes for softball and baseball games. An umpire will still be needed for the bases and to determine fair and foul balls. It is predicted that these automatic umpires will be coin operated, which will permit teams to go to the diamonds, and by inserting a coin they will have the services of an errorless balls and strikes umpire.

7. Closed-circuit television will be used in gymnasium facilities to aid in supervising the facilities from a central control point. A flick of the switch will place one in immediate contact with any area in the building.

8. Lighted gymnasium floor lines will eliminate the maze of lines that frequently confuse the players. Gymnasiums will have lines for basketball, volleyball, tennis, and badminton, but a new lighting system will produce only the lines of the court to be used by turning on a wall switch.

9. Outdoor fields, tracks, and playgrounds will be completely surfaced with synthetic materials such as Astroturf and Tartan. As the competition increases between manufacturers and the volume expands, costs of these materials will reach a level that will make them obtainable on a wide scale.

10. For those who do not have synthetic surfaces, moistureless synthetic dirt will be developed which will not turn to mud, but will have all other properties of nature's dirt.

11. Unrefrigerated plastic ice will enable ice hockey, figure skating, and other ice activities to take place in the warm climates as well as in the cold, and year-round rather than seasonal.

12. Throw-away paper clothing will be used by participants. Swim suits, shirts, and paper towels will be discarded after one use, thereby eliminating laundry charges.

13. The new synthetic surfaces will eliminate the need for cleats on shoes. Psychologically, players may wish to retain them, but eventually they will be proven unnecessary.

The following Evaluation Check List may be suggestive of the need for an evaluative instrument suitable for periodic use in any given situation. It is reproduced by permission of the publisher, Croft Educational Services, Inc., New London, Connecticut, 1971.

An Intramural Evaluation Check List

The successful intramural program requires careful planning before each season, constant appraisal during the season, and a motivating post-season awards program. To make sure he has left nothing to chance, Howard Parsons, Chairman of Boys' Physical Education and Youth Services Coordinator at Charles Maclay Junior High School, Pacoima, California, has made the following check list to evaluate his intramural program.

Before the Season
1. Do I have adequate facilities?
2. Do I have adequate supplies and equipment?
3. Have I a good storage system?
4. Are all items marked and identified?
5. Have I planned for adequate safety supervision?
6. Have I scheduled a variety of seasonal sports?

7. Have I informed my administrator as to what we plan to do?
8. Have I involved as many faculty members as possible?
9. Have I informed and involved the PTA whenever practical?
10. Have I advertised the program by daily bulletins, PE class announcements, signs, posters, and newspaper releases?
11. Have I checked all community agencies to reduce conflicts in scheduling?
12. Have I planned seasonal activities that are neither too long nor too short?
13. Am I really enthusiastic about the program?
14. Do I have a standings bulletin board in a prominent place?
15. Have I posted clear-cut rules governing all activities for all to see and do I insist that everyone understand and follow the rules?
16. Have I posted a schedule of all proposed intramural activities?
17. Do I have well-trained student officials?
18. Do I have good captains who know their jobs?
19. Do the captains and team members know the rules of the league and the sport they're playing?

Seasonal Organization and Operation

1. Have I organized teams using a system that will work in our school?
2. Have I planned so that all who want to participate may participate?
3. Have I included activities for all grades and abilities?
4. Have I made being on a team attractive for all?
5. Do I have an effective means of checking attendance?
6. Do all teams know who, when, and where they play?
7. Have I developed a system to control absenteeism?
8. Do I have a plan to reorganize leagues if teams drop out?
9. Do I have a method of publicizing games (photography and journalism clubs)?

After the Season

1. Do I have a good awards program?
2. Have I based my awards on attendance and participation as well as ability?
3. Do I have team awards and trophies?
4. Do I have an all-star vs. league champion game at the end of each season in each sport?
5. Do I have an awards day (father-son night, letter day)?
6. Have I kept up-to-date records?
7. Do I have sports clinics in all activities?
8. Have I evaluated the program to improve it?
9. Have I written thank you notes to all who have helped during the season?

REFERENCES

[1] *The Recreational Gym and You,* Purdue University, Lafayette, Ind., annual publication for students and faculty.

[2] William P. Fehring, "Club Sports," *Twentieth National Conference Proceedings,* National Intramural Association, 1969.

[3] George W. Haniford, "Pros and Cons of the Sports Club Program," Speech given at January, 1969, meeting of the NCPEAM.

[4] Stan Marshall, "Athletic Directors Survey," *National Association of Collegiate Directors of Athletics Quarterly,* III, Number 1, Part II.

[5] "Basic Olympics," *Twentieth National Conference Proceedings,* National Intramural Association, 1969, pp.143-46.

20

PRACTICAL AIDS AND SUGGESTIONS
TO FACILITATE COMPETITION

Any successful program of intramural and recreational sports and activities demands much more than the mere announcement of a coming event, the acceptance of entries, the selection of officials, and the scheduling procedure. A program will rise from mediocrity to far greater significance when attention is paid to details and the mechanical aspects of competition. Just as the interschool program takes on an added luster with the introduction of ceremony and color, so the intramural program will have distinction and appeal with a bit of planning and thoughtfulness. These little details need not be expensive or elaborate, and need not be designed to attract the public. Rather, it becomes a matter of individual ingenuity and inventiveness as the director attempts to provide little devices and aids to make competition more enjoyable and attractive.

All intramural departments can, in time, provide colored game jerseys for all contests, as well as striped shirts for all officials. Care in laundering will keep them in service for several seasons. Jerseys can be planned in several contrasting colors, and many of the permanent units will rise to the occasion and purchase colored game jerseys of their own. If there is no provision for the purchase of game jerseys with appropriate numbering and lettering, a satisfactory substitute can be made by gathering the assorted white cotton jerseys which always seem to accumulate around the locker room and dyeing them in assorted colors to add a distinctive touch to the game and to make play easier by the use of contrasts. One high school director solved this problem by having each basketball manager or captain purchase a package of colored dye, which is used to color each team's cotton game jerseys differently. The department constantly accumulates these older cotton jerseys which are used in the project. The team jersey system is much better than the lack of organization which permits odd conglomerations of colors often seen on one team, with the opponents often playing without jerseys. Intramural contests are now being watched by thousands of students and spectators during the year, and are deserving of more administrative attention in the future.

The following material is presented as an aid in facilitating competition. The list of suggestions on easily constructed pieces of equipment is not at all inclusive, nor are the designs exclusive. Many other devices can be worked out and constructed in the school shops. Junior and senior high schools often have a distinct advantage over the college or university in their ability to have pieces of equipment and apparatus made in school shops not always found on the college campus. Equipment, therefore, is often more expensive for the colleges to have built. Perhaps the brief

Fig. 117. Chico State College, California, provides special intramural jerseys for all sports and contests.

presentation of suggestions that follow will serve to stimulate other home-made paraphernalia which contributes so much to the smooth running of a modern program.

Administrative Aids

SLOGANS AND SIGNS

With the modern recognition of the value of visual aids in education, it should be obvious that there is real value in attractive slogans and signs about the department. Well-placed slogans and catchy phrases add something to the interest and motivation of the program and have an almost unconscious effect on student participation. These can be painted permanently on walls, or can be lettered on show cards and changed from time to time. A list of slogans that have been observed in the various physical education departments over the nation is shown here as suggestions:

It Pays To Play
An Hour A Day Devote To Play
Sports For Health
Learn To Relax
Stay Stronger Longer
The Man Who Is Wise Will Exercise
A Sport For Every Man—A Man For Every Sport
Do Your Bit To Stay Physically Fit
Relax The Healthful Way—Turn To Sports
Study Hard. Work Hard. Play Hard. Relax.
Take Up A Sport
Get Your Stimulation Through Competition
Treat Yourself To Better Health Through Recreation
Learn To Play Several Sports Well
Play An Hour A Day—Keep The Doctor Away
Tired Week Nights? Then On Week Ends Take Up A Sport
Exercise And Stay Healthy
You Can't Fly With The Eagles In The Daytime And Stay Out
   With The Owls At Night
Exercise Is The Best Tonic
Don't Miss The Fun Of Being Healthy—Exercise
Put More Power In Man Power Through Recreation

PRINTED AND STOCK FORMS TO
FACILITATE ADMINISTRATION

In the large intramural department which has several sports running simultaneously, it is well to have a stock of standard forms and printed supplies always on hand in anticipation of the time when they will be needed quickly. As the program varies it will become evident that new items must occasionally be planned and prepared, but there are many forms, blanks, cards, and materials that always should be quickly available. Stocks can be replenished in the slack periods of the year, although such a time rarely exists in the constantly busy intramural offices of a large university. As an aid to the director just developing a new program, the following check list will be of some assistance in determining what supplies and materials are most commonly used today:

1. Awards certificates which can be filled in whenever needed for all-star teams, records broken, and outstanding performances.
2. Pocket-sized award cards that can be filled in and endorsed as needed.
3. Score sheets for all sports. The team sports should have larger filing-size cards printed or mimeographed to include all pertinent game information. Ohio State and the University of Texas print up team scorecards on lightweight cardboard which are easier to use on field and floor and can later be filed as needed.
4. Scorecards for the more individual sports such as table tennis, squash, handball, badminton.

Fig. 118. Sample scorecard for individual sports arranged for team matches.

INTRAMURAL ATHLETICS

SCORE CARD

HANDBALL   **SQUASH**

Team _____ Team _____

	Rank	
	1	
	2	
	3	
	4	
	5	

Date _____ Winning Team _____

Team Match Score_____

5. Boxing scorecards should be on hand either printed or mimeographed for the use of judges at the ringside. These should be
filled in with the matches before being given to the judges.

6. Mimeographed sheets or cards should be on the shelf for the
speedy preparation of single or double elimination tournaments
(see Chapter 11).

7. Mimeographed sheets containing a dummy schedule for each type
of round-robin league, such as the four-team league, five-, six-,
seven-, or eight-team leagues, will save much scheduling time and
are indispensable to the director. Some of these are illustrated in
Chapter 11.

8. Printed or mimeographed daily intramural schedule sheets.

9. Printed forms to facilitate the checking out of equipment from the
cage or equipment room (see Figure 120).

10. Officials' cards to be used for every game. Officials endorse these
cards, which become a permanent record for payment, matters
of protest, and later reference (see Figure 121).

11. Swimming pool permit cards. Most schools require that every
student be examined at the student health center before reporting
to the pool for swimming. These cards are filed and valid only
for one semester.

12. Health permit cards which must be endorsed by the health
center before students are eligible for the more strenuous sports.

13. Individual record cards to be used as a participation record for
every student where individual point systems are used.

Fig. 119. Partial sample of daily intramural schedule sheets.

INTRAMURAL DAILY SCHEDULE

Sport _____Day _____ Date_____

TIME	LOCATION	TEAM	vs.	TEAM	LEAGUE

INTRAMURAL AND PHYSICAL EDUCATION EQUIPMENT CARD

Date_____

Basketballs_____	Ping Pong Balls_____
Baseballs_____	Ping Pong Paddles_____
Baseball Bats_____	Punching Bag_____
Baseball Masks_____	Punching Bag Mitts_____
Baseball Mitts_____	Golf Clubs_____
Baseball Bases_____	Golf Balls_____
Boxing Gloves_____	Squash Balls_____
Boxing Headgear_____	Squash Rackets_____
Footballs_____	Stop Watches_____
Game Gongs_____	Volley Balls_____
Horseshoes_____	Shuffleboard Set_____
Badminton Birds_____	Water Polo Ball_____
Badminton Rackets_____	Soccer Ball_____
Officials' Shirts_____	Whistles_____
IM Game Jerseys_____	Horns_____
Jumping Ropes_____	

I agree to be responsible for and return the equipment checked above. I will pay for all lost items.

_____

        Name   Address   Phone

Fig. 120.

Fig. 121. Sample official record card for all games.

INTRAMURAL OFFICIALS RECORD

Sport_____Date_____

PLACE	TIME	FORFEIT OR GAME SCORES

Signature_____

14. Printed or mimeographed entry sheets for all standardized annual sports. These eliminate the necessity of reprinting each season.
15. Printed or mimeographed rules and regulations covering all sports, unless these are all included in the handbook.
16. A supply of intramural handbooks for constant distribution and reference. These should be reprinted and reedited every year, or at least every other year.
17. Reservation cards to be used whenever courts and facilities are assigned and reserved at any time.
18. Printed forms to be used in testing for proficiency for such events as Sigma Delta Psi.
19. Scorecards for basketball free throws and basketball golf.
20. Printed or mimeographed events sheets for track meets and swimming events.
21. Cards for judges and timers at all track and swimming meets.
22. Postal cards imprinted for sending out notices of games scheduled.
23. Special printed or mimeographed bulletin heading sheets. A good supply should always be on hand, ready for quick mimeographing of current announcements and bulletins in all sports.

It should be noted that the above list is a partial memorandum of many forms that will be used more often in the department. The director undoubtedly will have to develop additional materials as needed.

Permanent Records of the Program

All of the year's bulletins and announcements should be filed away and preserved carefully. For that reason they should all be made up on regular letter-sized paper. At the end of the year's activity all materials should be gathered together; summaries of all events, together with statistics, should be arranged and indexed; and the whole year's program of printed results and materials should be bound for permanent reference. This device is of tremendous importance to the director as he seeks to check on how a particular event was operated in years gone by, or attempts to dig out statistical facts about each year's program as needed. This plan is far superior to the haphazard idea of letting the files accumulate with miscellaneous materials which are always difficult to find and which almost invariably find their way into the wastebasket periodically.

A Motivating Idea

An ingenious device which is being widely copied and used nationwide following its origin and development by Frank Griffin at Sequoia Union High School at Redwood City, California, is the Peg Board. This board is made with a series of numbered holes mounted high enough on gym wall or playground so that the participant cannot touch the floor or ground. The boy takes a peg, made from old baseball bat handles, and by a series of movements while suspended in air, moves from one numbered hole to the next, all arranged in such a way that progression is difficult and requires much practice. Complete details of this excellent device can be found in another publication.[1]

Fig. 122. Intramural action at Texas University. Note the arrangement for officiating volleyball—the stand, the striped shirt.

Sport Cuts, Photographs, and Illustrations

Every department should set aside a place where cuts, mats, photographs, and illustrations of all kinds can be filed and preserved for later use. Each year most school annuals discard a group of cuts on intramurals which might as well be gathered into the intramural department for later motivation and publicity work. The enterprising director will also keep his files full of pictures, sports illustrations, and comic sports drawings which can be used on future bulletins, to enliven a poster for the bulletin board, or to pep up the intramural handbook.

Arrangement and Construction of Equipment

All kinds and types of ingenious devices will occur to the director who is constantly thinking about efficiency in the department. In the equipment rooms all kinds of paraphernalia can be devised to provide for golf clubs, placement of the various rackets, and storage of the playing equipment. Special racks should be devised where tennis, squash, and badminton rackets can be placed, each in a frame to prevent warping and twisting. Special racks should be built where fencing weapons can be stored while not in use. Tennis rackets can be arranged in a lightweight wooden box which opens into two parts with hinges, and which can be transported to the courts as a single unit. This is especially practical for class instruction if the department furnishes all the rackets. A homemade cart can be made in the school shop for the transportation of larger field pieces wherever the fields are some distance from the gymnasium. A visit to the junk yard usually will produce an axle and old auto wheels, which can be equipped with rubber tires. The cart can be painted in school colors, and will greatly facilitate operation. This device is particularly helpful for schools playing six-man tackle football, permitting the carrying of pants, shoulder pads, helmets, and colored jerseys. Some departments may see fit to set up a few tools and a workbench for the construction of archery arrows, the repair of all kinds of equipment, the making of darts and targets, etc. High on the equipment room wall should be arranged racks with holes into which javelins can be stuck to prevent warp when laid horizontally. Special racks can easily be constructed into which all baseball and softball bats can be stored in and out of season. Extra parts always should be on hand when hurdles become broken, so that only a few minutes will be required for replacement in the midst of a meet. Movable softball backstops can be constructed with wheels to permit movement from diamond to diamond as needed. These can be built very much like the regular baseball batting cages. Frames and tripods can be built for archery targets.

Sturdy and practical special judges' stands for the tennis courts can be built in the school shop. These stands should be so arranged that two officials can sit on top, each facing a different court; cafeteria chair wooden arms should be built into the top to facilitate writing and scorekeeping.

A number of rather simple pieces of equipment are described and illustrated here as a suggestion for those who desire to improvise. The list is by no means complete, but may stimulate further ideas in home and school construction.

SCOREBOARDS FOR VOLLEYBALL AND WRESTLING

Two types of scoreboards are pictured in Figures 123 and 124. These devices are easily built and can be moved about as needed. In Fig. 123 the scoring device can be fixed to the top of the volleyball standard, with the official manipulating it from atop the officials' stand at the end of the net.

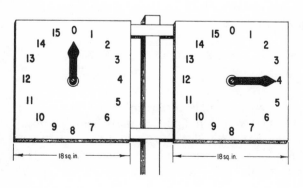

Figs. 123 and 124. Scoreboards for volleyball and wrestling.

STANDARDS FOR VOLLEYBALL
AND BADMINTON

There are many types of standards that can be built easily. Figure 125 pictures a simple arrangement. The upright pipe is equipped with rings and snaps for the net, and the lower end is set in a concrete base which was allowed to harden inside an old automobile tire casing. This

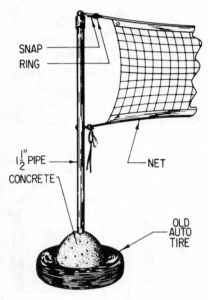

SNAP
RING

$1\frac{1}{2}"$ PIPE
CONCRETE

NET

OLD
AUTO
TIRE

Fig. 125. Homemade standard for volleyball or badminton.

can be painted attractively when completed. The rubber base will prevent floor scratching. This type of standard is good for badminton use, where a number of courts in series are desired, since the weight and construction of the base will not require fastenings.

MARKERS TO STIMULATE INTEREST
IN FIELD EVENTS

Figure 126 gives an idea of the simple construction of a broad-jump marker which will show the best recorded jump as the event progresses. A student assistant moves the indicator along as each mark is bettered. Similar markers can be made for the pole vault and high jump. These items of track equipment make the sport more interesting for competitor and spectator alike.

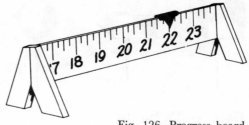

Fig. 126. Progress board
for broad jump.

MISCELLANEOUS HINTS FOR
ADDITIONAL FACILITIES

Figure 127 illustrates another way of arranging basketball goals for mass play. This piece of equipment can be constructed in a number of ways, and transported to the playing area whenever needed.

Figure 128 shows some ideas for the shop construction of markers for the school golf practice tee. These can be made in a variety of shapes, brightly enameled to give color to an intramural golf driving or pitching tournament, or merely to use on a permanent school driving range or tee. Benches should be brought out and placed near the tee area. A club rack also can be built for the tee. A portable scoreboard can be built which can be used at the tee for scorekeeping, and in a great number of ways later in the intramural program.

Fig. 127.

Fig. 128. Designs for making golf-tee markers.

The construction of shuffleboard courts and score markers can be undertaken by any school without difficulty. The vocational shop class at Tecumseh, Nebraska, built concrete tennis courts and shuffleboard courts for the high school. Many smaller schools lay out shuffleboard courts on one end or side of the gymnasium, while others lay out courts on the concrete or terrazzo corridors of the school building, and still others lay out courts on the school sidewalks. If one is constructing special courts outside, it is well to place them parallel to each other, built on a raised earthen spot which has been terraced and leveled for the purpose. The area up to the concrete courts can be landscaped and grassed. Benches should be placed at both ends of each court, and a shuffleboard score indicator can be built for each court to attract interest and increase participation. It is not difficult to construct discs and cues in the school shop. Figure 129 gives the specifications for the cue and Figure 130 shows plans for the disc. The cue should be made of $1\frac{1}{8}$-inch maple reinforced at the tips with a spline of maple 5/16 inch by $1\frac{1}{8}$ inches, the grain being at right angles to the cue handle. Circles for identification can be painted in a shallow depression turned into the wood on a lathe or other woodworking device. The discs

Fig. 129. Shuffleboard cue.

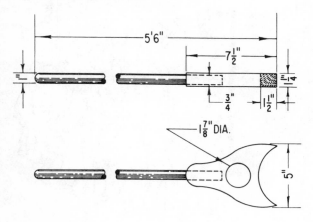

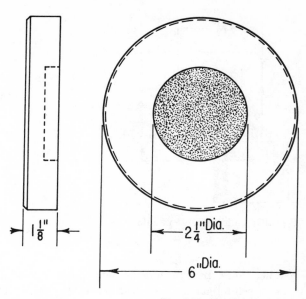

Fig. 130. Shuffleboard disc.

can be made with felt bottoms that have been given two coats of shellac and then have been waxed in order to protect the floors.

Figure 131 describes a simple way to construct table tennis bats, which can be made best from three-ply fir wood, pressed wood, or veneer. The handle and head should be cut from one piece, with a reinforcement of extra wood firmly glued in place on both sides of the handle and rounded off for a smooth grip. The surface of the head can be made up with a sandpaper or thin rough-surfaced rubbed matting face on either side.

Figure 132 shows specifications for a paddle tennis paddle which should be made of three- or five-ply fir wood. For strength the head and

Fig. 131. Table tennis bat.

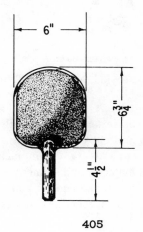

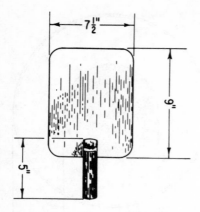

Fig. 132. Paddle tennis paddle.

handle should be cut from a single piece of wood, with each side of the handle reinforced as described for table tennis. The faces can be cross-barred with grooves to increase the surface contact with the ball.

Figure 133 illustrates a simple shop-made judges' and timers' stand for track events, equipped with two wheels to facilitate its easy movement from place to place. Care should be taken to use a light and strong wood which can be painted and neatly finished. Metal wheels can be mounted on improvised steel axles, or wooden wheels can be built in the shop.

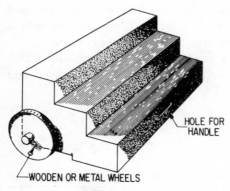

HOLE FOR HANDLE

WOODEN OR METAL WHEELS

Fig. 133. Movable track judges' stand.

A departmental post office for the junior and senior high school can be fastened to the wall in an appropriate hallway where students pass in and out of the department. Each section is lettered alphabetically, allowing students to communicate with opponents and partners to arrange for matches and games, and otherwise facilitating competition. The director can make good use of this device in sending notices to students on coming events, scheduled matches, etc.

A simple boxlike receptacle can be fastened to the department hall area, into which can be placed all kinds of announcements and cards for student use. The invitational words, "TAKE ONE," can be printed on the front face of the box, which should have an open top to facilitate distribution.

White enameled frames can be built for the permanent display of handball and squash rules. The frames can be screwed on a wall near the courts, and should be glass-covered to avoid soiling and tearing. A similar frame can be built out of wood, with a glass cover, with an open slot on the top into which can be inserted spot announcements from time to time. This eliminates the necessity of taking the frame apart to change notices.

Special equipment is now available for quickly arranging lines on the floor. These tools save much time and eliminate permanent line painting for many sports. Ordinary gummed paper rolls are used in any desired width. The paper lines rotate through a water receptacle, and moisture is spread over the paper as it passes through by means of a brush. Paper lines, which will remain usable for many weeks if desired, can be put down on any floor in a few minutes. All that is necessary for their removal is to wash over them with a bucket of hot water and a towel. The machine is ideal when a large number of badminton or volleyball courts must be laid quickly over a large basketball floor area and permanent painted lines would be objectionable.

Figure 134 illustrates a simple homemade arrangement for the cross-lining of a single lane in outdoor track. The white or colored lime is placed in the lower receptacle, and with a light tamp the color is transmitted quickly to the track. This is very useful for relay carnivals where a great

Fig. 134. Homemade one-lane track liner.

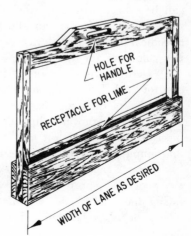

number of single-lane lines should be set for the various passing and starting areas of the many events. If the full-width line is considered objectionable, a shorter lining device can be made which will make a line of
one-foot length on either side of the lane. It might be well to make up two
or three of these liners so that different colored lime can be used in each.
A piece of wire screen is tacked across the bottom to act as a sieve.

Figure 135 describes a homemade paddle for aerial darts. The paddle
can be constructed similar to the paddle tennis and table tennis bats, with
the head and handle cut from a single piece, and with the additional work
required to complete a finished handle.

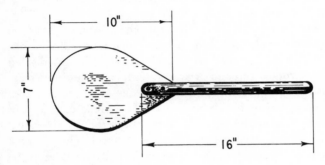

Fig. 135. Aerial darts paddle.

A satisfactory substitute for a regular starter's pistol which can be used
for all practice starts in interschool and intramural track is the construction
of two smooth pieces of wood hinged at one end, with a handle fastened
on the outside face of each half of the device. The two pieces are then
quickly slapped together, simulating the crack of the starter's gun.

Special racks can easily be built on which all softball or baseball bats
can be placed, either on the playing field or in the equipment room. A
special wooden frame can also be built for use in lining the batters' box.
Specifications for this device can be found by consulting the official baseball rule book for dimensions.

In the swimming pool, simple take-off starting boxes can be built,
one for each lane the pool affords. These are built to fit tightly over the
deck edge of the pool tile, with a thin rubber piece fitted on the underside
of the box to prevent slipping and movement, and another thin rubber
piece firmly fastened on top. These starting boxes provide better starting
and eliminate towels' being used on the tile deck.

Water polo goals may also be constructed simply to fit snugly over
the pool deck, or purchased, with white-painted rectangular face boards
facing the pool as the scoring area. They can then be removed quickly
when not in use. Water basketball goals can be built, using a regular fan-

shaped basketball board and goal, raised to 5 feet above the water edge and built into a movable platform which also fits snugly over the pool deck edge. Water basketball seems to have more appeal for intramural purpose and eliminates the usual tug-of-war that occurs around the shallow end in water polo. The swimming pool should also have a record board for intramural all-time swimming records. This can be made of slate, mounted in a white enameled wooden frame, and suspended or screwed into the pool wall. If slate is used, records can be changed quickly with chalk, and an occasional splash does not do much damage. For the swimming meet a simple flash scorecard device for the diving judges can be made. Instead of the usual clumsy set of cards, a container can be made of lightweight material, open at the top and on one side. The score cards are marked from one to ten, and fastened at one lower corner with a bolt. Each card can be marked on the upper back so the judge can see each card's number without looking over the top or turning the device around.

For the large gymnasium where several intramural basketball games are running simultaneously, and where electric scoreboards are not provided for each court, the simple table scoreboard illustrated in Figure 136 can be built. The device can be constructed out of lightweight material

Fig. 136. Portable intramural basketball score-board for table use.

to permit easy movement, so that boards may be stored away after each day's games. The scorecards are fastened by means of a soldered or brazed ring, and the numbers should be painted on thin metal plates which have been painted white. The stopwatch or game timer can be placed securely on the scorer's side of the device, together with a set of rules or instructions.

For the playing fields a large assignment board can be built on which information concerning the field assignments and other announcements can be placed daily. This board can be fixed firmly in the ground near the entrance to the playing area, and all teams will soon make it a habit to report there before proceeding to the proper field for their scheduled games. Appropriate field markers can be made by using gasoline filling station signs of metal which have heavy steel bases, easily moved about from field to field. Figure 137 illustrates such a metal field marker which has permanent numbers painted on for use in designating fields, but which also can be used as golf driving distance markers by merely placing a large cardboard disc over the top showing the number of yards.

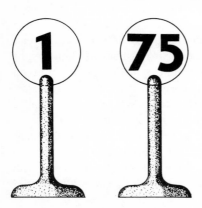

Fig. 137. Metal pedestal-type markers for designation of fields; also useful for golf distance markers.

Schools fortunate enough to be situated in the North have little trouble constructing an outdoor ice hockey rink. If funds are not available for a regular rink with wooden side bank boards, the snow can be banked up around the edges and sprinkled and frozen to form a retaining wall to facilitate play. The wooden ice hockey rink bank boards can be constructed in sections, remaining in place through the winter season, and being stored away during the warmer weather. Ice hockey goals of iron pipe and chicken wire netting can be built in the school shop.

For indoor golf putting competition and practice a simple putting apparatus can be constructed. The box is built in the school shop, with holes, cut to a depth of 6 inches, into which tin cans are placed securely. Old pieces of stairway carpeting are perfect as a putting surface, and give the desired length for putting competition. Games can be devised with each contestant getting any number of specified putts, with scores evaluated according to the holes scored. It is not difficult to construct an indoor golf driving range or cage, which can then be placed in some corner or little-used room and will be used constantly by many students throughout the winter months. The practice of golf shots can also be carried on by placing the students along a canvas wall at regular intervals and shooting off cocoa mats into the canvas.

For the outdoor touch football fields there are several commercial goal line flags for sale. However, a very inexpensive arrangement can be made by sinking a piece of iron pipe in the ground at each goal intersection. Into this sleeve an ordinary long and heavy screen-door spring can be inserted quickly. Flags made from bright red material can be tied on the spring. These are easily seen and eliminate the injury hazard since they bend easily when hit, springing back into place after impact. Another easily built and inexpensive arrangement is pictured in Figure 138. Again, a heavy screen door spring is inserted into a block of wood about 6 inches square. This is secured by a screw. This block is then mounted on a larger piece of wood about one inch thick. The entire unit can be transported easily to the goal lines daily and taken in afterwards.

Dart boards are easily built for the noon-hour or recreational program. These are constructed of plaster board or plywood, and the design can be found in many dart rules sets, or in sporting goods catalogs. Boards for dart baseball, dart bowling, and many other dart games can be built. It might also be possible to construct the darts in the school handicraft or woodworking shop.

Another easily made device is the bump board or ladder tournament board pictured in Figure 139. It can be made of three-ply fir wood, painted and lettered as desired. The metal plates are tacked on, and allow names to be inserted and moved from one position to another as the tournament progresses. The plates are slotted or flanged to hold name cards.

Another ingenious device is the Track Bump Board. This large and beautifully decorated board can be permanently mounted on the gymnasium wall for all to see. A series of track events are used and motivation comes

Fig. 138. Homemade goal line flags.

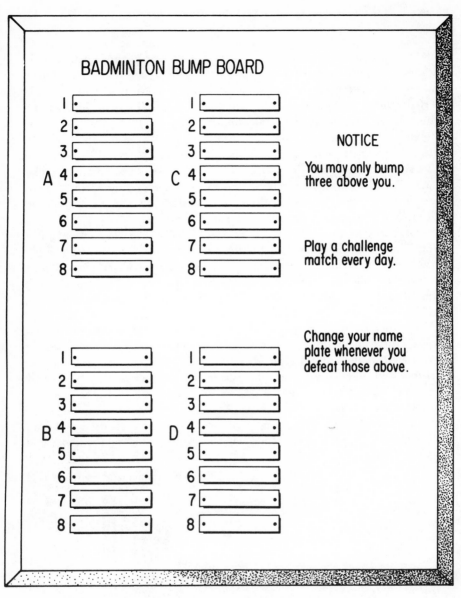

Fig. 139. Homemade bump board for ladder tournament in individual sports.

from the desire of hundreds of boys to find a place for their own names on this Roll of Honor by "bumping" another boy from the record spots on the board. All testing is done by the instructors only. Any boy may, at any time during several months, request the right to excel any track mark on the list. Spaces are provided for the best seven marks in each event. The boy's name card is inserted according to the record beaten.

Fig. 140. Traffic cones are used by many schools for goal markers, track lanes, circles for games, stanchions for maze running, targets, line markers, etc.

Fig. 141. Installing the batting post.

HOBBY SHOPS AND HANDICRAFT
ON THE CAMPUS

Many schools have made provisions for the individual who enjoys handicraft work or who would like to learn something of the art. At the University of Iowa a well-equipped workshop is available for students, who may putter with any desired project. Here can be made archery bows and arrows, targets, darts, and other items of recreational nature. Purdue University and the University of Nebraska both have a puttering room for handicraft work located in the Student Union Building. Few schools today lack some kind of practical arts shop where all kinds of equipment can be constructed. Often it is possible to make much of the equipment and apparatus used in the program, reducing to a small fraction the cost of such paraphernalia. Most school shops have students taking courses for credit who cannot afford to furnish their own materials for costly projects and the instructor is usually willing to have these students work on projects for the intramural department.

It is evident, therefore, that the director need not curtail his program drastically for want of many pieces of equipment that can be built easily, with a minimum of ingenuity, and without a great outlay of funds. Often the deeper meaning of recreation is enhanced as the student shares the responsibility of construction.

Fig. 142. Ready for "Post-ball" or "Post-softball" or "No-pitch softball" or use as an aid to correct batting form.

Fig. 143. Good construction design for a portable batting cage or backstage for multiple diamonds.

Fig. 144. Good construction design for multiple court goals, which could be made portable if desired by adding retractable wheels. Installed at the North Phoenix, Arizona, High School.

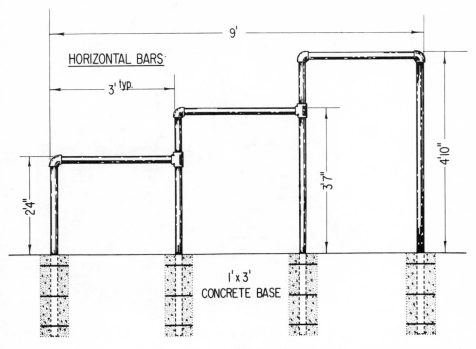

9'

HORIZONTAL BARS

3' typ.

4'10"

3'7"

2'4"

1' x 3'
CONCRETE BASE

Fig. 145. Construction and installation design for horizontal bars. Height can be varied to suit age level served. Good for physical fitness testing and general use.

Fig. 146. Ideal rack (on wheels) made in school shop for golf clubs. Can be used for equipment room storage and rolled out to scene of activity.

Fig. 147. Homemade portable rack for fishing and casting rods, which was developed at the University of Tennessee.

Fig. 148. Homemade portable cart rack for softball and baseball bats, balls, and gloves.

(Courtesy Jayfro Mfg. Co.)

Fig. 149. Mesh cord bag is ideal for carrying quantities of balls (soccer, volleyball, basketball) from equipment room to field or floor.

REFERENCE

1 Louis E. Means, *Physical Education Activities, Games and Sports* (Dubuque: William C. Brown Company, 1963).

SELECTED BIBLIOGRAPHY

This bibliography is classified into three sections: (1) books and publications, (2) theses and special studies, and (3) periodicals and shorter articles.

The 1952 edition of this book (The C. V. Mosby Company) included an exhaustive listing of everything significant written up to that time in the field of intramural sports, recreational activities adaptable to competitive organization, and outing activities. This list of references has been deleted. Those who wish to refer to a complete compendium of these writings may find value in using the 1952 edition together with this bibliography.

Books and Publications

AMERICAN ASSOCIATION FOR HEALTH, PHYSICAL EDUCATION AND RECREATION, *Intramural Sports For College Men and Women,* National Conference Report, Washington, D.C., AAHPER, 1956.

———, *Physical Education for High School Students,* Washington, D. C., Revised, 1960.

———, *School Athletics; Problems and Policies,* Washington, D.C., National Education Association and AASA, 1954.

————, *Standards in Sports for Girls and Women,* Washington, D.C., AAHPER, 1958.

BAUMER, WILLIAM H., *et al., Sports As Taught and Played at West Point.* Harrisburg, Pa.: Military Service Publishing Company, 1943.

BEEMAN, HARRIS F., *"An Analysis of Human Relations in the Administration of Intramurals in the Western Conference."* National Intramural Association, *Eleventh Annual Conference Proceedings,* 1960.

———— and JAMES H. HUMPHREY, *Intramural Sports:* A Text and Study Guide. Dubuque, Iowa: William C. Brown Company, 1954.

BEUTTLER, FRED C., *"Boy's Intramural Athletic Programs in Iowa's Secondary Schools"* (Special Field Study). National Intramural Association, *Eleventh Annual Conference Proceedings,* 1960.

BORST, EVELYNE, and ELMER MITCHELL, *Social Games for Recreation.* New York: The Ronald Press Company, 1959.

BOYDEN, E. DOUGLAS, and ROGER C. BURTON, *Staging Successful Tournaments.* New York: Association Press, 1957.

BRYANS, HELEN, and ROBERTA CHARLESWORTH, *Skill in Games.* Toronto: J. M. Dent and Sons, Ltd., 1950.

BUCHER, CHARLES, *Administration of School Health and Physical Education Programs* (2nd ed.). St. Louis: C. V. Mosby Co., 1958.

DAMKROGER, ERNEST L., *Recreation Through Competition.* New York: Association Press, 1947.

DAUGHTREY, GREYSON, and JOHN B. WOODS, *Physical Education Programs,* Philadelphia: W. B. Saunders Co., 1971.

Department of Physical Education for Women, Florida State University, *Physical Education Handbook for College Women.* Dubuque, Iowa: William C. Brown Company, 1955.

FAIT, HALLIS, *et al., A Manual of Physical Education Activties* (2nd ed.). Philadelphia: W. B. Saunders Co., 1961.

FORSYTHE, CHARLES E., *Administration of High School Athletics.* Englewood Cliffs, N.J.: Prentice-Hall, Inc., 1954.

GABRIELSEN, MILTON, and CASWELL MILES, *Sports and Recreation Facilities: for School and Community.* Englewood Cliffs, N.J.: Prentice-Hall, Inc., 1958.

GERI, FRANK, *Illustrated Games and Rhythms for Children.* Englewood Cliffs, N.J.: Prentice-Hall, Inc., 1955.

GRIEVE, ANDREW W., *Directing High School Activities.* Englewood Cliffs, N.J.: Prentice-Hall, Inc., 1963.

HACKENSMITH, C. W., *History of Physical Education.* New York: Harper & Row, Publishers, 1969.

HUNT, SARAH E., *Games and Sports the World Around* (3rd ed.). New York: The Ronald Press Company, 1964.

HUNT, VALERIE V., *Recreation for the Handicapped.* Englewood Cliffs, N.J.: Prentice-Hall, Inc., 1955.

KINSEY, DAN, *"Student Leadership Viewpoints."* Rural College, National Intramural Association *Eleventh Annual Conference Proceedings,* 1960.

KLIENDEIST, VIOLA, and ARTHUR WESTON, *Intramural and Recreation Programs for Schools and Colleges.* Indianapolis: Meredith Publishing Co., 1964.

KRAUS, RICHARD, *Recreation and Leisure in Modern Society.* New York: Appleton-Century-Crofts, 1971.

LARSON, MARJORIE S., *Speed-A-Way, A New Game for Boys and Girls.* Minneapolis: Burgess Publishing Co., 1961.

LEAVITT, NORMA M., and HARTLEY D. PRICE, *Intramural and Recreational Sports for College.* New York: The Ronald Press Company, 1958.

MEANS, LOUIS E., *Physical Education Activities, Sports and Games.* Dubuque, Iowa: William C. Brown Company, 1952; rev. 1963 and 1969.

MENKE, FRANK G., *The New Encyclopedia of Sports.* New York: A. S. Barnes & Co., 1948.

MILLER, DONNA MAE, and KATHRYN RUSSELL, *Sport: A Contemporary View,* Philadelphia: Lea & Febiger, 1969.

MITCHELL, ELMER D., *Sports for Recreation.* New York: A. S. Barnes & Co., 1952.

MUELLER, PAT, and ELMER D. MITCHELL, *Intramural Sports.* New York: The Ronald Press Company, 1960.

NASH, JAY B., *Philosophy of Recreation and Leisure.* Dubuque, Iowa: William C. Brown Company, 1960.

—— et al., *Physical Education Organization and Administration.* New York: A. S. Barnes & Co., 1951.

NEILSON, N. P., and WINIFRED VAN HAGEN, *Physical Education for Elementary Schools.* New York: The Ronald Press Company, 1956.

PATERSON, ANN, *Team Sports for Girls.* New York: The Ronald Press Company, 1958.

RICE, EMMETT A., *A Brief History of Physical Education,* rev. and enlarged. New York: The Ronald Press Company, 1958.

RICHARDSON, HAZEL A., *Games for Elementary School Grades.* Minneapolis: Burgess Publishing Co., 1951.

SAPORA, ALLEN, and ELMER MITCHELL, *The Theory of Play and Recreation.* New York: The Ronald Press Company, 1961.

SCHEERER, WILLIAM W., *High School Intramural Program.* Minneapolis: Burgess Publishing Co., 1951.

SCOTT, HARRY A., *Competitive Sports in Schools and Colleges.* New York: Harper & Row, Publishers, 1951.

SEATON, DON CASH, et al., *Physical Education Handbook.* Englewood Cliffs, N.J.: Prentice-Hall, Inc., 1959.

SHAW, JOHN, et al., *Individual Sports for Men.* Philadelphia: W. B. Saunders Co., 1950.

STAFFORD, GEORGE T., *Sports for the Handicapped.* Englewood Cliffs, N.J.: Prentice-Hall, Inc., 1947.

THOMPSON, JOHN C., *Physical Education for the 1970's.* Englewood Cliffs: Prentice-Hall, Inc., 1970.

TUNIS, JOHN R., *Sport for the Fun of It.* New York: A. S. Barnes & Co., 1940.

VERNIER, MARYHELEN, *Methods and Materials in Recreation Leadership.* Philadelphia: W. B. Saunders Co., 1956.

V-FIVE ASSOCIATION OF AMERICA, *Intramural Programs* (rev. ed.), U. S. Naval Institute, 1950.

VOLTMER, EDWARD F., and ARTHUR A. ESSLINGER, *Organization and Administration of Physical Education.* New York: F. S. Crofts & Co., 1954.

WILLIAMS, JESSE F., *Principles of Physical Education* (7th ed.). Philadelphia: W. B. Saunders Co., 1958.

YUKIC, THOMAS, *Fundamentals of Recreation* (2nd ed.). New York: Harper & Row, Publishers, 1969.

Theses and Special Studies

ANDERSON, JOHN DICKASON, *"An Evaluation of Participation in Extracurricular Activities by Secondary School Students."* Ph.D. thesis, University of Pittsburgh, 1941.

ATWELL, GLADYS, *"A Study to Determine Which Physical Education Activities Carry Over Two or Three Years After Graduation from High School."* Master's thesis, University of Michigan, 1938.

BAILEY, GORDON ARTHUR, *"Analysis of Data Basic to Organization of Intramural Athletics in a Senior High School."* Master's thesis, University of Texas, 1946.

BAKER, JOHN ALOYSIOS, *"Sociological Aspects of Intramural Sports."* Master's thesis, University of Kentucky, 1940.

BARIL, CHARLES ALTHONS, *"The Carry-Over of Recreational Activities from High School into College."* Master's thesis, University of Kentucky, 1940.

BARR, HELEN, *"A Survey of Outing Organizations and Activities in the Colleges and Universities of the United States."* Denison University, Granville, Ohio, 1940.

BEACH, LOWELL W., *"The Nature and Status of Co-Recreation in the Michigan High School Physical Education Program."* Master's thesis, University of Michigan, 1946.

BEAUDRY, FRANCES E., *"Relation Between Play Activities and the Development of Desirable Personality Traits."* Master's thesis, University of Michigan, 1940.

BERG, JAMES O., *"Differences Between Male Participants and Non-Participants in a College Intramural Sports Program in Regard to Academic Achievement and Academic Ability."* Ph.D. thesis, University of Missouri, 1969.

BLISS, C. H., *"A Survey of Extra-Curricular Duties of Men Physical Education Teachers in Public Schools of Indiana."* Master's thesis, Purdue University, 1940.

BOOMERSHINE, W. H., *"An Analysis of Junior and Senior High School Sports Activities."* Unpublished Master's thesis, Purdue University, 1942.

BREWSTER, MARGARET E., *"Activities in the Rural School Recreation Program,"* *The Research Quarterly,* XI (May, 1940), 142.

CLARK, BEULAH B., *"Extra-Curricular Activities in the United Lutheran Colleges of America."* Ph.D. thesis, Teachers College, Columbia University, 1944.

CLARK, EDWIN CREED, *"The Relationship of Recreational Participation to Industrial Efficiency."* Master's thesis, Purdue University, 1946.

DULLES, FOSTER R., *"America Learns to Play: A History of Popular Recreation."* Ph.D. thesis, Columbia University, 1940.

EDGREN, HARRY DANIEL, *"An Orientation in Recreation for Secondary School Youth."* Ed.D. thesis, New York University, 1944.

FEDERAL SECURITY AGENCY, OFFICE OF EDUCATION, *Camping and Outdoor Experiences in the School Program,* Bulletin No. 4, 1947.

FIELDS, FOREST E., *"The Cost of Intramural Sports Per Man Hour Participation."* Master's thesis, Purdue University, 1946.

HANHILA, MATT O., *"A Study of the Intramural Sport Programs in the High Schools of Arizona."* Master's thesis, University of Arizona, 1940.

HARROWELL, MARJORIE E., *"The Relationship of Intelligence, Scholarship, and the Ability of High School Girls to Play Team Games."* Master's thesis, New York University, 1940.

HENTHORN, EDWARD CHARLES, *"The Relative Value Received from Extra-Curricular Activities by Pupils in Large and Small Schools."* Master's thesis, University of Nebraska, 1940.

HUGHES, CHARLES I., *"Study of Intelligence and Extra-Curricular Participation of College Men."* Master's thesis, University of Michigan, 1934.

JONES, GALEN, *"Extra-Curricular Activities in Relation to the Curriculum,"* Ph.D. thesis, Columbia University, 1935.

KRAUS, JESS, C. E. MUELLER, and BRUCE ANDERSON, "An Experimental Epidemiological Investigation on a Head Injury Control Device in College Touch Football Athletics." Cincinnati, Ohio: U.S. Public Health Service, 1969.

LAITEN, YALE J., *"The Extra-Curricular Concomitants of Personality Adjustment and Socio-Economic Status Among High School Boys."* Ph.D. thesis, New York University, 1944.

LUCEY, MILDRED, and BETSEY KERSEY, *"The Status of Intramural Sports for Women in the Colleges and Universities of Pennsylvania."* Research project, Pennsylvania State College, 1948.

LUX, LLOYD H., *"The Application of Guides for Development of Intramural Activities for College Men."* Unpublished Ed.D. thesis, Teachers College, Columbia University, 1950.

MARTIN, LA VERLE, "An Evaluation and Comparison of Men's Intramural Programs in Four-Year State-Supported Institutions in the United States." Master's thesis, Texas Technological College, 1969.

MATHEWS, DAVID O., *"Programs of Intramural Sports in Selected Ohio Public Schools."* Ed.D. thesis, Western Reserve University, 1958.

McCLUGGAGE, MARSTON M., *"Motivating Forces in the Development of Collec-*

tivized Forms of Leisure-Time Activity." Ph.D. thesis, University of Kansas, 1941.

MEANS, LOUIS E., *Camping and Outdoor Education in California.* Sacramento: California State Department of Education, March, 1956.

MILLER, J. O., *"Study of College Recreation Programs."* Master's thesis, Indiana University, 1951.

MILLER, LEONARD, *"A Comparison of Academic and Intelligence Achievement of the Participants and Non-Participants in Intramural Athletics at the University of Kentucky."* Master's thesis, University of Kentucky, 1937.

NORDLY, CARL L., *"The Administration of Intramural Athletics for Men in Colleges and Universities."* Ph.D. thesis, Teachers College, Columbia University, 1937.

PEACE, JAMES S., *"A Manual of the Organization and Conduct of an Intramural Program for Colleges and Universities."* Ed.D. thesis, New York University, 1943.

PHELPS, DALE, "Current Practices and Recommended Guidelines for the Administration of Sports Clubs in Male and Co-educational Four-Year Colleges and Universities." Ph.D. thesis, Indiana University, 1969.

PINK, RALPH J., "A Survey to Determine the Current Status of Intramural Recreational Programs in Selected United States Colleges and Universities." Ph.D. thesis, University of Utah, 1969.

SEIDEL, BEVERLY L., *"Development of Intramural Sports for Women, with Particular Emphasis on Participation."* Master's thesis, University of Michigan, 1946.

SMITH, WARREN E., *"A Survey of Post-War Trends and Changes in College and University Intramural Programs."* Master's thesis, University of Michigan, 1947.

SOMERS, MADELINE R., *"A Comparative Study of Participation in Extracurricular Sports and Academic Grades,"* *The Research Quarterly,* XXII, No. 1 (March, 1951), 84.

SPRANDEL, WALTER B., *"Status of Intramural Sports in Ten Denominational Colleges of Michigan."* Master's thesis, University of Michigan, 1941.

STAFFORD, GEORGE T., *"Adapted Sports for Atypical Secondary School Boys."* Ed.D. thesis, New York University, 1937.

STUMPNER, ROBERT, *"Philosophy of Intramurals."* National Intramural Association, *Eleventh Annual Conference Proceedings,* 1960, p. 5.

SWENSON, HELEN JEAN, *"The Relationship of Participation in Sports to Certain Traits of Personality."* Master's thesis, Pennsylvania State College, 1941.

UHRLAUB, DAVID, "Recommended Criteria for Directors of College Intramural Activities for Men as Compared with Present Practices in Selected Colleges and Universities of the United States." Master's thesis, Kent State University, 1969.

WADLINGTON, J. E., *"Fishing as a Recreational Activity."* Master's thesis, University of Kentucky, 1942.

WEDEMEYER, ROSS, *"Philosophy of Intramurals."* National Intramural Association, *Eleventh Annual Conference Proceedings,* 1960, p. 10.

WEINSTEIN, REBECCA R., *"The Organization and Procedures in the Conduct of Play Days for High School Girls."* Ed.D. thesis, New York University, 1943.

WERNER, ALFRED C., and FRED M. COOMBS, *Recreational Interests of Male Alumni of Alleghany College.* Research project, Pennsylvania State College, 1948.

WILLIAMS, JACK, *"Evaluation of Intramural Sports of Colleges in the Lone Star Conference."* Master's thesis, University of Texas, 1947.

Periodicals

ADAMS, IRIS, "Dance Intramurals in Elementary School," *Journal of Health, Physical Education and Recreation (JOHPER),* XXVIII (March, 1958), 16.

ANDREWS, EMILY R., "The Pink Pig—An Adventure in Outing," *Journal of Health and Physical Education,* XX, No. 1, January, 1949.

ARNHOLTER, WYNNE, "Sports for Teen-Agers," *Recreation Magazine,* XLI, No. 4, July, 1947.

ASHCRAFT, J. HOLLEY, "Sane Competitive Program for Junior High School Boys," *JOHPER,* XXIV, November, 1952.

BACON, HAROLD, and TOM MAYES, "You Don't Have to 'Baby' Your Gym Floor," *JOHPER,* XXVI (March, 1955), 14.

BAILEY, MARTHA JEANNE, *Some Trends in Coeducational Recreation for Adolescents with Recommendations.* Purdue University, West Lafayette, Ind., 1941.

BERG, JUNE, "Are We Fair to Our Children?" *Recreation Magazine,* XLI, No. 11 (February, 1948), 530.

BIERHAUS, FREDERIC, "Mountain Recreation," *JOHPER,* XXVIII (March, 1958), 16.

BOOKWALTER, KARL W., "The Co-Educational and Co-Recreational Use of Physical Education Activties." *Proceedings of College Physical Education Association,* December, 1940, pp. 62-68.

BRUMBACH, WAYNE B., "Teachers Like to Play Too," *JOHPER,* XXIV (January, 1952), 24.

BUCHER, CHARLES A., "Field Days." *Journal of Health and Physical Education,* XIX, No. 1, January, 1948.

CALLERY, JOHN, "Intramural Programs for Smaller High Schools," *Athletic Journal,* XXX, No. 1 (September, 1949), 60.

CASETY, MARY Z., "Post-College Recreation," *Recreation Magazine,* XXXVIII, No. 8, November, 1944.

CHAPMAN, GARLAND R., "After-School Recreation for Elementary Children," *JOHPER,* XXVI (November, 1955), 14.

CHELLMAN, JOHN, "Competition in the Intramural Program," *The Physical Educator,* XVI, No. 2, May, 1959.

CHRISTLIEB, MARILYN, "Planning and Organizing Ski Events," *Journal of Health and Physical Education,* XIX, No. 2 (February, 1948), 84.

COPELAND, DODD, "Intramurals Through Sports Clubs," *Scholastic Coach,* XVIII, No. 2 (October, 1948), 50.

CREED, C. E., "Relationship of Recreational Participation to Industrial Efficiency," *Research Quarterly of the American Association for Health, Physical Education, and Recreation,* XVII, No. 3 (October, 1946), 199.

DABNEY, MARY B., "Leisure-Time Sports Clubs," *JOHPER,* XXIV, December, 1952.

DALTHORP, CHARLES J., "Athletics for All," *Athletic Journal,* XXI, No. 1, September, 1940.

DAUGHTREY, GREYSON, "Sports Preferences in Intramurals," *Scholastic Coach,* XI, No. 8, April, 1942.

DAVIS, BOB, "Lunch Period Recreation," *Aim Magazine,* VII, No. 2, February, 1948.

DELIUS, ROBERT D., "Lunch-Period Activities," *Aim Magazine,* VI, No. 5 (May, 1947), 17.

DODSON, TAYLOR, "Public Relations for Intramural Programs," *The Physical Educator,* IX, No. 1 (March, 1952), 16.

ELBEL, E. R., "Intramural Athletics for High School Boys," *Athletic Journal,* XXII, No. 8, April, 1942.

ELVEDT, RUTH, "Skiing at Mount Holyoke," *JOHPER,* XXII, No. 1 (January, 1951), 46.

————, *Winter Sports, Part of the Physical Education Program,* Official Winter Sports and Outing Activities Guide, 1947-1949. Published for NSWA by A. S. Barnes & Co., 1947.

ERICKSON, RALPH J., "Intramural Sports and Life," *Peabody Journal of Education,* LXXII (January, 1960), 216-21.

ESSLINGER, ARTHUR A., "The Program at West Point," *JOHPER,* XXII, No. 5 (May, 1951), 20.

FAIT, HOLLIS F., "The Case for Corecreation," *JOHPER,* XXII, No. 5 (May, 1951), 20.

FARRIS, JEFF, "Bait Casting Golf," *JOHPER,* XX, No. 8 (October, 1949), 515.

FLAGG, BARBARA, *Let's Have a Skating Party,* Official Winter Sports and Outing Activities Guide. Published for NSWA by A. S. Barnes & Co., 1949.

GEISSINGER, RUTHANN R., "Increasing Interest in Dance Through a Dance Intramural," *Journal of Health and Physical Education,* XX, No. 1 (January, 1949), 44.

GEIST, ROLAND C., "How to Start a Bicycle Club in Schools and Colleges," *Recreation,* XLIII, No. 7 (October, 1949), 346.

GIAUQUE, C. D., "Student Recreation on Our College Campuses," *Journal of Health and Physical Education,* XI, No. 2, February, 1940.

GRAMBEAU, RODNEY J., "Paddleball," *Athletic Journal,* Vol. XXIX, No. 9 (May, 1949), 50.

GRAZAN, JOE, "Intramurals at the University of South Carolina," *Southern Coach and Athlete,* X, No. 1, September, 1947.

GUILD, BRUCE, "Suggestions for a Community Winter Carnival," *Athletic Journal,* XXI, No. 5, January, 1941.

HAIDT, MARIE, "Riflery for Women in the Colleges," *Journal of Health and Physical Education,* XIX, No. 6, June, 1948.

HALLIBURTON, JACK, "Individual Doubles Tournament Plan," *Scholastic Coach,* XVII, No. 1, September, 1947.

HANIFORD, GEORGE, "Problems in Co-Recreational Sports," *College Physical Education Proceedings,* LIX, 1956, 152-54.

HAUCK, MARY B., "Americans All—A High School Club System," *Recreation,* XLII, No. 9 (December, 1948), 418.

HENDERSON, EDWIN B., "An Experiment in Elementary School Athletics," *JOHPER,* XXII, No. 6 (June, 1951), 21.

HILL, IVAN W., "Unique Co-Operation in School and Community Recreation," *JOHPER,* XXIV (March, 1952), 14.

HOUSTON, LAURENCE E., "Youth Education," *JOHPER,* XXII, No. 3 (March, 1951), 54.

IRWIN, LESLIE W., "New Directions in Physical Education," *Jaurnal of Health and Physical Education,* XVII, No. 5, May, 1946.

JACKSON, EDGAR B., "New Trier Shows the Way," *Athletic Journal,* XXVI, No. 7, March, 1946.

JAEGER, ELOISE, and ELSE BOCKSTRUCK, "Effective Student Leadership," *JOHPER,* XXX, Decembeer, 1959.

JANSEN, LAURENCE, "Planning an Intramural Track and Field Program in a Large High School," *Athletic Journal,* XXV, No. 6, February, 1945.

JOHNSON, W. P., "The Club Approach to Intercollegiate Athletics In a New Community College," *JOHPER,* XLII, No. 3, March, 1971.

KAUFMAN, KARL, JR., "Recreation in Today's Schools," *JOHPER,* XXIII, No. 3 (March, 1952), 15.

KAYWOOD, RICHARD, "Awards in the College Intramural Program," *JOHPER,* XXI, No. 8 (October, 1950), 11.

KENDIG, ROBERT S., "A Physical Education Program for All Students," *Journal of Health and Physical Education,* XVIII, No. 10, December, 1947.

KENT, JOHN H., "A Few Feathers From an Old Bird," *Southern Coach and Athlete,* VII, No. 8, April, 1945.

KILROY, THOMAS J., "Child Leaders Take Over the Noon-Hour Playground," *Recreation,* XLV, No. 4 (September, 1951), 219.

KRABLIN, GEORGE H., "A Winter Sports School," *Journal of Health and Physical Education,* XIX, No. 3, March, 1948.

LIEGERAT, GILES F., "Water Basketball," *The Scholastic Coach,* XVII, No. 7, March, 1948.

LIMBERT, PAUL M., "The Place of Recreation in the Total College Curriculum," *Recreation,* XLIII, No. 6 (September, 1949), 283.

LOFT, BERNARD, "A Positive Approach to Safety" (in Intramurals), *JOHPER,* XXXII, June, 1961, pp. 34-35.

LOVELESS, JAMES C., and ESTER G. POST, "The College Outing Club," *Recreation,* XLIV, No. 9 (March, 1941), 558.

MACAULAY, MINNIE MAUDE, "Co-Recreation at Berea College," *Recreational Games and Sports Guide, Official Sports Library for Women.* New York: A. S. Barnes & Co., 1945.

MALLORY, PATRICIA, "Co-Recreational Intramurals," *School Activities,* XXXV (November, 1963), 68.

MAROUS, RICHARD S., "After-School Recreation," *JOHPER,* XXIV, February, 1953.

MATHEWS, DAVID O., "Lima's Intramural Program," *Athletic Journal,* XXXIX (February, 1959), 38, 46, 54-57.

McCOOE, DAVID L., and C. E. HUTCHINSON, "An Experiment in Noon-Time Recreation," *JOHPER,* XXII, No. 8 (October, 1951), 28.

McCOY, MARY ELIZABETH, "Fitness Through Intramurals," *JOHPER,* XXVIII, June, 1957.

———, "Fitness Through Intramurals," *JOHPER,* XXVIII (October, 1958), 16.

McDONOUGH, THOMAS, "The College Intramural Program," *Journal of Health and Physical Education,* XVII (October, 1946), 471, 499-501.

MEANS, LOUIS E., "California Goes Forward in Recreation," *JOHPER,* XXV, September, 1953.

———, "Extramural Athletics," *JOHPER,* XX ,No. 1, January, 1949.

———, "The Fourth R—Recreation," *JOHPER,* XXIII, No. 4 (April, 1952), 7.

———, Inter Civic-Club Recreational Jamboree," *Recreation Magazine,* XL, No. 10, January, 1947; and *Athletic Journal,* XXVII, No. 2, October, 1946.

———, "National Conference on Education for Leisure," *JOHPER,* XXVIII, September, 1957.

———, "Noon Hour Recreational Program," *Scholastic Coach,* XVII, Nos. 3 and 4, November and December, 1947.

———, "Play Them Out," *Recreation Magazine,* XL, No. 5, August, 1946; and *Scholastic Coach,* XVII, No. 1, September, 1947.

———, "Post War Survey of College and University Intramurals," *Athletic Journal,* XXVIII, No. 8, April, 1948.

———, "School-Community Planning for Facilities at Long Beach," *JOHPER,* XXIII, No. 4, April, 1952.

———, "Summer Fun for Teen Agers," JOHPER, XXVII, April, 1956.

MEEK, DORIS, "Organizing Our Campus Recreation Program," *JOHPER,* XXVII (April, 1956), 84.

MENDELSOHN, ELLIS J., "Recent Trends and Developments in Extramural Activities," *College Physical Education Proceedings,* LIX (1956), 155-60.

MEREDITH, WILLIAM F., "Highlights of the College Intramural Sports Conference," *JOHPER,* XXVII (January, 1956), 22.

———, "Highlights of the College Intramural Sports Conference," *JOHPER,* XXVII, January, 1957.

MEYER, ROSE D., "They Bowl Cut-Rate," *Recreation,* XLII, No. 7 (October, 1948), 318.

MUNDT, HOWARD G., "The Future of Intramural Programs," *Athletic Journal,* XXV, No. 6, February, 1945.

NATIONAL INTRAMURAL ASSOCIATION, *Fifteenth Annual Conference Proceedings,* March, 1964:

HAIGH, BARTON, "Co-Educational Program," pp. 14-15.

HARPER, DON, "Co-Recreational Activities Stagnation," p. 13.

NATIONAL INTRAMURAL ASSOCIATION, *Nineteenth Annual Conference Proceedings.* Austin, Texas: William C. Brown Company, 1968:

BOYCHEFF, KOOMAN, "Program Administrative Procedures," p. 22-25.

FLORY, C. M., "The Social Aspect," Contributions of Intramurals to Education, p. 49-51.

GOEHRS, WARREN, "Recreational Aspects," Contributions of Intramurals to Education, p. 53-55.

HANIFORD, GEORGE, "Organization and Finance," Future Trends in Intramurals, p. 16-19.

HUDDER, GERALD, "Activities, Programs and Participating Units," Future Trends in Intramurals, p. 27-31.

KEEN, PAUL V., "Contributions to Educational Progress," Contributions of Intramurals to Education, p. 55-58.

REES, TREVOR, "Training Intramural Officials at Kent State," p. 32.

SEZAK, SAM, "Training Intramural Officials at the University of Maine," p. 31-32.

TOWNES, ROSS, NORMAN FREDERICK, WILLARD HOLSBERRY, and AL SHERIFF, "Training Student Leaders," p. 61-63.

UNRUH, DAN, "Research and Development," Future Trends in Intramurals, p. 19-22.

NATIONAL INTRAMURAL ASSOCIATION, *Twentieth Annual Conference Proceedings.* Los Angeles, Calif., 1969:

BUCK, CHARLES R., "Co-Educational Intramurals—Trend or Topic," p. 52-56.

FEHRING, WILLIAM P., "Club Sports," p. 49-52.

GRUBER, ALAN J., "Proposals for Improving Fairness in Single and Double Elimination Tournaments," p. 98-99.

MUELLER, C. E., "Ideation in Intramurals," pp. 193-99.

TOWNES, ROSS, "Fitness Programs—A Way of Life," pp.138-42.

NETHERTON, CLIFFORD L., "Bait Casting, Winter and Summer," *JOHPER,* XXI, No. 9 (November, 1950), 12.

NEWMAN, YALE J., "Recreation Leadership in Secondary Schools," *JOHPER,* XXV, March, 1954.

NICHOLS, WALTER S., "Fly Tying for Recreation," *Recreation Magazine,* XLI, No. 1, April, 1947.

OGAN, ALICE P., "Playday for the Elementary School," *JOHPER,* XXIV (May, 1954), 18.

OLDS, EDWARD B., "How Do Young People Use Their Leisure Time?" *Recreation,* XLII, No. 10 (January, 1949), 458.

OLSON, DOROTHY ANN, "The Place of Recreation in the Total College Curriculum, Student Program Evaluation," *Recreation,* XLIII, No. 12 (March, 1950), 582.

PETERSON, GUNNAR, and JOHN SHAW, "In the Winter Syracuse Moves Outdoors," *JOHPER,* XXII, No. 1, January, 1951.

PRICE, HARTLEY, "The Intramural 'V' Physical Fitness Test at the University of Illinois," *Athletic Journal,* XXII, No. 9, May, 1942.

RAGLIN, JIM, "Extramural Meet," *Athletic Journal,* XXXII, No. 7 (March, 1952), 38.

RAYMER, MILTON, "Bowling, A Recreation for Youth," *JOHPER,* XXII, No. 7 (September, 1951), 11.

"Recreation On the Campus," A Report From the National Recreation Congress, *Recreation,* XLIV, No. 8 (January, 1951), 453.

RHOADES, A. H., "The Safety Aspects of the Experimental Touch Football Helmet," *Eighteenth Annual Proceedings of the National Intramural Association,* 1967.

RICE, ROBERT J., "Extramurals," *JOHPER,* XXX, October, 1958.

RICKER, WILLIAM, "Basket Volleyball," *JOHPER,* XXIII, No. 1 (January, 1952), 39.

ROGERS, C. R., "How to Start a Rifle Club," *Scholastic Coach,* XVII, No. 2, October, 1947.

ROMINE, CHARLES, "The Fate of Intramurals Lies in the Spice,"*Athletic Journal,* XXIV, No. 6, February, 1944.

SCOTT, HARRY A., "The School as a Coordinating Agency for Leisure-Time Activities," *Journal of Health and Physical Education,* IX, No. 8, October, 1938.

SCOTT, M. GLADYS, "Competition for Women in American Colleges and Universities," *Research Quarterly,* March, 1945, pp. 49-71.

SHAINWALD, DICKIE, "The Development of a Co-Recreation Committee," *Journal of Health and Physical Education,* XIX, No. 1, 1948.

SIMON, J. MALCOLM, "Student Leadership in College Intramurals," *JOHPER,* XXXII, June, 1961, pp. 35-36.

SMALLING, RAY, "Complete Intramural Program," *Scholastic Coach,* XIX, No. 1 (September, 1949), 50.

SMITH, FRANK E., "Setting Up Game Schedules," *Industrial Sports Journal,* XI, No. 8 (August, 1950), 10.

SPRANKLE, DALE, "Albion's Touch Football," *Athletic Journal* XXX, No. 10 (June, 1950), 6.

STARR, HELEN M., *The Purposes of Competitive Athletics in American Education.* Washington, D.C.: AAHPER, American Academy of Physical Education, Professional Contributions No. 7, 1961, pp. 28-41.

STEIN, JULIAN V., "Boy's Intramural Sports Association," *JOHPER,* XXVI, January, 1955.

SWENSON, JEAN, "A Coeducational Sports Day," *Journal of Health and Physical Education,* XVIII (April, 1947), 266-68.

TAYLOR, NANETTE, "A Ski School in Action," *JOHPER,* XXIII, No. 2 (February, 1952), 16.

TODD, TOM, "Student-Guided Activity Program," *Scholastic Coach,* XV, No. 4, December, 1945.

WALKER, PAUL, "Intramural Panacea," *Scholastic Coach,* XVII, No. 9, May, 1948.

WATKINS, JAMES H., "Intramurals in Junior High School," *JOHPER,* XXI, No. 5 (May, 1950), 281.

WELLS, L. JANET, "Boating in the School Program," *JOHPER,* XXIX, May, 1958.

WHITMAN, HOWARD, "Play As You Go," *Recreation Magazine,* XLI, No. 11, February, 1948.

WILLGOOSE, CARL E., "A Community Ski School," *Journal of Health and Physical Education,* XX, No. 1, January, 1949.

WILSON, PAUL C., "Backboard Tennis," *JOHPER,* XXIII, No. 3 (March, 1952), 8.

INDEX
OF INDIVIDUALS AND SCHOOLS

SUBJECT INDEX